£30.00

D1621148

ALLITERATIVE POETRY
OF THE
LATER MIDDLE AGES

ROUTLEDGE MEDIEVAL ENGLISH TEXTS

General editor: Malcolm Andrew

*Professor of English Language and Literature,
The Queen's University of Belfast*

This series is intended to respond to a need. Its purpose is to broaden the range of medieval English literature which can be studied at undergraduate and graduate level by offering sound, attractive editions of major works which are at present inaccessible. Texts are unmodernized except for punctuation, edited in accordance with rigorous scholarly standards, and supported by textual annotation. Explanatory footnotes are full but concise, and designed to provide the kind of explanation and elucidation which will facilitate critical response to the text. Each volume has a comprehensive glossary, with ample cross-referencing and line references. Introductory material, succinct and incisive, supplies essential information; used in conjunction with the carefully selected bibliography, it should also encourage further reading.

The alliterative tradition is one of the most significant in medieval English poetry. This collection meets a longstanding need in presenting a number of little-known Middle English alliterative poems that have been overshadowed by the three masterpieces *Pearl, Sir Gawain and the Green Knight*, and *Piers Plowman*. It illustrates the great range and variety of alliterative verse, both rhymed and unrhymed. The poems range from descriptions of armies on the march, bloody battles, and dramatic storms, to quieter scenes – the silent stalking of a deer, a dream of goddesses. Whatever the subject – social and political satire, theological controversy, moral admonition – it is always given a lively and interesting setting, inviting us, in the words of *The Parlement of the Thre Ages*, 'riche romance to rede and rekken the sothe off kempes and of conquerours'.

ALLITERATIVE POETRY
OF THE
LATER MIDDLE AGES

An Anthology

THORLAC TURVILLE-PETRE
Lecturer in English, University of Nottingham

ROUTLEDGE
London

First published 1989
by Routledge
11 New Fetter Lane, London EC4P 4EE

© 1989 Thorlac Turville-Petre

Printed in Great Britain by TJ Press (Padstow) Ltd,
Padstow, Cornwall
Disc conversion by Columns Typesetters of Reading

British Library Cataloguing in Publication Data

Turville-Petre, Thorlac
Middle English alliterative poetry: an
anthology.
1. Poetry in English, 1066–1400 –
Anthologies
I. Title
821'.1'08

ISBN 0 415 01304 6
ISBN 0 415 01305 4 Pbk

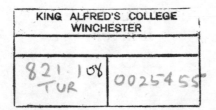

CONTENTS

Contents

ILLUSTRATIONS

ACKNOWLEDGEMENTS

For valuable advice and criticism I am very grateful to the general editor of this series, Malcolm Andrew, and to John Burrow, Hoyt Duggan and Ralph Hanna. I owe a special debt to Professor Duggan for his generosity in allowing me to make use of our joint work on the text of *The Wars of Alexander* for the selection here, which differs in presentation, but not greatly in substance, from our edition for EETS.

Many librarians gave me help by allowing me access to their manuscripts and supplying me with photographs. The generosity of the Pierpont Morgan Library in supplying photographs without charge must not go unrecorded. David Weston, of Glasgow University Library, gave me helpful information about Hunterian MS. 380.

Thorlac Turville-Petre

ABBREVIATIONS

For abbreviations of texts cited, see pp. xi–xiii.

AN	Anglo-Norman
AV	The Authorized Version of the Bible
BL	British Library
DOST	*Dictionary of the Older Scottish Tongue*
EETS	Early English Text Society
ELH	*English Literary History*
ES	*English Studies*
Fr	French
Gk	Greek
JEGP	*Journal of English and Germanic Philology*
LALME	*A Linguistic Atlas of Late Medieval English*
Lat	Latin
LSE	*Leeds Studies in English*
MÆ	*Medium Ævum*
ME	Middle English
MED	*The Middle English Dictionary*
MLN	*Modern Language Notes*
MP	*Modern Philology*
MS	*Mediaeval Studies*
NM	*Neuphilologische Mitteilungen*
NQ	*Notes and Queries*
NT	New Testament
NWMidl	North West Midlands
OE	Old English
OED	*The Oxford English Dictionary*
OFr	Old French

Abbreviations

ON	Old Norse
OT	Old Testament
RES	*Review of English Studies*
SN	*Studia Neophilologica*
SP	*Studies in Philology*
STS	Scottish Text Society

TEXTS CITED WITH
THEIR ABBREVIATIONS

Awntyrs	*The Awntyrs off Arthure at the Terne Wathelyn*, ed. R. Hanna III (Manchester, 1974)
BD	Chaucer, *The Book of the Duchess* (see *CT*)
Bede, *History*	Bede, *A History of the English Church and People*, trans. L. Sherley-Price (revised edn, Harmondsworth, 1968)
CA	*Confessio Amantis*, ed. G. C. Macaulay, *The Complete Works of John Gower* (Oxford, 1901)
Cleanness	ed. J. J. Anderson (Manchester, 1977)
CT	Chaucer, *The Canterbury Tales*, ed. L. D. Benson, *The Riverside Chaucer* (3rd edn, Oxford, 1988)
Death and Liffe	ed. J. H. Hanford and J. M. Steadman, *SP*, xv (1918), 221–94
Dest Troy	*The 'Gest Hystoriale' of the Destruction of Troy*, ed. G. A. Panton and D. Donaldson, EETS 39 & 56 (1869, 1874)
Erkenwald	*St. Erkenwald* (see pp. 101–19 below)
Henryson, *Fables*	in *The Poems of Robert Henryson*, ed. D. Fox (Oxford, 1981)
HF	Chaucer, *The House of Fame* (see *CT*)
HKB	Geoffrey of Monmouth, *The History of the Kings of Britain*, trans. L. Thorpe (Harmondsworth, 1966)

Abbreviations

Kings	*The Three Dead Kings* (see pp. 148–57 below)
Kyng Alisaunder	ed. G. V. Smithers, EETS 227 & 237 (1952, 1957)
Malory	*The Works of Sir Thomas Malory*, ed. E. Vinaver (2nd edn. Oxford, 1967)
Manning, *Chronicle*	*The Chronicle of Robert Manning of Brunne*, pt i, ed. F. J. Furnivall, Rolls Ser. 87 (London, 1887)
LGW	Chaucer, *The Legend of Good Women* (see *CT*)
Morte A	*Morte Arthure*, ed. M. Hamel (New York, 1984)
Mum	*Mum and the Sothsegger*, ed. M. Day and R. Steele, EETS 199 (1936)
Parlement	*The Parlement of the Thre Ages* (see pp. 67–100 below)
Patience	ed. J. J. Anderson (Manchester, 1969)
Pearl	ed. E. V. Gordon (Oxford, 1953)
PF	Chaucer, *The Parliament of Fowls* (see *CT*)
PPCrede	*Pierce the Ploughmans Crede*, ed. W. W. Skeat, EETS 30 (1867)
PPl A	*Piers Plowman: The A Version*, ed. G. Kane (London, 1960)
PPl B	*Piers Plowman: The B Version*, ed. G. Kane and E. T. Donaldson (London, 1975)
PPl C	*Piers Plowman by William Langland: An Edition of the C-text*, ed. D. Pearsall (London, 1978)
Rom Rose	*The Romance of the Rose*, in *The Riverside Chaucer* (see *CT*)
St. Albans	*The Boke of St. Albans*, ed. R. Hands, *English Hawking and Hunting in The Boke of St. Albans* (Oxford, 1975)
SGGK	*Sir Gawain and the Green Knight*, ed. J. R. R. Tolkien and E. V. Gordon, revised N. Davis (2nd edn, Oxford, 1967)

Abbreviations

Siege J	*The Siege of Jerusalem*, ed. E. Kölbing and M. Day, EETS 188 (1932)
Susan	*A Pistel of Susan* (see pp. 120–39 below)
TC	Chaucer's *Troilus and Criseyde* (see *CT*)
The Towneley Plays	ed. G. England and A. W. Pollard, EETS ES 71 (1897)
Trevisa, *Properties*	John Trevisa, *On the Properties of Things*, ed. M. C. Seymour *et al.* (Oxford, 1975)
Voeux	*Les Voeux du Paon*, ed. R. L. Graeme Ritchie, *The Buik of Alexander*, STS, 2nd ser., 12, 17, 21, 25 (1921–9)
Wars	*The Wars of Alexander*, ed. H. N. Duggan and T. Turville-Petre, EETS SS 10 (1989)
Wil Pal	*William of Palerne*, ed. G. H. V. Bunt (Groningen, 1985)
Wynnere	*Wynnere and Wastoure* (see pp. 38–66 below)
The York Plays	ed. R. Beadle (London, 1982)

INTRODUCTION

The purpose of this collection is to present a number of less well-known Middle English alliterative poems that have been overshadowed by the three masterpieces, *Pearl, Sir Gawain and the Green Knight* and *Piers Plowman*. The Arthurian poems and the works of Langland's followers are reserved for other volumes in this series, and so are not included in this anthology. There has in consequence been room for a varied collection of alliterative poems of the fourteenth and fifteenth centuries, all of which are worthy of more attention than they generally receive. By concentrating on the shorter pieces it has been possible to present most works complete, though I have also included selections from three long alliterative histories, which in some ways actually benefit from being presented in extract.

In particular the aim has been to illustrate the great range and variety of alliterative verse, both rhymed and unrhymed. The power of the line to describe scenes of violent action has often received favourable comment, and in the three histories will be found armies on the march, bloody battles and dramatic storms. But other and quieter scenes are equally well represented: for example, the silent stalking of the deer in *The Parlement of the Thre Ages*, the delights of the garden in *A Pistel of Susan*, and Paris's dream of the three goddesses in *The Destruction of Troy*. With the dream of Paris may be compared the two dream-vision debates, *Wynnere and Wastoure* and the *Parlement*, as well as two other visions, *Somer Soneday* and *The Three Dead Kings*, that are not formally set within the framework of a dream. The poets' interests range over social and political satire, heroes of romance, theological controversy, ancient history and moral admonition.

Whatever the subject, it is always given a lively and interesting setting. The issue at the heart of *St Erkenwald* is the question of the salvation of the heathen; the poet entices the reader into considering this subject by describing workmen rebuilding St Paul's, the strange discovery of a corpse miraculously preserved, the wonder of the crowd, the healing tears of a bishop. In *Wynnere* the arguments that are ultimately to do with the proper management of the economy are played out against a rich and colourful background of decorated tents and armies with bright banners, and the points are made by two vitriolic and disreputable opponents. In *Kings* the stern moral warning about the need to think further than the pleasures of this world is given in a dark and stormy wood by three grisly bodies taken up from their graves. These writers know that the task of poetry is to instruct by entertaining, so that, as the prologue of *Morte Arthure* announces, their poems must be 'Plesande and profitabill to the pople that them heres'.

DATES AND PLACES

The dating of many of these poems is difficult, in particular because there are in most cases no allusions to contemporary events, and the manuscripts are often much later than the poems themselves. Furthermore, the formulaic nature of the language makes it almost impossible to demonstrate that one work is indebted to another, and there are no obvious developments in technique, style or theme to allow dating on literary grounds. Much the earliest manuscript is Harley 2253, a collection made in about 1340, and some of the *Harley Lyrics* date back to the beginning of the century or even earlier. They illustrate the variety of rhyming alliterative stanzas current in the first half of the fourteenth century, and in some aspects of vocabulary and technique they are precursors of later verse, though exactly how they relate to the rhymed alliterative poems from late in the fourteenth century is not clear.

The earliest of the unrhymed poems, apart from the short *Erceldoun's Prophecy* in the Harley MS., is perhaps *Wynnere*, which was almost certainly composed in the 1350s. *The Siege of Jerusalem, Susan* and *Somer Soneday* must be fourteenth-century compositions since they are preserved in manuscripts dating from around the end of the century. There are probable allusions in *Dest Troy* to Chaucer's *Troilus and Criseyde*, which would place it after 1385, perhaps considerably after, since the manuscript was copied in about 1540. *Kings* was copied after 1426, but the poem may be a much earlier composition. The remaining works, *Parlement, Erkenwald* and *The Wars of Alexander*, are all in manuscripts no earlier than the mid-fifteenth century, and there are no secure grounds for dating them earlier than that.

The provenance is often equally hard to determine. Scribes generally copied out the texts in their own dialects, and if there are no rhymes there is often very little evidence to show what dialectal alterations the scribes have made. The poet's vocabulary may indicate a general area of composition, but it can never be conclusive proof because it is in part the shared diction of a school of poets. There is enough cumulative evidence from dialect, vocabulary and allusions to make it certain that some of the poems presented here are from the West Midlands; with the exception of some of the *Harley Lyrics* there is no conclusive evidence to show that any were written outside that broad area, though one or two of them might have been.

The scribe who copied the *Harley Lyrics* worked in Ludlow in Shropshire, though he seems to have collected the poems from all over the country. Nearly a century later, John Audelay, living at Haughmond Abbey a little further north in the same county, included *Kings* among a collection of his own poems, but in this case the rhymes show that the poem must have come to him from somewhere to the north. The narrator of *Wynnere* describes himself as a westerner, and allusions in the poem suggest Cheshire as a likely provenance. *Erkenwald* is probably from the same county, where the manuscript of the poem was later copied. The rhymes of *Susan* place that poem a little further north, perhaps in south Yorkshire. The author of *Dest Troy* came from Whalley in central Lancashire, and this county is likely to have been the provenance of the *Wars* and possibly also of *Siege J*, though the evidence for the latter is very slight.

AUTHORS AND AUDIENCES

It is a feature of this poetry that it treats of topics that are learned and sophisticated, but presents them in a way that will have wide appeal. So the histories of Troy and Alexander that had previously been recounted for a clerical and aristocratic readership in Latin prose are translated into English verse, the Old Testament account of Susannah and the Elders is given a fashionably elaborate setting, and the theological arguments about the destination of the just pagan, in which Wycliffe and others participated, forms the basis of the story of *Erkenwald*. With the rise in the status of English after the mid-fourteenth century, an audience that lacked an easy familiarity with Latin and French, but yet had educated interests in theology, history and romance, an understanding of political issues and an appreciation of the finer techniques of such arts as hunting and siege-warfare, could turn to the alliterative poets to provide them with suitable entertainment and edification 'in ese of Englysch men in Englysch speche' (*William of Palerne* 168).

Into this general picture of the social setting must be fitted the few facts we know about authors and their patrons. *Dest Troy* was translated from a Latin history at the request of an unidentified knight by a Lancashire poet called John Clerk, just as many years earlier Humphrey de Bohun, Earl of Hereford, had commissioned a certain William to translate *Wil Pal* from French. Both John Clerk and William may have been priests or chaplains, like John Audelay, chantry priest to Lord Strange of Knokin, who wrote his poems for the instruction of the monks at Haughmond. The scribe of MS. Harley 2253 has been judged to be a cleric with legal training, and since he copied texts in Latin and French as well as English, and some of these texts seem to count on an understanding of legal procedures, at least one section of the audience for whom the manuscript was compiled must have possessed a considerable degree of learning. Perhaps some of them were clerics in a large ecclesiastical or gentry household, although the lyrics of social comment express a sympathy for the condition of country people burdened by royal and seigneurial exactions that does not fit entirely comfortably into this proposed setting. The author of *Wynnere* more clearly

4

takes up the worries of the gentry at the uncertain future awaiting them, making an appeal to a nostalgic provincialism under threat from a tide of mercantile acquisitiveness that is about to sweep away the old feudal relationship of the lord to his lady, to his retainers, and indeed to his poet.

Both author and audience were firmly rooted in their provincial culture, their local society, their language, their landscapes of woods and hills and valleys; at the same time they were keenly aware of the impingement of events in a wider world, the decisions of a king and his ministers, the effects of national and local taxation, the battles in distant countries, and the abiding theological and moral issues in an age so preoccupied with its own material values.

THE METRE

A modern reader lacks that instinctive understanding of the alliterative line that a contemporary audience must have had, and so it is important to analyse how the metre works. In essence it is very straightforward, though the finer points are more complex and not yet fully investigated. All examples cited are from *Erkenwald*.

The line is divided into half-lines, which may be referred to as the a-verse and the b-verse. Each half-line has two stresses, and is bound to its partner by alliteration of both stresses of the a-verse and the first stress (or rarely both stresses) of the b-verse:

Ther was a **b**yschop in þat **b**urgh ~ **b**lessyd and sacryd (3)

This pattern is represented as aa/ax. Consonants alliterate with identical consonants or with consonant groups such as /sk/ or /sp/; any vowel can alliterate with any other or with /h/, though some poets tend to alliterate identical vowels:

Now of þis **A**ugustynes **a**rt ~ is **E**rkenwolde bischop (33)

The rhythm of the half-line is determined by the arrangement of the group of unstressed syllables, the 'dips', around the stresses. Stresses are marked as /, unstressed syllables as x, so that l. 3 quoted above would be denoted as: xxx/xxx/ ~ /xx/x.

The rhythm of the b-verse is quite tightly controlled. Poets avoided the alternating rhythms of xx/xx/ and x/x/x, and therefore one of the dips preceding the stresses is long, consisting of two or more syllables, and the other is short, consisting of one syllable, or more often is entirely omitted. If there is a dip after the last stress, it is short. Some common b-verse patterns are ~ x/xx/x, e.g. ' ~ and Cristendome stablyd' (2), and ~ xx//x, e.g. '~ haden sende hyder' (8).

There are a number of common variations on the basic pattern. The a-verse is frequently extended, so that there are three prominent syllables, often with alliteration on all three:

He turnyd temples þat tyme ~ (15)

In many cases it would be natural to subordinate one of the alliterating syllables, as *summe* in this half-line:

Bot summe segge couthe say ~ (100)

In other cases it may be that all three syllables should receive full metrical stress.

In the b-verse the rhythmic pattern of alternating stresses, generally avoided, is found when an adjective (or participial adjective) of two syllables precedes its noun, as in l. 277, '~ psalmyde writtes' (~/x/x).

Irregular patterns of alliteration and rhythm occur in the manuscripts, but where there are good grounds for determining the authorial reading, many such irregular patterns can be shown to be the products of scribal error. In the case of *Siege J* extant in eight manuscripts, and *Wars* in two, the evidence indicates that all such irregularities are scribal. In the *Parlement* the evidence is less decisive, perhaps because the archetype from which the two manuscripts descend is a poorer one, or perhaps because the poet himself was responsible for some of the variant patterns. Poems surviving in only one copy show the same kinds of variation. It is not a necessary conclusion that all poets adopted the same metrical constraints and that therefore all such variant patterns are scribal corruptions, but it is likely that at least many of them are. For a fuller analysis of alliterative patterns, see Turville-Petre (1980), Duggan (1986b); for rhythmic patterns see Duggan (1986a, 1988).

The alliterative line was used also in rhymed verse, in particular in stanzas of thirteen lines. The examples edited here are *Susan*, *Somer Soneday* and *Kings*. In this stanza eight four-stress lines are followed by five shorter lines, and it is no doubt from this model that the author of *Gawain* derived his unique stanza of unrhymed lines completed by a five-line 'bob and wheel'. In the thirteen-line stanza, the long lines have the structure of the unrhymed lines discussed above, though there is more variation; in particular there is frequent alliteration of the final stressed and rhyming syllable:

Of alle riches þat renke ~ arayed was riht (*Susan* 4)
He hed a wif hiʒt Susan ~ was sotil and sage (*Susan* 14)

This stanza may have developed from earlier experimental stanzaic forms that combine alliteration and rhyme in lines of variable length, as in many of the *Harley Lyrics*, some of which are only a step away from the thirteen-line stanza.

EDITORIAL PROCEDURES

Only two of the poems here are extant in full in more than one manuscript: *Siege J* in eight (one of which lacks the first 961 lines), and *Susan* in five (one lacking the first 104 lines). *Parlement* and *Wars* are both recorded in part in two manuscripts; all the other poems are found in one copy only.

Where there are several texts available, I have attempted to determine the authorial reading from among the variants, and from that cumulative evidence to establish the principles on which the author composed. This procedure, which works best with *Siege J* and *Wars*, has been explained in detail in Turville-Petre (1987a).

Where there is only one text, an editor has less evidence to draw on. I have therefore followed the manuscript reading unless there seemed to me to be clear indications of error. Such indications might be failure in sense, in alliteration, rhythm or (in a few poems) rhyme, or variance from the reading of the source.

I have consulted all the manuscripts or photographs of them, considered their readings, and recorded all departures from the manuscript on which the text is based, together with a few variants that seem of special significance from other manuscripts. Emendations conform to the spelling of the base text. In the listing of variants, the spelling is that of the manuscript whose sigil immediately follows. Thus, in *Parlement*, the base manuscript, Thornton, has *thaire*, the Ware manuscript has *þey*, and the emended text reads *thay*; this is listed as: 252 þey] W, thaire T. If the text is extant only in one manuscript, the emended reading is followed by the manuscript reading without sigil.

In the edited texts all abbreviations have been expanded without notice, including the expansion of *&* to *and* (or *ant* in the *Harley Lyrics*), *Ihs* and *Ihu* to *Jesus* and *Jesu*, and *q* to *quod*. Capitalization, word-division and punctuation are modern, so that ms. *no noþer* is printed *non oþer*, and *a nerand*, *a nox* (both alliterating on /n/) are printed *an erand*, *an ox*. The letter forms *þ* and *ʒ* have been retained, but in view of the variation and uncertainty in scribal forms, *i* and *j* have been standardized according to modern usage. An accent has been added to final *-e* in words such as *cité*, *affinité*, *semlé*, to indicate that it must be sounded.

THE HARLEY LYRICS

INTRODUCTION

Manuscript

BL MS. Harley 2253 is an anthology of verse and prose in French, Latin and English, and contains the most important and varied collection of medieval English lyrics. The scribe worked in Ludlow, on the Shropshire-Herefordshire border, from at least 1314 to 1349, and compiled this ms. in about 1340; see Revard (1979, 1981, 1982). Historical references in the text range from the Battle of Lewes of 1264 to the taxation of 1337–8; see Stemmler (1962:30). The scribe evidently collected his poems from a wide area; Brook (1933) judges the dialects of the poems edited here to be as follows: south-east or south midlands III, IV; north-west and north midlands II, VI; northern V, VIII. Subject-matter and language show that IX is also northern.

The lyrics selected here are presented in the order they appear in the ms.

Verse-forms

The most heavily alliterated lyrics, nine of which are edited here, use a wide variety of verse-forms, and these can be compared to the forms of later rhyming alliterative poems; see Turville-Petre (1977a, 18–21); Osberg (1984). The patterns are as follows: I: four monorhymed long-lines with medial rhyme, followed by a bob and two shorter lines all rhyming together. Cf. the 13-line stanza of the *Towneley Plays*. II: eight lines on one rhyme

9

followed by a couplet. III: 12-line stanzas with alternating rhymes, rather similar to the *Pearl* stanza. IV: 12-line stanzas with alliteration of pairs of lines, pararhyme and consonance throughout the octave in the first stanza; cf. *Kings*. V: 6-line stanzas with alternating rhymes. VI: verses of eighteen lines, made up of the tail-rhyme stanza followed by a 6-line wheel. VII: 8-line stanzas with alternating rhymes. VIII: monorhymed stanzas of four lines. IX: the earliest fourteenth-century example of the unrhymed line, of variable length and with irregular alliteration.

Themes

None of the most heavily alliterated lyrics is on religious topics. Several that express social comment or satire are important precursors of *Wynnere*, *PPl* and *Mum and the Sothsegger*. They attack the extravagance of women's fashions (I), the disastrous effects of taxation (III), the vexatious intrusion of ecclesiastical courts (VI) and the baseness of retainers (VIII). Lyric VII conveys a sharp impression of rural life, while IX is an early example of the type of alliterative prophecy later included in *Wynnere* and *PPl*. Lyrics II, IV and V are all witty and often surprising poems of love, the first two in praise of women and the last an impassioned exchange between a frustrated lover and his fleetingly reluctant mistress.

The virtues of the love-lyrics have long been recognized, e.g. by Stemmler (1962), but the satires, oddly, have, been regarded as 'crude' and 'popular'. Although they draw upon a popular mood of social alienation, they are in style and technique the most sophisticated poems in English of their age. Abuse is not necessarily crude, as Dunbar so wittily demonstrated 150 years later. There is a good, brief discussion in Pearsall (1977:120–32), and in Kane (1986).

BIBLIOGRAPHY

Facsimile

Facsimile of British Museum MS. Harley 2253, introduction by N. R. Ker, EETS 255 (1965)

Introduction

Editions

J. A. W. Bennett and G. V. Smithers, *Early Middle English Verse and Prose* (2nd edn, Oxford, 1968) (V, VII)

K. Böddeker, *Altenglische Dichtungen des MS. Harl. 2253* (Berlin, 1878) (I–VIII)

G. L. Brook, *The Harley Lyrics* (4th edn, Manchester, 1968) (II, IV, V, VII)

C. Brown, *English Lyrics of the XIIIth Century* (Oxford, 1932) (I, II, IV, VII)

B. Dickins and R. M. Wilson, *Early Middle English Texts* (London, 1951) (I, VII)

R. H. Robbins, *Historical Poems of the XIVth and XVth Centuries* (New York, 1959) (III, VI, VIII, IX)

C. and K. Sisam, *The Oxford Book of Medieval English Verse* (Oxford, 1970) (II, III, V, VII)

Studies

G. L. Brook, 'The original dialects of the Harley Lyrics', *LSE*, 2 (1933:38–61)

G. Kane, 'Some fourteenth-century "political" poems', in *Medieval English Religious and Ethical Literature*, ed. G. Kratzmann and J. Simpson (Cambridge, 1986:82–91)

J. R. Maddicott, 'The English peasantry and the demands of the Crown 1294–1341', *Past and Present*, Supplement 1, 1975

R. J. Menner, 'The Man in the Moon and hedging', *JEGP*, 48 (1949:1–14)

R. H. Osberg, 'Alliterative technique in the lyrics of MS Harley 2253', *MP*, 82 (1984:125–55)

D. Pearsall, *Old English and Middle English Poetry* (London, 1977)

D. J. Ransom, *Poets at Play* (Norman, Okla., 1985)

C. Revard, 'Richard Hurd and MS. Harley 2253', *NQ*, 224 (1979:199–202)

C. Revard, 'Three more holographs in the hand of the scribe of MS Harley 2253 in Shrewsbury', *NQ*, 226 (1981:199–200)

C. Revard, '*Gilote et Johane*: an interlude in BL MS. Harley 2253', *SP*, 79 (1982:122–46)

T. Stemmler, *Die englischen Liebesgedichte des MS. Harley 2253* (Bonn, 1962)

R. Woolf, 'The construction of *In a fryht as y con fare fremede*', *MÆ*, 38 (1969:55–9)

I THE FOLLIES OF FASHION

Lord þat lenest vs lyf ant lokest vch an lede,
Forte cocke wiþ knyf nast þou none nede,
Boþe wepmon ant wyf sore mowe drede
Lest þou be sturne wiþ strif for bone þat þou bede
    In wunne,   5
      Þat monkune
    Shulde shilde hem from sunne.

Nou haþ prude þe pris in euervche plawe,
By mony wymmon vnwis Y sugge mi sawe,
For ȝef a ledy lyne is leid after lawe   10
Vch a strumpet þat þer is such drahtes wl drawe;
    In prude
      Vch a screwe wol hire shrude
    Þah he nabbe nout a smok hire foule ers to hude.

Furmest in boure were boses ybroht,   15
Leuedis to honoure Ichot he were wroht,
Vch gigelot wol loure bote he hem habbe soht,
Such schrewe fol soure ant duere hit haþ aboht;

1–7 i.e. God who watches over everyone has no need to act with violence, since men and women must stand in dread of the commandment to avoid sin. The sinfulness of extravagant dress is often attacked, e.g. *Wynnere* 410–22.
5 'In bliss', i.e. in the Garden of Eden.
9 *By*: 'by the example of'.
10 'For if a lady's clothing is fitted according to fashion.'
11 '. . . will play such tricks', as in *York Plays* xxxvii. 399.
14 *he*: 'she', as in l. 17 and frequently in this ms.
15 The term 'boss' was applied to a projection or bun of hair over each cheek. See C. W. and P. Cunnington, *Handbook of English Mediaeval Costume* (London, 1952:p. 74 and pl. 30). The bosses were held in place by the hair-net (*chelle*, l. 21). Round the head was the fillet (l. 32), and the barbette of linen (l. 31) went from the top of the head under the chin. The total result looked remarkably like a pig with drooping ears (l. 23); see fig. 1.
16 *he*: 'they'.
17 *soht*: 'obtained'? (see III. 63). Or emend to *oht*, 'possessed'.

In helle
Wiþ deueles he shule duelle   20
For þe clogges þat cleueþ by here chelle.

Nou ne lackeþ hem no lyn boses in to beren,
He sitteþ ase a slat swyn þat hongeþ is eren,
Such a joustynde gyn vch wrecche wol weren,
Al hit comeþ in declyn þis gigelotes geren.   25
        Vpo lofte
    Þe deuel may sitte softe
Ant holden his halymotes ofte.

3ef þer lyþ a loket by er ouþer e3e
Þat mot wiþ worse be wet for lac of oþer le3e,   30
Þe bout ant þe barbet wyþ frountel shule fe3e.
Habbe he a fauce filet he halt hire hed he3e.
        To shewe
    Þat heo be kud ant knewe
For strompet in rybaudes rewe.   35

30 lac] lat.

21 'Because of the lumps (the bosses) that are held in place by her hair-
net.'
22 'Now they are not short of linen (barbettes) to support bosses.'
24 *joustynde gyn*: lit. 'jousting device'; one sense of *joust* (from Fr) was
'join, unite'; hence *MED justen* v. 3(c) suggests '? some kind of linen
headgear or chin-band used to bind plaits of hair to the sides of the face'.
There is the same use of *gyn*, together with other similarities of subject-
matter, vocabulary and stanza-form, in *Towneley Plays* xxx. 260–4.
25 *comeþ in declyn*: 'gets worse', with a play on 'hangs down low (round
her cheeks)'. The contrast is with the devil sitting in proud possession on
high.
29–30 'If there lies a hair-curl by the ear or by the eye, that must be
wetted with something worse for lack of any other lye.' Lye was an
alkaline solution used for washing and bleaching hair; the most available
form of it was urine, hence 'something worse', as explained by R. J.
Menner, *MLN*, 55 (1940:244). Perhaps, though, emend *worse* to *wouse*,
'plant sap (for tanning, etc.)'.
32 *fauce filet*: 'false' in that the headband is not made of silk (unlike
Alysoun's fillet, Chaucer, *CT* i. 3243)? More probably it is a particular
fashionable kind of fillet.
34 *kud ant knewe*: 'well-known and recognised'.

II ANNOT AND JOHN

Ichot a burde in a bour ase beryl so bryht,
Ase saphyr in seluer semly on syht,
Ase jaspe þe gentil þat lemeþ wiþ lyht,
Ase gernet in golde ant ruby wel ryht.
Ase onycle he ys on yholden on hyht,   5
Ase diamaund þe dere in day when he is dyht,
He is coral ycud wiþ cayser ant knyht,
Ase emeraude amorewen þis may haueþ myht.
Þe myht of þe margarite haueþ þis mai mere;
For charbocle Ich hire ches bi chyn ant by chere.   10

Hire rode is ase rose þat red is on rys,
Wiþ lilye-white leres lossum he is,
Þe primerole he passeþ, þe peruenke of pris,
Wiþ alisaundre þareto, ache ant anys.
Coynte ase columbine such hire cunde ys,   15
Glad vnder gore in gro ant in grys,
He is blosme opon bleo, brihtest vnder bis,
Wiþ celydoyne ant sauge, ase þou þiself sys.
Þat syht vpon þat semly to blis he is broht,
He is solsecle to sauue ys forsoht.   20

Verse by verse the poet compares the lady to precious stones, flowers,
birds, spices and famous people. Such comparisons of the lady (or the
Virgin) are traditional, though usually less elaborate.
5 'As an onyx she is one who is highly regarded.'
6 *in day when*: 'whenever', as also in l. 36. Cf. *SGGK* 80: *in daye*,
'ever'.
9 Precious stones were believed to have medicinal powers; see *English
Mediaeval Lapidaries*, EETS 190, *passim*; and (with special reference to
this poem) Stemmler (1962:204–14).
10 *For*: 'before, in preference to'.
11–30 See *Susan* 66–117 for similar association of the lady with birds and
flowers.
16 *Glad vnder gore*: 'beautiful under her dress', i.e. 'physically
beautiful'.
19 *Þat syht*: 'he who looks'.
20 'She is a marigold who is sought out for healing'. Cf. l. 34. Herbals
dealt with the healing properties of plants; marigold was an antidote for
venom and a remedy for the plague; see *MED mari-gold(e*.

II Annot and John

He is papejai in pyn þat beteþ me my bale,
To trewe tortle in a tour Y telle þe mi tale,
He is þrustle þryuen ant þro þat singeþ in sale,
Þe wilde laueroc ant wolc ant þe wodewale.
He is faucoun in friht, dernest in dale   25
Ant wiþ eueruch a gome gladest in gale,
From Weye he is wisist into Wyrhale,
Hire nome is in a note of þe nyhtegale.
In Annote is hire nome; nempneþ hit non!
Whose ryht redeþ, roune to Johon.   30

Muge he is ant mondrake þourh miht of þe mone,
Trewe triacle ytold wiþ tonges in trone,
Such licoris mai leche from Lyne to Lone,
Such sucre mon secheþ þat saueþ men sone.
Bliþe yblessed of Crist, þat bayþeþ me mi bone   35
When derne dedis in day derne are done.

23 ant] in.   31 þourh] þouh.   35 bayþeþ] bayeþ.   36 dedis]
dede is; day] dayne.

21 *in pyn*: i.e. 'in *my* torment'. The parrot's song traditionally brought
happiness; see Chaucer's tongue-in-cheek commendation, *CT* vii. 766–8,
where other songbirds are the thrush and the sparrowhawk.
22 'To thee, faithful turtle-dove in a castle . . .' — a suitable setting for
a courtly lady.
24 *wolc*: generally interpreted as the only English occurrence of Welsh
gwalch, 'hawk'. The Sisams very plausibly emend *ant wolc* to *in wolcn*,
'in the sky'.
25 *dernest*: 'most hidden', introducing the concept of secrecy so
important to the medieval lover.
27 The River Wye runs through south Wales; the Forest of Wirral lies to
the north of Chester; cf. *SGGK* 701.
28–9 In the ms. *a note* is written *Anote*, a common diminutive of Agnes.
The lover is less scrupulous than Troilus in preserving the secrecy of the
relationship; cf. Chaucer, *TC* iii. 281–322.
30 'Whoever interprets it correctly, whisper to John.'
31–40 There is a very similar list of spices in *Kyng Alisaunder* 6782–6.
Mandrake root was used in both medicine and magic; it should be dug
up after sunset (Trevisa, *Properties*, p. 996) since the moon has a strong
influence on the compounding of medicines; see Gower, *CA* v. 4115–45.
32 *in trone*: 'in throne', i.e. 'in court', as in l. 39.
33 The River Lyn is in north Devon; the Lune runs north of Lancaster.
35–6 '. . . who grants my entreaty whenever secret deeds are done
secretly.'

15

Ase gromyl in greue grene is þe grone,
Ase quibibe ant comyn cud is in crone,
Cud comyn in court, canel in cofre,
Wiþ gyngyure ant sedewale ant þe gylofre.   40

He is medicine of miht, mercie of mede,
Rekene ase Regnas resoun to rede,
Trewe ase Tegeu in tour, ase Wyrwein in wede,
Baldore þen Byrne þat oft þe bor bede.
Ase Wylcadoun he is wys, dohty of dede,   45
Feyrore þen Floyres folkes to fede,
Cud ase Cradoc in court carf þe brede,
Hendore þen Hilde, þat haueþ me to hede.
He haueþ me to hede, þis hendy anon,
Gentil ase Jonas, heo joyeþ wiþ Jon.   50

41 medicine] medierne.   44 oft] of.

38 '. . . which is remarkable in its flower-head.'
41–50 Among these names of heroes and heroines, the references to
Tegeu and Cradoc are particularly interesting. In Welsh sources Tegau
Eurvron is the wife of Caradawc Vreichvras; see R. Bromwich, *Trioedd
Ynys Prydein* (Cardiff, 1961:512–14). In the later story of the Boy and
the Mantle, the test of the mantle shows that of all the ladies in Arthur's
court only Craddocke's lady is faithful, and the test of the knife which
only in Craddocke's hands cuts the boar's head (cf. l. 47) shows that he
alone is no cuckold. See F. J. Child, *The English and Scottish Popular
Ballads* (repr. New York, 1957:i, 257–74).
    The identities of the other figures are less certain. For suggestions see
Brown, *XIII*, 226–8; R. M. Wilson, *The Lost Literature of Medieval
England* (2nd edn, London, 1970:133–4).

III   THE EVILS OF TAXATION

Ich herde men vpo mold make muche mon
Hou he beþ itened of here tilyynge;
Gode ȝeres ant corn boþe beþ agon,
Ne kepeþ here no sawe ne no song synge.
Nou we mote worche, nis þer non oþer won,   5
Mai Ich no lengore lyue wiþ mi lesinge;
ȝet þer is a bitterore bit to þe bon,
For euer þe furþe peni mot to þe kynge.
Þus we carpeþ for þe kyng ant carieþ ful colde,
Ant weneþ forte keuere ant euer buþ acast,   10
Whose haþ eny god, hopeþ he nout to holde,
Bote euer þe leuest we leoseþ alast.

Luþer is to leosen þer ase lutel ys,
Ant haueþ monie hynen þat hopieþ þerto;
Þe hayward heteþ vs harm to habben of his,   15

7 bit] bid.

The complaint is that in a time of poor harvest the exactions of the lord
and the king are cripplingly heavy. Maddicott (1975:3, 7, 13), shows that
during the years of the great famine of 1315–17 taxation was particularly
high, and he suggests this as an appropriate date for the poem, though it
may be noted that the complaint in the Towneley *Second Shepherds'
Play*, ll. 10–37, is very similar.
2 *he beþ*: 'they are'.
4 'Nor (do they) wish to hear any story nor sing any song.' For *kepeþ
here*, cf. V. 8.
7 'There is a yet more grievous cut to the bone.'
8 *mot*: 'must go'.
13–14 'It is dreadful to lose where there is little, and (we) have many
farm-workers who rely (for wages) on it.' The narrator is not a starving
peasant but a modest farmer; he has a farm, labourers, land and corn,
cattle and a mare, and he can afford a mark to bribe the bailiff. See
Maddicott (1975:13).
15–17 'The hayward threatens us with suffering from his men, the bailiff
promises us misery and intends indeed to inflict it, the woodward who
keeps watch under the bough brings us sorrow.' The hayward supervised
the enclosed land and the work on it: 'haue an horn and be hayward and
lygge þeroute nyhtes/And kepe my corn in my croft fro pykares and
theues' (*PPl* C v. 16–17). The bailiff managed the manor; the woodward

17

Harley Lyrics

Þe bailif beckneþ vs bale ant weneþ wel do,
Þe wodeward waiteþ vs wo þat lokeþ vnder rys,
Ne mai vs ryse no rest, rycheis ne ro.
Þus me pileþ þe pore þat is of lute pris;
Nede in swot ant in swynk swynde mot swo.   20
Nede he mot swynde þah he hade swore
Þat naþ nout en hod his hed forte hude;
Þus wil walkeþ in lond ant lawe is forlore,
Ant al is piked of þe pore þe prikyares prude.

Þus me pileþ þe pore ant pykeþ ful clene,   25
Þe ryche me raymeþ wiþouten eny ryht,
Ar londes ant ar leodes liggeþ fol lene,
Þorh biddyng of baylyfs such harm hem haþ hiht.
Men of religioun me halt hem ful hene,
Baroun ant bonde, þe clerc ant þe knyht;   30
Þus wil walkeþ in lond ant wondred ys wene,
Falsshipe fatteþ ant marreþ wyþ myht.
Stont stille y þe stude ant halt him ful sturne,
Þat makeþ beggares go wiþ bordon ant bagges;
Þus we beþ honted from hale to hurne;   35
Þat er werede robes, nou wereþ ragges.

16 beckneþ] bockneþ.   28 biddyng] bddyng.   29 Men] mem.

---

looked after the plantations. All were officials of the lord. See Bennett
(1937:162–7, 179–80, 182).
19 'Thus the poor who are of little account are oppressed'; *me* is indef.
pron. (OE *man*), as also in l. 56.
20 *Nede*: 'poverty, the poor man'. In l. 21 *Nede* is adv., 'of necessity'.
21–2 'He is bound to waste away, even though he had affirmed that he is
without a hood to shelter his head.'
24 'The proud array of the horsemen (i.e. the retainers, cf. VIII) is
plundered from the poor.'
25–36 The effects of taxation on rich and poor alike.
26 'The rich are wrongfully fleeced.' See Kane (1986:86).
27 *Ar*: 'their'.
29 'Men in holy orders are treated very wretchedly.'
33–4 'He who makes beggars go with staff and bags stands unmoved and
behaves very cruelly.' Taxation was so oppressive that some farmers
were forced to leave the land; cf. l. 67, and see Maddicott (1975: 15, 19).

18

3et comeþ budeles wiþ ful muche bost:
'Greyþe me seluer to þe grene wax!
Þou art writen y my writ, þat þou wel wost!'
Mo þen ten siþen told Y my tax.   40
Þenne mot ych habbe hennen arost,
Feyr on fyhsh-day launprey ant lax.
Forþ to þe chepyn – geyneþ ne chost,
Þah Y sulle mi bil ant my borstax.
Ich mot legge my wed wel 3ef Y wolle,   45
Oþer sulle mi corn on gras þat is grene,
3et I shal be foul cherl, þah he han þe fulle;
Þat Ich alle 3er spare, þenne Y mot spene.

Nede Y mot spene þat Y spared 3ore,
A3eyn þis cachereles comeþ þus Y mot care;   50
Comeþ þe maister-budel brust ase a bore,
Seiþ he wole mi bugging bringe ful bare.
Mede Y mot munten a marke oþer more
Þah Ich at þe set dey sulle mi mare;
Þus þe grene wax vs greueþ vnder gore,   55
Þat me vs honteþ ase hound doþ þe hare.
He vs honteþe ase hound hare doþ on hulle,

57 doþ] doh.

37 *budeles*: 'beadles', the hundred-bailiffs who collected the king's taxes.
The poet now discusses the effects of royal taxation.
38 The document by which the Exchequer called in unpaid debts was
sealed with green wax.
40 'I have payed over my tax more than ten times.' Bailiffs would
demand payment again and pocket the proceeds themselves; Maddicott
(1975:12).
41 'Then I must have roast hens (as bribes for the bailiffs).'
42 *fyhsh-day*: see *Wynnere* 311n. The bailiff eats lamprey and salmon.
43 'Off to the market; no argument helps.'
45 *legge my wed*: 'lay down my pledge', i.e. pawn valuable possessions.
46 To raise money quickly he must sell his green corn in the field as a
'future'.
47 *he han*: 'they (the bailiffs) have'.
50 'Thus I must worry in expectation that these tax-collectors are
coming.'
53 'I must offer a bribe of a mark or more' — a sizeable sum; see
Wynnere 356n.
55 *vnder gore*: 'to the quick'; for the usual sense see II. 16.

Seþþe Y tok to þe lond such tene me wes taht;
Nabbeþ ner budeles boded ar fulle,
For he may scape ant we aren euer caht.   60

Þus Y kippe ant cacche cares ful colde
Seþþe Y counte ant cot hade to kepe;
To seche seluer to þe kyng Y mi seed solde,
Forþi mi lond leye liþ ant leorneþ to slepe.
Seþþe he mi feire feh fatte y my folde,   65
When Y þenke o mi weole welneh Y wepe;
Þus bredeþ monie beggares bolde,
Ant vre ruȝe ys roted ant ruls er we repe.
Ruls ys oure ruȝe ant roted in þe stre,
For wickede wederes by broke ant by brynke;   70
Þer wakeneþ in þe world wondred ant wee,
Ase god is swynden anon as so forte swynke.

58 tok] tek.

59 'Bailiffs have never demanded their fill.'
63 He was forced to sell his seed-corn to pay his taxes.
65 'Then they took my fine cattle in my fold.'
68–9 The effects of taxation are compounded by severe weather, as they
were in 1315–17. *in þe stre*: 'in the straw', i.e. before it is threshed.
72 'It is as good to waste away at once as to labour thus.'

IV THE POET'S REPENTANCE

Weping haueþ myn wonges wet
For wikked werk ant wone of wyt,
Vnbliþe Y be til Y ha bet
Bruches broken – ase bok byt –
Of leuedis loue þat Y ha let,   5
Þat lemeþ al wiþ luefly lyt.
Ofte in song Y haue hem set,
Þat is vnsemly þer hit syt.
   Hit syt ant semeþ noht
   Þer hit ys seid in song;   10
   Þat Y haue of hem wroht
   Ywis hit is al wrong.

Al wrong Y wrohte for a wyf
Þat made vs wo in world ful wyde,
Heo rafte vs alle richesse ryf   15
Þat durþe vs nout in reynes ryde.
A styþye stunte hire sturne stryf
Þat ys in heouene hert in hyde.
In hire lyht on ledeþ lyf
Ant shon þourh hire semly syde.   20

3–6 'I shall be unhappy until I have made amends for sins I've
committed – as the book (the Bible?) commands – in respect of ladies'
love that I've forfeited, who all shine with a lovely light.' The poet
repents of 'shewynge how that wemen han don mis' (Chaucer, *LGW*,
Prol. G 266). For discussion see Stemmler (1962:194–9).
8 'Which is improper where it's placed.'
11 'What I've composed about them.'
13–18 The poet has been led astray by the archetypal temptress (Eve),
but put right by the emblem of female virtue (the Virgin). For the theme
of Mary as second Eve (just as Christ is second Adam), see Woolf
(1968:115–16).
15–16 'She deprived us of all abundant wealth, she who should not take
control of us.' The forms and senses of *dare* and *þar* became confused;
for *durþe*, 'should, must', see *MED durren* 2(a).
17–19 'An excellent lady who is hidden in the heart of heaven stopped
her vicious attack. In her alighted one who lives.'

Þourh hyre side he shon
Ase sonne doþ þourh þe glas;
Wommon nes wicked non
Seþþe he ybore was.

Wycked nis non, þat Y wot,   25
þat durste for werk hire wonges wete,
Alle heo lyuen from last of lot
Ant are al hende ase hauke in chete.
Forþi on molde Y waxe mot
Þat Y sawes haue seid vnsete;   30
My fykel fleish, mi falsly blod,
On feld hem feole Y falle to fete.
    To fet Y falle hem feole
    For falsleke fifti folde,
    Of alle vntrewe on tele   35
    Wiþ tonge ase Y her tolde.

Þah told beon tales vntoun in toune –
Such tiding mei tide, Y nul nout teme –
Of brudes bryht wiþ browes broune,
Our blisse heo beyen, þis briddes breme.   40
In rude were roo wiþ hem to roune
Þat hem mihte henten ase him were heme.
Nys kyng, cayser, ne clerk wiþ croune

28 hauke] hake.   40 Our] or.   41 to] *om.*

21–2 This image of Mary's virginity, attributed to St Augustine, is often
used.
25–6 'I know that no-one is wicked who has had to wet their cheeks for
sorrow.' *Non* is construed first as sg. then as pl.
27–8 'They live entirely free from sinfulness of conduct, and are as
obedient as hawk in hall.' The same image of meekness is in *Pearl* 184.
31–2 'My sinful flesh, my deceitful blood, I make them very submissive.'
On feld, 'on the ground', extends the image of *falle to fete*, 'make fall to
the feet'; *feole* is adv., 'greatly'.
35–6 'For everything false in wicked speech which I formerly (*her* = *er*)
uttered.'
37–48 The stanza presents difficulties. 'Though improper tales are told
in company – such events may happen, I don't wish to vouch for it (?) –
about lovely ladies with brown eyebrows, yet they restore our joy, these
excellent ladies. In boorish society (?) it would be relaxing to talk

IV The poet's repentance

Þis semly seruen þat mene may seme.
  Semen him may on sonde   45
  Þis semly seruen so,
  Boþe wiþ fet ant honde
  For on þat vs warp from wo.

Nou wo in world ys went away
Ant weole is come ase we wolde   50
Þourh a mihti, methful mai
Þat ous haþ cast from cares colde.
Euer wymmen Ich herie ay,
Ant euer in hyrd wiþ hem Ich holde,
Ant euer at neode Y nyckenay   55
Þat Y ner nemnede þat heo nolde.
  Y nolde ant null yt noht,
  For noþyng nou a nede
  Soþ is þat Y of hem ha wroht,
  As Richard erst con rede.   60

Richard, rote of resoun ryht,
Rykening of rym ant ron,
Of maidnes meke þou hast myht,
On molde Y holde þe murgest mon.
Cunde comely ase a knyht,   65
Clerk ycud þat craftes con,

---

44 mene] me ne.

___

confidentially with them, whoever might treat them as would be fitting
for him. There is no king, emperor nor tonsured cleric for whom it might
appear demeaning to serve these fine ladies. It would befit him to
minister to (*seruen on sonde*) these fine ones in every way possible, for
the sake of one (i.e. Mary) who rescued us from sorrow.'
49–72 For observations on the last two stanzas see E. G. Stanley, *NQ*,
220 (1975:155–7).
54–60 'And I always support (*holde wiþ*) them publicly, and whenever
necessary I deny that I ever made remarks they didn't like. I didn't want
and don't want it (viz. to make unwelcome remarks), for nothing now is
necessarily true that I've written of them, as Richard was the first to
point out.'
61–72 An elaborate series of compliments to 'Richard', whose noble
poetry is so well known. *Sic transit gloria mundi.*
62 *Rykening of*: 'taking account of', i.e. 'with regard to'.

23

In vch an hyrd þyn aþel ys hyht,
Ant vch an aþel þin hap is on.
  Hap þat haþel haþ hent
  Wiþ hendelec in halle;   70
  Selþe be him sent
  In londe of leuedis alle!

71 him] hem.

67–8 'In every assembly your excellence is acknowledged, and your
happiness resides in every good action.'
72 *of*: 'by'.

V THE MEETING IN THE WOOD

In a fryht as Y con fare fremede
Y founde a wel feyr fenge to fere,
Heo glystnede ase gold when hit glemede;
Nes ner gome so gladly on gere.
Y wolde wyte in world who hire kenede,   5
Þis burde bryht, ȝef hire wil were;
Heo me bed go my gates lest hire gremede;
Ne kepte heo non henyng here.

'Yhere þou me nou, hendest in helde,
Nauy þe none harmes to heþe.   10
Casten Y wol þe from cares ant kelde,
Comeliche Y wol þe nou cleþe.'

'Cloþes Y haue on forte caste,
Such as Y may weore wiþ wynne.
Betere is were þunne boute laste   15
Þen syde robes ant synke into synne.
Haue ȝe or wyl, ȝe waxeþ vnwraste;
Afterward or þonke be þynne.
Betre is make forewardes faste
Þen afterward to mene ant mynne.'   20

'Of munnyng ne munte þou namore.
Of menske þou were wurþe, by my myht.
Y take an hond to holde þat Y hore

For an analysis of structure and meaning see Woolf (1969), where the emendations of l. 40 are proposed. The poem, with its 'combinations of narrative and dramatic with lyric elements', is a *chanson d'aventure*; see H. E. Sandison, *The "Chanson d'Aventure" in Middle English* (Bryn Mawr, Pennsylvania, 1913).
4 'Never was a man in such a happy mood.'
6 '. . . if she were agreeable to it' (viz. my asking).
8 'She wished to hear no insulting suggestions.'
15 'It is better to wear thin clothes without sinfulness.'
17 *or*: 'your' (and in l. 18). 'If you have your way, you will become deceitful.'
22 *by my myht*: 'as much as I can (provide it).'
23 *þat*: 'until'.

Of al þat Y þe haue byhyht.
Why ys þe loþ to leuen on my lore   25
Lengore þen my loue were on þe lyht?
Anoþer myhte ȝerne þe so ȝore
Þat nolde þe noht rede so ryht.'

'Such reed me myhte spaclyche reowe
When al my ro were me atraht,   30
Sone þou woldest vachen an newe
Ant take anoþer wiþinne nyȝe naht.
Þenne miht I hongren on heowe,
In vch an hyrd ben hated ant forhaht,
Ant ben ycayred from alle þat Y kneowe   35
Ant bede cleuyen þer Y hade claht.'

'Betere is taken a comeliche y cloþe
In armes to cusse ant to cluppe
Þen a wrecche ywedded so wroþe;
Þah he þe slowe ne myhtu him asluppe.   40
Þe beste red þat Y con to vs boþe
Þat þou me take ant Y þe toward huppe.
Þah Y swore by treuþe ant oþe,
Þat God haþ shaped mey non atluppe.'

31 þou] þo.   33 hongren] hengren.   40 þe] me; myhtu] myhti.

26 'For longer than my love would be settled on you'; i.e. 'why do you think my promises will last no longer than my desire'.
31 *vachen*: 'search for'; *MED fecchen* 4(a). The alliteration suggests emendation to *sechen*.
32 Cf. the expression 'nine days' wonder', and Chaucer, *TC* iv. 588.
33–6 For the motif of the abandoned mistress shunned by family and friends, see Woolf (1969:56).
36 'And be told to stick to what I had grasped hold of.'
37–40 In answer, the lover warns of another danger, the unloved and violent husband. For the motif see Woolf (1969:57).
40 'You would never get free of him even if he killed you.'
42 'That you take me and I spring to you.'
44 'No-one may escape what God has ordained.'

'Mid shupping ne mey hit me ashunche.   45
Nes Y neuer wycche ne wyle.
Ych am a maide, þah me ofþunche.
Luef me were gome boute gyle.'

47 þah] þat.

45–6 'One may not escape from it (God's decree) even by shape-shifting; I was never a witch or a sorceress.' Woolf (1969:58), draws a parallel with the *chanson des transformations*, 'in which the maiden posits various shapes that she will assume in order to elude her suitor'.
48 'A man without deceit would be pleasing to me.' Does she persuade herself that he is honest, or is she resigned to taking what she can get?

VI IN THE ECCLESIASTICAL COURT

Ne mai no lewed lued libben in londe,
Be he neuer in hyrt so hauer of honde,
　So lerede vs biledes;
3ef Ich on molde mote wiþ a mai
Y shal falle hem byfore ant lurnen huere lay　　　　　5
　Ant rewen alle huere redes;
Ah bote Y be þe furme day on folde hem byfore,
Ne shal Y nout so skere scapen of huere score,
　So grimly he on me gredes,
Þat Y ne mot me lede þer wiþ mi lawe　　　　　10
On alle maner oþes þat heo me wulleþ awe,
　Heore boc ase vnbredes.
　Heo wendeþ bokes vnbrad
　Ant makeþ men a moneþ amad,
　Of scaþe Y wol me skere　　　　　15
　Ant fleo from my fere,

The speaker, having had dealings with a girl (l. 4), is brought before the
court to answer the charges of two women (l. 57). Presumably both are
claiming valid contract to him. In the end he is punished (l. 82) and
formally married by a priest (ll. 87–8). For the general background see
B. L. Woodcock, *Medieval Ecclesiastical Courts in the Diocese of
Canterbury* (London, 1952), and for the courts' concern with
matrimonial cases, see M. M. Sheehan, 'The Formation and Stability of
Marriage in Fourteenth-Century England', *MS*, 33 (1971: 228–63).
Problems concerning the validity of clandestine marriages arose
particularly frequently, since private betrothal followed by intercourse
might constitute marriage, even though not solemnized by the Church.
1 *lewed lued*: 'layman', in contrast to *lerede*, l. 3.
9–18 The meaning of these lines is obscured by uncertainties over forms
of the pron. and v., since the scribe has altered many of the forms of the
northern author. Thus *he* may be 'he', 'she' or 'they', *heo* 'she' or 'they';
the pr.pl. ending is occasionally northern *-es* in rhyme (e.g. l. 4), more
usually *-eþ* or *-en*. So *he gredes* (9) and *heo wulleþ* (11) may both be sg.,
but in context are probably pl.
10–11 Perhaps: 'That I may not bring testimony for my own defence,
with all the kinds of oaths with which they will frighten me.'
12 'As they close their book'? The *bok* is perhaps the court-register; *ase*
is for *as he*; *vnbredes*, pp. *vnbrad*, from *breden*, 'to open (a book)'.
15–16 'I wish to clear myself of a damning charge and flee from my
mistress.'

Ne rohte he whet yt were
  Boten heo hit had.

Furst þer sit an old cherl in a blake hure,
Of alle þat þer sitteþ semeþ best syre,   20
  Ant leyþ ys leg olonke.
An heme in an herygoud wiþ honginde sleuen,
Ant mo þen fourti him byfore my bales to breuen,
  In sunnes ȝef Y songe.
Heo pynkes wiþ heore penne on heore parchemyn   25
Ant sayen Y am breued ant ybroht yn
  Of al my weole wlonke;
Alle heo bueþ redy myn rouþes to rede,
Þer Y mot for menske munte sum mede
  Ant þonkfulliche hem þonke.   30
  Shal Y þonke hem þer er Y go?
  ȝe, þe maister ant ys men bo!
  ȝef y am wreit in heore write,
  Þenne am Y bac bite,
  For moni mon heo makeþ wyte   35
    Of wymmene wo.

ȝet þer sitteþ somenours syexe oþer seuene,
Mysmotinde men alle by here euene,
  Ant recheþ forþ heore rolle.
Hyrdmen hem hatieþ, ant vch mones hyne,   40
For eueruch a parossh heo polkeþ in pyne

33 weit] wreint.

17–18 Obscure. Is *hit* the form of the alleged betrothal?
19–24 The judge and the clerks of the court who record the man's sins
and threaten to confiscate his property until he bribes them and
expresses his gratitude.
24 *songe*: for *sonke*, 'sank'; cf. V.16.
29 Cf. III.53.
33 *wreit in heore write*: cf. III.39.
35–6 'For they lay the blame on many men for the misfortunes of women.'
37 The summoners who ferreted out offences and ensured that the
accused appeared before the ecclesiastical court; see Chaucer, *CT* iii.
1301–31. There are innumerable attacks on their corruption, especially
from Langland; e.g. *PPl* B ii. 57–62, iii. 134–52. See L. A. Haselmayer,
'The Apparitor and Chaucer's Summoner', *Speculum*, 12 (1937:43–57).

Ant clastreþ wyþ heore colle.
Nou wol vch fol clerc þat is fayly
Wende to þe bysshop ant bugge bayly,
   Nys no wyt in is nolle;   45
Come to countene court, couren in a cope,
Ant suggen he haþ priuilegie proud of þe pope,
   Swart ant al toswolle.
   Aren heo toswolle forswore?
   Ʒe, þe hatred of helle beo heore!   50
   For þer heo beodeþ a boke
   To sugge ase Y folht toke.
   Heo shulen in helle on an hoke
      Honge þerefore!

Þer stont vp a ʒeolumon, ʒeʒeþ wiþ a ʒerde,   55
Ant hat out an heh þat al þe hyrt herde,
   Ant cleopeþ Magge ant Malle;
Ant heo comeþ bymodered ase a morhen
Ant scrynkeþ for shome ant shomeþ for men,
   Vncomely vnder calle.   60
Heo biginneþ to shryke and scremeþ anon
Ant saiþ by my gabbyng ne shal hit so gon,
   Ant 'Þat beo on ou alle,
Þat þou shalt me wedde ant welde to wyf!'

43–54 The immoral summoners turn for support to the bishop; when
they are themselves summoned before the county court, they claim that
by privilege of clergy they cannot be tried by the secular authorities. In
the bishop's court they commit perjury and accuse the poet of
fornication. Gower complains of this abuse in *Vox Clamantis*, iii. 3.
43 Cf. *clerc fayllard*, Bennett and Smithers (1968:XV. 8).
44 *bayly*: here a court official. The meaning of *bugge* is unknown.
51 *beodeþ a boke*: either 'affirm on the Bible', or 'ask for a Bible' (in
order to affirm).
52 *folht toke*: 'had intercourse'; *folht* is a characteristic scribal spelling of
folth, 'filth, lechery etc.'. For the phrase see *MED filth* n. 3b.
55–7 The court crier calls for Magge (a form of Margaret) and Malle (a
diminutive of Mary).
58–62 The verbs may be sg. or pl.; see 9–18n.
60 For the conventional epithet of which this is the reverse, see II.16.
62–3 'And say(s) it (the court business) will not be conducted by my
lying testimony, and "Let that be the responsibility of you all (in
court) . . ."'

Ah me were leuere wiþ lawe leose my lyf   65
  Þen so to fote hem falle.
  Shal Y to fote falle for mi fo?
  3e, monie byswykeþ heo swo!
  Of þralles Y am þer þrat
  Þat sitteþ swart ant forswat,   70
  Þer Y mot hente me en hat
    Er Ich hom go.

Such chaffare Y chepe at þe chapitre
Þat makeþ moni þryue mon vnþeufol to be
  Wiþ þonkes ful þunne,   75
Ant seþþe Y go coure at constory
Ant falle to fote vch a fayly,
  Heore is þis worldes wynne.
Seþþen Y pleide at bisshopes plee,
Ah me were leuere be sonken y þe see   80
  In sor wiþouten synne.
At chirche ant þourh cheping ase dogge Y am dryue
Þat me were leuere of lyue þen so forte lyue
  To care of al my kynne.
  Atte constorie heo kenneþ vs care   85
  Ant whissheþ vs euele ant worse to fare.
  A pruest proud ase a po
  Seþþe weddeþ vs bo.
  Wyde heo worcheþ vs wo
    For wymmene ware!   90

68 'Yes, they (or she) persuade(s) many to that effect.'
71 *en hat*: 'a judicial order', viz. to marry.
82 Woodcock, p. 98, cites a case where the offender in a matrimonial suit was sentenced to be whipped seven times round the market-place and the church.
83 *of lyue*: i.e. 'be dead'; *MED lif* n. 1b (d).
90 *ware*: takes up the commercial image of l. 73, and has also a sexual meaning, 'private parts' (*OED ware* sb.[3] 4c).

VII MAN IN THE MOON

Mon in þe mone stond ant strit,
On is bot-forke is burþen he bereþ;
Hit is muche wonder þat he n'adoun slyt,
For doute leste he valle he shoddreþ ant shereþ.
When þe forst freseþ muche chele he byd,   5
Þe þornes beþ kene, is hattren totereþ.
Nis no wyþt in þe world þat wot wen he syt,
Ne – bote hit bue þe hegge – whet wedes he wereþ.

Whider trowe þis mon ha þe wey take?
He haþ set is o fot is oþer toforen;   10
For non hiþte þat he haþ ne syþt me hym ner shake,
He is þe sloweste mon þat euer wes yboren!
Wher he were o þe feld pycchynde stake
For hope of ys þornes to dutten is doren,
He mot myd is twybyl oþer trous make,   15
Oþer al is dayes werk þer were yloren.

Þis ilke mon vpon heh when er he were,
Wher he were y þe mone boren ant yfed,
He leneþ on is forke ase a grey frere;
Þis crokede caynard sore he is adred!   20

1 *stond ant strit*: he appears to be striding yet he stands still. So l. 11,
'Despite any haste that he has, one never sees him move'. See fig. 2,
showing the man striding with his bundle of thorns.
4 The man shudders as the moon glimmers.
7 *wyþt*: a spelling of *wyht*, 'person'. So, too, l. 11 *hiþte* for *hiht*,
'haste', *syþt* for *syht*, 'sees'; l. 35 *heþ* for *heh*, 'high'. Conversely, l. 39
teh for *teþ*, 'teeth'.
8 In folk-belief the man was banished to the moon as a penalty for
stealing brushwood as he was making hedges. See Menner (1949) for a
full discussion. Only the hedge knows what clothes he wears, since half
of them have been left on the thorns (l. 6).
9 'Whither (do you) believe this man to have gone?'
13–16 In making a hedge, the framework of stakes has first to be set up.
The newly growing thorns are protected from cattle by laying another
bundle (*oþer trous*) on top. The process is fully described by Menner
(1949).
14 'In the hope of growing thorns to close up the openings or gaps in his
hedges' (Menner).

Hit is mony day go þat he was here,
Ichot of his ernde he naþ nout ysped;
He haþ hewe sumwher a burþen of brere,
Þarefore sum hayward haþ taken ys wed.

Ȝef þy wed ys ytake, bring hom þe trous!   25
Sete forþ þyn oþer fot, stryd ouer sty!
We shule preye þe haywart hom to vr hous
Ant maken hym at heyse for þe maystry,
Drynke to hym deorly of fol god bous,
Ant oure dame Douse shal sitten hym by.   30
When þat he is dronke ase a dreynt mous,
Þenne we shule borewe þe wed ate bayly.

Þis mon hereþ me nout, þah Ich to hym crye.
Ichot þe cherl is def; þe del hym todrawe!
Þah Ich ȝeȝe vpon heþ, nulle nout hye;   35
Þe lostlase ladde con nout o lawe.
Hupe forþ, Hubert, hosede pye!
Ichot þart amarscled into þe mawe.
Þah me teone wiþ hym þat myn teh mye,
Þe cherld nul nout adoun er þe day dawe.   40

23–4 The hayward (see III.15–17n) has caught the man cutting briars
and has taken a pledge for the payment of the fine. For the hayward's
wed, see *PPl* C xiii. 41–8, where the merchant who is caught crossing the
cornfield must surrender his hat or gloves to the hayward.
25–32 The plan is that the man should bring his bundle home, the
hayward will be invited in for a drink, and when he is as drunk as a
drowned mouse he will be persuaded to redeem the *wed* from the bailiff,
whose job it was to keep such pledges.
30 *Douse*: her name means 'Sweetheart'.
33–6 The man shows no signs of responding to the poet's offer. Perhaps
he is deaf.
35 *nulle*: for *null he*, 'he will not'.
36 *con . . . lawe*: 'knows nothing of what is right'?
37 *hosede pye*: like a magpie the man in the moon is black and white
and is a thief; unlike the magpie he is wearing hose. Gail Duggan has
privately suggested the reading *hodede*, with reference to the bird's black
head.
38 Perhaps: 'I know you are bewitched (hence "paralysed"?) through
and through'; *amarscled* is possibly related to *malscred*, 'bewildered'.
See Menner (1949:13–14).
40 'The fellow will not come down before daybreak.'

VIII   RETAINERS

Of rybaudz Y ryme ant rede o my rolle,
Of gedelynges, gromes, of Colyn ant of Colle,
Harlotes, hors-knaues, bi pate ant by polle;
To Deuel Ich hem tolyuer ant take to tolle!

Þe gedelynges were gedered of gonnylde gnoste,   5
Palefreiours ant pages ant boyes wiþ boste,
Alle weren yhaht of an horse þoste;
Þe Deuel huem afretye, rau oþer aroste!

Þe shuppare þat huem shupte, to shome he huem shadde
To fles ant to fleye, to tyke ant to tadde;   10
So seyþ romaunz, whose ryht radde,
'Fleh com of flore, ant lous com of ladde'.

Þe harlotes bueth horlynges ant haunteþ þe plawe,
Þe gedelynges bueþ glotouns ant drynkeþ er hit dawe,
Sathanas huere syre seyde on is sawe,   15
'Gobelyn made is gerner of gromene mawe'.

Þe knaue crommeþ is crop er þe cok crawe,
He momeleþ ant moccheþ ant marreþ is mawe;

4 tolyuer] tolyure.

Maddicott (1975:59), describes the demands made on farmers by the
king's and nobles' horsemen as they travelled through the country. The
complaint is repeated in the Towneley *Second Shepherds' Play*, ll. 19–45.
3 '. . . one and all.'
5 *gonnylde gnoste*: meaning uncertain. *OED*, s.v. *gun sb.*, interprets as
'Gunnhild's spark', ingeniously taking Gunnhild as a pet name for a
cannon. This is neither meaningful nor sufficiently abusive. The
reference may be to Queen Gunnhild, who in Icelandic sources has a
reputation for gross licentiousness. Or the first word may be a formation
of *gonen*, 'to gape, open wide, to desire greedily', + *-ilde* (cf. *grucchild*,
motild, etc.), hence 'a woman who gapes (or desires)'. The phrase is no
doubt dredged from the gutter, where records are poorly kept.
12 Previously interpreted as 'a butterfly comes from a flower'. In view of
l. 10, it is more probably 'a flea comes out of the floor'.
16 For Gobelyn as a devil's name, see *PPl* B xviii. 293.

When he is al forlaped ant lad ouer lawe
A doseyn of doggen ne myhte hym drawe.   20

Þe rybaudz aryseþ er þe day rewe,
He shrapeþ on is shabbes ant draweþ huem to dewe,
Sene is on is browe ant on is eȝe-brewe
Þat he louseþ a losynger ant shoyeþ a shrewe.

Nou beþ capel-claweres wiþ shome toshrude,   25
Hue boskeþ huem wyþ botouns ase hit were a brude,
Wiþ lowe-lacede shon of an hayfre hude
Hue pykeþ of here prouendre al huere prude.

Whose rykeneþ wiþ knaues huere coustage,
Þe luþernesse of þe ladde, þe prude of þe page,   30
Þah he ȝeue hem cattes dryt to huere companage,
Ȝet hym shulde arewen of þe arrerage.

Whil God wes on erþe ant wondrede wyde,
Whet wes þe resoun why he nolde ryde?
For he nolde no grom to go by ys syde,   35
Ne grucchyng of no gedelyng to chaule ne to chyde!

Spedeþ ou to spewen, ase me doþ to spelle!
Þe fend ou afretie wiþ fleis ant wiþ felle!
Herkneþ hideward, horsmen, a tidyng Ich ou telle,
Þat ȝe shulen hongen ant herbarewen in helle!   40

20 hym] hyre.

19 *lad ouer lawe*: 'brought to the ground'; *MED loue* n.(3).
22–4 'He scratches his scabs and draws liquid from them (?); it is evident
from his forehead and eyebrow that he is delousing a reprobate (himself)
and putting shoes on a villain.' His scabby face betrays his immorality,
since, like Chaucer's Summoner, *CT* i. 623–33, he suffers from the
effects of lechery. See Mann (1973:138–9, 274).
28 Apparently 'They get all their finery from their food', since their
fancy shoes are made of the skin of the heifer they have just eaten.
37 'Hurry up and vomit, just as it makes me (vomit) to relate it.'(?)

IX THOMAS OF ERCELDOUNE'S PROPHECY

La countesse de Donbar demanda a Thomas de Essedoune quant la guere de scoce predreit fyn e yl la respoundy e dyt:

When man as mad a kyng of a capped man,
When mon is leuere oþer mones þyng þen is owen,
When Loudyon ys forest ant forest ys felde,
When hares kendles o þe herston,
When wyt ant wille werres togedere,   5
When mon makes stables of kyrkes ant steles castles wyþ styes,
When Rokesbourh nys no burgh ant market is at Forwyleye,
When þe alde is gan ant þe newe is come þat don noþt,
When Bambourne ys donged wyþ dede men,
When men ledes men in ropes to buyen ant to sellen,   10

The earliest of a long line of alliterative prophecies. A different version is printed in *Reliquiæ Antiquæ* i, 30. For references to others, see Turville-Petre (1977a:143). There are close parallels in *Wynnere* and in 'Vpon Loudon Law' printed in *The Whole Prophesie of Scotland* in 1603 (repr. Bannatyne Club, 1833).

Rubric 'The Countess of Dunbar asked Thomas of Erceldoune when the Scottish war would end, and he answered her and said.' The contemporary countess was 'Black Agnes', who famously defended the Castle of Dunbar against the English in 1337–8. Presumably the reference here is to her predecessor, Marjory, who finally surrendered the castle in 1296. A document dated 1294 refers to Thomas de Ercildoun, son and heir of Thomas Rymour de Ercildoun. For consideration of the many prophetic works attributed to him see J. A. H. Murray, EETS 61 (1875).

1 'When a king has been made of a madman.' For this sense of *capped*, see note to *Kings* 127. The reference may be to Edward II.

2 An example of the topsy-turviness that is always with us; cf. also ll. 8, 12, 14.

3 *Loudyon*: 'Lothian'.

4 Cf. *Wynnere* 13.

7 *Rokesbourh*: 'Roxburgh'. *Forwyleye* is unidentified.

9 *Bambourne*: 'Bannockburn', suggesting that the prophecy was written to encourage the English after their disastrous defeat in 1314, perhaps during the Roxburgh campaign of 1334 when the Earl of Dunbar was on the English side.

When a quarter of whaty whete is chaunged for a colt of ten
    marke,
When prude prikes ant pees is leyd in prisoun,
When a Scot ne may hym hude ase hare in forme þat þe
    Englyssh ne shal hym fynde,
When ryþt ant wrong ascenteþ togedere,
When laddes weddeþ leuedis,   15
When Scottes flen so faste þat for faute of ship hy drouneþ
    hemselue.
Whenne shal þis be? Nouþer in þine tyme ne in myne,
Ah comen ant gon wiþinne twenty wynter ant on.

11 *whaty*: 'mildewed'? (not otherwise recorded). Wheat-prices rose
astronomically during the floods and famine of 1315–16.
15 Cf. Wynnere 14–15.

WYNNERE AND WASTOURE

INTRODUCTION

Manuscript

The poem follows the *Parlement* as the last item in BL MS.
Addit. 31042, fols. 176b-181b, a large anthology including the
Siege J, romances and religious works; see Stern (1976), and J. J.
Thompson, *The London Thornton Manuscript* (Woodbridge,
1987). The scribe, Robert Thornton, a country gentleman from
East Newton in Yorks, also copied another large collection,
Lincoln Cath. Lib. MS. 91, which includes *Morte A* and *Awntyrs*.
Both mss. date from *c.* 1425–50.

Date, place and context

Wynnere and Wastoure have served Edward III for 25 years (l.
206), and this, together with a reference to Sir William Shareshull
(l. 317), and allusions to the Statute of Treasons (ll. 131–3) and
the general economic state of the country following the Black
Death, seems to give secure grounds for the belief that the action
is set in 1352 or shortly after, though this is questioned from time
to time, most recently by Salter (1978), and Trigg (1986). The
poem begins with an account of the difficulties facing those from
the north-west (ll. 7–8), but at the same time the author exhibits
knowledge of national affairs and in particular of the customs and
ceremonial of the royal court; see Vale (1982:73–5). Contacts
between the north-west midlands and London were strong, since
the Black Prince was Earl of Chester and he employed many

Cheshire men in administration and the army. See M. J. Bennett, *Community, Class and Careerism* (Cambridge, 1983). Perhaps the writer was part of the administration at Chester Castle dealing with the affairs of the Black Prince; see note to ll. 117–18.

Structure and theme

Like the *Parlement*, the poem is a dream-vision enclosing a debate, on the nature of which see Jacobs (1985). The prologue establishes the poet as a prophet-figure who will tell the truth about the desperate state of the nation; see Turville-Petre (1987b). He relates his dream of two opposing armies: one, consisting of clergy, lawyers and merchants is described in great detail, the other, of 'men of armes', very cursorily. The two leaders, respectively Wynnere and Wastoure, are led to the king to present their cases. Each argues that his activities are essential to the economic health of society while his opponent's will result in catastrophe. The king, looking on them with affection, encourages both of them to continue their ways of life, and, as far as the extant text goes, makes no criticism of either. The last lines of the text are lost, but it is probable that not a great deal is missing.

Wynnere and Wastoure represent personal attitudes to life as well as class and sectional interests in the country; see Speirs (1957:263–89). More particularly they are emblems of the forces of a society that is at the same time acquisitive and extravagant. Edward III made constant and heavy demands on his people to finance wars in pursuance of his claim to the French crown and to pay for the rich display and ceremonial of the court circle. Bestul (1974:62–5), cites examples of contemporary condemnation of the King's extravagance.

BIBLIOGRAPHY

Editions

Sir Israel Gollancz, *A Good Short Debate between Winner and Waster* (2nd edn, London, 1931)
J. Burrow, *English Verse 1300–1500* (London, 1977:32–45 (ll. 218–453))

Studies

T. H. Bestul, *Satire and Allegory in Wynnere and Wastoure* (Lincoln, Neb., 1974)

N. Jacobs, 'The typology of debate and the interpretation of *Wynnere and Wastoure*', *RES*, n.s. 36 (1985:481–500)

E. Salter, 'The timeliness of *Wynnere and Wastoure*', *MÆ*, 47 (1978:40–65)

J. Speirs, *Medieval English Poetry: The Non-Chaucerian Tradition* (London, 1957:263–89)

S. Trigg, 'Israel Gollancz's "Wynnere and Wastoure": political satire or editorial politics?', in *Medieval English Religious and Ethical Literature*, ed. G. Kratzmann and J. Simpson (Cambridge, 1986:115–27)

T. Turville-Petre, 'The prologue of *Wynnere and Wastoure*', *LSE*, n.s. 18 (1987:19–29)

J. Vale, *Edward III and Chivalry* (Woodbridge, 1982)

HERE BEGYNNES A TRETYS AND GOD SCHORTE
REFREYTE BYTWIXE WYNNERE AND WASTOURE

Sythen that Bretayne was biggede and Bruyttus it aughte
Thurgh the takynge of Troye with tresone withinn,
There hathe selcouthes bene sene in seere kynges tymes,
Bot neuer so many as nowe by the nynedele;
For nowe alle es witt and wyles that we with delyn,   5
Wyse wordes and slee and icheon wryeth othere.
Dare neuer no westren wy while this werlde lasteth
Send his sone southewarde to see ne to here
That he ne schall holden byhynde when he hore eldes.
Forthi sayde was a sawe of Salomon the wyse   10
(It hyeghte harde appone honde, hope I non oþer):
'When wawes waxen schall wilde and walles bene doun,
And hares appon herthe-stones schall hurcle in hire fourme,
And eke boyes of no blode with boste and with pryde
Schall wedde ladyes in londe and lede at hir will,   15

14 no] *om.*   15 at hir] hir at.

1–3 The opening lines of *SGGK* describe in more detail how Brutus,
descendant of Aeneas who fled from Troy after treason, founded
Britain. Many strange events have taken place since 'þis Bretayn watz
bigged bi þis burn rych' (*SGGK* 20).
4 The brilliant victories over the French at Crécy and Calais in 1346–7
were succeeded in 1348 and the following years by the horrors of the
Black Death, when it seemed that, with starvation, increased crime and
a severe shortage of labour, economic and moral order was collapsing.
5 *witt*, 'intellect', can be misused: 'Ac Wyles and Wyt were aboute
faste/To ouercome þe kyng thorw catel yf they myhte' (*PPl* C iv. 77–8).
6 'Wise and cunning words, and each person denounces the other'. Thus
the wisdom is self-serving, as in *PPl* A xi. 17–18; see Turville-Petre
(1987b).
9 *holden byhynde*: 'remain behind', i.e. 'be worse off'. *hore eldes*:
'grows old and grey'.
11 'It rapidly approaches, I firmly believe.'
12 These saws, which have nothing to do with Solomon, are popular
images of doom; see Turville-Petre (1987b:23–4). Two of the Fifteen
Signs of Judgement illustrated in the *Holkham Bible Picture Book* are
the sea rising and the buildings falling.
13–15 For these two manifestations of topsy-turviness see *Harley Lyrics*,
IX.4, 15, above.

Wynnere and Wastoure

Thene dredfull domesdaye it draweth neghe aftir.'
Bot whoso sadly will see and the sothe telle
Say it newely will neghe or es neghe here.
Whylome were lordes in londe þat loued in thaire hertis
To here makers of myrthes þat matirs couthe fynde,   20
And now es no frenchipe in fere bot fayntnesse of hert,
Wyse wordes withinn þat wroghte were neuer
Ne redde in no romance þat euer renke herde.
Bot now a childe appon chere withowtten chyn-wedys,
Þat neuer wroghte thurgh witt thre wordes togedire,   25
Fro he can jangle als a jaye and japes telle
He schall be leuede and louede and lett of a while
Wele more þan þe man that made it hymseluen.
Bot neuer-þe-lattere at the laste when ledys bene knawen,
Werke wittnesse will bere who wirche kane beste.   30

Bot I schall tell ȝow a tale þat me bytyde ones,
Als I went in the weste wandrynge myn one
Bi a bonke of a bourne, bryghte was the sone
Vndir a worthiliche wodde by a wale medewe.
Fele floures gan folde ther my fote steppede.   35

25 thre] thies.

19–28 For parallels to this complaint at the neglect of true poets, see Turville-Petre (1987b:23–6).
21 *frenchipe*: i.e. 'patronage'.
22–3 '(Falsely) wise words in that company that were never uttered nor read in any romance of the past.' See Turville-Petre (1987b:25).
24 *chyn-wedys*: lit. 'chin-garments', a unique compound, derisively modelled on such heroic vocabulary as *here-wedys*, 'armour' (e.g. *Parlement* 201).
27 *lett of*: 'appreciated'.
28 *made it*: 'composed the poem'.
29–30 'Nevertheless, in the end when men are revealed for what they are, work will bear witness to the one who can best work.' In context *werke* and *wirche* both have reference to composing literary works.
32 *the weste*: cf. l. 7. However, adventures were conventionally located in the west; for examples and references see *King Horn*, ed. J. Hall (Oxford, 1901), note to l. 5, and *The Poems of John Audelay*, ed. E. K. Whiting, EETS 184 (1931:note to 18. 482–3).
35–44 The spring setting for the dream-vision should be compared especially with *Death and Liffe* 22–36, and *Parlement* 1–20. In each case

42

Wynnere and Wastoure

I layde myn hede one ane hill ane hawthorne besyde,
The throstills full throly they threpen togedire,
Hipped vp heghwalles fro heselis tyll othire,
Bernacles with thayre billes one barkes þay roungen,
Þe jay janglede one heghe, jarmede the fowles,   40
Þe bourne full bremly rane þe bankes bytwene.
So ruyde were þe roughe stremys and raughten so heghe
That it was neghande nyghte or I nappe myghte
For dyn of the depe watir and dadillyng of fewllys.
Bot as I laye at the laste þan lowked myn eghne   45
And I was swythe in a sweuen sweped belyue;
Me thoghte I was in the werlde, I ne wiste in whate ende,
One a loueliche lande þat was ylike grene
Þat laye loken by a lawe the lengthe of a myle.
In aythere holte was ane here in hawberkes full brighte,   50
Harde hattes appon hedes and helmys with crestys,
Brayden owte thaire baners bown for to mete,
Schowen owte of the schawes in schiltrons þay felle,
And bot the lengthe of a launde thies lordes bytwene;
And alle prayed for the pese till the prynce come,   55
For he was worthiere in witt than any wy ells
For to ridde and to rede and to rewlyn the wrothe

---

40 fowles] foles.

---

there is a profusion of birds and flowers and a river. For general
discussion of the tradition see R. Tuve, *Seasons and Months* (Paris,
1933).
36 In *Death and Liffe* the narrator 'settled me to sitt/Vnder a huge
hawthorne' (30–1). In *Rom Rose* the churl Daunger is discovered asleep
'undir an hawethorn' (4002).
38 'Woodpeckers hopped up from hazel-trees to other (trees).'
39 Barnacle-geese were supposedly engendered on trees: 'I tolde hem
that [in] oure contree weren trees that baren a fruyt that becomen
briddes fleeynge'; *Mandeville's Travels*, ed. M. C. Seymour (Oxford,
1967:191). Such geese attach themselves to the tree by their *billes*.
48 *lande*: 'glade, clearing' (OFr *lande*), to be distinguished in this text
from *londe*, 'land, country' (OE *land, lond*).
50–4 The armies of Wynnere and Wastoure are sheltering in the woods
(*aythere holte*) separated by the *la(u)nde* of ll. 48, 54. The setting is
discussed by R. V. W. Elliott, 'The Topography of *Wynnere and
Wastoure*', *ES*, 48 (1967:134–40).

That aythere here appon hethe had vntill othere.
At the creste of a clyffe a caban was rerede,
Alle raylede with rede the rofe and the sydes   60
With Ynglysse besantes full brighte betyn of golde,
And ichone gayly vmbygone with garters of inde,
And iche a gartare of golde gerede full riche.
Then were the wordes in þe webbe werped of he,
Payntted of plunket and poyntes bytwene,   65
Þat were fourmed full fayre appon Frensche lettres;
And alle was it one sawe appon Ynglysse tonge:
'Hethyng haue the hathell þat any harme thynkes'.

Now the kyng of this kythe, kepe hym oure Lorde!
Vpon heghe one the hale ane hathell vp stondes,   70

58 hethe] hate.   64 the] thre.   66 Frensche] fresche.   70 hale] holt.

58 *here appon hethe*: cf. l. 196.
61 *besantes*: small gold ornaments on dress etc., described and
illustrated in Newton (1980:25, 37, figs. 9 and 12). Cf. *Parlement* 123. In
1348 Princess Joan's bed was decorated with gold bezants; Vale
(1982:74). *Ynglysse* bezants are perhaps representations of the new gold
coinage issued in England in 1344.
62–8 On the tent are representations of the Order of the Garter
(illustrated in fig. 3). The Garter is blue circumscribed with gold, as in
the BL postcard from *Bruges' Garter Book* (*c.* 1430). The motto, as
recorded at the end of *SGGK*, is 'hony soyt qui mal pence', which is
translated here in l. 68. The Order was apparently promulgated in April
1349, though it may have been less formally established two years
earlier; see Vale (1982: 76–91).
63 *of golde gerede*: 'decorated with gold'.
66 *Frensche*: the Garter motto was, of course, in French, and there was
special point to this; Vale (1982:81). The narrator, having noted the
language, offers his own translation of the motto. Without the
emendation of *fresche*, we must suppose the motto was, uniquely, in
English. For the sense of *lettres*, 'words', see *Dest Troy* 59–60.
70 For *hale*, 'tent', the ms. has *holt*, 'wood', but this causes problems.
Who is the *hathell* and why is he with the armies (cf. l. 50)? With the
emendation he becomes a decorative emblem of the king on top of the
tent, fashioned (*wroghte*) in the figure of a wild man, and bearing the
royal arms (ll. 78–81). By this device the king can be identified (l. 83).
Such highly decorated tents appear elsewhere; one topped with an eagle
is described in *Sir Launfal* 265–76, and an even more elaborate pommel
of an eagle on a gold apple with dragons and lions is displayed on the
tents in *Siege J* 326–32.

Wroghte als a wodwyse alle in wrethyn lokkes,
With ane helme one his hede ane hatte appon lofte,
And one heghe one þe hatte ane hattfull beste,
A lighte lebarde and a longe, lokande full kene,
ȝarked alle of ȝalowe golde in full ȝape wyse;   75
Bot that þat hillede the helme byhynde in the nekke
Was casten full clenly in quarters foure:
Two with flowres of Fraunce before and behynde,
And two out of Ynglonde with sex egre bestes,
Thre leberdes one lofte and thre on lowe vndir;   80
At iche a cornere a knoppe of full clene perle,
Tasselde of tuly silke tuttynge out fayre.
And by þe cabane I knewe the kynge that I see,
And thoghte to wiete or I went wondres ynewe;
And als I waytted withinn, I was warre sone   85

79 egre] grym.

71 The *wodwyse* was a figure at pageants, court-games and tournaments, and developed as a decorative and heraldic emblem. See Bernheimer (1952), esp. pl. 40 depicting King Wenceslas seated on a throne with wild men behind him holding up his arms and crested helmet. Edward III's wardrobe accounts record an order for livery of white velvet worked with blue garters and patterned throughout with *wodewoses*, and for the Christmas games in 1348 an order for twelve heads of *wodewoses*; see N. H. Nicolas, *Archaeologia*, 31 (1845:41, 43); and further, Vale (1982:73–5, 175), who relates the setting of the poem to court-games and pageants. Lord Berners' translation of Froissart's account of the disastrous wild-man pantomime at the court of Charles VI is in D. Gray, *The Oxford Book of Late Medieval Verse and Prose* (Oxford, 1985:397–9).
72–82 For an understanding of the armour and heraldry see the funerary badge of Edward, the Black Prince (fig. 3). On the Black Prince's helm is his 'cap of maintenance', surmounted by a lion (as in ll. 72–5). His shield bears the quarterly arms of the fleurs-de-lis of France (first and last quarters, *before and behynde*, l. 78) and the three leopards (heraldically called lions) of England. In the poem these arms are instead displayed on the mantling which hangs down behind the neck (ll. 76–82), illustrated in Poole (1958: figs. 80, 91–3). The arms of France were quartered with those of England in 1340 with reference to Edward III's claims to the French throne.
83 'By the (heraldry of) the pavilion I recognized the king that I was looking at.'
85 'As I looked inside (the tent) I quickly noticed . . .'

Of a comliche kynge crowned with golde,
Sett one a silken bynche with septure in honde,
One of the louelyeste ledis, whoso loueth hym in hert,
That euer segge vnder sonn sawe with his eghne.
This kynge was comliche clade in kirtill and mantill,   90
Bery-brown was his berde, brouderde with fewlys,
Fawkons of fyne golde flakerande with wynges,
And ichone bare in ble blewe, als me thoghte,
A grete gartare of ynde girde in the myddes.
Full gayly was that grete lorde girde in the myddis,   95
A brighte belte of ble broudirde with fewles,
With drakes and with dukkes, daderande þam semede
For ferdnes of fawkons fete lesse fawked þay were.
And euer I sayd to myselfe, 'full selly me thynke
Bot if this renke to the reuere ryde vmbestonde.'   100
The kyng biddith a beryn by hym þat stondeth,
One of the ferlyeste frekes þat faylede hym neuer,
'Thynke, I dubbede the knyghte with dynttis to dele!
Wende wightly thy waye my willes to kythe.
Go bidd þou 3ondere bolde batell þat one þe bent houes   105
That they neuer neghe nerre togedirs;
For if thay strike one stroke stynte þay ne thynken.'
'3is, lorde!' said þe lede, 'While my life dures!'
He dothe hym doun one þe bonke and dwellys a while
Whils he busked and bown was one his beste wyse.   110
He laped his legges in yren to the lawe bones,

91 '(His clothes were) embroidered with birds.' Gollancz notes that in
1351 the King's robes were decorated with eagles holding garters with
the Garter motto.
93 'Each one (of the falcons) bore in a blue colour . . .'
97–8 'They seemed to be trembling for fear of the falcons' feet, lest they
were caught.' The Dauphin had an equally decorative belt in 1352, made
of cloth-of-gold and embroidered with fleurs-de-lis and birds; see
Newton (1980:35).
100 'If this man does not sometimes ride to the river (to go hawking).'
108 An elliptical expression of devotion and service: '(I shall obey you)
as long as I live'. Cf. *PPl* A xi. 101–02; also 'Þi man y wil be &
serue þe ay/Þer while mi liif lest may', *Guy of Warwick*, EETS ES
59 (1891: p. 572, v. 229).
111–18 The knight arms himself, first covering his legs, then his neck
and chest with the *pysayne* and his stomach with the *pawnce*, then his

With pysayne and with pawnce polischede full clene,
With brases of broun stele brauden full thikke,
With plates buklede at þe bakke þe body to ȝeme,
With a jupown full juste joynede by the sydes,   115
A brod chechun at þe bakke, þe breste had anoþer,
Thre wynges inwith, wroghte in the kynde,
Vmbygon with a gold wyre. When I þat gome knewe,
What, he was ȝongeste of ȝeris and ȝapeste of witt
Þat any wy in this werlde wiste of his age!   120
He brake a braunche in his hande and broched in swythe,
Trynes one a grete trotte and takes his waye
There bothe thies ferdes folke in the felde houes.

Sayd, 'Loo! The kyng of this kyth – þer kepe hym oure
    Lorde! –
Send his erande by me als hym beste lyketh   125
That no beryn be so bolde, one bothe his two eghne,
Ones to strike one stroke, no stirre none nerre
To lede rowte in his rewme, so ryall to thynke
Pertly with ȝoure powers his pese to disturbe.

121 broched in] caughten it.

---

arms with *brases*. He finally puts on his tunic (*jupown*), which has his
coat of arms depicted front and back. See Poole (1958:pls. 51, 52, 53b).
The arming of the knight is a favourite topic of alliterative poets; e.g.
SGGK 566–89, *Morte A* 900–15.
117–18 The knight's arms are precisely described: 'Three wings inside,
done in their natural form, encircled with a gold wire'. It is clear that the
narrator — and by implication the audience — recognizes these arms at
once. Salter (1978:53–4), shows that the Wingfield family bore arms of
three pairs of wings. Sir John Wingfield was from 1351 until his death ten
years later the chief administrator for the Black Prince, responsible for
all aspects of his winning and wasting. He visited Cheshire (e.g. in 1351
and 1353), and dealt constantly with Chester business. See Booth
(1981:73–9).
121 *broched in swythe*, 'urged his horse in quickly'; cf. *Dest Troy* 7690.
The ms. reading fails in both alliteration and grammar.
124 Þer introduces the wish, 'May the Lord preserve him!'; cf. *SGGK* 839.
125 *erande*: Gollancz plausibly emends to *bodword*, comparing
Parlement 558. Cf. also *Erkenwald* 105, and *MED*'s quotation s.v. *bodeword*: 'Jhesu . . . sendes þe þus bodword by me'.
126–33 These lines give precise grounds on which a charge of treason

For this es the vsage here, and euer schall worthe,   130
If any beryn be so bolde with banere for to ryde
Withinn þe kyngdome riche bot the kynge one,
That he schall losse the londe and his lyfe aftir.
Bot sen ȝe knowe noghte this kythe ne the kynge ryche,
He will forgiffe ȝow this gilt of his grace one.   135
Full wyde hafe I walked amonges thies wyes one,
Bot sawe I neuer siche a syghte, segge, with myn eghne,
For here es alle þe folke of Fraunce ferdede besyde,
Of Lorreyne, of Lumbardye and of lawe Spayne,
Wyes of Westwale þat in were duellen,   140
Of Ynglonde, of Yrlonde, Estirlynges full many
Þat are stuffede in stele, strokes to dele.
And ȝondere a banere of blake þat one þe bent houes
With thre bulles of ble white brouden withinn,
And iche one hase of henppe hynged a corde   145

---

144 bulles] bibulles.

---

might be brought. Crucial to the case is that banners are displayed
(l. 131). This was evidence of the levying of open war, which was the
prerogative of the sovereign (l. 132) and therefore constituted an attack
on royal authority. This had long been and continued to be (l. 130)
considered treasonable by international military law. Punishment was
execution, usually by drawing and hanging, and forfeiture of lands
(l. 133). The parliament of Jan. 1352 met to discuss the problem of 'les
destourbours de la pees et meintenours des quereles et des riotes'
(l. 129), and passed the Statute of Treasons, which was particularly
concerned to determine whether lands should be forfeited to the king or
to the lord of the fee. See M. H. Keen, 'Treason Trials under the Law of
Arms', *Trans. Roy. Hist. Soc.* 5th ser. 12 (1962:85–103); J. G. Bellamy,
The Law of Treason in England in the Later Middle Ages (Cambridge,
1970). Salter (1978:41–3), misses the significance of the banners.
140–1 'Men of Westphalia who live by fighting, (men) of England, of
Ireland, very many Hanseatic merchants' (from northern Germany and
the Baltic).
144 *bulles*: Gollancz's emendation of ms. *bibulles*. The power and
financial demands of the papacy represented by papal bulls were
increasingly resented during the pontificate of Clement VI (1342–52),
and anti-papal feeling was expressed in the Statutes of Provisors (1351)
and Praemunire (1353). At the Smithfield jousts in 1343, knights
disguised as the Pope and twelve cardinals took part; see Vale (1982:67).
145–6 From each bull hangs a cord of hemp with a heavy lead seal.
Clement VI had been keeper of the seals before his election; see

Seled with a sade lede, I say als me thynkes,
That hede es of Holy Kirke I hope he be there
Alle ferse to the fighte with the folke þat he ledis.
Anoþer banere es vpbrayde with a bende of grene,
With thre hedis white-herede with howes one lofte,   150
Croked full craftyly and kembid in the nekke;
Thies are ledis of this londe þat schold oure lawes ȝeme,
That thynken to dele this daye with dynttis full many.
I holde hym bot a fole þat fightis whils flyttynge may helpe,
When he hase founden his frende þat fayled hym neuer.   155

The thirde banere one bent es of blee whitte
With sexe galegs I see of sable withinn,
And iche one has a brown brase with bokels twayne;
Thies are Sayn Franceys folke þat sayen alle schall fey worthe.
They aren so ferse and so fresche þay feghtyn bot seldom.   160
I wote wele for wynnynge thay wentten fro home;
His purse weghethe full wele that wanne thaym all hedire.

157 galegs] galeys.

G. Barraclough, *The Medieval Papacy* (London, 1968:152). For
illustration of a bull, see *The New Catholic Encyclopedia*, s.v. *bulla*.
149 The green stripe on the lawyers' banner possibly alludes to the
green wax seal of notices of taxation from the Exchequer; cf. *Harley
Lyrics* III.38 above.
155 *his frende*: Wynnere's. For Wastoure's enmity towards the lawyers,
see ll. 314–18.
157 The Franciscans' banner depicts six sandals (with Gollancz's
emendation of ms. *galeys*). These are *sable*, i.e. 'black' (not 'sable-
lined'), each with a brown strap and two buckles. The Minorites were
not normally permitted to wear shoes, but sandals were accepted. Cf.
the attack in *PPCrede*: 'Fraunces bad his breþeren barfote to
wenden;/Now han þei bucled schon for bleynynge of her heles' (298–9).
159 Friars were known for their persuasive tongue, but generally they
relied on pleasant words and cajolery rather than hell-fire sermons. See
Mann (1973:37–54); and P. R. Szittya, *The Antifraternal Tradition in
Medieval Literature* (Princeton, N.J., 1986).
161–2 The avariciousness of the Franciscans is a commonplace; cf.
PPCrede 287–9.

The fourte banere one the bent es brayde appon lofte
With bothe the brerdes of blake, a balle in the myddes,
Reghte siche as the sone es in the someris tyde   165
When it hase moste of þe mayne one Missomer Euen;
Thynkes Domynyke this daye with dynttis to dele.
With many a blesenande beryn his banere es stuffede.
And sythen the pope es so priste thies prechours to helpe,
And Fraunceys with his folke es forced besyde   170
And alle the ledis of the lande ledith thurgh witt,
There es no man appon molde to machen þaym agayne
Ne gete no grace appon grounde vndir God hymseluen.

And ȝitt es the fyfte appon þe folde þe faireste of þam alle,
A brighte banere of blee whitte with three bore-hedis;   175
Be any crafte þat I kan, Carmes thaym semyde,

163 es] was.   164 balle] balke.   166 mayne] maye.
167 Thynkes] That was.   176 *transposed with 186.*

163–6 The banner of the Dominicans (the Black Friars, from the colour
of their cloak) has black borders with a ball shining as bright as the sun.
N. R. Havely, *NQ*, 228 (1983:207–9), shows that a symbol of light was
associated with the Dominicans. It may additionally symbolize their
pride for which they were often criticised; cf. *PPCrede* 256–66. Costumes
for Dominicans and merchants (see l. 190) were provided for the royal
Christmas games in 1352; see Vale (1982:74).
166 'When it has most strength on Midsummer's Eve.' The emendation
suggested by F. Holthausen, *Anglia Beiblatt*, 34 (1923:15).
168 'His banner is supported by many illustrious men.' *Blesenande*: lit.
'shining', with punning reference to the Dominicans' symbol.
169 English Dominicans were favoured by both king and pope, so that
there were Dominican cardinals, bishops and royal confessors. 'Þey
ben counseilours of kinges' (*PPCrede* 364). See D. Knowles, *The
Religious Orders in England* (Cambridge, 1948:167–70).
170 *es forced besyde*: 'is backed up (by the pope) in addition'.
171 The subject of *ledith* is either *Fraunceys* or more probably *the pope*.
175 A boar's head was a respectable and popular heraldic symbol. E.g.
Degaré's father has a 'sscheld of asur/And þre bor-heuedes þerin' (*Sir
Degaré*, ed. French and Hale, ll. 995–6). It was also food for a banquet
(see l. 332) and hence a popular tavern sign. In *PPCrede* the supposedly
abstemious Carmelites are found 'wiþ a full coppe' in a tavern (ll.
339–40); 'Glotony is her God, wiþ gloppyng of drynke' (l. 92). They are
the White Friars; hence the white banner.
176–7 A scribe has transposed ll. 176 and 186. Members of the Order of

For þay are the ordire þat louen oure Lady to serue.
If I scholde say þe sothe, it semys non othire
Bot þat the freris with othere folke schall þe felde wynn.

The sexte es of sendell, and so are þay alle,   180
Whitte als the whalles bone, whoso the sothe tellys,
With beltys of blake bocled togedir,
The poyntes pared off rownde, þe pendant awaye,
And alle the lethire appon lofte þat one lowe hengeth
Schynethe alle for scharpynynge of the schauynge iren;   185
The ordire of þe Austyns for oughte þat I wene,
For by the blussche of the belte the banere I knewe.
And othere synes I seghe sett appon lofte,
Some of wittnesse of wolle and some of wyne tounnes,
Some of merchandes merke, so many and so thikke   190
That I ne wote in my witt, for alle this werlde riche,
Whatt segge vnder the sonne can the sowme rekken.
And sekere one þat other syde are sadde men of armes,
Bolde sqwyeres of blode, bowmen many,
Þat if thay strike one stroke stynt þay ne thynken   195
Till owthir here appon hethe be hewen to dethe.

Forthi I bid ȝow bothe that thaym broghte hedir
That ȝe wend with me are any wrake falle
To oure comely kyng that this kythe owethe;

197 broghte hedir] hedir broghte.

Our Lady of Mount Carmel are also called 'Mary's Men'; see *PPCrede*
48, and 382–4, 'We Karmes . . . lyven by our Lady'.
180–5 The banner of the Austin Friars is white with black belts that
shine from the stropping of their razors. The Augustinians wore a belt
round their black cloak over their white habit.
189–90 'Some emblems as an indication of wool, some of wine casks,
some emblems of the marks of merchants, so many and so profuse . . .'
Merchants set their marks upon their goods and also used them as quasi-
heraldic symbols; cf. *PPCrede* 176–7 where the stained-glass windows in
the Dominican church 'schynen wiþ schapen scheldes to schewen
aboute,/Wiþ merkes of marchauntes ymedled bytwene'. See E. M.
Elmhirst, *Merchants' Marks*, Harleian Soc. 108 (London, 1959).
193 *þat other syde*: Wastoure's army.

And fro he wiete wittirly where þe wronge ristyth,   200
Thare nowthir wye be wrothe to wirche als he demeth!'
Off ayther rowte ther rode owte a renke als me thoghte,
Knyghtis full comly one coursers attyred,
And sayden, 'Sir sandisman, sele the betyde!
Wele knowe we the kyng. He clothes vs bothe,   205
And has vs fosterde and fedde this fyve and twenty wyntere.
Now fare þou byfore and we schall folowe aftire.'
And now are þaire brydells vpbrayde and bown one þaire
    wayes;
Thay lighten doun at þe launde and leued thaire stedis,
Kayren vp at the clyffe and one knees fallyn.   210
The kynge henttis by þe handes and hetys þam to ryse,
And sayde, 'Welcomes, heres, as hyne of oure house bothen!'
The kynge waytted one wyde and the wyne askes;
Beryns broghte it anone in bolles of siluere.
Me thoughte I sowpped so sadly it sowede bothe myn eghne!   215
And he þat wilnes of this werke to wete any forthire,
Full freschely and faste, for here a fitt endes!

Bot than kerpede the kynge, sayd 'Kythe what ʒe hatten
And whi the hates aren so hote ʒoure hertis bytwene.
If I schall deme ʒow this day, dothe me to here.'   220
'Now certys, lorde,' sayde þat one, 'the sothe for to telle,
I hatt Wynnere, a wy that alle this werlde helpis,
For I lordes cane lere thurgh ledyng of witt.
Thoo þat spedfully will spare and spende not to grete,
Lyve appon littill-whattes, I lufe hym the bettir.   225
Witt wiendes me with and wysses me faire;

201 wye] wyes; demeth] doeth.   215 sowed] sowred.

200–01 'And when the King knows for certain where the wrong lies,
neither man must (*thare*) be angry at (i.e. opposed to) acting as he
advises.'
206 Edward III came to the throne on 25 January 1327.
208 *bown*: '(they are) gone' (ppl. of *bowe*).
211 *henttis*: 'seizes (them)'.
222 '. . . who helps all this world.'
223 Wynnere repeatedly insists on his close association with *witt*, 'good
sense' (though see note to l. 5), semi-personified in l. 226.

Aye when gadir my gudes than glades myn hert.
Bot this felle false thefe þat byfore ʒowe standes
Thynkes to strike or he stynt and stroye me for euer.
Alle þat I wynn thurgh witt, he wastes thurgh pryde;   230
I gedir, I glene, and he lattys goo sone,
I pryke and I pryne, and he the purse opynes.
Why, hase this cayteffe no care how men corne sellen?
His londes liggen alle ley, his lomes aren solde,
Downn bene his dowfehowses, drye bene his poles,   235
The deuyll wounder one the wele he weldys at home,
Bot hungere and heghe howses and howndes full kene!
Safe a sparthe and a spere sparrede in ane hyrne,
A bronde at his bede-hede, biddes he non oþer
Bot a cuttede capill to cayre with to his frendes.   240
Then will he boste with his brande and braundesche hym ofte,
This wikkede weryed thefe that Wastoure men calles,
That if he life may longe this lande will he stroye.
Forthi deme vs this daye, for Drightyns loue in heuen,
To fighte furthe with oure folke to owthire fey worthe.'   245

'ʒee, Wynnere', quod Wastoure, 'thi wordes are hye,
Bot I schall tell the a tale that tene schall the better.
When thou haste waltered and went and wakede alle þe
  nyghte,
And iche a wy in this werlde that wonnes the abowte,
And hase werpede thy wyde howses full of wolle sakkes –   250
The bemys benden at the rofe, siche bakone there hynges,
Stuffed are sterlynges vndere stelen bowndes –

227 'All the time my goods accumulate . . .'
228 *thefe* need be no more than a general term of abuse. See also l. 242.
230 Wynnere, guided by *witt*, claims Wastoure is guided by *pryde*.
232 *pryke and pryne*: 'sew and stitch up' (the purse which Wastoure
opens). Both verbs mean primarily 'to pierce' (*MED priken, prenen*).
233 Wynnere complains that Wastoure has no regard for the profits of
corn, just as Wastoure ridicules Wynnere for his preoccupation with
them (ll. 368–74).
236 'Let the Devil marvel at the wealth he has at home', since Wastoure
has nothing left 'except hunger . . .' etc.
245 'To go and fight with our armies until (*to*) one of us is killed.'
247 *the . . . the*: 'thee . . . thee'.
251–62 Wastoure argues that wasting (i.e. consumption) is necessary for

What scholde worthe of that wele if no waste come?
Some rote, some ruste, some ratons fede.
Let be thy cramynge of thi kystes, for Cristis lufe of heuen!   255
Late the peple and the pore hafe parte of thi siluere,
For if thou wydwhare scholde walke and waytten the sothe
Thou scholdeste reme for rewthe, in siche ryfe bene the pore.
For and thou lengare thus lyfe, leue thou non oþer,
Thou schall be hanged in helle for that thou here spareste;   260
For siche a synn haste þou solde thi soule into helle,
And there es euer wellande woo, worlde withowtten ende.'

'Late be thi worde, Wastoure,' quod Wynnere the riche;
'Thou melleste of a mater, thou madiste it thiseluen.
With thi sturte and thy stryffe thou stroyeste vp my gudes   265
In playinge and in wakynge in wynttres nyghttis,
In owttrage, in vnthrifte, in augarte pryde.
There es no wele in this werlde to wasschen thyn handes
That ne es gyffen and grounden are þou it getyn haue.
Thou ledis renkes in thy rowte wele rychely attyrede;   270
Some hafe girdills of golde þat more gude coste
Than alle þe faire fre londe that ȝe byfore haden.
ȝe folowe noghte ȝoure fadirs þat fosterde ȝow alle,
A kynde herueste to cache and cornes to wynn
For þe colde wyntter and þe kene with gleterand frostes,   275
Sythen dropeles drye in the dede monethe;

264 thou(2)] tho.   270 rychely] ryhely.

---

a sound economy, and that winning is a cover for the deadly sin of
avarice.
260 *that*: 'what'.
264 'You speak of a problem that you yourself created.' That is, poverty
is a result of extravagance not of avarice.
268–9 The general sense is that Wastoure disposes of all his wealth
before he gets it, though l. 268 is obscure.
269 *grounden*: either from *grinden*, 'to grind', hence 'consume' (so
Gollancz), or, more probably, from *graunten*, 'to give away' (so
Burrow).
275 *For*: 'in preparation for'. *gleterand*: possibly /gl/ alliterates with /k/,
but Gollancz's emendation to *clengande*, 'clinging', is attractive.
276 The 'dede monethe' of drought is probably March; cf. Chaucer, *CT*
i. 2.

And thou wolle to the tauerne byfore þe toune-hede,
Iche beryne redy with a bolle to blerren thyn eghne;
Hete the whatte thou haue schalte and whatt thyn hert lykes,
Wyfe, wedowe or wenche þat wonnes thereaboute.   280
Then es there bott "fille in!" and "feche forthe florence to
   schewe!"
"Wee hee!" and "worthe vp!", wordes ynewe.
Bot when this wele es awaye, the wyne moste be payede fore;
Than lympis ȝowe weddis to laye or ȝoure londe selle.
For siche wikked werkes wery the oure Lorde!   285
And forthi God laughte that he louede and leuede þat oþer,
Iche freke one felde ogh þe ferdere be to wirche.
Teche thy men for to tille and tynen thyn feldes,
Rayse vp thi rent-howses, ryme vp thi ȝerdes,
Owthere hafe as þou haste done and hope aftir werse,   290
Þat es firste þe faylynge of fode and than the fire aftir
To brene the alle at a birre for thi bale dedis.
The more colde es to come, als me a clerke tolde!'

'Ȝee, Wynnere,' quod Wastoure, 'thi wordes are vayne;

288 tynen] tymen.

277 *wolle*: 'will go'. Gollancz reads *wolle te to* for the alliteration.
278 i.e. 'to get you drunk'.
281 *florence*: 'florins'. 'Then there is nothing else (to be heard) but "fill up" and "bring out your money so that it can be seen".'
282 The reference is sexual, following on from l. 280. *Wee hee!* is the noise of an amorous horse (cf. Chaucer, *CT* i. 4066); *worthe vp*: 'climb up'. Cf. *PPl* A viii. 73–5: 'Þei wedde no womman þat hy wiþ delen/But as wilde bestis wiþ wehe & worþ vp togideris/And bringen forþ barnes þat bois ben holden'. *Wordes ynewe*: i.e. 'no more words are necessary'.
284 'Then you have to lay down a security', i.e. 'pawn valuables'.
286–7 Christ's prophecy of the Last Days includes: 'Then two shall be in the field; one shall be taken and one shall be left' (Matthew xxiv. 40). Hence Wynnere cunningly threatens Wastoure not just with economic downfall but also with divine rejection and final damnation.
290 *as þou haste done*: 'what you've earned'.
291–3 Famine, burning and extreme cold are all features of apocalyptic prophecy.
294–304 Wastoure argues that it is better to distribute money to the community than to hoard it and have it dispersed after death by friars or by heirs.

With oure festes and oure fare we feden the pore.   295
It es plesynge to the Prynce þat Paradyse wroghte.
When Cristes peple hath parte hym payes alle the better
Then here ben hodirde and hidde and happede in cofers
That it no sonn may see thurgh seuen wyntter ones;
Owthir freres it feche, when thou fey worthes,   300
To payntten with thaire pelers or pergett with thaire walles.
Thi sone and thi sektours ichone slees othere,
Maken dale aftir thi daye, for thou durste neuer
Mawngery ne myndale ne neuer myrthe louediste.
A dale aftir thi daye dose the no mare   305
Þan a lighte lanterne late appone nyghte
When it es borne at thi bakke, beryn, be my trouthe.
Now wolde God that it were als I wisse couthe,
That thou, Wynnere, thou wriche, and Wanhope thi brothir,
And eke ymbryne dayes and euenes of sayntes,   310
The Frydaye and his fere one the ferrere syde,
Were drownede in the depe see there neuer droghte come,
And dedly synn for thayre dede were endityde with twelue,
And thies beryns one the bynches with howes one lofte
That bene knowen and kydde for clerkes of the beste,   315
Als gude als Arestotle or Austyn the wyse,

300 freres] it freres.

298 'Rather than that it should here be. . .'
303 *durst neuer*: 'never dared to have'.
305 i.e. '. . . is no more good to you'.
308 'Would to God that I could arrange it.'
309 *Wanhope*: defined by Chaucer's Parson as 'despeir of the mercy of God that comth somtyme of to muche outrageous sorwe' (*CT* x. 693). The accusation is that Wynnere leads a life so full of worry and so lacking in good fun (cf. ll. 322–3) that he will be drawn to the unforgivable sin. Wastoure is carried away into a denunciation of penances imposed by the Church.
310 Days set aside for fasting were those preceding a saint's day and, in certain weeks of the year, the ember days of Wednesday, Friday and Saturday.
311 Fridays and Saturdays throughout the year were days of abstinence, i.e. 'fysch dayes'. Saturday is Friday's 'companion on the further side'.
313 Wastoure wishes that deadly sin might be indicted by a jury of twelve for causing the death (*dede*) of Friday etc.
314 i.e. the lawyers. The defective b-verse is repeated from l. 150.

That alle schent were those schalkes, and Scharshull it wiste
Þat saide I prikkede with powere his pese to distourbe.
Forthi, comely kynge that oure case heris,
Late vs swythe with oure swerdes swyngen togedirs,   320
For nowe I se it es full sothe þat sayde es full ȝore:
"The richere of ranke wele the rathere will drede;
The more hauande þat he hathe, the more of hert feble".'

Bot than this wrechede Wynnere full wrothely he lukes,
Sayse 'Þis es spedles speche to speken thies wordes.   325
Loo, this wrechide Wastoure that wydewhare es knawenn!
Ne es nothir kaysser ne kynge ne knyghte þat the folowes,
Barone ne bachelere ne beryn that thou loueste,
Bot foure felawes or fyve that the fayth owthe.
And he schall dighte thaym to dyne with dayntethes so many 330
Þat iche a wy in this werlde may wepyn for sorowe.
The bores hede schall be broghte with plontes appon lofte,
Buk-tayles full brode in brothes there besyde,
Venyson with the frumentee and fesanttes full riche,
Baken mete therby one the burde sett,   335

317 Sir William Shareshull was Chief Justice of the King's Bench
1350–61. He framed the Statute of Treasons (cf. ll. 126–33), incurring
much unpopularity among the knights; see B. H. Putnam, *The Place in
Legal History of Sir William Shareshull* (Cambridge, 1950). Together
with Sir John Wingfield, he was deeply involved in the legal and financial
administration of Cheshire, where he held a general eyre in 1353. See
Booth (1981:73, 120–2).
   it wiste: 'knew about it'. Wastoure, who has already tangled with
Shareshull (l. 318), is defying him to do his worst.
322–3 'Riches bringeth oft harm and ever feare' (Whiting, R117).
330–57 Wastoure's feast consists of the usual three courses; first the
really substantial meat dishes, then roast meats, swans and tarts, and
finally smaller birds, pastries and confections. Essentially the same are
the menus from fourteenth-century cook-books in EETS SS 8
(1985:39–41). There is an even more elaborate description in *Morte A*
176–206.
332 Gollancz perhaps rightly emends *plontes* to *bayes*, though for
alliteration of voiced and voiceless consonants see l. 334.
334 *frumentee*, made of boiled wheat and milk, was the usual
accompaniment to venison.

Chewettes of choppede flesche, charbiande fewlis,
And iche a segge þat I see has sexe mens dole.
If this were nedles note anothir comes aftir,
Roste with the riche sewes and the ryalle spyces,
Kiddes clouen by þe rigge, quarterd swannes,   340
Tartes of ten ynche þat tenys myn hert
To see þe borde ouerbrade with blasande disches
Als it were a rayled rode with rynges and stones.
The thirde mese to me were meruelle to rekken,
For alle es Martynmesse mete þat I with moste dele,   345
Noghte bot worttes with the flesche, withowt wilde fowle
Saue ane hene to hym that the howse owethe.
And he will hafe birdes bownn one a broche riche,
Barnakes and buturs and many billed snyppes,
Larkes and lyngwhittes lapped in sogoure,   350
Wodcokkes and wodwales full wellande hote,
Teeles and titmoyses to take what hym lykes,
Caudels of conynges and custadis swete,
Dariols and dische-metis þat ful dere coste,
Maumene þat men clepen ȝour mawes to fill,   355

337 dole] doke.   353 Caudels] . . . . .ls.   354 Dariols] . . . . .ls.
355 Maumene] . . . . .ene.

336 *chewettes*: small pies filled with chopped meat or fish and eggs.
charbiande: uncertain; perhaps an early form of Fr *c(h)arbonade*, 'grilled meat'.
343 The crucifix richly studded with jewels is a curiously troubling image in the context of Wastoure's feast.
345 *Martynmesse*: Nov. 11, when meat was cured for winter use.
347 The owner of the house (i.e. Wynnere himself) is allowed chicken.
349–50 King Arthur also provides 'bernakes and botures' (*Morte A* 189), but his knights listen to the song 'of larkes, of lynkwhyttez' rather than eat them (l. 2674).
353–60 Letters have been lost where a corner of the leaf is torn away. Reconstructed readings are Gollancz's, except in ll. 356 and 357.
353 *custadis*: (Fr *crustade*), open tarts of meat, eggs etc.
354 Arthur offers *dariolls endoride*, 'glazed pastries' (*Morte A* 199).
355 'What men call *maumene*' – a dish of chopped chicken often flavoured with wine and almond milk. The reconstructed line is not wholly satisfactory.

58

Wynnere and Wastoure

Aye a mese at a merke bytwen twa men;
Siche bot brynneth for bale ȝour bowells within.
Me tenyth at ȝour trompers þay tounen so heghe
Þat ich a gome in þe gate goullyng may here.
Þan wil þay say to þamselfe as þay samen ryden,   360
Ȝe hafe no hope of þe helpe of þe heuen-kyng.
Þus are ȝe scorned by skyll and schathed þeraftir
Þat rechen for a repaste a rawnson of siluer.
Bot ones I herd in a haule of a herdmans tong:
"Better were meles many þan a mery nyghte".'   365
And he þat wilnes of þis werke for to wete forthire,
Full freschely and faste, for here a fit endes.

'Ȝee, Wynnere,' quod Wastour, 'I wote wele myseluen
What sall lympe of þe, lede, within a lite ȝeris
Thurgh þe poure plenté of corne þat þe peple sowes.   370
Þat God will graunt of his grace to growe on þe erthe
Ay to appaire þe pris þat it passe nott to hye,

---

356 Aye a] *lost.*   357 Siche] . . .he.   358 Me tenyth] . . . . . .yth.
359 Þat ich] *lost.*   360 Þan] *lost.*   361 hope] myster.   364 ones]
one.   366 forthire] forthe.   369 a lite] fewe.   372 þat it] and.

---

356 Diners were served in pairs (cf. 'Ay two had disches twelue', *SGGK*
128). Here each course for each pair costs a mark, i.e. two-thirds of a
pound. In 1349 during the plague two horses could be bought for a
mark; see M. McKisack *The Fourteenth Century* (Oxford, 1959:334).
The b-verse is corrupt; perhaps read *twa men bytwen* or *amonges twa
men.*
358 Cf. 'þe first cors come with crakkyng of trumpes', *SGGK* 116.
361 *hope:* ms. *myster,* 'need', neither alliterates nor makes sense.
364 *herdmans:* Gollancz glosses 'herdsman's', but it probably means
'retainer's' (OE *hired-*) as Burrow suggests. The saying is proverbial:
'Better are meales many than one to mery' (Whiting, M434).
369–74 In times of abundant harvest, corn-prices will fall and with them
the value of Wynnere's hoarded grain. Wastoure skilfully portrays
Wynnere as grudging God's munificence and accuses him again of the sin
of *wanhope* (cf. l. 309). In 1349–50 prices dropped sharply with falling
demand after the Black Death.
369 *a lite:* Gollancz's emendation, supported by the identical b-verse in
Wars 4523.
371 *Þat:* 'that (corn) which'.

59

Schal make þe to waxe wod for wanhope in erthe,
To hope aftir an harde ȝere, to honge þiseluen.
Woldeste þu hafe lordis to lyfe as laddes on fote?   375
Prelates als prestes þat þe parischen ȝemes?
Prowde marchandes of pris as pedders in towne?
Late lordes lyfe als þam liste, laddes as þam falles;
Þay þe bacon and beefe, þay botours and swannes,
Þay þe roughe of þe rye, þay þe rede whete,   380
Þay þe grewell gray, and þay þe gude sewes,
And þen may þe peple hafe parte in pouert þat standes,
Sum gud morsell of mete to mend with þair chere.
If fewlis flye schold forthe and fongen be neuer,
And wild bestis in þe wodde wone al þaire lyue,   385
And fisches flete in þe flode and ichone frete oþer,
Ane henne at ane halpeny by halfe ȝeris ende,
Schold not a ladde be in londe a lorde for to serue.
Þis wate þu full wele witterly þiseluen,
Whoso wele schal wyn a wastour moste he fynde,   390
For if it greues one gome it gladdes anoþer.'

'Now,' quod Wynner to Wastour, 'me wondirs in hert
Of thies poure penyles men þat peloure will by,
Sadills of sendale with sercles full riche.
Lesse and ȝe wrethe ȝour wifes, þaire willes to folowe,   395
Ȝe sellyn wodd aftir wodde in a wale tyme,
Bothe þe oke and þe assche and all þat þer growes.

386 frete] ete.

375–83 Now Wastoure argues that his activities are necessary to
preserve the social order.
379 The author of *The Simonie* (ed. T. Wright, Camden Soc. vi,
1839:323–45), complains that errand-boys will no longer do a job 'for
beof ne for bakoun' (l. 387).
386 *frete*: emended by Gollancz.
387 'A hen would be sold at a halfpenny by the end of half a year.'
388 'There would not be a servant in the land . . .', because they would
all find food without having to work for it.
390 i.e. 'every winner needs a waster'. Gollancz compares a German
proverb.
394 *sercles*: 'circlets' to go round knights' helmets. Cf. *SGGK* 615–18.
395 *Lesse and*: 'lest'.

Þe spyres and þe ȝonge sprynge ȝe spare to ȝour children
And sayne God wil graunt it his grace to grow at þe last
For to saue to ȝour sones, bot þe schame es ȝour ownn.   400
Nedeles saue ȝe þe soyle, for sell it ȝe thynken.
Ȝour forfadirs were fayne when any frende come
For to schake to þe schawe and schewe hym þe estres,
In iche holt þat þay had ane hare for to fynde,
Bryng to þe brode lande bukkes ynewe   405
To lache and to late goo to lightten þaire hertis.
Now es it sett and solde, my sorowe es þe more,
Wastes alle wilfully ȝoure wyfes to paye.
That are were lordes in londe and ladyes riche,
Now are þay nysottes of þe new gett so nysely attyred   410
With sleȝe slabbande sleues sleght to þe grounde,
Ourlede all vmbtourne with ermyn aboute,
Þat es as harde, as I hope, to handil in þe derne
Als a cely symple wenche þat neuer silke wroghte.
Bot whoso lukes on hir lyre, oure Lady of Heuen,   415
How scho fled for ferd ferre out of hir kythe

409 were] had.   411 sleȝe] elde.

407 *sett*: 'leased'. With a steady decline in profits from farming, owing to
low grain prices, rising labour costs and perhaps also exhaustion of the
soil, landowners increasingly abandoned direct farming in favour of
leasing.
409 'Those who previously were . . .' The landowners have sold up and
bought fancy clothes.
411 There are attacks on the fashion of hanging sleeves from the 1340s;
see Newton (1980:4, 9, 11, and fig. 4). At the end of the century Richard
II was accused of being guided by fashionable young lords whose 'slevis
slide on þe erthe' (*Mum* iii. 152).
413–14 The elaborate clothing is 'as difficult, I believe, to handle in the
dark. . .' But the comparison in the next line makes no sense. 'As a poor
unsophisticated girl who never worked with silk.' The line may be
corrupt or a passage omitted.
415–22 Wynnere contrasts the elegance of the new sophisticates with the
humility of the Virgin Mary as she rode with Joseph and the infant Jesus
into Egypt (Matthew ii. 13–14). The scene was often illustrated, e.g. in
The Holkham Bible Picture Book.
415 *lyre*: this is either *MED lire n.* (1), 'loss', here in the sense
'misfortune, hardship' (so Burrow), or *MED ler*, 'face, countenance'. If
the latter, the poet perhaps alludes to a picture of the Flight.

Appon ane amblande asse withowtten more pride,
Safe a barne in hir barme and a broken heltre
Þat Joseph held in hys hande þat hend for to ȝeme,
Allþofe scho walt al þis werlde hir wedes wer pore   420
For to gyf ensample of siche for to schewe oþer
For to leue pompe and pride; þat pouerte ofte schewes.'

Than þe Wastour wrothly werpes vp his eghne
And said 'Þou Wynnere, þou wriche, me wondirs in hert,
What hafe oure clothes coste þe, caytef, to by,   425
Þat þou schal birdes vpbrayd of þaire bright wedis,
Sithen þat we vouche safe þat þe siluer payen?
It lyes wele for a lede his leman to fynde,
Aftir hir faire chere to forthir hir herte;
Then will scho loue hym lelely as hir lyfe one,   430
Make hym bolde and bown with brandes to smytte,
To schonn schenchipe and schame þer schalkes ere gadird.
And if my peple ben prode me payes alle þe better
To fee þam faire and free tofore with myn eghne.
And ȝe negardes appon nyghte ȝe nappen so harde,   435
Routten at ȝour raxillyng, raysen ȝour hurdes;
Ȝe beden wayte one þe wedir, þen wery ȝe þe while

420 wedes] wordes.   423 werpes] castes.

421–2 'In order to give example of such things to show others that they
should abandon pomp and pride; poverty often demonstrates that.'
423 *werpes*: emended by Gollancz.
427–9 'Since we who pay the silver allow it. It is fitting for a man to
provide for his lady, to gladden her heart in response to her gracious
behaviour.'
430 '. . . as her life itself.'
436 'Snore as you stretch (lit. at your stretching), lift up your bums.' In
l. 248 Wastoure had mocked Wynnere for being unable to sleep for
worry. Here he accuses him of the sleep of sin that will put him into the
hands of the Devil. 'When the old enemy sees that our reason is asleep,
he makes his way to her at once'; *The Ancrene Riwle*, trans. M. B. Salu
(London, 1963:121).
437–8 Wynnere makes a virtue of his slothfulness, instructing his men to
wait for the weather before taking action, then cursing because it is too
late to do anything about it. And so the miser saves money in repairs
and labour.

Þat 3e nade hightilde vp 3our houses and 3our hyne raysed.
Forthi, Wynnere, with wronge þou wastes þi tyme,
For gode day ne glade getys þou neuer.   440
Þe deuyll at þi dede-day schal delyn þi gudis,
Þo þou woldest þat it were wyn þay it neuer;
Þi skathill sectours schal seuer þam aboute,
And þou hafe helle full hotte for þat þou here saued.
Þou tast no tent one a tale þat tolde was full 3ore: 445
I hold hym madde þat mournes his make for to wyn;
Hent hir þat hir haf schal and hold hir his while,
Take þe coppe as it comes, þe case as it falles;
For whoso lyfe may lengeste lympes to feche
Woodd þat he waste schall to warmen his helys   450
Ferrere þan his fadir dide by fyvetene myle.
Now kan I carpe no more; bot, Sir Kyng, bi þi trouthe,
Deme vs where we duell schall; me thynke þe day hyes.
3it harde sore es myn hert and harmes me more
Euer to see in my syghte þat I in soule hate.'   455

The kynge louely lokes on þe ledis twayne,
Says 'Blynes, beryns, of 3our brethe and of 3oure brode worde
And I schal deme 3ow this day where 3e duelle schall,
Aythere lede in a lond þer he es loued moste.

442–3 'Those you wish to inherit it will never get it; your wicked executors will disperse the goods.' Wastoure returns to the argument of l. 302.
445–51 The *tale* is to take life as it comes without worrying and saving up for the future.
447 'Let him who shall have her take her and keep her while he lasts.'
448 *coppe*: i.e. 'what is to happen'. The image derives from Matthew xxvi. 39, 'let this cup pass from me'.
449–51 A long life means only that he will have to go further to fetch the firewood that will all be burnt up anyway to warm his heels. The extra journey is not surprising, since Wastoure is progressively cutting down all his trees (ll. 396–8).
457 *Wars* 5491 provides a close parallel.

Wende, Wynnere, þi waye ouer þe wale stremys,   460
Passe forthe by Paris to þe Pope of Rome.
Þe cardynalls ken þe wele, will kepe þe ful faire
And make þi sydes in silken schetys to lygge,
And fede þe and foster þe and forthir thyn hert,
As leefe to worthen wode as þe to wrethe ones.   465
Bot loke, lede, be þi lyfe, when I lettres sende
Þat þou hy þe to me home on horse or one fote;
And when I knowe þou will come, he schall cayre vttire
And lenge with anoþer lede til þou þi lefe take.
For þofe þou bide in þis burgh to þi berde hore,   470
With hym happyns þe neuer a fote for to passe.
And thou, Wastoure, I will þat þou wonie euire
Þer moste waste es of wele, and wyng þervntill.
Chese þe forthe into þe Chepe, a chamber þou rere.
Loke þi wyndowe be wyde and wayte þe aboute   475
Where any botet beryn þurgh þe burgh passe;

468 come] co. . .   469 take] *lost.*   470 berde hore] ber. . . . .
471 to passe] *lost.*   472 wonie euire] woni. . . . . . .   473 þervntill]
. . . . ntill.   476 botet] potet.

460–5 Wynnere is to go to his supporters at the papal court (cf. l. 147)
where amassing money (through papal taxes etc.) is properly
appreciated.
461 From 1305 the 'Pope of Rome' had been resident in Avignon in
south-east France.
465 They would 'as willingly go mad as ever anger you'.
469–73 The leaf is torn.
470 '. . . until your beard grows grey.'
471 The alliteration fails.
472–95 Wastoure is to encourage his followers to further extravagance.
Such waste will benefit the suppliers who are Wynnere's followers
(l. 495). In effect this supports Wynnere's argument of ll. 390–1.
473 '. . . and hurry there.' No more satisfactory reconstruction comes to
mind.
474 *þe Chepe*: Cheapside in London, where markets were held, and
where the 'white wyn of Lepe' was sold (*CT* vi. 563–4). Cheapside runs
east from St Paul's Cathedral, and continues into Poultry (l. 490). Bread
Street (l. 480) runs off it to the south.
476 *botet*: 'booted', i.e. 'equipped for riding'; see *MED boten v.* (2),
'ocreo: to boten'. Wastoure is to look after his supporters, the knights
and 'bolde sqwyeres of blode' (l. 194).

Teche hym to þe tauerne till he tayte worthe,
Doo hym drynk al nyȝte þat he dry be at morow,
Sythen ken hym to þe crete to comforth his vaynes,
Brynge hym to Bred Strete, bikken þi fynger,   480
Schew hym of fatt schepe scholdirs ynewe
Hotte for þe hungry, a hen oþer twayne,
Sett hym softe one a sege and sythen send after,
Bryng out of þe burgh þe best þou may finde,
And luke thi knave hafe a knoke bot he þe clothe spred;   485
Bot late hym paye or he passe, and pik hym so clene
Þat fynd a peny in his purse and put owte his eghe!
When þat es dronken and don, duell þer no lenger,
Bot teche hym owt of the townn to trotte aftir more,
Then passe to þe Pultrie, þe peple þe knowes,   490
And ken wele þi katour to knawen þi fode:
The herons, þe hasteletez, þe henne wele serue,
Þe pertrikes, þe plouers, þe oþer pulled byrddes,
Þe albus, þis oþer foules þe egretes dere.
Þe more þou wastis þi wele, þe better þe Wynner lykes.   495
And wayte to me, þou Wynnere, if þou wilt wele chefe,
When I wende appon werre my wyes to lede,
For at þe proude pales of Parys þe riche

---

481 schepe] chepe.   485 spred] spre. .

479 *crete*: a sweet wine as the hair of the dog.
483 *send after*: 'send out for supplies'.
487 The *beryn* is to be persuaded to spend all he has so that 'may anyone who finds a penny in his purse be damned'. Cf. 'And but his cnaue be prest, put out myne eiȝe', *PPCrede* 288.
491 The *katour* was the officer who bought the food for the household.
492 *hasteletez*: roasted entrails of a boar; cf. *SGGK* 1612.
494 *albus*: perhaps a kind of finch (so *MED*), or perhaps, in this context, a white bird (Lat *albus*, 'white'). *egretes*: white herons, extinct in Britain since the eighteenth century.
496–503 After his victorious campaign in 1346 in which the English army reached the outskirts of Paris, Edward was keener than ever to press his claim to the French crown. But the costs were astronomical, and soldiers and investors had to be tempted by the thought of the rich profits that could be made. The *proude pales* is the Palais de la Cité illustrated in *Les Tres Riches Heures de Duc de Berry*, ed. J. Longnon (London, 1969:pl. 7 (June)).

65

I thynk to do it in ded and dub þe to knyghte
And giff giftes full grete of gold and of siluer   500
To ledis of my legyance þat lufen me in hert,
And sythen kayren as I come with knyghtis þat me foloen
To þe kirke of Colayne þer þe kynges ligges. . .
The last lines are lost

500 siluer] si. . . . .   502 kayren] layren.

499 *do it in ded*: 'put it into effect'.
503 Cologne Cathedral with the shrine of the Three Magi. On his great
diplomatic coup of an alliance with the Emperor Lewis IV in 1338,
Edward had heard Mass at the Cathedral. Presumably he intended to
return there in gratitude for final victory in France. He never did.

THE PARLEMENT OF THE
THRE AGES

INTRODUCTION

Manuscripts

The *Parlement* precedes *Wynnere* in Robert Thornton's MS. BL
Addit. 31042, fols. 169a–176b (T), on which the text here is
based. Another copy, lacking ll. 1–225, is in the Ware MS., BL
Addit. 33994, fols. 19a-26a (W), written in the late fifteenth
century.

Date and place

There are no precise indications of the date of the poem. On the
basis of the description of 3outhe's clothes, Lewis (1968) argues
for a late fourteenth-century date, which is likely enough, but the
evidence is inconclusive. Nor is there clear evidence of the
original dialect, though it is generally assumed to be north
midland.

Sources

The major source is Jacques de Longuyon's *Les Voeux du Paon*
(*c.* 1312), an account of the Battle of Epheson fought by
Alexander the Great against Clarus of Ind and his son Porrus. In
the course of lauding the virtues of Porrus, Longuyon compares
him favourably with the Nine Worthies (*Voeux* 7484–579). The
author of the *Parlement* bases Elde's enumeration (ll. 300–579)
on this passage, though at some points he adds to the brief

French account much information taken from other French romances and some English legends. The account in *Morte A* 3278–437 also depends on *Voeux*, and several verbal parallels suggest the possibility of a relationship with the *Parlement* (e.g. *Morte A* 3418–19, *Parlement* 444–5).

Lines 25–92, describing the deer and its dismembering, may be drawn directly from experience, though the passage is in many respects close to instructions in hunting manuals, in particular in *The Boke of Huntyng*, extant from the fifteenth century and in 1486 printed as part of *The Boke of St. Albans*. See *St. Albans*, ed. R. Hands, pp. xxxii–xliv.

Structure and theme

A dream-vision debate, like *Wynnere*. The long and lively prologue establishes the worldly concerns of the narrator and yet, by describing his activities as a poacher, characterises him as a figure in some ways outside society and therefore perhaps as an observer detached from the specific concerns of the disputants within his dream. See Waldron (1972), and Scattergood (1983). The dream itself opens with portraits of 3outhe, Medill Elde and Elde, with the bias to begin with heavily in favour of handsome 3outhe and his elegant sport of hawking, which is lovingly described. The greater part of the dream is taken up by Elde's account of the Nine Worthies, which is, by comparison, long-winded and strangely incompetent. Elde argues that each of the Nine achieved distinction, but they all ended up equally dead, as did the Wise and the Lovers whom he also enumerates. Therefore, he concludes, worldly preoccupations and achievements are vain. The dreamer wakes up to his Maytime landscape and makes off home, not commenting, though presumably reflecting, on the message of his dream. The time-scale of the action, beginning at dawn (l. 6) and ending at sunset (l. 654), underlines the thematic time-scale from youth to death, for, in the popular image discussed by Burrow (1986:56–72), 'mannis liif here is but a day'.

BIBLIOGRAPHY

Editions

Sir Israel Gollancz, *The Parlement of the Thre Ages* (London, 1915)
M. Y. Offord, *The Parlement of the Thre Ages*, EETS 246 (1959)

Studies

J. A. Burrow, *The Ages of Man* (Oxford, 1986)
A. Kernan, 'Theme and structure in *The Parlement of the Thre Ages*',
  NM, 75 (1974:253–78)
R. E. Lewis, 'The date of the *Parlement of the Thre Ages*', *NM*, 69
  (1968:380–90)
R. A. Peck, 'The careful hunter in *The Parlement of the Thre Ages*',
  ELH, 39 (1972:333–41)
B. Rowland, 'The three ages of *The Parlement of the Three Ages*',
  Chaucer Review, 9 (1975: 342–52)
V. J. Scattergood, '*The Parlement of the Thre Ages*', *LSE*, n.s. 14
  (1983:167–77)
T. Turville-Petre, 'The ages of man in *The Parlement of the Thre Ages*',
  MÆ, 46 (1977:66–76)
T. Turville-Petre, 'The nine worthies in *The Parlement of the Thre Ages*',
  Poetica, 11 (1979:28–45)
R. A. Waldron, 'The prologue to *The Parlement of the Thre Ages*', *NM*,
  73 (1972:786–94)

THE PARLEMENT OF THE THRE AGES

In the monethe of Maye when mirthes bene fele,
And the sesone of somere when softe bene the wedres,
Als I went to the wodde my werdes to dreghe,
Into þe schawes myselfe a schotte me to gete
At ane hert or ane hynde, happen as it myghte,   5
And as Dryghtyn the day droue frome þe heuen,
Als I habade one a banke be a bryme syde
There the gryse was grene, growen with floures –
The primrose, the pervynke and piliole þe riche –
The dewe appon dayses donkede full faire,   10
Burgons and blossoms and braunches full swete,
And the mery mystes full myldely gane falle.
The cukkowe, the cowschote, kene were þay bothen,
And the throstills full throly threpen in the bankes,
And iche foule in that frythe faynere þan oþer   15
That the derke was done and the daye lightenede.
Hertys and hyndes one hillys þay gon,
The foxe and the filmarte þay flede to þe erthe,
The hare hurkles by hawes and harde thedir dryues
And ferkes faste to hir fourme and fatills hir to sitt. 20
Als I stode in that stede, one stalkynge I thoughte;
Bothe my body and my bowe I buskede with leues
And turnede towardes a tree and tariede there a while,
And als I lokede to a launde a littill me besyde
I seghe ane hert with ane hede, ane heghe for the nones, 25

1 monethe] monethes T.   17 gon] gonen *or* gouen T.

1–103 On the function of the prologue and the figure of the narrator-as-poacher, see Waldron (1972), Peck (1972), and Scattergood (1983). As in *Somer Soneday* and *Kings*, a hunting prologue introduces a vision of mortality; see Turville-Petre (1974:5–12).
3 *my werdes to dreghe*: lit. 'to suffer my fate'; cf. *Cleanness* 1224. The immediate sense is 'to try my luck' (in poaching), but the phrase also applies to the sharp warning administered within the dream.
6 i.e. 'at dawn'.
14, 19–20 Cf. *Wynnere* 37 and 13.
21 *one*: 'on, about'.
25 'I saw a hart with a head of antlers, a high head indeed.'

70

The Parlement of the Thre Ages

Alle vnburneschede was þe beme, full borely þe mydle,
With iche feetur as thi fote, forfrayed in the greues,
With auntlers one aythere syde egheliche longe;
The ryalls full richely raughten frome the myddes,
With surryals full semely appon sydes twayne,   30
And he assommet and sett of six and of fyve,
And þerto borely and brode and of body grete,
And a coloppe for a kynge, cache hym who myghte.
Bot there sewet hym a sowre þat seruet hym full ȝerne,
That woke and warned hym when the wynde faylede   35
That none so sleghe in his slepe with sleghte scholde hym
    dere,
And went the wayes hym byfore when any wothe tyde.
My lyame than full lightly lete I doun falle
And to the bole of a birche my berselett I cowchide.
I waitted wiesly the wynde by waggynge of leues,   40
Stalkede full stilly no stikkes to breke,
And crepite to a crab-tre and couerede me thervndere.
Then I bende vp my bowe and bownede me to schote,
Tighte vp my tylere and taysede at the hert,
Bot the sowre þat hym sewet sett vp the nese   45
And wayttede wittyly abowte and wyndide full ȝerne;
Then I moste stonde als I stode and stirre no fote ferrere,

26–7 The hart has not yet 'burnished' (polished) the main beam of his antlers, but each projecting tine (*iche feetur*) has been rubbed free (*forfrayed*) of its protective furry skin. The comparison *as thi fote* perhaps indicates the great length of the tines.
28–31 The 'antler' is the tine nearest the head, above that is the 'royal', and finally the 'surroyal'. At the top of each beam are clustered the *troches* (l. 67), by which the head is reckoned. This hart has a massive head with six and five troches. It is *assommet*, 'summed up', i.e. has its full complement. See *St. Albans* 1238–53 and note pp. 120–1.
34–7 The *sowre* (a stag in its fourth year) guards the older hart. Offord quotes from Edward of York's *Master of Game*: 'And sometyme a greet hert hath anoþer felawe that is called his squiere'.
43–54 The poacher uses a crossbow. He sets up the *tylere*, the stock of the bow, and takes aim, but he has to keep quite still while the younger deer sniffs around nervously. Then he releases the *hokes*, the catches of the bow, hitting the deer behind the shoulder – the recommended shot. For an account with illustrations of the procedure, see Gaston Phébus, *Livre de Chasse*, ed. G. Tilander (Karlshamn, 1971:269–79).

For had I myntid or mouede or made any synys,
Alle my layke hade bene loste þat I hade longe wayttede.
Bot gnattes gretely me greuede and gnewen myn eghne,   50
And he stotayde and stelkett and starede full brode,
Bot at the laste he loutted doun and laughte till his mete,
And I hallede to the hokes and the hert smote,
And happenyd that I hitt hym byhynde þe lefte scholdire
Þat þe blode braste owte appon bothe the sydes,   55
And he balkede and brayed and bruschede thurgh þe greues
As alle had hurlede one ane hepe þat in the holte longede.
And sone the sowre þat hym sewet resorte to his feris,
And þay forfrayede of his fare to þe fellys þay hyen,
And I hyede to my hounde and hent hym vp sone   60
And louset my lyame and lete hym vmbycaste.
The breris and the brakans were blody byronnen,
And he assentis to þat sewte and seches hym aftire
There he was crepyde into a krage and crouschede to þe
     erthe.
Dede als a dore-nayle doun was he fallen,   65
And I hym hent by þe hede and heryett hym vttire,
Turned his troches and tachede thaym into the erthe,
Kest vp that keuduart and kutt of his tonge,
Brayde oute his bewells my bereselet to fede,
And I slitte hym at þe assaye to see how me semyde,   70
And he was floreschede full faire of two fyngere brede.

48 myntid] mytid T.   69 oute] *om.* T.   70 slitte] sisilte T.

66–96 The description of the 'undoing' or brittling of the hart should be
compared with the instructions in *St. Albans* 1749–844, and the poetic
treatments in *SGGK* 1325–61, and in Gottfried von Strassburg's *Tristan*,
trans. A. T. Hatto (Harmondsworth, 1960:78–82). Despite his fear of
discovery, the poacher works skilfully and according to 'the noble
customys of jantylmen', as Malory calls them (*Works*, p. 375). For
illustration of the process, see Phébus, p. 177.
66–71 The hart is laid on its back, its tongue and bowels are removed,
and the breast is cut open at the 'assay' in order to test the thickness of
the fat. As in *SGGK* 1328–9, the fat is to a depth of two fingers.
68 *keuduart*: meaning uncertain, perhaps an error for *keuenart*. See
A. McIntosh, 'Some Words in the *Northern Homily Collection*', *NM*, 73
(1972:197) '*cauenard*, term of abuse, scoundrel?'.

I chese to the chawylls chefe to begynn
And ritte doun at a rase reghte to the tayle,
And þan þe herbere anone aftir I makede;
I raughte the righte legge byfore, ritt it þeraftir,   75
And so fro legge to legge I lepe thaym aboute,
And þe felle fro þe fete fayre I departede
And flewe it doun with my fiste faste to the rigge.
I tighte owte my trenchore and toke of the scholdirs,
Cuttede corbyns bone and keste it awaye;   80
I slitte hym full sleghely and slyppede in my fyngere
Lesse the poynte scholde perche the pawnche or the guttys;
I soughte owte my sewet and semblete it togedire
And pullede oute the pawnche and putt it in an hole.
I grippede owte the guttes and graythede thaym besyde,   85
And than the nombles anone name I thereaftire,
Rent vp fro the rygge reghte to the myddis,
And then the fourches full fayre I fonge fro þe sydes
And chynede hym chefely and choppede of the nekke
And þe hede and the haulse homelyde in sondree.   90
Þe fete of the fourche I feste thurgh the sydis
And heuede alle into ane hole and hidde it with ferne,
With hethe and with hore-mosse hilde it about
Þat no fostere of the fee scholde fynde it theraftir,
Hid the hornes and the hede in ane hologhe oke   95
Þat no hunte scholde it hent ne haue it in sighte.

84 pawnche] pawche T.

72–8 For a similar account of the flaying, cf. *St. Albans* 1759ff.
74 To 'make the arber' is to remove the gullet and first stomach, tying it
to prevent the contents escaping and spoiling the flesh. See *SGGK*
1330–1.
79–81 'Than take owt the shulderis and slyttith anoon/The baly to the
syde from the corbyn bone/That is corbyns fee', *St. Albans* 1775–7. The
'ravens' bone' was a piece of gristle thrown up to the birds. Cf. *SGGK*
1355.
86 *nombles*: edible innards with their attached flesh; see *St. Albans*
1792ff and note.
88–91 The haunches (*fourches*) are cut from the sides, the backbone is
removed, the neck cut from the body and the head from the neck.
Finally the hind legs are fastened to the sides. Cf. *St. Albans* 1817–23,
1838–40, *SGGK* 1357.

I foundede faste therefro for ferde to be wryghede
And sett me oute one a syde to see how it cheuede,
To wayte it frome wylde swyne that wyse bene of nesse.
And als I satte in my sette the sone was so warme,   100
And I for slepeles was slome and slomerde a while;
And there me dremed in that dowte a full dreghe sweuynn,
And whate I seghe in my saule the sothe I schall telle.

I seghe thre thro men threpden full ȝerne
And moten of mychewhate and maden thaym full tale;   105
And ȝe will, ledys, me listen bot a littill while,
I schall reken thaire araye redely forsothe
And to ȝowe neuen thaire names naytly thereaftire.
The firste was a ferse freke, fayrere than thies othire,
A bolde beryn one a blonke bownne for to ryde,   110
A hathelle on ane heghe horse with hauke appon hande.
He was balghe in the breste and brode in the scholdirs,
His axles and his armes were iliche longe,
And in the medill als a mayden menskfully schapen,
Longe legges and large and lele for to schewe.   115
He streghte hym in his sterapis and stode vprightes;
He ne hade no hode ne no hatte bot his here one,
A chaplet one his chefelere chosen for the nones,
Raylede alle with rede rose richeste of floures,
With trayfoyles and trewloues of full triede perles,   120
With a chefe charebocle chosen in the myddes.

106 bot a littill] ane hande T.

101 *for slepeles*: 'because of lack of sleep'. An adj. is sometimes used as
a noun after *for*; cf. *for radde* l. 429, and see Mustanoja (1960:381–2).
102 *dowte*: 'anxiety' (of being apprehended). It was well recognized that
the dreamer's state of mind affected the dream: see Chaucer, *PF* 99–105,
HF 29–35.
104–65 For discussion of the division into *three* ages see Turville-Petre
(1977b), and Burrow (1986:66–72). ȝouthe's hawk, Medill Elde's money-
bags and Elde's beads are all traditional emblems.
106 For the emended half-line, see *SGGK* 30, *Wil Pal* 224.
118–21 In ll. 179–81 ȝouthe explains why he wears no hat. With his
chaplet, cf. Gawain's *vrysoun* and *cercle* (*SGGK* 608–18).

He was gerede alle in grene, alle with golde byweuede,
Enbroddirde alle with besanttes and beralles full riche;
His colere with calsydoynnes clustrede full thikke,
With many dyamandes full dere dighte one his sleues.   125
Þe semys with saphirs sett were full many,
With emeraudes and amatistes appon iche syde,
With full riche rubyes raylede by the hemmes;
Þe price of that perry were worthe powndes full many.
His sadill was of sykamoure that he satt inn,   130
His bridell alle of brente golde with silke brayden raynes,
His trapoure was of tartaryne þat traylede to þe erthe,
And he throly was threuen of thritty ʒere of elde
And therto ʒonge and ʒape, and ʒouthe was his name,
And the semelyeste segge that I seghe euer.   135

The seconde segge in his sete satte at his ese,
A renke alle in rosette þat rowmly was schapyn
In a golyone of graye girde in the myddes,
And iche bagge in his bosome bettir than othere.
One his golde and his gude gretly he mousede,   140
His renttes and his reches rekened he full ofte:
Off mukkyng, of marlelyng and mendynge of howses,

---

132 trapoure] cropoure T.   135 semelyeste] semely T.

122 Gold and green are the colours of vigour, elegance and beauty. See
l. 615, *SGGK* 151–72, and Burrow (1965:15–16).
123 *besanttes*: see *Wynnere* 61n.
124 *colere*: either a neckband (the modern sense), or a chain worn
round the neck, as in *Cleanness* 1569; see *MED coler*, and Lewis (1968).
132 *trapoure*: a decorative cloth over the horse, as illustrated in Poole
(1958:pl. 71). Cf. Barbour, 'trappit horss richt to the feit' (*Bruce* xvi,
185). The emendation is by Gollancz.
133 *thritty* (and cf. ll. 150, 164): Peck (1972:338), argues that as each of
the ages is 'at the extremity of his measure', the poet 'keeps us mindful
of the inevitability of each one's passing on to the next degree'. Kernan
(1974) and Rowland (1975) relate the years to the Parable of the Sower,
Matthew xiii. 8.
137 *rosette*: a coarse wollen cloth; cf. 'Thus yrobed in russet Y romede
about', *PPl* C x. 1. Medill Elde's clothes are practical.

Off benes of his bondemen, of benefetis many,
Off presanttes of polayle, of pufilis als,
Off purches of ploughe-londes, of parkes full faire,   145
Off profettis of his pasturs that his purse mendis,
Off stiewarde, of storrours, stirkes to bye,
Off clerkes, of countours his courtes to holde –
And alle his witt in this werlde was one his wele one.
Hym semyde for to see to of sexty зere elde,   150
And þerfore men in his marche Medill Elde hym callede.

The thirde was a laythe lede lenyde one his syde,
A beryne bownn alle in blake with bedis in his hande,
Croked and courbede, encrampeschett for elde.
Alle disfygured was his face and fadit his hewe,   155
His berde and browes were blanchede full whitte,
And the hare one his hede hewede of the same.
He was ballede and blynde and alle babirlippede,
Totheles and tenefull I tell зowe for sothe,
And euer he momelide and ment and mercy he askede   160
And cried kenely one Criste and his crede sayde
With sawtries full sere tymes to sayntes in heuen,
Envyous and angrye, and Elde was his name.
I helde hym be my hopynge a hundrethe зeris of age,
And bot his cruche and his couche he carede for no more.   165
Now hafe I rekkende зow theire araye redely the sothe,

166 I] *om.* T.

143 *benes*: extra services or 'boon-works' that the lord could demand of
his peasants, especially during the harvest. See Bennett (1937:106).
146 *his purse mendis*: 'puts money into his purse'.
147–8 The *stiewarde* ran the estates. *Storrours* are 'store-keepers', i.e.
reeves, whose powers are described by Chaucer, *CT* i. 597–9. The
countours are the lord's auditors, who, sometimes together with the lord
himself and assisted by the *clerkes*, held the manorial court to adjudicate
in local matters. On the duties of all these officials see Bennett
(1937:159–62, 167–73, 195–221).
158 *babirlippede*: 'with swollen lips', as in the description of Covetise,
PPl C vi. 198.
163 In 1571 Thomas Fortescue noted in his account of the ages in *The
Foreste* that Old Age is 'angrye, weamishe, harde to please, and
enuious'. On the general tradition see Turville-Petre (1977b:71–3).

And also namede ȝow thaire names naytly thereaftire,
And now thaire carpynge I sall kythe, knowe it if ȝowe liste.

Now this gome alle in grene so gayly attyrede,
This hathelle one this heghe horse with hauke one his fiste, 170
He was ȝonge and ȝape and ȝernynge to armes,
And pleynede hym one paramours and peteuosely syghede.
He sett hym vp in his sadill and seyde theis wordes:
'My lady, my leman, þat I hafe luffede euer,
My wele and my wirchip in werlde where þou duellys, 175
My playstere of paramours, my lady with pappis full swete,
Alle my hope and my hele, myn herte es thyn ownn!
I byhete the a heste and heghely I avowe
There schall no hode ne no hatt one my hede sitt
Till þat I joyntly with a gesserante justede hafe with onere 180
And done dedis for thi loue, doghety in armes!'

Bot then this gome alle in graye greued with this wordes
And sayde: 'Felowe, be my faythe þou fonnes full ȝerne,
For alle es fantome and foly that thou with faris!
Where es þe londe and the lythe þat þou arte lorde ouer? 185
For alle thy ryalle araye renttis hase þou none,
Ne for thi pompe and thi pride penyes bot fewe,
For alle thi golde and thi gude gloes one thi clothes.
And þou hafe caughte thi kaple þou cares for no fothire.
Bye the stirkes with thi stede and stalles thaym make! 190
Thi brydell of brent golde wolde bullokes the gete,
The pryce of thi perrye wolde purches the londes;
And wonne, wy, in thi witt, for wele-neghe þou spilles!'

Than the gome alle in grene greued full sore
And sayd: 'Sir, be my soule, thi consell es feble. 195

173 seyde] seyden T.   180 with (2)] *om.* T.   184 es] *om.* T.

184 Cf. 'All it is fantam þat we mid fare', Brown, *XIV*, no. 43.
189–90 'As long as you have got your horse you don't bother about a
cart-load (i.e. its agricultural use). Buy yourself cattle in exchange for
your steed and make stalls for them!' Cf. *Wynnere* 236–40.
192 *purches the*: 'buy for yourself'.
193 'And keep your wits about you, sir, for you are close to ruin.'

Bot thi golde and thi gude thou hase no god ells!
For be þe Lorde and the laye þat I leue inne,
And by the Gode that me gaffe goste and soule,
Me were leuere one this launde lengen a while,
Stoken in my stele-wede one my stede bakke,   200
Harde haspede in my helme and in my here-wedys
With a grym grownden glayfe graythely in myn honde,
And see a kene knyghte come and cowpe with myseluen,
Þat I myghte halde þat I hafe highte and heghely avowede,
And perfourme my profers and prouen my strengthes,   205
Than alle the golde and the gude that thoue gatt euer,
Than alle the londe and the lythe that thoue arte lorde ouer;
And ryde to a reuere redily thereaftir
With haukes full hawtayne that heghe willen flye;
And when þe fewlis bene founden, fawkoneres hyenn   210
To lache oute thaire lessches and lowsen thaym sone
And keppyn of thaire caprons and casten fro honde.
And than the hawteste in haste hyghes to the towre
With theire bellys so brighte blethely thay ryngen,
And there they houen appon heghte as it were heuen
   angelles.   215

204 'So that I might keep to what I've promised . . .' Cf. ll. 178–81.
208–45 There is no other literary treatment of hawking in ME, but there
are a number of treatises, many of them still unedited. *St. Albans* deals
mostly with avian ailments, feeding and the like.
209 The *hawtayne* (i.e. 'aristocratic') hawks are the long-winged 'hawks
of the tower' that soar and swoop down on their prey; cf. Chaucer's
'gentil hawtein faucoun heroner', *LGW* 1120. See R. Hands, *NQ*, 216
(1971:85–8).
211–12 The falconers release the leashes attached to the jesses that are
tied to the hawks' legs by means of small rings called varvels (l. 238).
Then they remove the hoods that hawks wear to keep them quiet when
carried.
213 *towre*: the position where the hawk circles high above waiting to
stoop. It is OFr *tour*, 'turn', blended with OE *tur*, 'tower'.
214 Hawks wear bells on their legs to draw attention to their position.
See *St. Albans* 1145–61.

Then the fawkoners full fersely to floodes þay hyen,
To the reuere with thaire roddes to rere vp the fewles,
Sowssches thaym full serely to seruen thaire hawkes.
Than tercelettes full tayttely telys doun stryken,
Laners and lanerettis lightten to thes endes,   220
Metyn with the maulerdes and many doun striken.
Fawkons þay founden freely to lighte,
With "hoo" and "howghe" to the heron þay hitten hym full
    ofte,
Buffetyn hym, betyn hym and brynges hym to sege,
And saylen hym full serely and sesyn hym thereaftire.   225
Then fawkoners full fersely founden þam aftire,
To helpen thaire hawkes thay hyen thaym full ȝerne,
For with the bitt of his bill bitterly he strikes.
They knelyn doun one theire knees and krepyn full lowe,
Wynnen to his wynges and wrythen thaym togedire,   230
Brosten the bones and brekyn thaym in sondire,
Puttis owte with a penn þe maryo one his gloue,

226 *here W begins.*   228 with] W, *om.* T.

216–18 The falconers drive up the game for their hawks. *Sowssches*: a technical term, 'drive into the air'; *seruen*: 'to drive out game into the view of the hawk' (*OED serve v.*[1] 53a).
220 *endes*: 'ducks' (OE *ened*).
222 *Fawkons*: here used specifically of the female peregrines which are capable of attacking the noblest game of all, the herons.
223 'Smyte youre tabur and cry "huff, huff, huff" and make the fowle to spryng' (*St. Albans* 1079–80).
224 *brynges hym to sege*: perhaps 'drive him down to the ground'. The 'siege' is 'the station of a heron on the watch for prey' (*OED*, 2c). The action of these lines is described by George Turbervile, *The Booke of Faulconrie or Hauking* (1575:164) 'As soone as the Hearon leaueth the siege, off with hir hood, and let hir flee: and if shee climb to the Hearon, and beate hir so that she bring hir downe, runne in apace to reskewe hir, thrusting the Hearons bil into the ground and breaking hir wings and legges.'
232 *maryo*: Gollancz's emendation to alliterative *pyth* is attractive, but 'marrow' is the word used to refer to the falcon's reward. Offord cites *Prince Edward's Book*: 'then kutte the grete bonys of the wynggis and with a penne draw oute the merowe' (*Reliquiæ Antiquæ*, i, 299).

And quopes thaym to the querrye that quelled hym to þe
   dethe.
He quyrres thaym and quotes thaym, quyppeys full lowde,
Cheres hym full chefely ecchekkes to leue,   235
Than henttis thaym one honde and hodes thaym theraftire,
Cowples vp theire cowers thaire caprons to holde,
Lowppes in thaire lesses thorowe vertwells of siluere;
Þan he laches to his luyre and lokes to his horse,
And lepis vpe one the lefte syde als þe laghe askes.   240
Portours full pristly putten vpe the fowlis
And taryen for theire tercelettis þat tenyn thaym full ofte,
For some chosen to þe echecheke, þoghe some chefe bettire;
Spanyells full spedily þay spryngen abowte,
Bedagged for dowkynge when digges bene enewede.   245
And than kayre to the courte that I come fro,
With ladys full louely to lappyn in myn armes,

233 quopes] whopis W, quotes T.   234 quyrres] T, wharris W.
235 cheres] He cheris W, Cheresche T; hym] T, þem W.

233 'And calls those (hawks) that killed him (the heron) to the quarry'.
The 'quarry' is the reward given to hounds or hawks; see *SGGK* 1324.
234 The meanings of the three verbs are uncertain. *quyrres*: either
'quarries' (i.e. gives them some of the game to eat), or 'calls with a
whirring sound' (ms. W has *wharris*). *quotes*: *MED* cites the verb under
both *houten*, 'shout to', and *quaten*! The latter is to be preferred, in the
sense 'make calm, bring to a settled state'. *quyppeys*: 'whips' (with the
roddes?), perhaps to direct the hawks; see next line.
235 *hym* is pl., 'them'. *ecchekkes*: 'base game such as rooks, crows,
doves etc.' (*OED check sb.* 6b).
237 The *cowers* are straps at the back of the hawks' *caprons*, 'hoods'.
238 The leashes are attached again; cf. ll. 211–12n. *Vertwells* does not
alliterate, but it is the correct term for the metal rings at the end of the
jesses.
239 *luyre*: 'a bait for recalling hawks, usually a bundle of leather and
feathers resembling a bird' (*MED lure* n. (1)a).
240 The correct way to mount with hawk on fist is illustrated in mss.; see
Frederick II, *De arte venandi cum avibus*, ed. in facs. C. A. Willemsen
(Graz, 1969:fols 98a and b).
245 'Bespattered from diving when ducks are driven down into the
water.' For *enewede* see *St. Albans* 1102n.
246 *kayre*: 'to go', infin. formally dependent on *me were leuere*, l. 199,
and parallel to *ryde*, l. 208.

The Parlement of the Thre Ages

And clyp thaym and kysse thaym and comforthe myn hert;
And than with damesels dere to daunsen in thaire chambirs,
Riche romance to rede and rekken the sothe   250
Off kempes and of conquerours, of kynges full noblee,
How thay wirchipe and welthe wanne in thaire lyues;
With renkes in ryotte to reuelle in haulle,
With coundythes and carolles and compaynyes sere,
And chese me to the chesse that chefe es of gamnes –   255
And this es life for to lede while I schalle lyfe here.
And thou with wandrynge and woo schalt wake for thi
    gudes,
And be thou doluen and dede thi dole schall be schorte,
And he that thou leste luffes schall layke hym therewith,
And spend that thou sparede, the deuyll spede hym ells!'   260
Than this renke alle in rosett rothelede thies wordes;
He sayde: 'Thryfte and thou haue threpid this thirtene
    wynter.
I seghe wele samples bene sothe that sayde bene full ʒore:
"Fole es that with foles delys." Flyte we no lengare.'

Than this beryn alle in blake bownnes hym to speke   265
And sayde: 'Sirres, by my soule, sottes bene ʒe bothe!
Bot will ʒe hendely me herken ane hande-while
And I schalle stynte ʒoure stryffe and stillen ʒour threpe.
I sett ensample bi myselfe and sekis it no forthire:
While I was ʒonge in my ʒouthe and ʒape of my dedys,   270

252 þey] W, thaire T.   260 sparid] W, haste longe sparede] T.
261 rothelede] T, ratild W.   263 ful] W, *om.* T.

254 Both *coundythes* and *carolles* are dance-songs; see *SGGK* 1655, and R. L. Greene, *The Early English Carols* (2nd edn, Oxford, 1977: esp. p. xxix).
257 The usual phrase is *wandreth and wo*, 'care and sorrow' (e.g. *Wars* 528). Cf. *Wynnere* 248.
258 'When you are dead and buried, mourning for you will be brief.'
259 *therewith*: i.e. 'with the *gudes*'. With ll. 259–60, cf. *Wynnere* 442–4.
260 'The devil help him if he doesn't!' An ironic exclamation; cf. Chaucer, *TC* iv. 630.
264 A saw recorded in Scotland; see B. J. Whiting, *MS*, 11 (1949:172).
269 *sekis*: pr.1sg.; a northern form.

81

I was als euerrous in armes as ouþer of ȝoureseluen
And as styffe in a stourre one my stede-bake,
And as gaye in my gere als any gome ells,
And as lelly byluffede with ladyse and maydens;
My likame was louely es lothe nowe to schewe,   275
And as myche wirchip I wane, iwis, as ȝe bothen.
And aftir irkede me with this, and ese was me leuere,
Als man in his medill elde his makande wolde haue;
Than I mukkede and marlede and made vp my howses
And purcheste me ploughe-londes and pastures full noble,   280
Gatte gude and golde full gaynly to honde;
Reches and renttes were ryfe to myseluen.
Bot elde vndireȝode me are I laste wiste,
And alle disfegurede my face and fadide my hewe,
Bothe my browes and my berde blawnchede full whitte;   285
And when he sotted my syghte than sowed myn hert,
Croked me, cowrbed me, encrampeschet myn hondes
Þat I ne may hefe þam to my hede ne noghte helpe
    myseluen,
Ne stale stonden one my fete bot I my staffe haue.
Makes ȝoure mirrours bi me, men, bi ȝoure trouthe,   290
This schadowe in my schewere schunte ȝe no while.
And now es dethe at my dore that I drede moste,
I ne wot wiche daye, ne when, ne whate tyme he comes,
Ne whedirwardes, ne whare, ne whatte to do aftire,
Bot many modyere than I, men one this molde   295
Hafe passed the pase þat I schall passe sone.
And I schall neuen ȝow the names of nyne of the beste
Þat euer wy in this werlde wiste appon erthe,
Þat were conquerours full kene and kiddeste of oþer.

279–82, 284–7 Cf. ll. 140–6, 154–6.
290 'Take warning from me . . .' See *MED mirour* 3(d), and cf. *Kings*
120, and Brown *XIV*, no. 101, ll. 57–60.
291 *schadowe* has the senses 'reflection', cf. *Rom Rose* 1529;
'foreshadowing' (esp. of death), cf. 'the shadwe of deeth', Chaucer, *CT*
x. 211; 'image of life's insubstantiality', cf. 'Þe joie of þis wrecchid
world is . . . likned to a schadewe', Brown, *XIV*, no 134, ll. 25–6.

The arste was Sir Ector and aldeste of tyme,   300
When Troygens of Troye were tried to fighte
With Menylawse þe mody kynge and men out of Grece
Þat þaire cité assegede and sayled it full ӡerne,
For Elayne his ownn quene that thereinn was halden,
Þat Paresche the proude knyghte paramours louede.   305
Sir Ectore was euerous, als the storye telles
And als clerkes in the cronycle cownten þe sothe,
Nowmbron thaym to nynetene and nyne mo by tale
Off kynges with crounes he killede with his handes,
And full fele oþer folke, als ferly were ellis.   310
Then Achilles his adversarye vndide with his werkes,
With wyles and no wirchipe woundede hym to dethe
Als he tentid to a tulke þat he tuke of were,
And he was slayne for that slaughte sleghely þeraftir
With the wyles of a woman as he had wroghte byfore.   315
Than Menylawse þe mody kynge hade myrthe at his hert
Þat Ectore hys enymy siche auntoure hade fallen,
And with the Gregeis of Grece he girde ouer the walles;
Þe prowde paleys dide he pulle plat to þe erthe,
Þat was rialeste of araye and rycheste vndir the heuen.   320

300 arste] firste TW.   308 nynetene] xix T, nynety W.   319 dide he
pulle] T, he pulled W; plat] doun TW.

300–11 The first half of the account of Hector is based on *Voeux*
7484–94; see Turville-Petre (1979:35–6). The *cronycle* (l. 307) that lies
behind the account is Guido de Columnis, *Historia Destructionis Troiae*;
see introduction to *Dest Troy*.
300 *arste*: see ll. 464 and 586, in both of which ms. W reads *eldist*.
308–10 *Voeux* claims that Hector killed nineteen kings and over a
hundred princes and earls.
311–31 The remainder of the account of Hector relies on Guido.
Achilles, stealing up on Hector, killed him as he was attending to a
prisoner. Hecuba, Hector's mother, tricked Achilles into coming to the
temple, where Paris slayed him. The Greeks persuaded the Trojans to
admit a bronze horse full of soldiers, and thus the walls of Troy were
broached, King Priam killed in the temple, and the buildings of the city
destroyed.
313 *of were*: 'by warfare'; cf. Chaucer, *TC* i. 134.
319 The emendation corrects the alliterative pattern. For the common
expression *plat to þe erthe*, see *MED plat* adv. 1a.

And þen þe Trogens of Troye teneden full sore,
And semblen þaym full sorely and sadly þay foughten,
Bot the lure at the laste lighte appon Troye;
For there Sir Priamus the prynce put was to dethe,
And Pantasilia the proude quene paste hym byfore,   325
Sir Troylus a trewe knyghte þat tristyly hade foghten;
Neptolemus a noble knyghte at nede þat wolde noghte fayle,
Palamedes a prise knyghte and preued in armes,
Vlixes and Ercules þat euerrous were bothe,
And oþer fele of þat ferde fared of the same,   330
As Dittes and Dares demedon togedir.

Aftir this Sir Alysaunder alle þe worlde wanne,
Bothe the see and the sonde and the sadde erthe,
Þe iles of the Oryent to Ercules boundes
(Ther Ely and Ennoke euer hafe bene sythen,   335
And to the come of Antecriste vnclosede be þay neuer),

325–6 Penthesilia, Queen of the Amazons, led her women in support of
the Trojans, but was finally killed by Pyrrhus. Troilus was killed by
Achilles.
327–9 The Greek heroes. Neoptolemus (i.e. Pyrrhus), son of Achilles,
was killed by Orestes long after the destruction of Troy. Palamedes, son
of the Greek king Nauplius, was slain by Paris, and Ulysses was killed
unwittingly by his son. Hercules is mentioned early in Guido's account.
He was poisoned by the shirt of Nessus, as recounted by Chaucer, *CT*
vii. 2119–26.
331 Dictys the Cretan and Dares the Phrygian wrote supposedly eye-
witness accounts of the Trojan war. Guido acknowledged them as his
sources.
332–405 The Alexander story is not from the short account of the
Worthies in *Voeux*, but in ll. 345–93 the poet gives a loose plot-summary
of the *Voeux* as a whole.
334–6 Alexander's legendary journeys extended from the Earthly
Paradise in the east, where Elias and Enoch await the coming of
Antichrist, to the pillars of Hercules in the west. On the former, see
Lascelles (1936); for the latter see *Dest Troy* 310–15, *Kyng Alisaunder*
5573–86.

And conquered Calcas knyghtly theraftire
Ther jentille Jazon þe Jewe wane þe flese of golde.
Then grathede he hym to Gadres the gates full righte,
And there Sir Godfraye the gude the Goderayns assemblet   340
And rode oute full ryally to rescowe the praye.
And þan Emenyduse hym mete and made hym full tame,
And girdes Gadyfere to the grounde, gronande full sore,
And there that doughty was dede and mekill dole makede.
Then Alixander the Emperour, þat athell kyng hymseluen,   345
Arayed hym for to ryde with renkes þat he hade.
There was the mody Meneduse, a mane of Artage,
He was duke of þat douth and a dussypere,
Sir Filot and Sir Florydase, full ferse men of armes,
Sir Clyton and Sir Caulus, knyghtis full noble,   350
And Sir Garsyene the gaye, a gude man of armes,
And Sir Lyncamoure thaym ledys with a lighte will.
And than Sir Cassamus thaym kepide, and the kyng prayede
To fare into Fesome his frendis to helpe,
For one Carrus the kynge was comen owte of Inde   355
And hade his fomen affrayede and Fozayne asegede
For dame Fozonase the faire that he of lufe bysoughte.

338 Jazon] T, Josue W; flese] T, slevis W.　346 with] W, with the T.
356 his fomen] W, fozome T.

337–8 Alexander's conquest of Colchis (*Calcas*) is unknown to history or
legend, and Jason was, of course, a Greek not a Jew. Gollancz emends
Jewe to *Grewe*, but the error is perhaps the poet's, and in any case l. 338
is unmetrical. The story of the Golden Fleece is in Guido.
339–44 The story of the *Fuerre de Gadres*. Gadifer of Larris (both mss.
have *Godfraye* in l. 340) is killed while attempting to retrieve the cattle
rustled by Alexander's men led by Emenidus of Arcage (*Emenyduse*,
l. 342, *Meneduse of Artage*, l. 347, *Amenyduse*, l. 359).
347–52 All these knights are listed in *Voeux* 182–5.
353–9 Cassamus, brother of the dead Gadifer of Larris, persuades
Alexander to go to Epheson, where King Clarus of Ind is besieging the
city for the love of Fesonas, one of Gadifer's three children. Alexander
agrees to go in reparation for the slaying of Gadifer by Emenidus.
354 *frendis*: 'kin'; Cassamus's niece and two nephews.
356 *Fozayne*: the same as *Fesome* (l. 354), i.e. Epheson. By the city
runs the river Faron (l. 360).
357 Emending *of lufe* to *to fere*, 'as wife' (cf. l. 388) would correct the
alliteration. So Duggan (1986b:99).

85

The kynge agreed hym to goo and graythed hym sone,
In mendys of Amenyduse þat he hade mysdone.
Then ferde he towarde Facron and by the flode abydes, 360
And there he tighte vp his tentis and taried there a while.
There knyghtis full kenely caughten theire leue
To fare into Fozayne dame Fozonase to see,
And Idores and Edease, alle bydene,
And there Sir Porus and his prynces to the poo avowede. 365
Was neuer speche byfore spoken sped bettir aftir,
For als þay demden to doo thay deden full euen;
For there Sir Porus the prynce into the prese thrynges
And bare the batelle one bake and baschede thaym swythe,
And than the bolde Bawderayne bowes to the kyng 370
And brayde owte the brighte brande owt of the beryns
    hande,
And Florydase full freschely foundes hym aftir
And hent the helme of his hede and the halse crakede.
Than Sir Gadefere the gude gripis his axe,
And into the Indyans ofte auntirs hym sone, 375
And thaire stiffe standerte to stikkes he hewes;
And than Sir Cassamus the kene Carrus releues –
When he was fallen appon fote he fet hym his stede,
And aftyr that Sir Cassamus Sir Carus he drepitt,
And for þat poynte Sir Porus perset hym to dethe. 380
And than the Indyans ofte vttire þam droghen
And fledden faste of the felde and Alexandere suede;
When þay were skaterede and skayled and skyftede in
    sondere,

364 alle] T, all þes W. 369 basshed] W, abaschede T. 371 beryns]
kynges TW.

364 Ydorus is betrothed to Betis, son of Gadifer of Larris. Edeas is the
niece of Fesonas.
365 Porrus, son of King Clarus, kills a peacock, and when it is brought
in at the banquet he and his companions make brave vows over it.
370–1 Cassiel, 'li Baudrains', lord of Baderis (l. 389), vows to take
Alexander's sword from him. So *bowes to the kyng* is 'goes up to
Alexander'. Both mss. erroneously repeat *kynges* in l. 371.
374 i.e. Gadifer the younger, son of Gadifer of Larris.
377–80 Cassamus, out of admiration for Porrus, allows Clarus to
remount, thus fulfilling his vow. In the end he kills him, but is himself
killed by Porrus.

Alyxandere oure athell kyng ames hym to lenge,
And fares into Fozayne festes to make,   385
And weddis wy vnto wy that wilnede togedire:
Sir Porus the pryce knyghte, most praysed of othere,
Fonge Fozonase to fere and fayne were thay bothe;
The bolde Bawderayne of Baderose, Sir Cassayle hymseluen,
Bele Edyas the faire birde bade he non oþer,   390
And Sir Betys the beryne the beste of his tyme
Idores his awnn lufe aughte he hymseluen;
Then iche lede hade the loue that he hade longe ȝernede.
Sir Alixander oure emperour ames hym to ryde
And bewes towardes Babyloyne with beryns þat were
    leuede,   395
Bycause of dame Candore that comforthed hym moste,
And that cité he bysegede and sayllede it aftire,
While hym the ȝatis were ȝete and ȝolden the keyes.   ,
And there that pereles prynce was puysonede to dede,
Þare he was dede of a drynke, as dole es to here,   400
That the curssede Cassander in a cowpe hym broghte.
He conquered with conqueste kyngdomes twelue,
And dalte thaym to his dussypers when he the dethe tholede,
And thus the worthieste of this werlde went to his ende.

Thane Sir Sezere hymseluen, that Julyus was hatten,   405
Alle Inglande he aughte at his awnn will
When the Bruyte in his booke Bretayne it callede.
The trewe toure of Londone in his tyme he makede,

395 with] W, with the T.   396 Candore] T, Cadace W.   397 saylid] W,
assayllede T.

386 *wilnede togedire*: 'wished (to be) together'.
396 In legend Alexander falls in love with Queen Candace. The odd
form *Candore* is repeated in l. 627.
401 Antipater persuaded his son Cassander to poison Alexander's wine.
405–21 This keeps close to the *Voeux* account of Caesar, but adds the
English references of ll. 408–13.
407 *the Bruyte*: not an author, as the poet seems to believe, but the term
for any chronicle dealing with the history of Britain from the time of its
foundation by Brutus. Cf. *SGGK* 1–19, and 2523–6, *Brutus bokez*.
408–13 The beliefs that Caesar built the Tower of London and Dover

And craftely the condithe he compaste thereaftire,
And then he droghe hym to Dovire and duellyde there a
    while,   410
And closede ther a castelle with cornells full heghe,
Warnestorede it full wiesely, als witnesses the sothe,
For there es hony in that holde holden sythen his tyme.
Than rode he into Romayne and rawnsede it sone,
And Cassabalount þe kynge conquerede thereaftire.   415
Then graythed he hym into Grece and gete hym belyue,
The semely cité Alexaunder seside he theraftire,
Affrike and Arraby and Egipt the noble,
Surry and Sessoyne sessede he togedir
With alle the iles of the see appon iche a syde.   420
Thies thre were paynymes full priste and passed alle othire.

Of thre Jewes full gentill jugge we aftir
In the Olde Testament as the storye tellis,
In a booke of the Bible that breues of kynges,
And renkes þat rede kane Regum it callen.   425
The firste was gentill Josue þat was a Jewe noble,
Was heryet for his holynes into heuenriche.
When Pharaoo had flayede the folkes of Israelle,
Thay ranne into the Rede See for radde of hymseluen;

416 hym(2)] T, þem W.

Castle are discussed by H. Nearing Jr, 'Local Caesar traditions in
Britain', *Speculum*, 24 (1949:218–27). For the Tower story, see
Shakespeare, *Richard II*, V. i. 2.
414–15 Caesar 'sousmist as Ronmains le roy Cassibilant', *Voeux* 7507.
Probably the poet is unaware that Cassivelaunus was a British chief. See
Geoffrey of Monmouth, *HKB* iv. 1–11.
416 *gete hym*: 'conquered them' (the Greeks). See l. 235n.
417–20 Directly from *Voeux* 7511–13. *Alexaunder*: Alexandria; *Surry
and Sessoyne*: Syria and Saxony.
425 *Regum*: the Books of Kings (together with Samuel). They do not
contain accounts of Joshua or Judas Maccabeus.
428–38 An extraordinary muddling of Joshua's crossing of the Jordan
(Joshua iii. 13–17) with Pharaoh's pursuit of Moses over the Red Sea
(Exodus xiv. 21–31). The image of the wall of water is also from Exodus.
Voeux mentions 'le flun Jourdan' (l. 7522), but there are other French
texts that refer to the Red Sea; see Turville-Petre (1979:39–40).

And than Josue the Jewe Jesu he prayed   430
That the peple myghte passe vnpereschede that tyme;
And than the see sett vp appon sydes twayne
In manere of a mode walle that made were with hondes,
And thay soughten ouer the see, sownnde alle togedir,
And Pharaoo full fersely folowede thaym aftire.   435
And efte Josue þe Jewe Jesus he prayede,
And the see satillede agayne and sanke thaym thereinn –
A soppe for the sathanas, vnsele haue theire bones!
And aftire Josue þe Jewe full gentilly hym bere
And conquerede kynges and kyngdomes twelue,   440
And was a conqueroure kene kyd in his tyme.

Than Dauid the doughty thurghe Drightyn sonde
Was caughte from kepyng of schepe and a kyng made;
The grete grym Golyas he to grounde broghte
And sloughe hym with his slynge and with no sleghte ells;   445
The stone thurghe his stele helme stonge into his brayne
And he was dede of that dynt, the Deuyll hafe that reche!
And than was Dauid full dere to Drightyn hymseluen
And was a prophete of pryse and praysed full ofte,
Bot ȝit greued he his God gretely theraftire,   450
For Vrye his awnne knyghte in aventure he wysede,
There he was dede at that dede as dole es to here;
For Bersabee his awnn birde was alle þat bale rerede.

The gentill Judas Machabee was a Jewe kene,
And thereto worthy in were and wyse of his dedis;   455
Antiochus and Appolyne aythere he drepide,

---

441 kene kid] W, full kene and moste kyd T.   446 stang] W, stongen T.

430 *Jesu* is more appropriate alliteratively than chronologically, though
Joshua is a prefiguration of Christ (Acts vii. 45; Hebrews iv. 8).
438 'I care nothing for the devils, bad luck to their bones!'
442–53 *Voeux* 7530–6 recounts the slaying of Goliath and calls David a
'holy sinner' without explicit reference to Uriah and Bathsheba. See 1
Samuel xvii, and 2 Samuel xi.
447 'May the devil take the one that cares!' (*reche*, pr.3sg.subj., 'may
reck, care'). A common phrase; cf. *PPl* B vi. 120.
454–8 Closely translated from *Voeux* 7537–45. See 1 and 2 Maccabees.

And Nychanore anoþer knyghte full naytly thereaftire,
And was a conquerour kydde and knawen with the beste.
Thies thre were Jewes full joly and justers full noble
That full loughe haue bene layde of full longe tyme;   460
Of siche doughety doers looke what es worthen.

Of the thre Cristen to carpe couthely theraftir
Þat were conquerours full kene and kyngdomes wonnen,
Areste was Sir Arthure and eldest of tyme,
For alle Inglande he aughte at his awnn will   465
And was kynge of this kythe and the crowne hade.
His courte was at Carlele comonly holden,
With renkes full ryalle of his Rownnde Table
Þat Merlyn with his maystries made in his tyme,
And sett the Sege Perilous so semely one highte,   470
There no segge scholde sitt bot hym scholde schame tyde,
Owthir dethe withinn the thirde daye demed to hymseluen,
Bot Sir Galade the gude that the gree wanne.
There was Sir Launcelot de Lake full lusty in armes,
And Sir Gawayne the gude that neuer gome harmede,   475
Sir Askanore, Sir Ewayne, Sir Errake Fytz Lake,
And Sir Kay the kene and kyd of his dedis,
Sir Perceualle de Galeys þat preued had bene ofte,
Mordrede and Bedwere, men of mekyll myghte,
And othere fele of that ferde, folke of the beste.   480
Then Roystone þe riche kyng, full rakill of his werkes,

457 knyght] W, kynge T.   460 of] W, sythen gane T.   461 *line om.* W.
481 Roystone] Rusten W, Boystone T.

461 The line does not alliterate and is not in ms. W. It may be scribal.
464–512 *Voeux* 7548–57 recounts that the giant Ruiston failed to add
Arthur's beard to his collection, and that Arthur killed one (viz. a giant)
on St Michael's Mount and others elsewhere. The English poet adds
many familiar Arthurian stories to this.
467 *at Carlele*: as in *Morte A* 64 and other texts.
470–5 The story of Sir Galahad and the Sege Perelous is retold by
Malory, *Works*, 102, 853–62.
476–9 All these knights appear in Malory, and all except Perceval in
Morte A. Ewayne is Chrétien's Yvain, and *Errake* is his Erec, son of
King Lac.
481–5 The story of King Royns and the beards is told by Malory, *Works*,
54–6. See also Geoffrey of Monmouth, *HKB* x. 3.

He made a blyot to his bride of berdes of kynges,
And aughtilde Sir Arthures berde one scholde be;
Bot Arthure oure athell kynge anoþer he thynkes,
And faughte with hym in the felde till he was fey worthen.   485
And þan Sir Arthure oure athell kynge ames hym to ryde,
Vppon Sayn Michaells Mounte meruaylles he wroghte,
There a dragone he dreped þat drede was full sore.
And than he sayled ouer the see into sere londes,
Whils alle the beryns of Bretayne bewede hym to fote;   490
Gascoyne and Gyane gatt he thereaftir,
And conquered kyngdomes and contrees full fele.
Than ames he into Inglonde into his awnn kythe,
The gates towardes Glasschenbery full graythely he rydes,
And ther Sir Mordrede hym mett by a more syde,   495
And faughte with hym in the felde to alle were fey worthen
Bot Arthur oure athell kyng and Ewayne his knyghte.
And when the folke was flowen and fey bot thaymseluen,
Than Arthure Sir Ewayne athes by his trouthe
That he swiftely his swerde scholde swynge in the
    mere,   500
And whatt selcouthes he see the sothe scholde he telle;
And Sir Ewayne swith to the swerde and swange it in the
    mere,

---

482 of(1)] W, of the T.   486 athell] *om*. TW.   497 Ewan] W,
Wawayne T (*so too in* 499, 502, 505).   498 folk] W, felde T.
502 swith] T, start swith W.

487–8 The story in Geoffrey, *HKB* x. 2–3, is that Arthur kills a *giant* on
St Michael's Mount, following a dream of a dragon (himself) overcoming
a bear (the giant).
490 'Until all the men of Brittany submitted to him.'
491 Gascony and Guienne formed the duchy of Aquitaine in south-west
France. See Geoffrey, *HKB* ix. 11, and *Morte A* 37.
493–512 The Fr *Mort Artu* gives the story of the battle with Mordred
near Glastonbury, 'the throwing of the sword into the lake, and Arthur's
passage to Avalon in a boat rowed by ladies.
497 *Ewayne*: ms. T consistently reads *Wawayne* (i.e. Gawain), but the
alliteration shows that this is wrong. In no other account does either
Ywain or Gawain throw the sword into the water; in the Fr *Mort Artu* it
is Gyrflet, in Malory it is Bedivere.
502 *swith*: 'quickly (goes)'. See the reading of ms. W.

91

And ane hande by the hiltys hastely it grippes
And brawndeschet that brighte swerde and bere it awaye;
And Ewayne wondres of this werke and wendes bylyue   505
To his lorde there he hym lefte, and lokes abowte,
And he ne wiste in alle this werlde where he was bycomen.
And then he hyghes hym in haste and hedis to the mere,
And seghe a bote from the banke and beryns thereinn;
Thereinn was Sir Arthure and othire of his ferys,   510
And also Morgon la Faye that myche couthe of sleghte;
And there ayther segge seghe othir laste, for sawe he hym
   no more.

Sir Godfraye de Bolenn siche grace of God hade
Þat alle Romanye he rode and rawnnsunte it sone,
Þe Amorelle of Antyoche aftire he drepit   515
Þat was called Corborant, kiluarde of dedis,
And aftir he was callede kynge and the crownn hade
Of Jerusalem and of the Jewes gentill togedir,
And with the wirchipe of this werlde he went to his ende.

Than was Sir Cherlemayne chosen chefe kynge of Fraunce   520
With his doghty doussypers to do als hym lykede:

503–4 *lines om.* W.   511 Morgon] W, Morgn T.   518 Jerusalem] W,
Jerasalem T; of the Jewes] T, Jury W.

513–19 The account of Godfrey of Bouillon is very close to *Voeux*
7567–72. In 1098, during the First Crusade, Godfrey defeated the emir
Kerbogha (*Corborant*) and won Antioch.
520–79 This account of Charlemagne is quite different from *Voeux*
7558–65, which briefly mentions his conquest of Spain, his victory over
the Saxons and the re-establishment of Christianity in Jerusalem.
521–30 *doussypers*: properly Charlemagne's 'twelve peers', but the poet
elsewhere uses the word to mean no more than 'noble knights' (ll. 348,
403). Roland and Oliver are the heroes of the *Chanson de Roland*,
together with Samson; Reiner of Genoa is Roland's father. Others are
Aubrey of Burgogne, Ogier the Dane, Naimes of Bavaria, Archbishop
Turpin of Rheims, Tierri of Ardennes, Berard of Mondisdier and Guy of
Burgundy. All of these, except Samson, figure in the ME *Sir Ferumbras*,
ed. S. J. Herrtage, EETS ES 34 (1879). The *Katur Fitz Emowntez*, 'four
sons of Aymon', are the heroes of the Fr prose romance *Les Quatres Fils
Aymon*.

Sir Rowlande the riche duke and Raynere of Jene,
Olyuer and Aubrye and Ogere the Deanneys,
And Sir Naymes at the nede that neuer wolde fayle,
Turpyn and Terry, two full tryed lordes,   525
And Sir Sampsone hymselfe of the Mounte Ryalle,
Sir Berarde de Moundres, a bolde beryn in armes,
And gud Sir Gy de Burgoyne, full gracyous of dedis,
The Katur Fitz Emowntez were kydde knyghtes alle,
And oþer moo than I may myne or any man elles.   530
And then Sir Cherlles þe chefe ches for to ryde,
And paste towardes Polborne to prouen his strenghte,
Salamadyne the Sowdane he sloghe with his handis,
And þat cité he bysegede and saylede it full ofte
While hym his ʒernynge was ʒett and the ʒates opynede.   535
And Witthyne thaire waryed kynge wolde nott abyde
Bot soghte into Sessoyne socoure hym to gete,
And Cherlemayne oure chefe kynge cheses into the burgh,
And dame Nioles anone he name to hymseluen
And maried hir to Maundevyle þat scho hade myche louede;   540
And spedd hym into hethyn Spayne spedely thereaftire,
And fittilled hym by Flagott faire for to loge.

522 duke and] duke & sir W, and Duke T.   523 the] W, *om.*
T.   529 knyghtes] W, kynges T.   534 cite] W, *om.* T.

522 Cf. l. 563. The readings of both mss. are unmetrical; see Duggan
(1986a:591).
531–40 In 777 Charlemagne went to Paderborn (*Polborne*) in Saxony
(*Sessoyne*), where he met the Governor of Barcelona Suleiman Ibn Al-
Arabi (*Salamadyne?*), with whom he entered an alliance. The Saxons led
by Widukind (*Witthyne*) continued their resistance for many years. The
poet's source for this information has not been identified, nor have
Nioles and *Maundevyle.*
541–57 A very sketchy account of the story in *Sir Ferumbras.* The giant
Saracen, Ferumbras, defeated by Oliver, agrees to be christened. Oliver
and other knights are captured and taken over the river Flagot to
Mautrible, then moved next day to Aigremont where they are
imprisoned by Balan, father of Ferumbras. Balan's daughter, Floripas,
takes pity on them and rescues them, and hands over the Holy Relics
that Ferumbras had taken from Jerusalem. Charlemagne arrives at
Aigremont and captures Balan, who refuses to be baptized and so is
killed by Ogier. Floripas is baptized, and Charlemagne returns to
St Denis with the Holy Relics.

There Olyuer the euerous aunterde hymseluen
And faughte with Sir Ferambrace and fonge hym one were,
And than they fologhed hym in a fonte and Florence hym
   called.   545
And than moued he hym to Mawltryple Sir Marchel to seche,
And that emperour at Egremorte aftir he takes,
And wolde hafe made Sir Marcel a man of oure faythe,
And garte feche forthe a founte byfore with his eghne,
And he dispysede it and spitte and spournede it to the erthe, 550
And one swyftely with a swerde swapped of his hede.
And dame Floripe þe faire was fologhed theraftire,
And kende thaym to the corownne þat Criste had one hede,
And the nayles anone nayttly thereaftire,
When he with passyoun and pyne was pynnede one the rode. 555
And than those relikes so riche redely he takes,
And at Sayne Denys he thaym dide and duellyd there foreuer.
And than bodworde vnto Balame full boldly he sendys
And bade hym Cristyne bycome and one Criste leue,

545 fologhed] T, halowd W. 546 Marchel] W, Balame T. 548 Sir
Marcel] Marcel W, Sir Balame T. 552 fologhed] cristened T, halowd
W. 555 pynnede one the rode] naylede one the rode T, on þe rode
naylid W. 556 redely] T, rathely W. 558 Balaam] W, Merthill T.

546 *Marchel*: the poet has reversed the names of Balan of the
Ferumbras story and Marsile from the *Chanson de Roland*. The scribe,
Robert Thornton, who had already transcribed two Charlemagne
romances, realized the poet's error and corrected the mistake, but the
alliterative patterns and the readings of ms. W reveal what the poet
wrote. See Turville-Petre (1979:43n).
552 For the emendation *fologhed*, cf. l. 545 and variants.
555 *pynnede*: 'nailed'. The scribes pick up *naylede* from l. 554.
557 'And he placed them at St Denis (near Paris) and (they) stayed
there forever.'
558–70 The story of the *Chanson de Roland*. Ganelon is sent to
Saragossa to demand that King Marsile (not Balan) should be baptized.
Returning with gifts to Charlemagne, he treacherously reports that the
Sultan has agreed to this. In fact the Saracens are preparing for battle,
and at Roncevaux they attack the rearguard of the French army led by
Roland. After deeds of great valour, the French leaders are killed before
Charlemagne can come to the rescue. He pursues the Saracens, taking
vengeance on them at Saragossa and destroying their idols.

Or he scholde bette doun his borowes and brenn hym
    thereinn,   560
And garte Genyone goo that erande that greuede thaym alle.
Thane rode he to Rowncyuale, þat rewed hym aftire,
There Sir Rowlande the ryche duke refte was his lyfe,
And Olyuer his awnn fere that ay had bene trewe,
And Sir Turpyn the trewe that triste was at nede,   565
And full fele othir folke, als ferly were elles.
Then suede he the Sarazenes seuen ʒere and more,
And the Sowdane at Saragose full sothely he fyndis,
And there he bett downn þe burghe and Balam he tuke,
And that daye he dide hym to the dethe als he had wele
    seruede.   570
Bot by than his wyes were wery and woundede full many,
And he fared into France to fongen thaire riste,
And neghede towarde Nerbone that noyede thayme full sore,
And þat cité he asseggede appone sere halfues
While hym the ʒates were ʒette and ʒolden the keyes,   575
And Emorye made emperour euen at that tyme
To haue it and to holde it to hym and to his ayers.
And then thay ferden into Fraunce to fongen thaire ese,
And at Sayn Denys he dyede at his dayes tyme.
Now hafe I neuened ʒow the names of nyne of þe beste   580
Þat euer were in this werlde wiste appon erthe,
And the doghetyeste of dedis in thaire dayes tyme,
Bot doghetynes when dede comes ne dare noghte habyde.

Of wyghes þat were wyseste will ʒe now here,

565 triste] trusty W, full triste T.   569 Balam] W, Sir Merthill
T.   570 hym] W, *om.* T.   577 haue] W, kepe T.

571–7 The taking of Narbonne is recounted in *Aymeri de Narbonne*. See
Turville-Petre (1979:43).
581 *were*: 'man'.
583 It is noteworthy that this line is repeated in a poem on the Nine
Worthies, ed. T. Turville-Petre, *Nottingham Medieval Studies*, 27
(1983:79–84, l. 32).
584–630 Included in *ubi sunt* lists of the famous dead are many of the
Wise and the Lovers enumerated by Elde. See, e.g., Thomas of Hales,
'Love Ron', ed. Brown, *XIII*, no. 43, ll. 65–72, and discussion in Woolf

And I schall schortly ȝow schewe and schutt me ful sone.   585
Arestotle he was arste in Alexander tyme,
And was a fyne philozophire and a fynour noble
The grete Alexander to graythe golde when hym liste,
And multiplye metalles with mercurye watirs
And with his ewe ardaunt and arsneke pouders,   590
With salpetir and sal-jeme and siche many othire,
And menge his metalles and make fyne siluere,
And was a blaunchere of the beste thurgh blaste of his fyre.
Then Virgill thurgh his vertus verraylé he maket
Bodyes of brighte brasse full boldely to speke,   595
To telle whate betydde had and whate betyde scholde
When Dioclesyane was dighte to be dere emperour –
Off Rome and of Romanye the rygalté he hade.

---

588 grathe] W, graythe and gete T.   593 blaunchere] blawcher W,
plaunchere T.   594 verrayle] veruayle *or* vernayle T, veryall W.

(1968:62, 71, 108–10). Elde's Wise consist of two pagans, a Jew and a
Christian.
587 *philozophire*: 'learned man', often more narrowly 'alchemist', and
used specifically of Aristotle, the supreme alchemist in the medieval
view. See *MED philosophre* (a), (c) and (f), and Chaucer, *CT* i. 294–8,
and v. 1561.
588 'To make gold for Alexander the Great when he wanted.'
589–93 *multiplye*: 'transmute base metals into gold and silver', the
ultimate aim of every alchemist. *mercurye watirs*: compounds of
mercury, such as mercuric chloride (prepared with *sal-jeme*, 'common
salt or sodium chloride') or mercuric oxide (prepared with *salpetir*,
'saltpetre'). Mercury was thought to be the basic constituent of all metals
and therefore fundamental to the alchemist; see E. J. Holmyard,
Alchemy (Harmondsworth, 1957:75, 94, 112). *ewe ardaunt*: 'alcohol',
heavily used by alchemists in their search for the philosopher's stone; see
ibid. (53, 219–20). *arsneke pouders*: 'arsenious oxide' and other
compounds, used for whitening metals as a step towards altering their
substance. Hence Aristotle was a *blaunchere*, 'whitener'.
594–8 Numerous stories were told about Virgil's magic devices,
including a number of heads and statues that would warn of approaching
danger. For the emperor Appolanius 'this Virgilie made by his crafte an
ymage or a statute . . . þe which sholde shewe and telle to þe messagers
of þe Emperour the namys of hem þat breke þe lawe', *Gesta
Romanorum*, ed. S. J. Herrtage, EETS ES 33 (1879:27). See
J. W. Spargo, *Virgil the Necromancer* (Cambridge, Mass., 1934). It may
be noted that Diocletian (l. 597) lived 300 years after Virgil.

Than Sir Salomon hymselfe sett hym by hym one,
His bookes in the Bible bothe bene togedirs;   600
That one of wisdome and of witt wondirfully teches,
His sampills and his sawes bene sett in the toþer;
And he was the wyseste in witt that wonnede in erthe,
And his techynges will bene trowede whills þe werlde
    standes
Bothe with kynges and knyghtis and kaysers therinn.   605

Merlyn was a meruayllous man and made many thynges,
And naymely nygromancye nayttede he ofte,
And graythed Galyan a boure to gete hyr þerin
That no wy scholde hir wielde ne wynne from hymseluen.
Theis were the wyseste in the worlde of witt þat euer were,   610
Bot dethe wondes for no witt to wende were hym lykes.

Now of the prowdeste in presse þat paramoures loueden
I schall titly 30w telle and tary 30w no lengere:
Amadase and Edoyne in erthe are thay bothe

602, 604–5 *lines om.* W.   603 wonnede in erthe] euer wonnede in erthe
T, yn erth was W.   608 grathid] W, graythen T; gete] W, kepe T.
610 euer] W, euer 3itt T.

599 'Then Solomon set himself apart (in eminence).'
600 The books of Wisdom and Ecclesiasticus were both attributed to
Solomon.
606–9 Possibly an inaccurate reference to the story in *La Suite de Merlin*
of Merlin's infatuation with Niviene, for whom he builds a 'manoir'. She
later traps him forever in a marble tomb. Less well known, but more
appropriate, is the story of another 'manoir' built by Merlin for his
unnamed mistress in *The Continuations of the Old French Perceval*, ed.
W. Roach (Philadelphia, 1971:vol. iv, ll. 31789–915). Here there is no
suggestion that Merlin's magic powers are finally overcome. 'Galienne' is
a name found in Fr romances, but no one of that name is associated with
Merlin.
612 *prowdeste in presse*: see *Susan* 117 and n.
614–25 In 'Love Ron', Brown *XIII*, no. 43, ll. 65–8, are listed Paris and
Helen, Amadas and Ydoine, and Tristram and Isolde. There is no ME
version of the Fr romance *Amadas et Ydoine*, but the pair are quite
frequently mentioned in English. Samson is usually cited as an example
of a great man who foolishly submitted to a woman (e.g. *SGGK*
2417–18). The reference here is prompted by his appearance in *ubi sunt*

That in golde and in grene were gaye in thaire tyme;   615
And Sir Sampsone hymselfe, full sauage of his dedys,
And Dalyda his derelynge, now dethe has þam bothe;
Sir Ypomadonn de Poele, full priste in his armes,
Þe faire Fere de Calabre, now faren are they bothe;
Generides þe gentill, full joly in his tyme,   620
And Clarionas þat was so clere are bothe nowe bot erthe;
Sir Eglamour of Artas, full euerous in armes,
And Cristabelle the clere maye es crept in hir graue;
And Sir Tristrem the trewe, full triste of hymseluen,
And Ysoute his awnn lufe in erthe are þay bothe.   625
Whare es now dame Dido was qwene of Cartage?
Dame Candore the comly, was called quene of Babyloyne,
Penolopie that was price and passed alle othere,
And dame Gaynore the gaye, nowe grauen are thay all,
And othere moo than I may mene or any man elles.   630

Sythen doughtynes when dede comes ne dare noghte habyde,

617 now] W, & now T; bothe] W, boghte T. 618 his] W, hir T.
626 *line om.* W. 628 passid] W, pasten T. 629 all] W, bothen T.

---

lists (e.g. Brown, *XIV*, no. 134, l. 13, where Caesar and Aristotle are also included). The AN romance *Ipomedon* was translated three times into English. There are two ME versions of *Generides*, presumably derived from a lost Fr poem; the reference here to Generides and Clarionas is probably the earliest. The romance of *Sir Eglamour of Artois* is only known in English; Thornton copied a text of it into his Lincoln ms. The only ME account before Malory of Tristram and Isolde is *Sir Tristrem*. Fuller details of all the ME romances can be found in J. B. Severs, *A Manual of the Writings in Middle English*, i (New Haven, 1967).
615 *golde and grene*: see l. 122n.
626–30 Lists of famous women of the past are common; Lydgate, after referring to 'the wourthy nyne', lists Candace, Dido and Penelopie as ladies 'fressh of face' ('Timor Mortis Conturbat Me', ed. H. N. MacCracken, EETS 192 (1934:830–1). For the form *Candore*, see l. 396. She and *Gaynore*, 'Guenevere', are appropriately mentioned following an account of the Worthies.
626 This non-alliterating line is not in ms. W and may be scribal.
631–4 Elde recapitulates the development of the poem: cf. 631 with 583 (the Worthies), 632 with 611 (the Wise), 633 with 612 and 172 (the Lovers and 3outhe), 634 with 141 (Medill Elde).

Ne dethe wondes for no witt to wende where hym lykes,
And therto paramours and pride puttes he full lowe,
Ne there es reches ne rent may rawnsone ȝour lyues,
Ne noghte es sekire to ȝoureselfe in certayne bot dethe,   635
And he es so vncertayne that sodaynly he comes,
Me thynke þe wele of this werlde worthes to noghte.
Ecclesiastes the clerke declares in his booke,
    Vanitas vanitatum et omnia vanitas,
Þat alle vayne and vanytes and vanyte es alle;
Forthi amendes ȝoure mysse whills ȝe are men here,   640
    Quia in inferno nulla est redempcio,
For in Helle es no helpe, I hete ȝow for sothe.
Als God in his gospelle graythely ȝow teches,
    Ite ostendite vos sacerdotibus,
To schryue ȝow full schirlé and schewe ȝow to prestis,
    Et ecce omnia munda sunt vobis,
And ȝe þat wronge wroghte schall worthen full clene.
Thou man in thi medill elde hafe mynde whate I saye!   645
I am thi sire and thou my sone, the sothe for to telle,
And he the sone of thiselfe þat sittis one the stede,
For Elde is sire of Midill Elde, and Midill Elde of ȝouthe.
And haues gud daye for now I go, to graue moste me wende;
Dethe dynges one my dore, I dare no lengare byde.'   650
When I had lenged and layne a full longe while,
I herde a bogle one a bonke be blowen full lowde,
And I wakkened therwith and waytted me vmbe;

638 *line om.* W.   653 *line om.* W.

638a Ecclesiastes i. 2; the classic statement of *contemptus mundi*.
640a 'For there is no redemption in hell'; a much-quoted response from the Office of the Dead.
642a 'Go show yourself to the priests.' (Luke xvii. 14), a text used as authority for the Sacrament of Penance; e.g Hoccleve, 'To Oldcastle', (ed. F. J. Furnivall, EETS ES 61 and 73 (revsd edn, 1970)), verse 11 (sidenote).
643a 'And behold, all things are clean unto you.' (Luke xi. 41)
652 The 'bugle on a bank' is the huntsman's horn. And yet in dream-visions dreamers are usually woken by a disturbance *within* the dream, where the horn sounds a much grimmer warning. 'I sey no more, but be ware of ane horne!' (Brown, *XV*, no. 149, l. 21). On these closing lines see Peck (1972:340–1); Turville-Petre (1977b:75).

Than the sone was sett and syled full loughe,
And I founded appon fote and ferkede towarde townn.   655
And in the monethe of Maye thies mirthes me tydde,
Als I schurtted me in a schelfe in þe schawes faire,
And belde me in the birches with bewes full smale,
And lugede me in the leues þat lighte were and grene.
There dere Drightyne this daye dele vs of thi blysse,   660
And Marie þat es mylde qwene amende vs of synn. Amen,
    amen.

Thus endes the Three Ages.

657 schurtted me in a schelfe] T, serchid me a shote W.   661 synn] T,
oure mysse W.

656–9 These lines syntactically and thematically recall the prologue. The
world is still beautiful.

1 A Lady of Fashion (third from left), early fourteenth century.
BL Addit. MS. 18719, by permission of the British Library.
(See *Harley Lyrics*, no. I: 'The follies of fashion'.)

2 The Man in the Moon. Seal of Walter de Grendon, *c*. 1330.
Reproduced from *Archaeological Journal* (1848).
(See *Harley Lyrics*, no. VII: 'Man in the moon'.)

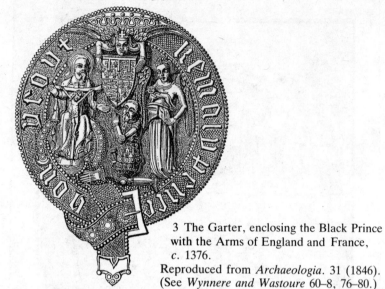

Hony soyt ke mal y pence.

3 The Garter, enclosing the Black Prince with the Arms of England and France, *c.* 1376.
Reproduced from *Archaeologia.* 31 (1846). (See *Wynnere and Wastoure* 60–8, 76–80.)

4 Lawyer's Dress, with Coif and Mantle. Brass of Sir John Cassy, Deerhurst, Glos., 1400.
Photo courtesy of Victoria and Albert Museum. (See *St Erkenwald* 78–84.)

5 The Wheel of Fortune, late fourteenth century.
Bodley MS. Douce 332.
(See *Somer Soneday*.)

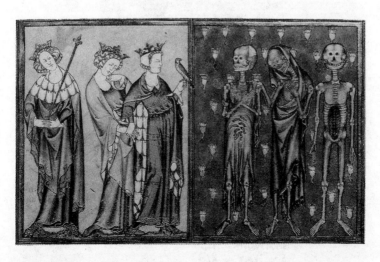

6 The Three Living and the Three Dead, early fourteenth century.
De Lisle Psalter, BL Arundel 83, by permission of the British Library.
(See *The Three Dead Kings*.)

7 Alexander's Fort on Boats, *c.* 1340.
Bodley MS. 264.
(See *Wars of Alexander* 1508–71.)

ST ERKENWALD

INTRODUCTION

Manuscript

The unique text of *St Erkenwald* is in BL MS. Harley 2250, fols.
72b-75b. Other contents are saints lives from *The South English
Legendary*, a life of Christ and works of religious instruction in
English and Latin; see Peterson's edition (1977:3–6). *St Erkenwald*
is the only alliterative poem in the ms.

The date of the ms. is given as 1477 by the scribe. In about
1530 Thomas Bowker recorded his ownership. He was a priest in
Eccles, Lancs., who was associated with the family of Booth of
Barton, Lancs. It is possibly significant that Laurence Booth, an
earlier member of this family, became Dean of St Paul's
Cathedral in 1456 and died in 1480. The name Elisabeth Booth,
from the branch of the family at Dunham Massey, Cheshire, was
also noted in the ms. in the 1530s. See Luttrell (1958:38–42).

Date, dialect and authorship

The poem cannot be precisely dated. The suggestion that it may
be associated with the Bishop of London's attempt in 1386 to re-
establish the cult of St Erkenwald is not conclusive. Peterson
(1977:13–14), shows that there was considerable interest in the
cult of the saint throughout the last quarter of the fourteenth
century and the first quarter of the fifteenth.

The dialect of this part of the ms. is assigned by *LALME* to
Cheshire, and the opening reference to 'London in Englond'

suggests that the poet may also have come from Cheshire, which considered itself rather separate from the rest of the country; see H. J. Hewitt, *Cheshire under the Three Edwards* (Chester, 1967:3).

Much discussion has centred on authorship. The earlier view that the *Gawain* poet also wrote *St Erkenwald*, while not demonstrably wrong, has nothing to support it; see Benson (1965). Clearly the writer had an interest in and knowledge of London and St Paul's, and was quite possibly connected with the Cathedral. A recently discovered alliterative poem was written on a rent account from St Paul's in about 1397; see R. Kennedy, 'A Bird in Bishopswood', in *Medieval Literature and Antiquities*, ed. M. Stokes and T. L. Burton (Woodbridge, 1987:71–87).

Sources

The poem describes how workmen renovating St Paul's discover a tomb containing an uncorrupted body. Bishop Erkenwald is summoned and commands the body to speak. The man relates that he was a pagan judge venerated for his honesty and righteousness, but now excluded from Heaven as a consequence of his lack of faith. Weeping, Erkenwald wishes that the judge might have life for as long as it would take to baptize him, and as he utters the words of baptism, a tear splashes on the body, and the soul is immediately received into Heaven as the body crumbles into dust.

This is a version of a story with widespread appeal in the Middle Ages because of its applicability to the arguments about salvation through grace or through merit. It is most often told of the pagan emperor Trajan, whose soul is released from Hell by the prayers of St Gregory who has learned of Trajan's virtue. Langland gives the story as a demonstration of the saving power of goodness even without faith (*PPl* C xii. 73–98; xiv. 205–17), thus opposing the views of Thomas Bradwardine, archbishop of Canterbury in 1348–9, who took the extreme position that there could be no salvation through good works alone; see Morse's edition (1975:19–31).

Dante places Trajan in Heaven, describing how, as a reward for his virtue, he was resuscitated to give him an opportunity to believe (*Purgatorio* x. 73–96; *Paradiso* xx. 106–17). In the closest analogue to *St Erkenwald*, the early commentary on Dante by Jacopo della Lana (*c.* 1330), workmen find a coffin containing the living tongue of Trajan, whereupon Gregory prays that Trajan might live again and be baptized. For a full account see Whatley (1986:334–7).

No similar story is related in the surviving *vitae* of St Erkenwald. Bede's brief account of his episcopate was supplemented by later lives and miracles, which include a story of the removal of the saint's body to St Paul's. St Erkenwald was commemorated as a builder and a converter of the people in the liturgy of his festival; see Whatley (1986:353–9).

Theme and structure

The issue of salvation through works or through grace was hotly debated in the fourteenth century (and again at the Reformation). The uncorrupted body discovered during the rebuilding of St Paul's Cathedral is that of a pagan judge, a model of righteousness and an ideal figure of earthly justice, who even so is denied a place at the banquet of Heaven. Nevertheless, because of his unswerving goodness, he has been granted a miraculous life-in-death so that he may receive the sacrament of baptism from Bishop Erkenwald. The poet's position is therefore the conservative one, that the judge can only be saved through the miraculous conferring of grace, and this contrasts with the liberal viewpoint expressed by Langland. See the illuminating discussion by Whatley (1986). Fittingly for a poem centring on St Paul's, the basis of this argument is the Pauline Epistles, especially Romans iv. Other references to the Epistles will be found in the notes.

This unattractive theology is most attractively expressed. The story of London's past and its struggle with paganism demonstrates the workings of grace through the activities of the Church, and shows Erkenwald as a successor to St Augustine, as he extends and deepens the faith of Londoners through the miracle of the judge's salvation. The old *lagh* that the judge administers (ll. 203, 216) is overturned by the new *lagh* that Erkenwald teaches (l. 34). The references to sounds that run through the poem underline how much the disorder of human life is in need of the regularity and control of the Church, as the disturbed cries of the

populace (l. 110) are displaced by the ringing of the day-bell
(l. 117), the lovely singing of the choir (l. 133), and in the last
line the great celebratory ringing of the city bells when Church
and citizens unite in celebration. See Petronella (1967:538); and
for the imagery of dark and light see McAlindon (1970:488–9).

In the ms. the poem is divided into two exactly equal halves by
a large capital at l. 177. This is the point at which the bishop
turns to address the body. The first half of the poem describes the
wonder and confusion among the Londoners, which is resolved
by Erkenwald's exploration of divine grace in the second half.
See further on structure McAlindon (1970:484–5). The poet, like
the authors of *Cleanness*, *Patience*, *Siege J* and the *Wars*, shows a
marked tendency to compose in units of four lines. This can be
satisfactorily indicated by punctuation.

BIBLIOGRAPHY

Editions

Sir Israel Gollancz, *St. Erkenwald* (London, 1922)
H. L. Savage, *St. Erkenwald* (New Haven and London, 1926)
R. Morse, *St. Erkenwald* (Cambridge, 1975)
C. Peterson, *Saint Erkenwald* (Philadelphia, 1977)

Studies

L. D. Benson, 'The Authorship of *St. Erkenwald*', *JEGP*, 64
   (1965:393–405)
C. A. Luttrell, 'Three north-west midland manuscripts', *Neophilologus*,
   42 (1958: 38–50)
T. McAlindon, 'Hagiography into art: a study of *St. Erkenwald*', *SP*, 67
   (1970: 472–94)
R. A. Peck, 'Number structure in *St. Erkenwald*', *Annuale Medievale*,
   14 (1973:9–21)
V. F. Petronella, '*St. Erkenwald*: style as the vehicle for meaning',
   JEGP, 66 (1967:532–40)
G. Whatley, 'Heathens and Saints: *St. Erkenwald* in its legendary
   context', *Speculum*, 61 (1986:330–63)

SAINT ERKENWALD

At London in Englond noȝt full long sythen
Sythen Crist suffrid on crosse and Cristendome stablyd,
Ther was a byschop in þat burgh, blessyd and sacryd;
Saynt Erkenwolde as I hope þat holy mon hatte.
In his tyme in þat toun þe temple alder-grattyst   5
Was drawen doun, þat one dole, to dedifie new,
For hit hethen had bene in Hengyst dawes
Þat þe Saxones vnsaȝt haden sende hyder.
Þai bete oute þe Bretons and broȝt hom into Wales
And peruertyd all þe pepul þat in þat place dwellid;   10
Þen wos this reame renaide mony ronke ȝeres,
Til Saynt Austyn into Sandewich was send fro þe pope.
Þen prechyd he here þe pure faythe and plantyd þe trouthe,
And conuertyd all þe communnates to Cristendame newe,
He turnyd temples þat tyme þat temyd to þe deuell,   15
And clansyd hom in Cristes nome and kyrkes hom callid.
He hurlyd owt hor ydols and hade hym in sayntes,
And chaungit cheuely hor nomes and chargit hom better;
Þat ere was of Appolyn is now of Saynt Petre,

1–24 Bede's *History* (i. 15) describes how the pagan Saxons, led by Hengist and Horsa, invaded Britain, destroyed its buildings and killed priests and people. In 596 Pope Gregory sent Augustine to convert the English (i. 23), and also issued instructions on the purification of heathen temples (i. 30). Bede gives a brief account of the episcopate of Erkenwald, 670–93 AD (iv. 6).
1–2 *sythen/Sythen*: 'after the time that'. For correlative *sythen*, cf. *Seege of Troye* (EETS 172), ll. 1–3. The poet's references to dates are puzzling; cf. ll. 206–10.
6 *þat one dole*: 'one part of it'.
8 *vnsaȝt*: adv. 'in hostility'; cf. *Morte A* 1457.
9–32 These lines deal with the conversion of Britain by St Augustine, before returning in l. 33 to his successor St Erkenwald.
12 *Sandewich*: one of the Cinque Ports. Bede gives the landing-place as the Isle of Thanet, a few miles to the north.
19 Gollancz (p. xv) notes the 'tradition that a church to St. Peter was erected . . . out of the remains of a temple of Appolo that stood on its site at . . . Westminster'. *Appolyn* alliterates on the vowel, as four times in *Wars* and twice in *Alex B*. The b-verse alliteration falls on *is*.

Mahoun to Saynt Margrete oþir to Maudelayne,   20
Þe Synagoge of þe Sonne was sett to oure Lady,
Jubiter and Jono to Jesu oþir to James.
So he hom dedifiet and dyght all to dere halowes
Þat ere wos sett of Sathanas in Saxones tyme.
Now þat London is neuenyd hatte þe New Troie,   25
Þe metropol and þe mayster-toun hit euermore has bene;
Þe mecul mynster þerinne a maghty deuel aght,
And þe title of þe temple bitan was his name,
For he was dryghtyn derrest of ydols praysid,
And þe solempnest of his sacrifices in Saxon londes.   30
Þe thrid temple hit wos tolde of Triapolitanes:
By all Bretaynes bonkes were bot othire twayne.
Now of þis Augustynes art is Erkenwolde bischop
At loue London toun and the lagh teches,
Syttes semely in þe sege of Saynt Paule mynster   35
Þat was þe temple Triapolitan as I tolde are.
Þen was hit abatyd and beten doun and buggyd efte new,
A noble note for þe nones and New Werke hit hatte;
Mony a mery mason was made þer to wyrke,
Harde stones for to hewe with eggit toles,   40
Mony grubber in grete þe grounde for to seche

20 *Mahoun*: widely used as a name of a pagan god (e.g. *Patience* 167), though etymologically a shortened form of *Mahomet*.
24 *sett of Sathanas*: 'established for Satan'.
25 'What is now named London was called "the New Troy".' After settling in Britain, Brutus named his principal city Troia Nova, according to Geoffrey of Monmouth, *HKB* i. 17. A much more circumstantial account of its naming is given by Robert Manning, *Chronicle* i. 1889–932.
29 *ydols* is stressed and alliterated on the second syllable.
31 'It was reckoned as the third temple of the Triapolitans', i.e. of the three metropolitan cities. King Lucius supposedly converted the three pagan archflamens at London, York and the City of Legions into archbishoprics (Geoffrey, *HKB* iv. 19).
32 i.e. 'Throughout the whole of Britain were only two others'.
33 'Now Erkenwald is bishop of Augustine's province.' The poet in this way associates Erkenwald with Augustine's conversion of London.
38 *New Werke*: in fact the thirteenth-century rebuilding of St Paul's was referred to as 'the New Work'.
41–2 The *fundement*, 'foundation', rests on the *grounde*, and on it is laid þe *fote*, 'the footings of the building'.

Þat þe fundement on fyrst shuld þe fote halde;
And as þai makkyd and mynyd a meruayle þai founden
As ʒet in crafty cronecles is kydde þe memorie,
For as þai dyʒt and dalfe so depe into þe erthe   45
Þai founden fourmyt on a flore a ferly faire toumbe;
Hit was a throgh of thykke ston thryuandly hewen,
With gargeles garnysht aboute alle of gray marbre.
The sperl of þe spelunke þat spradde hit olofte
Was metely made of þe marbre and menskefully planed   50
And þe bordure enbelicit with bryʒt golde lettres;
Bot roynyshe were þe resones þat þer on row stoden.
Full verray were þe vigures þer auisyd hom mony,
Bot all muset hit to mouth and quat hit mene shuld,
Mony clerke in þat clos with crownes ful brode   55
Þer besiet hom aboute noʒt to bryng hom in wordes.
Quen tithynges token to þe toun of þe toumbe-wonder
Mony hundrid hende men highid þider sone;
Burgeys boghit þerto, bedels and othire,
And mony a mesters mon of maners dyuerse;   60
Laddes laften hor werke and lepen þiderwardes,
Ronnen radly in route with ryngand noyce;
Þer comen þider of all kynnes so kenely mony
Þat as all þe worlde were þider walon within a
    hondequile.
Quen þe maire with his meynye þat meruaile aspied,   65
By assent of þe sextene þe sayntuaré þai kepten,

49 The] thre.

49 'The fastening of the tomb that secured it on top.' *Spradde* is for
sparde, 'fastened', either a metathesised form or a scribal error, as first
suggested by *OED*, s.v. *sperel*.
53–4 'The letters were quite plain to see and many studied them there,
but everyone wondered aloud about it and what it could mean.' The
contrast is between the *verray* ('clear') characters and their *roynyshe*
('mysterious') import.
56 'Busied themselves to no purpose there to make words out of them'
(the *vigures*).
66 i.e. with the sexton's permission the mayor and his retinue took
possession of the sanctuary where the tomb was found.

Bede vnlouke þe lidde and lay hit byside;
Þai wold loke on þat lome quat lengyd withinne.
Wyȝt werkemen with þat wenten þertill,
Putten prises þerto, pinchid one-vnder,   70
Kaghten by þe corners with crowes of yrne,
And were þe lydde neuer so large þai laide hit by sone.
Bot þen wos wonder to wale on wehes þat stoden
That myȝt not come to to knowe a quontyse strange,
So was þe glode within gay, al with golde payntyd,   75
And a blisfull body opon þe bothum lyggid,
Araide on a riche wise in riall wedes;
Al with glisnande golde his gowne wos hemmyd,
With mony a precious perle picchit þeron,
And a gurdill of golde bigripid his mydell;   80
A meche mantel on lofte with menyuer furrit,
Þe clothe of camelyn ful clene with cumly bordures,
And on his coyfe wos kest a coron ful riche
And a semely septure sett in his honde.
Als wemles were his wedes withouten any tecche   85
Oþir of moulyng oþir of motes oþir moght-freten,
And als bryȝt of hor blee in blysnande hewes
As þai hade ȝepely in þat ȝorde bene ȝisturday shapen;
And als freshe hym þe face and the flesh nakyd
Bi his eres and bi his hondes þat openly shewid   90
With ronke rode as þe rose and two rede lippes,
As he in sounde sodanly were slipped opon slepe.
Þer was spedeles space to spyr vschon oþir

67–8 'Ordered the lid to be opened and placed to one side; they wished to look in that container (to see) what was in it.'
69 *with þat*: 'then'.
72 'And however large the lid was . . .'
73 *to wale*: lit. 'at one's choice', i.e. 'very much'.
74 *come to to knowe*: 'manage to understand'. For *come to*, 'succeed', see Robert Manning, *Handlyng Synne* 2672, 'He myȝt neuer come to to do', cited in *MED comen* v., 4a(d).
75 *glode within*: 'open space inside (the tomb)'.
78–84 The coif and the mantle lined with miniver would immediately suggest that the figure was a judge – see the brass of Sir John Cassy, fig. 4 – but the crown and sceptre would be puzzling. The judge explains later, ll. 245–56.
93 'There was time spent without success as each one asked the other'.

Quat body hit myȝt be þat buried wos ther;
How long had he þer layne, his lere so vnchaungit,   95
And al his wede vnwemmyd? Þus ylka weghe askyd.
'Hit myȝt not be bot such a mon in mynde stode long.
He has ben kyng of þis kith, as couthely hit semes;
He lyes doluen þus depe; hit is a derfe wonder
Bot summe segge couthe say þat he hym sene hade.'   100
Bot þat ilke note wos noght, for nourne none couthe,
Noþir by title ne token ne by tale noþir,
Þat euer wos breuyt in burgh ne in boke notyd
Þat euer mynnyd such a mon, more ne lasse.
Þe bodeword to þe byschop was broght on a quile   105
Of þat buried body al þe bolde wonder;
Þe primate with his prelacie was partyd fro home,
In Esex was Sir Erkenwolde an abbay to visite.
Tulkes tolden hym þe tale with troubull in þe pepul,
And suche a cry aboute a cors crakit euermore,   110
The bischop sende hit to blynne by bedels and lettres
And buskyd þiderwarde bytyme on his blonke after.
By þat he come to þe kyrke kydde of Saynt Paule,
Mony hym metten on þat meere þe meruayle to tell,
He passyd into his palais and pes he comaundit   115
And deuoydit fro þe dede and ditte þe durre after.

97 mynde] myde.   103 boke] boko.   104 mon] more.

97 'Such a man must have been long remembered.' The onlookers are
puzzled because they have no record of a man of such evident
importance and apparently so recently buried; cf. ll. 157–8.
99–100 'It is very strange, unless someone were able to say that he had
seen him.'
102 'Neither by written document nor historical evidence nor oral
report.'
104 'That such a man was ever referred to at all.'
108 Bede, *History* iv. 6, notes that Erkenwald built the abbey at
Barking, Essex, for his sister.
109–11 'With perplexity among the people, men told him the story, and
such an uproar about a body resounded all the time that the bishop sent
a message by beadles and letters to put a stop to it.'
113 *By þat*: 'when'; *kydde of*: 'named after'.
116–21 Instead of rushing in to inspect the body, Erkenwald goes to the
Bishop's Palace and spends most of the night in prayer. The *houres* (l.
119) are prayers recited at the canonical hours.

St Erkenwald

Þe derke nyȝt ouerdrofe and day-belle ronge,
And Sir Erkenwolde was vp in þe vghten ere þen,
Þat welnegh al þe nyȝt hade naityd his houres
To biseche his souerayn of his swete grace   120
To vouchesafe to reuele hym hit by a visoun or elles.
'Þagh I be vnworthi', al wepand he sayde,
'Thurgh his deere debonerté digne hit my Lorde;
In confirmyng þi cristen faith, fulsen me to kenne
Þe mysterie of þis meruaile þat men opon wondres.'   125
And so long he grette after grace þat he graunte hade
An ansuare of þe Holy Goste, and afterwarde hit dawid.
Mynster-dores were makyd opon quen matens were songen,
Þe byschop hym shope solemply to synge þe hegh masse.
Þe prelate in pontificals was prestly atyrid,   130
Manerly with his ministres þe masse he begynnes
Of *Spiritus Domini* for his spede on sutile wise,
With queme questis of þe quere with ful quaynt notes.
Mony a gay grete lorde was gedrid to herken hit,
As þe rekenest of þe reame repairen þider ofte,   135
Till cessyd was þe seruice and sayde þe later ende;
Þen heldyt fro þe autere all þe hegh gynge.
Þe prelate passid on þe playn þer plied to hym lordes,
As riche reuestid as he was he rayked to þe toumbe,
Men vnclosid hym þe cloyster with clustred keies,   140
Bot pyne wos with þe grete prece þat passyd hym after.
The byschop come to þe burynes, him barones besyde,
Þe maire with mony maȝti men and macers before hym;

119 naityd] nattyd.

123–5 'May my Lord grant it through his dear mercy. To confirm
Christian belief, help me to explain the mystery of this strange thing that
men are wondering about.' Erkenwald requests divine help so that his
explanation of the mystery will strengthen the faith of his flock. See
Whatley (1986:340).
130 *prestly*: 'promptly', perhaps with a pun on 'priestly', i.e.
'ecclesiastically'.
132 *Spiritus Domini* is the Mass of the Holy Spirit that opens with these
words. It is a natural choice for the bishop; cf. l. 127.
138 *plied to*: 'assembled around'; see *MED ap(p)lien* v. 1(a) and (b);
OED ply v.[2], 5.
140 *cloyster*: 'enclosed area (around tomb)'. Cf. *SGGK* 804.

110

St Erkenwald

Þe dene of þe dere place deuysit al on fyrst,
Þe fyndynge of þat ferly with fynger he mynte.   145
'Lo, lordes,' quod þat lede, 'suche a lyche here is,
Has layn loken here on logh, how long is vnknawen;
And ȝet his colour and his clothe has caȝt no defaute,
Ne his lire ne þe lome þat he is layde inne.
Þer is no lede opon lyfe of so long age   150
Þat may mene in his mynde þat suche a mon regnyd,
Ne noþir his nome ne his note nourne of one speche,
Queþer mony porer in þis place is putte into graue
Þat merkid is in oure martilage his mynde foreuer;
And we haue oure librarie laitid þes long seuen dayes,   155
Bot one cronicle of þis kyng con we neuer fynde.
He has non layne here so long, to loke hit by kynde,
To malte so out of memorie bot meruayle hit were.'
'Þou says soþe,' quod þe segge þat sacrid was byschop,
'Hit is meruaile to men þat mountes to litell   160
Toward þe prouidens of þe prince þat paradis weldes,
Quen hym luste to vnlouke þe leste of his myȝtes.
Bot quen matyd is monnes myȝt and his mynde passyd,
And al his resons are torent and redeles he stondes,
Þen lettes hit hym ful litell to louse wyt a fynger   165
Þat all þe hondes vnder heuen halde myȝt neuer.
Þereas creatures crafte of counsell oute swarues,
Þe comforth of þe Creatore byhoues þe cure take;

154 'Whose record (*mynde*) is inscribed in our burial-register for ever.'
157–8 'To look at it (the body) from its physical appearance, he has not been lying here so long as to vanish so entirely from memory, unless something extraordinary has taken place.'
161 *Toward*: 'in respect of'.
165–6 'Then it causes him (God) very little trouble to set free with a finger that which all the hands on earth could never hold on to.' The contrasts are between *a fynger/all þe hondes*, and *louse/halde*. From Luke xi. 20, the 'finger of God' is the power of the Holy Spirit, which Erkenwald has invoked.
167–8 Whatley (1986:341), suggests that *of þe Creatore* is dependent upon *cure take*, 'take heed'. 'In a situation where the cleverness of created beings turns aside from understanding, the relief (from this perplexity) makes it necessary for you (the dean) to pay attention to the Creator.' The dean has failed to explain the mystery by consulting his library and chronicles. Erkenwald rebukes him by stressing that a

111

And so do we now oure dede, deuyne we no fyrre;
To seche þe soth at oureselfe ȝee se þer no bote;   170
Bot glow we all opon Godde and his grace aske,
Þat careles is of counsell and comforthe to sende;
And þat in fastynge of ȝour faith and of fyne bileue,
I shal auay ȝow so verrayly of vertues his
Þat ȝe may leue vpon long þat he is lord myȝty,   175
And fayne ȝour talent to fulfille if ȝe hym frende leues.'

Then he turnes to þe toumbe and talkes to þe corce,
Lyftand vp his egh-lyddes he loused such wordes:
'Now, lykhame þat þus lies, layne þou no lenger!
Sythen Jesus has juggit today his joy to be schewyd,   180
Be þou bone to his bode, I bydde in his behalue,
As he was bende on a beme quen he his blode schadde,
As þou hit wost wyterly and we hit wele leuen,
Ansuare here to my sawe, concele no trouthe!
Sithen we wot not qwo þou art, witere vs þiselwen   185
In worlde quat weghe þou was and quy þow þus ligges,
How long þou has layne here and quat lagh þou vsyt,
Queþer art þou joyned to joy oþir juggid to pyne.'
Quen þe segge hade þus sayde and syked þerafter,
Þe bryȝt body in þe burynes brayed a litell,   190
And with a drery dreme he dryues owte wordes
Þurgh sum lant goste of lyfe of hym þat lyfe redes.

179 þus] þu.   192 of(1)] *om*; lyfe(2)] al.

---

miracle can only be referred to the power of God. The bishop's purpose throughout is to stress man's dependence upon God; cf. ll 124–5 and 173–5.

169–70 'And so let us get on with our business and speculate no further. You find no solution in seeking the truth among ourselves.'

173–6 'And in order to confirm your faith and true belief, I shall so convincingly inform you of his powers that before long you may believe that he is Almighty Lord and is ready to fulfil your desire if you believe him to be your friend.' In l. 173 *þat* is correlative, anticipating *Þat* in l. 175.

192 As it stands in the ms., the line is deficient in sense and alliteration. In support of the emendation *goste of lyfe*, 'breath of life', cf. *Cleanness* 325, 'Alle þat . . . gost of lyf habbeȝ'; and for the idea of *lant goste*, 'spirit of life (temporarily) granted', cf. *SGGK* 2250. Translate:

'Bisshop,' quod þis ilke body, 'þi boode is me dere;
I may not bot bogh to þi bone for bothe myn eghen.
To þe name þat þou neuenyd has and nournet me after   195
Al heuen and helle heldes to and erthe bitwene.
Fyrst to say the þe sothe quo myselfe were,
One þe vnhapnest hathel þat euer on erth ȝode,
Neuer kyng ne cayser ne ȝet no knyȝt nothyre,
Bot a lede of þe lagh þat þen þis londe vsit.   200
I was committid and made a mayster-mon here
To sytte vpon sayd causes, þis cité I ȝemyd
Vnder a prince of parage of paynymes lagh,
And vche segge þat him sewid þe same fayth trowid.
Þe lengthe of my lying here þat is a lewid date,   205
Hit is to meche to any mon to make of a nombre;
After þat Brutus þis burgh had buggid on fyrste,
Noȝt bot fife hundred ȝere þer aghtene wontyd
Before þat kynned ȝour Criste by cristen acounte:
A þousand ȝere and þritty mo and ȝet threnen aght.   210

206 is] *om.*

'Through some breath of life borrowed from Him who controls life'. The
poet is perhaps deliberately vague about whether the judge is in some
sense actually still alive; see W. A. Quinn, 'The psychology of
St Erkenwald', *MÆ*, 53 (1984:180–91).
198 *One þe vnhapnest*: 'the most unfortunate'. For intensifying *one* see
Mustanoja (1960:297–9), and cf. *SGGK* 137.
202 *sayd causes*: 'accusations brought to trial'; *MED seien* v(1), 2b(g).
205 *lewid date*: perhaps 'worthless period of time', because spent in
Limbo. *MED*, following Savage, glosses *lewid* '?unknown, ?forgotten',
but these senses are not found elsewhere. Gollancz emends to *lappid*,
'hidden'.
206–10 The date of the founding of Britain was supposed to be around
1200 BC. (see, e.g., Manning's *Chronicle* i. 1749). Since King Belinus
fought the Romans, the date of his reign during which the judge says he
lived must have been after the foundation of Rome in the 8th century
BC. The judge appears to say *either* that he was buried 482 (500 − 18)
years after the founding of Britain and 1054 (1000 + 30 + [3 × 8]) years
before the birth of Christ, *or* (with the punctuation adopted here) 482 BC
and 1054 years before the discovery of his body. Neither can be quite
right (cf. 1–24n), and editors have resorted to various unconvincing
emendations. The important point is that the judge was a pre-Christian
Briton.

I was an heire of anoye in þe New Troie
In þe regne of þe riche kyng þat rewlit vs þen,
The bolde Breton Sir Belyn – Sir Berynge was his brothire;
Mony one was þe busmare boden hom bitwene
For hor wrakeful werre quil hor wrath lastyd.   215
Þen was I juge here enjoynyd in gentil lawe.'
Quil he in spelunke þus spake, þer sprange in þe pepull
In al þis worlde no worde ne wakenyd no noice,
Bot al as stille as þe ston stoden and listonde
With meche wonder forwrast, and wepid ful mony.   220
The bisshop biddes þat body: 'Biknowe þe cause,
Sithen þou was kidde for no kynge, quy þou þe croun weres.
Quy haldes þou so hegh in honde þe septre
And hades no londe of lege men ne life ne lym aghtes?'
'Dere sir,' quod þe dede body, 'deuyse þe I thenke,   225
Al was hit neuer my wille þat wroght þus hit were.
I wos deputate and domesmon vnder a duke noble,
And in my power þis place was putte altogeder.
I justifiet þis joly toun on gentil wise

---

211 *an heire of anoye*: 'one who inherits suffering'. The phrase may be
understood as the reverse of such expressions as 'heirs of heaven's bliss',
'heir of salvation', quoted by *MED heir* n. 1(e). This use rests on the
Pauline doctrine of Justification by Faith that lies at the heart of the
poem: only through faith confirmed by baptism do Christians become
heirs of Abraham to *inherit* the Kingdom. See esp. Romans iv. 13–16,
and Ephesians ii. 3, 'children of wrath'.
213–15 Belinus, king of Britain, quarrelled with his brother Brennius,
but at last the two were reconciled and joined forces to conquer Rome
(Geoffrey, *HKB* iii. 1–10). Belinus was a great builder in London,
constructing Billingsgate (supposedly named after him), and 'he ratified
his father's laws everywhere throughout the kingdom, taking pleasure in
the proper administration of his own justice' (*HKB* iii. 10). Later Arthur
refers to him as 'that most glorious of the Kings of the Britons' (*HKB* ix.
16; cf. *Morte A* 277). To be a judge in the reign of Belinus was therefore
to represent the summit of pagan justice.
224 *ne life ne lym aghtes*: 'owned neither life nor limb'; cf. 'Eche a kyng
haþ goddis power, Of lyf and leme to saue and spille', quoted *MED lif*
n. 1c (a).
226 'Although it was never my desire that it should be done thus' (i.e.
that he should be arrayed in crown and sceptre).
229 *gentil*: as in l. 216, the sense is 'gentile', i.e. heathen. The judge's
point is that he did as well as a pagan could be expected to do, though

114

And euer in fourme of gode faithe, more þen fourty wynter;   230
Þe folke was felonse and fals and frowarde to reule –
I hent harmes ful ofte to holde hom to riȝt;
Bot for wothe ne wele ne wrathe ne drede,
Ne for maystrie ne for mede ne for no monnes aghe,
I remewit neuer fro þe riȝt by reson myn awen   235
For to dresse a wrang dome, no day of my lyue.
Declynet neuer my consciens for couetise on erthe
In no gynful jugement no japes to make;
Were a renke neuer so riche, for reuerens sake,
Ne for no monnes manas, ne meschefe ne routhe,   240
Non gete me fro þe hegh gate to glent out of ryȝt
Als ferforthe as my faith confourmyd my hert.
Þagh had bene my fader bone, I bede hym no wranges,
Ne fals fauour to my fader, þagh fell hym be hongyt;
And for I was ryȝtwis and reken and redy of þe laghe,   245
Quen I deghed for dul denyed all Troye;
Alle menyd my dethe, þe more and the lasse,
And þus to bounty my body þai buriet in golde,
Cladden me for þe curtest þat courte couthe þen holde,
In mantel for þe mekest and monlokest on benche,   250
Gurden me for þe gouernour and graythist of Troie,
Furrid me for þe fynest of faith me withinne.

---

this was not good enough (cf. l. 242). There may also be a pun on the
other sense of *gentil*, 'noble'. Cf. *Cleanness* 1432, and *Patience* 62.
234 *no monnes aghe*: 'fear of no man'.
235 *by reson myn awen*: 'according to my own judgement', which is
necessarily limited by his paganism. The idea is expanded in l. 242.
237–8 'My conscience never deviated, for any kind of avarice, into any
treacherous judgement that led me to make false decisions.'
239 'However powerful a man might be, out of deference to him.'
241 *hegh gate*: 'true path'; cf. *Pearl* 395.
242 'In so far as my faith moulded my conscience'. Inevitably, with such
imperfect knowledge of the Supreme Judge, he did depart from the *hegh
gate* in his ignorance.
243–4 'Even though *he* had been my father's murderer I offered him no
injuries, nor (did I offer) false favour to my father though *it* fell to him
to be hanged.' The striking rhetorical *chiasmus* is heightened by
omission of the subject-pronoun in the two subordinate clauses; see
Mustanoja (1960:141, 143).
247 '. . .the greater and lesser (citizens).'
248 *to bounty*: 'in honour'.

For þe honour of myn honesté of heghest enprise,
Þai coronyd me þe kidde kynge of kene justises
Þer euer wos tronyd in Troye oþir trowid euer shulde,   255
And for I rewardid euer riȝt þai raght me the septre.'
Þe bisshop baythes hym ȝet with bale at his hert,
Þagh men menskid him so, how hit myȝt worthe
Þat his clothes were so clene. 'In cloutes, me thynkes,
Hom burde haue rotid and bene rent in rattes long sythen.   260
Þi body may be enbawmyd, hit bashis me noght
Þat hit thar ryne no rote ne no ronke wormes;
Bot þi coloure ne þi clothe – I know in no wise
How hit myȝt lye by monnes lore and last so longe.'
'Nay, bisshop,' quod þat body, 'enbawmyd wos I neuer,   265
Ne no monnes counsell my cloth has kepyd vnwemmyd,
Bot þe riche kyng of reson, þat riȝt euer alowes
And loues al þe lawes lely þat longen to trouthe;
And moste he menskes men for mynnyng of riȝtes
Þen for al þe meritorie medes þat men on molde vsen,   270
And if renkes for riȝt þus me arayed has,
He has lant me to last þat loues ryȝt best.'
'Ȝea, bot sayes þou of þi saule,' þen sayd þe bisshop;
'Quere is ho stablid and stadde, if þou so streȝt wroghtes?
He þat rewardes vche a renke as he has riȝt seruyd   275
Myȝt euel forgo the to gyfe of his grace summe brawnche.
For as he says in his sothe psalmyde writtes:

262 no(1)] ne.

255 '. . .or (was) believed ever would (be throned).' For non-expression
of the infinitive *be* see *SGGK* 1544, and Mustanoja (1960:543).
262 'That no rot nor foul worms may touch it.' The reading was
suggested to me by John Burrow.
264–72 Man's wisdom (*lore* l. 264, *counsell* l. 266) is a mere shadow of
the powers of the *kyng of reson*, who 'always gives credit for justice'
(l. 267) above all other good deeds (*medes* l. 270). Because God so loves
the just, he has prolonged the judge's existence (l. 272).
276 'Could hardly avoid giving you some share of his grace.' The bishop
wrongly supposes the judge will have gained salvation through good
works.
277 *psalmyde writtes*: 'writings set down in the Psalms'.

"Þe skilfulle and þe vnskathely skelton ay to me."
Forþi say me of þi soule, in sele quere ho wonnes,
And of þe riche restorment þat raȝt hyr oure Lorde.'   280
Þen hummyd he þat þer lay and his hedde waggyd,
And gefe a gronyng ful grete and to Godde sayde:
'Maȝty maker of men, thi myghtes are grete;
How myȝt þi mercy to me amounte any tyme?
Nas I a paynym vnpreste þat neuer thi plite knewe,   285
Ne þe mesure of þi mercy ne þi mecul vertue,
Bot ay a freke faitheles þat faylid þi laghes
Þat euer þou, Lord, wos louyd in? Allas þe harde stoundes!
I was non of þe nombre þat þou with noy boghtes
With þe blode of thi body vpon þe blo rode;   290
Quen þou herghdes helle-hole and hentes hom þeroute,
Þi loffynge oute of limbo, þou laftes me þer,
And þer sittes my soule þat se may no fyrre,
Dwynande in þe derke deth þat dyȝt vs oure fader,
Adam oure alder, þat ete of þat appull   295
Þat mony a plyȝtles pepul has poysned for euer.
Ȝe were entouchid with his teche and take in þe glotte,

286 þe] þi.   292 me] ne.   297 teche] tethe.

278 Psalm xiv (AV xv) 1–2: 'Lord . . . who shall rest in thy holy hill? He
that walketh without blemish and worketh justice'. Cf. *Pearl* 673–84.
Earlier editors compare Psalm xxiii (AV xxiv) 3–4, but this is not so
close.
279 *quere*: usefully ambiguous: either 'where', or a contracted form of
'whether'.
280 *restorment*: 'restitution', alluding to Acts iii. 21.
287–8 'But always a man without faith who was without (*faylid*) your
doctrines in which you, Lord, were glorified.'
291–2 The finest ME account of the Harrowing of Hell is in *PPl* B xviii.
The source is the apocryphal Gospel of Nicodemus. Christ released souls
from a region of hell, the 'limbo of the fathers' (*limbus patrum*).
292 *þi loffynge*: perhaps 'your praiseworthy ones'; cf. *MED loving(e* ger.
(2), 1(c), although *MED loffinge* ger. follows Savage in interpreting it as
'remnant'.
296 *plyȝtles*: 'guiltless', perhaps with a play on the sense 'without
covenant'; cf. *plite*, 'covenant', l. 285.
297 'You were poisoned by his sin and you swallow in the foul stuff.'
Baptism is the medicine required by each person as a remedy for the
poisoning of Original Sin. See Romans v. 12–17.

117

Bot mendyd with a medecyn ȝe are made for to lyuye –
Þat is fulloght in fonte with faitheful bileue,
And þat han we myste alle merciles, myselfe and my soule. 300
Quat wan we with oure wele-dede þat wroghtyn ay riȝt,
Quen we are dampnyd dulfully into þe depe lake,
And exilid fro þat soper so, þat solempne fest,
Þer richely hit arne refetyd þat after right hungride?
My soule may sitte þer in sorow and sike ful colde, 305
Dymly in þat derke dethe þer dawes neuer morowen,
Hungrie inwith helle-hole, and herken after meeles
Longe er ho þat soper se oþir segge hyr to lathe.'
Þus dulfully þis dede body deuisyt hit sorowe
Þat alle wepyd for woo þe wordes þat herden, 310
And þe bysshop balefully bere doun his eghen,
Þat hade no space to speke, so spakly he ȝoskyd,
Til he toke hym a tome and to þe toumbe lokyd,
To þe liche þer hit lay, with lauande teres.
'Oure Lord lene', quod þat lede, 'þat þou lyfe hades, 315
By Goddes leue, as longe as I myȝt lacche water,
And cast vpon þi faire cors and carpe þes wordes:
"I folwe þe in þe Fader nome and his fre Childes
And of þe gracious Holy Goste", and not one grue lenger.
Þen þof þou droppyd doun dede, hit daungerde me lasse.' 320

306 Dymly] dynly.

300 *merciles*: 'lacking God's mercy'.
301 See Romans iv. 2–4 for the argument that there is no justification by works.
302 *lake*: 'pit (of Hell)'; see *MED lak(e* n. (1), 3(c). The usage derives from *lacus* in the Vulgate OT; e.g. Psalm xxix. 4 (AV xxx. 3).
304 The judge alludes to Matthew v. 6, 'Blessed are they that hunger and thirst after justice, for they shall have their fill', in order to underline his point that without faith even they are not called to the table of the Kingdom (Luke xxii. 30).
308 'For a long time, before she (the soul) may see that supper or find someone to invite her to it.'
309 *hit*: 'its'.
319 *not one grue*: 'not one little bit'. The construction is *as longe* (l. 316) . . . 'and not a moment longer'. The bishop is only asking for a small miracle.
320 '. . .it would make me less liable to punishment.' The bishop has spiritual responsibility for *all* those in his diocese.

With þat worde þat he warpyd, þe wete of his eghen
And teres trillyd adoun and on þe toumbe lighten,
And one felle on his face, and þe freke syked;
Þen sayd he with a sadde soun: 'Oure Sauyoure be louyd!
Now herid be þou, hegh God, and þi hende Moder,   325
And blissid be þat blisful houre þat ho the bere in!
And also be þou, bysshop, þe bote of my sorowe
And þe relefe of þe lodely lures þat my soule has leuyd in!
For þe wordes þat þou werpe and þe water þat þou sheddes,
Þe bryȝt bourne of þin eghen, my bapteme is worthyn.   330
Þe fyrst slent þat on me slode slekkyd al my tene;
Ryȝt now to soper my soule is sette at þe table;
For with þe wordes and þe water þat wesche vs of payne,
Liȝtly lasshit þer a leme loghe in þe abyme,
Þat spakly sprent my spyrit with vnsparid murthe   335
Into þe cenacle solemply þer soupen all trew;
And þer a marciall hyr mette with menske alder-grattest,
And with reuerence a rowme he raȝt hyr foreuer.
I heere þerof my hegh God and also þe, bysshop,
Fro bale has broȝt vs to blis, blessid þou worth!'   340
Wyt this cessyd his sowne, sayd he no more,
Bot sodenly his swete chere swyndid and faylid
And all the blee of his body wos blakke as þe moldes,
As roten as þe rottok þat rises in powdere.
For as sone as þe soule was sesyd in blisse,   345
Corrupt was þat oþir crafte þat couert þe bones,
For þe ay-lastande life þat lethe shall neuer
Deuoydes vche a vayneglorie þat vayles so litelle.
Þen wos louyng oure Lord with loves vphalden,
Meche mournyng and myrthe was mellyd togeder;   350
Þai passyd forthe in procession and alle þe pepull folowid,
And all þe belles in þe burgh beryd at ones.

321 of his] *followed by space.*

336–8 The *cenacle* is the Vulgate *cenaculum*, 'dining-room', of the Last
Supper and hence of the eschatological banquet (Luke xxii. 12). The
marciall was the officer in charge of seating arrangements etc. in a
medieval hall; cf. *Cleanness* 91. He finds the soul a *rowme*, not a 'room'
but a 'place at table'.

A PISTEL OF SUSAN

INTRODUCTION

Manuscripts

The poem is preserved in five manuscripts. The two earliest are huge anthologies of English religious writings, the Vernon MS., Bodl. Eng. Poet. a.1, fol. 317a–b (denoted by V), which also includes *PPl* A, *Joseph of Arimathie*, legends and homilies; and the companion volume, the Simeon MS., BL Addit. 22283, fols. 125b–126a (A). These two were copied at the end of the fourteenth century by Worcestershire scribes who appear to have used the same exemplar of *Susan*; see Doyle (1974). MS. Huntington HM 114, fols. 184b–190b (P), is dated 1425–50, and also contains *PPl* B; it was written by the Essex scribe who copied the Lambeth Palace ms. of *Siege J*; see Seymour (1974), and Doyle (1982:94). Of the same date is the Ingilby MS., Pierpont Morgan M 818, fols. 1a–5a (I), by a south Lincolnshire scribe according to *LALME*. It also contains *PPl* A; see Doyle (1982:96). The text in BL MS. Cotton Caligula A ii (pt. I), fols. 3a–5a (C), which has lost the first 104 lines of the poem, was copied in the mid fifteenth century, and is followed by a miscellaneous collection including several romances, some Lydgate, *Chevalere Assigne* and the *Siege J*; see Guddat-Figge (1976:169–72). All the scribes are from further south than the poet who, on the evidence of the rhymes, may be located in the southern part of the north of England (e.g. southern Yorkshire); see Dobson (1971:110).

The edited text is based on V. A gives essentially the same text (see above); P shares a number of errors with VA. C and I have some common errors but are independent of the group VAP. I shows a marked inclination to rewrite.

All departures from V are recorded in the variants, together with a selection of readings from other mss. which are of particular interest for the establishment of the text.

Authorship, date and verse-form

Andrew of Wyntoun, writing before 1420, ascribes to a certain 'Huchon of the Awle Ryale' a work called 'þe Pistil of Suet Susane' (*Orygynale Chronykil of Scotland*, 1414). Much has been speculated but nothing is known of this author; see MacCracken (1910). The date of the poem cannot be after *c.* 1400, the date of the mss. V and A.

Susan is written in the 13-line 'bob-and-wheel' stanza, for a study of which see Turville-Petre (1974). Eight four-stress lines, rhyming a b a b a b a b, are followed by a one-stress 'bob', and a 'wheel' of three-stress lines and a final two-stress line, the whole rhyming c d d d c. One common feature of these rhymed alliterative poems needs special comment: where a final disyllabic word alliterates on the first syllable and rhymes on the second, it receives level stress: thus the b-verse *of þat lynage* (l. 16) is stressed on *lyn-* for the alliteration and *-age* for the rhyme, in exactly the same way as *with a dep dich* (l. 5) is stressed x x / /. So, too, ll. 41, 136, 210 etc., and in the 'bob and wheel' ll. 114–16, 364 etc.

Source and theme

Susan is based on the story of Susan and the Elders, which in the Vulgate is placed at the end of the Book of Daniel, but is excluded from the Authorized Version. The poet makes two notable alterations. In place of an account of how the Elders secretly burned with lust for Susan, eventually admitting their desires to one another and conspiring to assault her (Daniel xiii. 10–14), the poet substitutes an extended description of Susan's garden (ll. 66–117). He also adds a moving stanza describing Susan's farewell-meeting with her husband Joachim after her condemnation (ll. 248–60). The effect of both alterations is to focus attention and sympathy on Susan. She becomes a romance heroine; for the beautiful lady in the garden setting, compare Emily in Chaucer's *Knight's Tale* (*CT* i. 1034–55). Susan's youth and beauty are constantly stressed; she is associated with the freshness of nature, but a nature that is cultivated, tamed and refined. Her love is pure and directed wholly towards her husband. The wicked and unnatural desires of the elders are shown up in contrast to the joys and beauties of the natural world associated with Susan. The poet emphasizes the contrast between youth and age: Susan and the boy Daniel oppose the strength of their purity and honesty to the cunning and treacherousness of the foul old judges.

BIBLIOGRAPHY

Editions

F. J. Amours, *Scottish Alliterative Poems*, Scottish Text Society 27 & 38 (1892, 1897)
A. Miskimin, *Susannah* (New Haven, 1969)

Studies

E. J. Dobson, *NQ*, 216 (1971:110–16)
H. N. MacCracken, 'Concerning Huchown', *PMLA*, 25 (1910:507–34)
T. Turville-Petre, 'Three poems in the thirteen-line stanza', *RES*, n.s. 25 (1974:1–14)

A PISTEL OF SUSAN

Þer was in Babiloine a bern, in þat borw riche,
Þat was a Jeuȝ jentil, and Joachin he hiht,
He was so lele in his lawe þer liued non him liche,
Of alle riches þat renke arayed was riht.
His innes and his orchardes were with a dep dich,   5
Halles and herbergages heiȝ vppon hiht,
To seche þoru þat cité þer nas non sich
Of erbes and of erberi so auenauntliche idiht
    Þat day,
      Wiþinne the sercle of sees,   10
      Of erberi and alees,
      Of alle maner of trees,
        Soþely to say.

He hed a wif hiȝt Susan, was sotil and sage,
Heo was Elches douȝter, eldest and eyre,   15
Louelich and lilie-whit, of þat lynage,
Of alle fason of foode frelich and feire.
Þei lerned hire lettrure of heore langage,
Þe maundement of Moises, marked to þat mayre

4 riches] AI, ricchesses P, riche V; arayed] API, arayes V; was] AP, he
was V, was he I. 6 hight] PI, heiht VA. 16 of] PI, out of A, on of
V. 18 heore] þeir I, þat VA, *line om.* P. 19 m. to þat] þei m. to þat
VAP, to menske hir as I; mayre] I, may VA, lair P.

3 'He was so loyal in his faith that there lived no one like him.'
5 The poet envisages Joachim's land as a moated estate.
10 The phrase means 'on earth', since the land-masses were visualized as
encircled by the ocean.
16 *lilie-whit*: the lily is the symbol of purity and, in particular, of the
Virgin. See ll. 66–117n; and cf. *Harley Lyrics* II.12 above.
17 *foode*: 'young woman' (cf. l. 283); thus 'Noble and lovely in every
womanly feature'.
19–22 The second half of l. 19 is corrupt in all the mss. The emended
line means '(they taught her) the Mosaic Law imparted to that Patriarch
(Moses) who went on a mission to Mount Sinai and on whom the Trinity
bestowed a pair of tablets to read'. The sense of *mayre*, 'mayor', is
sometimes extended to include Old Testament judges and doctors of the
Law; see *MED mair(e* n. 2(a). The biblical text alluded to is Exodus
xxxiv.

To þe mount of Synai þat went in message,   20
Þat þe Trinité bitok of tables a peire
    To rede.
    Þus thei lerne hire þe lawe
    Cleer clergye to knawe;
    To God stod hire gret awe,   25
      Þat wlonkest in weede.

He hedde an orchard newe, þat neiȝed wel nere
Þer Jewes with Joachim priueliche gon playe,
For he was real and riche of rentes to rere,
Honest and auenaunt and honorablest aye.   30
Iwis, þer haunted til his hous, hende, ȝe mai here,
Two domesmen of þat lawe, þat dredde were þat day,
Preostes and presidens preised als peere,
Of whom vr souerein Lord sawes gan say,
    And tolde   35
    How heor wikkednes comes
    Of þe wrongwys domes
    Þat þei haue gyue to gomes,
      Þis juges of olde.

Þus þis derf domesmen on daies þider drewe,   40
Al for gentrise and joye of þat Juwesse,

29 was] PI, *om.* VA; to rere] I, euer þere VA, euery wher P.   31 his]
API, her V.   32 domesmen] PI, domes VA.   40 derf domysmen] P,
domesmen ful derf I, dredful demers VA.

24 *cleer clergye*: 'theology'. The usual phrase is *pure clergy*; e.g.
Cleanness 1570.
25 'She stood in great awe of God'; lit. 'great awe towards God was
present to her'. The regular construction with *awe* (*OED awe*, *sb.* 4a).
26 *in weede*: lit. 'in dress'; used with superl. adjs (*worthiest, wlonkest*
etc.) in the sense 'of women'.
27 *neiȝed wel nere*: 'lay close by'.
29 *of rentes to rere*: 'in the income that he raised'. The expression means
that Joachim was prosperous, not that he was a landlord.
31 *hende*: 'gracious listeners'. Formally an adj., so without pl. inflexion.
34–8 'The Lord said of them that their wickedness derives from the
corrupt judgements that they have handed out to men.' The Vulgate has:
'Of whom the Lord said: Iniquity came out from Babylon from the
ancient judges that seemed to govern the people' (Daniel xiii. 5).

To go in þat gardeyn þat gayliche grewe,
To fonge floures and fruit þouȝt þei no fresse;
And whon þei seiȝ Susan, semelich of hewe,
Þei weor so set vppon hire, miȝt þei not sese;   45
Þei wolde enchaunte þat child hou schold heo eschewe,
And þus þis cherles vnchaste in chaumbre hir chese
    To fere.
      Wiþ two maidenes al on,
      Semelyche Suson,   50
      On dayes in þe merion
        Of murþes wol here.

Whon þeos perlous prestes perceyued hire play,
Þo þouȝte þe wrecches to bewile þat worly in wone;
Heore wittes wel waiwordes þei wrethen awai   55
And turned fro his teching þat teeld is in trone;

42 þat gardyn] I, his g. VA, þo gardyns P.   46 wolde . . . eschewe]
VAP, thouth to chaumpen þat schene wiþ chinchif & chewe I.   48 To
fere] I, Wiþ chere VAP.

46 'They wished to delude that girl however she might shun them'. The I
ms. has a quite different and striking line, though its *chinchif* is
unexplained. It may be a misreading of a noun *chinches* (OFr
chinchesse), from the adj. *chinche*, 'avarice'. Cf. *MED chinchehede*,
'greediness', *chinchenesse*, 'miserliness', and other derived forms. A line
based on I would read: 'Þei þouȝte to chaumpen þat child wiþ
chinches and chewe'; 'they intended to crunch up that child with
greediness and chewing'.
47–8 'Thus these unchaste villains chose her as a companion in the
bedroom'. The VAP reading in l. 48, *With chere*, is attractive in that it
continues the alliteration, but it makes weaker sense.
53–9 *hire*: 'her'; *heore* and *here*: 'their'.
54 *worly in wone*: 'lady esteemed in the world'. On the form and
associations of *worly* see J. A. Burrow, *Essays on Medieval Literature*
(Oxford, 1984:74–8). The tag *in wone* means lit. 'in the homes of men',
hence 'in society' or even 'on earth'. Cf. *truest in town, bright in bower*
and similar phrases.
55–60 The Vulgate reads: 'And they perverted their own mind and
turned away their eyes that they might not look unto heaven nor
remember (*recordarentur*) just judgements' (Dan. xiii. 9).
55 *waiwordes*: 'aside', hence 'wickedly, pervertedly'.
56 *teeld is in trone*: 'is seated in the throne (of heaven)'.

For siht of here souerayn, soþli to say,
Heore hor heuedes fro heuene þei hid apon one.
Þei cauȝt for heor couetyse þe cursyng of Kai,
For riȝtwys jugement recordet þei none,   60
    Þey two.
    Euery day bi day
    In þe pomeri þei play,
    Whiles þei mihte Susan assay
      To worchen hire wo.   65

In þe seson of somere with Sibell and Jane
Heo greiþed hire til hire gardin þat growed so grene,
Þer lyndes and lorers were lent vpon lane,
Þe sauyne and sypres, selcouþ to sene,

59 þe c. of Kai] VA, þe c. of cayme I, cristis curs for ay P.   66 Jane]
Jone VAPI.   67 greiþed hire] VAP, glode I.   68 lane] lone
VAPI.

57 *For*: 'in fear of, to avoid'.
59 *þe cursyng of Kai*: 'Cain's curse' (Gen. iv. 11–12); cf. l. 330. Both I
and P reject the poet's odd form *Kai*; I thus destroys the rhyme and P
rewrites the line.
66–72 The alteration in all the mss. of the rhyme-word *Jane* to the much
commoner *Jone*, together with the adoption of the west midl. rounded
form *lone* (OE *lane*), prompted the VA scribes to write the meaningless
plone for 'plane tree' (OFr *plane*), and to choose *rone* for *rane*, 'thicket'.
66–117 The Vulgate says only that Susan 'walked in her husband's
orchard' (Dan. xiii. 7). The poet's long description of the enclosed
garden depends in general terms on three seminal texts: the Book of
Genesis, the Song of Songs and the *Roman de la Rose*, on the influence
of which see D. Pearsall and E. Salter, *Landscapes and Seasons of the
Medieval World* (London, 1973:esp. 76–118). By association with the
Song of Songs and its medieval interpretations, Susan in the garden is an
emblem of a love that is pure and holy; she is the Virgin set against a
millefiore background of lilies, roses, apples, figs, parrots and
turtledoves. And yet the serpent lurks in the garden of paradise. By
association with the *Roman de la Rose*, the garden is a place of romantic
love, and hence, in the minds of old men, inspires thoughts of lust. The
locus classicus is Chaucer's *Merchant's Tale*, where old January
constructs a private, walled garden for his sex-games with May. See
A. L. Kellogg, 'Susannah and the *Merchant's Tale*', *Speculum*, 35
(1960:275–9).
68 *lent vpon lane*: 'situated over the path'. The ppl. is from *lenden*,
'dwell', not *lenen*.

Þe palme and þe poplere, þe pirie, þe plane,   70
Þe junipere jentel, jonyng bitwene,
Þe rose ragged on rys, richest in rane,
Iþeuwed with þeþorn thriuand to sene,
    So tiht.
      Þer weore popejayes prest,   75
      Nihtyngales vppon nest,
      Bliþe briddes o þe best,
        In blossoms so briht.

Þe briddes in blossoms þei beeren wel loude,
On olyues and amylliers and al kynde of trees,   80
Þe popejayes perken and pruynen for proude,
On peren and pynappel þei pyken in pees,
On croppes of canel keneliche þei croude,
On grapes þe goldfinch þei gladen and glees;
Þus schene briddes in schawe schewen heore schroude,   85
On firres and fygers þei fongen heore fees,
    In fay.
      Þer weore growyng so grene
      Þe date wiþ þe damesene,
      Turtils troned on trene   90
        By sixti I say.

70 plane] I, plone VA, plowme P.   72 in rane] I, on rone VA, in soume
P. 73 thriuand] I, thryvyng P, trinaunt VA.   77 Blithe] PI, Bliþest
VA.   82 pykyn] I, prikkyn P, ioyken VA; pees] VAI, prees P.   86 fees]
I, sees P, seetes VA.   91 say] API, say3 V.

72 *rane*: 'thicket'. The same form is in *Morte A* (see Hamel's edn, l.
923n). It appears to be the same word as *rone* (e.g. *SGGK* 1466, and
later Scottish texts). Proposed etymons are ON *runnr*, OFr *rain* and OE
rān, but none of these fully accounts for the meanings and forms.
73 *Iþeuwed*: 'trained, cultivated'. The rose grows around the thorn bush
and is supported by it. *þeþorn*: 'thevethorn', here whitethorn or
hawthorn.
81 *for proude*: see *Parlement* 101n for this construction of *for* followed
by an adj. used as a noun.
82 *pyken*: 'peck'; cf. *Cleanness* 1466. This reading is supported by the
sense of the whole passage (ll. 82–7) describing the birds eating the fruit
on the trees.
86 *fongen heore fees*: 'take their rewards', viz. the fir-cones and figs. The
phrase is used in this sense in *SGGK* 1622.

Þe fyge and þe filbert were fodemed so fayre,
Þe chirie and þe chestein þat chosen is of hewe,
Apples and almaundes þat honest are of ayre,
Grapes and garnettes gayliche þei grewe; 95
Þe costardes comeliche in cuþþes þei cayre,
þe britouns, þe blaunderers, braunches þei bewe,
Fele floures and fruit, frelich of flayre,
With wardons winlich and walshenotes newe,
    At wille 100
      Ouer heor hedes gon hyng
      Þe wince and þe wederlyng,
      Spyces speden to spryng
        In erber on hille.

Þe chyue and þe chollet, þe chibolle þe cheue, 105
Þe chouwet, þe cheuerol, þat schaggen on niht,
Þe persel, þe passenep, poretes to preue,
Þe pyon, þe peere, wel proudliche ipiht;
Þe lilye, þe louache, launsyng wiþ leue,
Þe sauge, þe sorsecle so semeliche to siht, 110
Columbyne and caraway in clottes þei cleue,
With ruwe and rubarbe raunged ariht,
    No lees;
      Daysye and ditoyne,
      Ysope and aueroyne, 115

---

92 fodemed] VA, formed I, found P.   97 þei] API, þe V.   100 At wille] I, As y telle P, Þey waled VA.   104 In erber on hille] I, In erbers enhaled VA, And in herbere þei felle P.   105 *Here* C *begins*.   106 schaggen] VA, chaungyn P, chaungeth C, schon I; on niht] VP, out n. A, at n. C, opon heyght I.   111 caraway in] CI, charuwe VA; cleue] CI, creue VA, P *rewrites*.   112 rawnged] CI, ragget VA, raylid P.

96 *in cuþþes þei cayre*: 'they go in families', i.e. are arranged by species. See Dobson (1971:113).
100, 104 The readings vary widely in these lines. The sense of VA is not apparent; P lacks the pointedness and the alliteration of I. *At wille*: 'according to desire', i.e. 'just as one would like'.
106 'The little cabbage (?), the chervil (a tall herb), that wave about during the night.' The other mss. offer nothing that is more meaningful.
111 *in clottes þei cleue*: 'they cling together in clumps'.

Peletre and plauntoyne
 Proudest in pres.

Als þis ȝonge ȝepply ȝede in hire ȝerde,
Þat was hir hosbondes and hire, þat holden were hende,
'Nou folk be faren from us, þar us not be ferde;   120
Aftur myn oynement warliche ȝe weende.
Aspieþ nou specialy þe ȝates ben sperde,
For we wol wassche us, iwis, bi þis welle strende.'
Forþi þe wyf werp of hir wedes vnwerde,
Vnder a lorere ful lowe þat ladi gan leende   125
  So sone.
 By a wynliche welle
 Susan caste of hir kelle;
 Bote feole ferlys hire bifelle
  Bi midday or none.   130

Nou were þis domesmen derf drawen in derne
Whiles þei seo þat ladi was laft al hire one,
Forte heilse þat hende þei hiȝed ful ȝerne,
With wordes þei worshipe þat worliche in wone:
'Wolt þou, ladi, for loue on vre lay lerne,   135
And vnder this lorere ben vr lemmone?
Þe þarf wonde for no wiȝt vr willes to werne,

118 ȝonge ȝepply] C, schaply þing VA, ȝarly & ȝouthe I, aray rapely P; ȝerde] PCI, ȝarde VA. 119 were] AP, with V. 137 Þe] PC, ȝe ne VA.

117 'Most splendid in the group', i.e. 'finest of all', as also in *Parlement* 612.
118 *ȝonge*: 'young woman'.
119 'That belonged to her and her husband who were highly regarded'.
120 *þar us not*: 'there is no need for us'.
121–3 This follows the Vulgate: 'So she said to the maids: "Bring me oil and washing balls and shut the doors of the orchard that I may wash me" (Dan. xiii. 17).
131 *drawen in derne*: 'withdrawn in secret', i.e. 'hidden'.
132 *Whiles*: 'until'.
135 *lay*: here the sense is 'way of life, practice', with an ironic play on the primary sense '(Jewish) faith'. The judges *worshipe* Susan.
137 'You needn't hesitate for anyone, and so refuse what we desire'.

For alle gomes þat scholde greue of gardin ar gone
    In feere.
        ȝif þou þis neodes deny,   140
        We schal telle trewely
        We toke þe wiþ avoutri
            Vnder þis lorere.'

Þen Susan was serwful and seide in hire þouȝt:
'I am with serwe biset on eueriche syde.   145
ȝif I assent to þis sin þat þis segges haue souȝt,
I be bretenet and brent in baret to byde;
And ȝif I nikke hem with nai hit helpeþ me nouȝt –
Such torfer and teone takeþ me þis tyde!
Are I þat worthlich wrethe, þat al þis world wrouȝt,   150
Betere is wemles weende of þis world wyde.'
        Wiþ þis
        Þo cast heo a carful cri,
        Þis loueliche ladi;
        Hir seruauns hedde selli;   155
            No wonder, iwis!

Whon kene men of hir court comen til hir cri,
Heo hedde cast of hir calle and hire keuercheue;
In at a priué posterne þei passen in hi
And findes þis prestes wel prest her poyntes to preue.   160
Þo seid þes loselles aloude to þe ladi:
'Þou hast gon wiþ a gome, þi God to greue,
And leyn with þi lemon in avoutri,
Bi þe lord and þe lawe þat we onne leeue!'
            Þey swere.   165

147 baret] VAP, bales CI.   149 torfer] toret VA, turment P, tray I,
Trybulacyon C.   150 wrethe] APCI, wrech V.   161 þes] P, þos I, þe
VA; losels] PCI, loselle VA.   163 leyn] C, ligge VA, lyes I, lyvid P.

142 'We caught you committing adultery'.
148 *nikke hem with nai*: 'say no to them'. Cf. also *SGGK* 706, 2471.
150–1 'Rather than that I should anger that Holy One who made all this
world, it is better that I should leave this world spotless.'
155 'Her servants were amazed'.
160 'And they find those priests well prepared to prove their
accusations.'

130

Alle hire seruauns þei shont
And stelen awey in a stont;
Of hire weore þei neuer wont
    Such wordes to here.

Hir kinrede, hir cosyns and al þat hire knewe   170
Wrong handes, iwis, and wepten wel sare,
Sykeden for Susan, so semeliche of hewe,
Al wyes for þat wyf wondred þei ware.
Þei dede hire in a dungon þer neuer day dewe,
While domesmen were dempt þis dede to declare,   175
Marred in manicles þat made wer newe,
Meteles whiles þe morwen to middai and mare,
    In drede.
      Þer com hir fader so fre
      Wiþ al his affinité,   180
      Þe prestes sauns pité
        And ful of falshede.

Þo seide þe justises on bench to Joachim þe Jewe
Þat was of Jacobes kynde, gentil of dedes:
'Let senden after Susan, so semelych of hewe,   185
Þat þou hast weddet to wif, wlankest in wedes.
Heo was in trouþe, as we trowe, tristi and trewe,

171 sare] C, sore VAPI.   173 wyes for þat wyfe] I, onwyse of þat wyf
VAP, wyues and wydowes C; ware] C, wore VP, were
AI.   175 declare] PC, clare VAI.   187 we] VAP, I CI.

173 *wyes*: 'men'. This word found rarely outside alliterative verse has
confused the scribes.
174 *dewe* is pa.t. of *dawen*, 'to dawn', usually a weak vb, but here with a
strong pa.t. for the rhyme, formed on the analogy of *knawen*, *blawen*
etc. The form is found also in Scottish texts; cf. *DOST daw v*.(b).
177 'Without food throughout the morning until midday and more'.
183–8 In the Biblical text it is the wicked priests who summon Susan
(Dan. xiii. 28–9). In the English judicial system the accusers cannot also
be the judges, so the poet invents impartial *justises* who summon Susan
to court and express their trust in her fidelity. The form *iustice* in the I
ms. may be original. The I scribe has taken it as sg. (hence *I* for *we* in
l. 187), but the word is often unchanged in the pl.
185 'Have Susan sent for'.

Hir herte holliche on him þat the heuene hedes.'
Þus þei brouȝt hire to the barre, hir bales to brewe;
Nouþer dom ne deþ þat day heo ne dredes   190
  Als ȝare.
  Hir here was ȝolow as wyre,
  Of gold fyned wiþ fyre,
  Hire scholdres schaply and schire,
   Þat bureliche was bare.   195

Nou is Susan in sale sengeliche arayed
In a selken schert, with scholdres wel schene.
Þo ros vp with rancour þe renkes reneyed,
Þis comelich accused with wordes wel kene.
Homliche on hir heued heor hondes þei leyed,   200
And heo wepte for wo, no wonder I wene.
'We schul presenten þis pleint, hou euer þou be paied,
And sei sadliche þe soþ, riȝt as we haue sene,
  O sake.'
  Þus wiþ cauteles waynt   205
  Preostes presented þis playnt;
  ȝit schal trouþe hem ataynt,
   I dar vndertake.

'Þorwout þe pomeri we passed us to play,
Of preiere and of penaunce was vre purpose.   210

191 ȝare] CI þare VA, yare *or* þare P. 192 here] PCI, hed VA.
195 was] VA, were PC, stode I. 202 euer þou] P, þou euer VA,
so euer þou C.

189 *hir bales to brewe*: 'to contrive her destruction'.
190–1 'That day she fears neither Judgement nor death as greatly (as she
fears the court).'
195 *was* is probably a northern pl. form (altered in P and C to *were*):
'that were beautifully bare'. Alternatively: 'that excellent lady was bare
(to the shoulders)'. The Vulgate has: 'Now Susanna was exceeding
delicate and beautiful to behold' (Dan. xiii. 31).
196 *sengeliche arayed*: 'set apart'.
202 The sense of *paied* includes 'rewarded'; hence, here, 'punished'.
203–4 *O sake*: 'Of the accusation'. The sense is 'And we shall fully
recount the truth of the accusation, just as we have seen it'.
205 *waynt*: a spelling of *quaint*, 'cunning'.

Heo com with two maidens dressed þat day,
In riche robes arayed, red as þe rose.
Wylyliche heo wyled hir wenches away
And comaunded hem kenely þe ȝates to close.
Heo eode to a ȝong mon in a valay;   215
Þe semblaunt of Susan wolde no mon suppose,
     For soþ!
       Be þis cause þat we say,
       Heo wyled hir wenches away;
       Þis word we witnesse for ay,   220
         Wiþ tonge and wiþ toþ.

'Whon we þat semblaunt seiȝ we siked wel sare,
For sert of hir souereyn and for hir owne sake.
Vr copes weore cumberous and cundelet vs care,
But ȝit we trinet a trot þat traytur to take.   225
He was borlich and bigge, bold as a bare,
More miȝti mon þen we his maistris to make.
To the ȝate ȝaply þei ȝeoden ful ȝare,
And he lift vp þe lach and leop ouer þe lake,
     Þat ȝouthe.   230
       Heo ne schunte for no schame
       But bouwed aftur for blame;
       Heo nolde cuyþe vs his name
         For craft þat we couþe.'

Now heo is dampned on deis, with deol þei hir deue,   235

211 dressyd] C, dressand I, deftly P, al richeli VA.   216 no man] PCI,
non VA.   225 to] APCI, *om.* V.   228 ful] APCI, wel V.   235 deol]
VAP, dyn C; þey] PC, þauȝ VA.

216 'Nobody could imagine the deceitful behaviour of Susan'.
218 *Be þis cause*: 'With this intention (of meeting the young man)'.
223 'For the sake of her husband . . .' *Sert* is an aphetic form of *desert*.
224 *cundelet vs care*: 'caused us trouble'. For the same phrase see
Awntyrs 90.
227 *his maistris to make*: 'to use his superior strength' (*MED maistrise*).
229 The *lake* is the moat, the *dep dich* of l. 5.
232 'But followed (him) in a disgraceful way.'
235 *with . . . deue*: 'they stun (lit. deafen) her with sorrow'. Cf. *York
Plays*, v. 129.

And hir domesmen vnduwe do hir be withdrawen.
Loueliche heo louted and lacched hir leue
At kynred and cosyn þat heo hed er knawen.
Heo asked merci with mouþ in þis mischeue:
'I am sakeles of syn,' heo seide in hir sawen,   240
'Grete God of his grace þis gomes forgeue
Þat doþ me derfliche be ded and don out of dawen
        Wiþ dere.
        Wolde God þat I miht
        Speke wiþ Joachim a niht.   245
        And siþen to deþ me be diht
            I charge hit not a pere.'

Heo fel doun flat in þe flore, hir feere whon heo fand,
Carped to him kyndeli as heo ful wel couþe:
'Iwis I wraþþed þe neuere, at my witand,   250
Neiþer in word ne in werk, in elde ne in ȝouþe.'
Heo keuered vp on hir kneos and cussed his hand:
'For I am dampned, I ne dar disparage þi mouþ.'
Was neuer serwfuller segge bi se nor bi sande,
Ne no soriore siht bi norþ ne bi souþ;   255
        Þo þare
        Þei toke þe feteres of hire feete,
        And euere he cussed þat swete.

238 er] CI, euere VAP; knawyn] PCI, iknawen VA.   241 þese gomes]
CI, ȝor gultus VAP; forgyfe] CI, foryeve P, forȝiue VA.   248 fand] PI,
fond] VAC.   254 sorowfuller] PI, more serwful VA, soryer C.
255 no] P, a CI, neuer a VA.

242 *don out of dawen*: 'deprived of life', as in *Pearl* 282. *Dawen* is
dat.pl. of *day*.
247 'I don't care a fig', lit. 'a pear'.
252 *keuered vp*: 'got up'. Having fallen to the floor in submission (l.
248), Susan kneels before her husband and kisses his hand.
253 *disparage*: 'sully'. Since the original sense is 'to marry a social
inferior', the word implies that the disgraced Susan will no longer claim
equality with her husband. The touching symbolism of this scene is
completed in the 'wheel', where Joachim kisses Susan and simply affirms
his faith in her innocence in the sight of God. The Vulgate makes no
mention of Joachim's reaction to the trial and condemnation.

134

'In oþer world schul we mete.'
    Seide he no mare.   260

Þen Susan þe serwfol seide uppon hiȝt,
Heef hir hondes on hiȝ, biheld heo to heuene:
'Þou Maker of Middelert þat most art of miht,
Boþe þe sonne and þe see þou sette vppon seuene.
Alle my werkes þou wost, þe wrong and þe riht;   265
Hit is nedful nou þi names to neuene.
Seþþe I am deolfolich dampned and to deþ diht,
Lord hertelich tak hede and herkne my steuene
    So fre.
    Seþþe þou maiȝt not be sene   270
    Wiþ no fleschliche eyene,
    Þou wost wel I am clene.
        Haue merci on me.'

Nou þei dresse hire to deþ withouten eny drede,
And lede forþ þat ladi, louesum of lere;   275
Grete God of his grace, of gyftes vngnede,
Help with þe Holi Gost and herde hir preyere.
He directed þis dom and þis derf dede
To Danyel þe prophete, of dedes so dere;
Such ȝiftes God him ȝaf in his ȝouþehede,   280

261 uppon hiȝt] VAPC, in his syght I.   266 neuene] PCI, nempne V,
nemene A.   272 I] CPI, þat I VA.   273 on] PCI, nou on VA.
276 gyftes] CPI, gultes VA.   278 derf] PC, delful VA, (278–81
lost in I).

261 The Vulgate 'Then Susanna cried out with a loud voice' does not
support I's more heavily alliterated line.
264 'You created both sun and sea in seven days.'
266 *þi names to neuene*: Susan calls for protection upon the names of
God used in the Old Testament. God's 'names seven' are often
mentioned; e.g. *Chester Plays*, EETS SS 3 (1974:xxii. 332).
274 *withouten eny drede*: 'certainly'; a tag. Again in l. 326.
276 *of gyftes vngnede*: 'unstinting in his bounty'. So, in *Cursor Mundi*,
EETS 62 (1876), l. 17218, Christ is 'noght of giftes gnede'.
277 *Help*: pa.t. 'helped'.

ʒit failed him of fourten fullich a ʒere,
> Nouht to layne.
> Þo criede þat freoly foode:
> 'Whi spille ʒe innocens blode?'
> And alle þei stoteyd and stode   285
> > Þis ferlys to frayne.

'What signefyes, gode sone, þese sawes þat þou seith?'
Þus þese maisterful men with mouþes gan mele.
'ʒe be fendes, al þe frape, I sei it in feiþ,
And in folk of Irael be foles wel fele.   290
Vmbiloke ʒou, lordes, such lawes ben leiþ,
Me þinkeþ ʒor dedes vnduwe such domes to dele.
Agein to þe gild-halle þe gomes vngreiþ!

---

281 hym] P, he C, hit VA; of fourten] a fourteniht VAPC; fullich a] ful of
þe VA, ful of a P, of a full C.   282 to] PCI, *om*. VA.   285 þei] API, þe
V.   287 þat þou] VAPI, & what hyt C; seyth] CI, seis VAP.   288 wiþ]
PCI, *om*. VA; gan] APCI can V.   289 ʒe] PCI, Þei VA; fendes]
VAP, fonned CI.   293 Agayn] PI, Aʒein VA, Haue agayn C; geld-] PCI,
ʒild- VA; þe (2)] VPC, ʒe AI.

281 'Yet he was fully a year short of fourteen.' Emendation proposed by
J. T. T. Brown, *Athenaeum* (1902:part 2, p. 254). The patristic view that
Daniel was aged twelve is discussed by C. Gnilka, *Aetas Spiritalis* (Bonn,
1972:236–8). Daniel is the pre-eminent example of the *puer senex*, on
which see Burrow (1986:95–134).
283 *freoly foode*: 'noble youth'; cf. l. 17.
285–6 'And they all hesitated and stopped to enquire into these strange
events'.
287 *þou seith*: see variant readings. The scribes were uneasily aware that
the form should be *seis* (Northern) or *seist* (Midland). However,
occasional 2 sg. endings in *-th* are found from OE times in Northern
texts; see A. Campbell, *Old English Grammar* (Oxford 1959:301, n. 1).
Later ME dialectal variation may also have played a part; Amours' note
is worth quoting: 'A Northern poet, accustomed to the forms *thou sayes,
he sayes*, with the same ending, may have believed that in the South *thou
sayth* was as correct as *he sayth*, and have used the word for the sake of
the rime. This is not a wild guess of my own: I have read such an
explanation of a similar licence; unfortunately I have lost the reference'
(p. 383).
293 'Back to the guild-hall with the wicked men!' The primary sense of
vngreiþ is 'unprepared', and this is not impossible here; the judges are to
be caught off guard by Daniel's questions.

I schal be proces apert disproue þis apele
    For nede.   295
      Lat twinne hem in two,
      For now wakneþ heor wo;
      Þei schal graunte ar þei go
        Al heore falshede.'

Þei diseuered hem sone and sette hem on sere   300
And sodeynly a seneke þei brouȝt into sale.
Bifore þis ȝonge prophete þis preost gon apere,
And he him apeched sone with chekes wel pale.
'Þou hast ibe presedent, þe peple to steere;
Þou dotest nou on þin olde tos in þe dismale.   305
Nou schal þi couetys be knowen, þat euer was vnclere;
Þou hast in Babiloygne on benche brewed muche bale,
      Wel bolde.
      Nou schal ȝor synnes be seene
      Of fals domes bideene,   310
      For ȝe in Babiloyne han bene
        Jugges of olde.

'Þou seidest þou seȝe Susanne sinned in þi siht;
Tel nou me trewly, vnder what tre?'
'Mon, bi þe muche God þat most is of miht,   315
Vnder a cyne, soþli, myseluen I hir se.'

296 twinne] VA, disseuere PCI.   300 on sere] C, sere VAP, in sondere
I.   301 a seneke] P, þat senek C, askede VA, asined I; into] PC, into þe
VA, to þe I.   306 couetyse] CI conscience VAP.   311 ye] PC, þeose V,
eose A.   312 Juggis] PCI, Jugget VA.

294 *be proces apert*: 'by open legal procedure'. *apele*: 'accusation'.
296 'Separate them!'
301 *seneke*: 'old man, elder' (Lat *senex*). The Vulgate calls them *senes*.
305 'You are going senile in your old age in evil days.' For the evidently
colloquial expression *On þin olde tos*, see also *Towneley Plays*, xxx. 592.
In þe dismale (Lat *dies mali*, OFr *dis mal*) is suggested by the Vulgate
'inveterate dierum malorum', 'thou that art grown old in evil days' (Dan.
xiii. 52). *Dismal*, originally a n. as here, developed as an adj. 'unlucky,
evil', hence 'gloomy, low spirited' (see *OED*).
306 *couetys*: 'lust'; see l. 331.
316 *cyne*: reproducing the Biblical *schino*, 'mastic tree'. This was
variously interpreted in the Middle Ages as a hawthorn, blackthorn,
birch etc.

A Pistel of Susan

'Nou þou lyest in þin hed, bi heuen vppon hiht,
An angel with a naked swerd þe neiȝes ful ne.
He haþ brandist his brond brennynde so briȝt
To marke þi middel at a mase in more þen in þre,   320
  No lese.
 þou brak Godes comaundement
 To sle such an innocent
 Wiþ eny fals juggement
  Vnduweliche on dese.'   325

Nou is þis domesmon withdrawen withouten eni drede
And put into prison aȝeyn to his place,
þei brouȝten þe toþer forþ whon þe barn bede,
Tofore þe folk and þe faunt freli of face.
'Cum forþ, þou corsed caytif, of Canaan sede!   330
Bicause of þi couetise þou art in þis case.
þou hast disceyuet þiself with þin oune dede;
Of þi wit for a wyf biwiled þou wase
  In wede.
 þou sey nou, so mote þou þe,   335
 Vnder what kynde of tre
 Semeli Susan þou se
  Do þat derne dede.

'þou gome of gret elde, þin hed is grei-hored,
Tel hit me treweli, ar þou þi lyf tyne.'   340

318 þe n. full ne] C, þe n. wel nere VA, he n. nere þe I, is ful ny þe P.
327 to hys] CI, in his P, into V, into a A. 330 of Canaan sede] PI, of
Caymes sede C, þou Canaan he sede VA.

320 'To cut your waist at a blow into more than three pieces.'
326–7 The judge is returned to his place in prison.
330–3 These lines paraphrase 'O thou seed of Chanaan and not of Juda,
beauty hath deceived thee and lust hath perverted thy heart' (Dan. xiii.
56).
333 Of þi wit . . . biwiled: 'deluded out of your wits'. There is a
suggestion of the anti-feminist commonplace of men duped by women,
as in SGGK 2425–6.
334 In wede is to be taken with a wyf.
335 so mote þou þe: 'so may you thrive', i.e. 'on your life' (OE þēon, 'to
prosper').

138

Þo þat reþly cherl ruydely rored
And seide bifore þe prophet: 'Þei pleied bi a prine.'
'Nou þou liest loude, so helpe me vr Lord!
For fulþe of þi falshed þou schalt ha euel fine,
Þou and þi cursed cumpere, ȝe mou not acorde.   345
ȝe schul be drawen to þe deþ þis dai ar we dine,
     So raþe.
       An angel is neih honde
       Takes þe domes of ȝor honde
       Wiþ a brennynge bronde   350
        To bryten ȝou baþe.'

Þen þe folk of Israel felle vppon knes
And lowed þat loueli Lord þat hire þe lyf lent.
All þe gomes þat hire god wolde gladen and glees
Þis prophete so pertli proues his entent.   355
Þei trompe bifore þis traiters and traylen hem on tres
Þorwout þe cité bi comuyn assent.
Hose leeueþ on þat Lord, þar him not lees,
Þat þus his seruaunt saued þat schold ha be schent
     Vnsete.   360
       Þis ferlys bifel
       In þe days of Danyel,
       Þe pistel witnesseþ wel
        Of þat profete.

---

341 reþly] V, roþly A, rodely C, loþely P, rewful I.   344 fynel PCI, pine
VA.   351 brittyn] CPI, byte VA.   360 Vnsete] I, In sete VAP, So
swete C.

342 *prine*: reproducing the Biblical *prino*, 'holm-oak'. Not recorded
elsewhere by *MED*.
344 *euel fine*: 'a bad end'.
349 'Removes the powers of judgement from you'.
351 *bryten*: 'destroy', translating the Vulgate *interfeciat*.
354 *hire god wolde*: 'wished her well'.
356–7 For particularly heinous crimes the victim was tied to a 'hurdle'
and dragged behind a cart around the city before execution.
358 'Whoever believes in the Lord need not be damned'. *þar him*:
(impers.) 'it is necessary for him'; cf. ll. 120, 137. *lees*: 'come to
perdition'; *MED lesen* v.(4), 9c(c).

SOMER SONEDAY

INTRODUCTION

Manuscript

The poem is the last item in Bodley MS. Laud Misc. 108, on fol. 237. The same late fourteenth- or early fifteenth-century scribe copied three saints lives to follow the earlier texts of *Havelok* and *King Horn*. The dialect of *Somer Soneday* shows some west midland features; see Oakden (1930:116–17); and M. Görlach, *The Textual Tradition of the South English Legendary* (Leeds, 1974:89).

Verse-form

A thirteen-line bob-and-wheel stanza, as *Susan*, with two eight-line stanzas marked *versus* by the scribe. The poet ends with eight short lines and five long lines, making up a sort of reversed thirteen-line stanza. While it is possible that the poem, ending at the foot of the last page, is incomplete, as argued by Smallwood (1973), the abrupt and dramatic ending is effective and unlikely to be the result of accident.

Theme

The narrator goes out hunting, but having wandered from the hunt comes across Lady Fortune with her wheel. He describes the four figures on the wheel that are traditional in illustrations of

Somer Soneday

the subject, as in fig. 5. See Patch (1927:164–7); and for the relationship with the motif of the four ages of man, see Dove (1986:67–73). There is no support for the earlier belief that any particular king is being commemorated; see Smallwood (1973), Turville-Petre (1974).

BIBLIOGRAPHY

Editions

C. Brown, in *Studies in English Philology*, ed. K. Malone and
  M. B. Ruud (Minneapolis, 1929:362–74)
R. H. Robbins, *Historical Poems of the XIVth and XVth Centuries* (New
  York, 1959:98–102)

Studies

T. M. Smallwood, 'The interpretation of *Somer Soneday*', *MÆ*, 42
  (1973:238–43)
T. Turville-Petre, '"Summer Sunday", "De Tribus Regibus Mortuis",
  and "The Awntyrs off Arthure": three poems in the thirteen-line
  stanza', *RES*, n.s. 25 (1974:1–14)

SOMER SONEDAY

HERE BIGYNNEÞ SOMER SONEDAY

Opon a somer soneday se I þe sonne
Erly risinde in þe est ende,
Day daweþ ouer doune, derknes is donne,
I warp on my wedes, to wode wolde I wende;
Wiþ kenettes kene þat wel couþe crie and conne 5
I hiede to holte wiþ honteres hende,
So ryfly on rugge roon and raches ronne
Þat in launde vnder lynde me leste to lende,
And lenede.
Kenettes questede to quelle 10
Al so breme so any belle,
Þe deer daunceden in þe delle
Þat al þe downe denede.

Denede dale and downe for dryft of þe deer in drede,
For meche murþe of mouþ þe murie moeth made; 15
I ros and romede and sey roon raches toȝede,
Þei stalken vnder schawe schatereden in schade,
And lordes lenged and ladies, leces to lede
Wiþ griþele grehoundes gode to game and glade,
And I cam to þe game þer gromes gonne grede, 20
And at a water wilde I wende ouer han wade,
Þer was.
I stalked be þe strem and be þe strond,

1 Opon] pon. 3 derknes is donne] derk is in towne. 18 lenged]
lenged lenged.

1–19 As in the *Parlement*, *Kings* and *Awntyrs*, the pleasures of the hunt
precede a grim reminder of mortality. See Turville-Petre (1974).
3 *derknes is donne*: the phrase as emended improves alliteration, rhyme
and sense, and can be widely paralleled; see Turville-Petre (1977a:86).
15 *moeth*: the same word as *mote*, 'a blast of a hunting horn', in *SGGK*
1141. The spelling for /t/ is *th* again in l. 131 *ȝeth*, 'yet', and is *ȝt* in l. 85
flyȝtte, 'flite, combat'.
16 '. . . and saw how roe deer fled from hounds.' Cf. *Kings*, l. 15n.
21 '. . . I intended to have crossed over.' *Han* is infin., *wade* is ppl.

Fer I be þe flod fond
A bot doun be a lond;   25
So passede I þe pas.

So passede I þe pas priuely to pleye
And ferde forþ in þat frith folk for to fynde,
Lawly longe I lustnede and vnder lowe lay,
Þat I ne herde hond, horn, hunte, hert ne hynde.   30
So wyde I walkede þat I wax wery of þe wey;
Þanne les I my layk and lenede vnder lynde,
And als I sat beside I say, soþ for to sey,
A wifman wiþ a wonder whel weue with þe wynde,
    And wond.   35
      Opon þe whel were, I wene,
      Merye men and madde imene;
      To hire I gan gon in grene,
      And Fortune Y fond.

Fortune, frend and fo, fayrest fere,   40
Ferli fals, fikel to fonde is ifounde;
Þe whel ʒe torneþ to wo, fro wo into wele þat were,
In þe ronynge rynge of þe roe þat renneþ so rounde.
A lok of þat leuedy wiþ louelich lere
Mi gode gameliche game gurte to grounde;   45
Couþe I carpe carpyng creftly and clere,

24 *Fer*: 'a long way off'.
32 *les I my layk*: 'I lost my quarry' (cf. *Parlement* 49), or perhaps 'I lost my enjoyment'.
33 The spelling of 'say' is always *sey(e)*, but the spelling of 'saw' varies between *say* (here and in ll. 87, 131) and *sey* (ll. 16, 64, 66).
34–9 In many illustrations the four figures on the Wheel of Fortune are titled *Regnabo*, 'I shall reign' (cf. ll. 66–86), *Regno*, 'I reign' (ll. 87–107), *Regnavi*, 'I have reigned' (ll. 108–30), and the dead figure of *Sum Sine Regno*, 'I am without sovereignty' (ll. 131–3). See Patch (1927:164–5).
46–52 The poet expresses fear of the vengeance that Fortune may take on him if he relates what he saw. 'If I were to utter complaints skilfully and clearly, verses about that lady would bind me in torment very quickly. Nevertheless I shall not desist; before I leave I will quickly make fitting remarks in due sequence.' The past tense of *bounde* in the main clause of a conditional sentence in pres. tense is paralleled by *SGGK* 1768–9, which has been seen as problematical.

Of þat birde bastons in bale me bounde
    Ful bowne.
  Naþeles ne mene I nat nay,
  I wile ar I wende away   50
  Redy resons in aray
  Radely to rowne.

Redely to roune, rounes to rede,
A loueloker leuedi liuiþ non in lond;
I wolde han went wiþ þat whyt in worþlich wede,   55
So ferly fair of face tofore hire I fond;
Þe gold of hire gurdel gloud as a glede,
Þat blisful burde in bale me bond
Or hire lyȝthhed in herte I hadde hede,
And wiþ a wonderful whel þat worþi wyth wond   60
    Wyþ mayn.
  A wifman of so muche myȝth,
  So wonder a whelwryȝth,
  Sey I neuere wiþ syȝth,
  Soþ for to seyn.   65

Soþ to seye, sitte I sey, as my sicȝthe sente,
A begyngge gome gameliche gay,
Bryȝt as þe blostme, with browes ibente,
On þe whel þat þe wyȝth weuede in þe wey.
Wyterly him was wel whan þe whel wente,   70

59 lyȝthhed] lyȝth heued.

55 *whyt*: 'wight, creature'. The word is also spelt *wyth*, l. 60, and *wyȝth*,
l. 69. Other spellings of *-ght* as *-t* are l. 109 *sout*, 'sought', and l. 113
iwrout, 'wrought'; as *-th* l. 100 *knyth*, 'knight', l. 111 *browth*, 'brought',
and l. 115 *nawth*, 'nought'; as *-ȝth* ll. 62–4 *myȝth*, 'might' etc., l. 84
flyȝth, 'flight', and others.
56 'I found her so very beautiful of face *in front*.' But Fortune may be
two-faced, as in Tristram (1976:pl. 17). See also Patch (1927:42–3, and
pl. 1).
59 'Before I had taken note of her fickleness in heart.'
63 In *Awntyrs* 271 Fortune is 'that wonderfull whelewright'. Only in
these two instances is a *wheelwright* one who *turns* a wheel.
67 *begyngge*: 'supplicating, pleading' (that Fortune will favour him)?
Probably an error.

For he layked and low, lenyng als he lay;
Loueliche lokyngges þe loueli me lente,
A meriere man on molde monen I ne may
    In mynde.
      Þe gome I gaf a gretyng,   75
      He seyde, 'Sestou, swetyng,
      Þe crowne of þat comely kyng
      I cleyme be kynde.

        Versus

    'Be kynde it me come
    To cleyme kyngene kyngdom,   80
    Kyngdom be kynde;
    To me þe whel wile wynde,
    Wynd wel, worþliche wyȝth,
    Fare Fortune, frendene flyȝth,
    Flitte forþ flyȝtte   85
    On þe selue sete to sitte.'

Sitte I say and seþe on a semeli sete,
Ryȝth on þe rounde on þe rennyng ryng,
Caste kne ouer kne as a kyng kete,
Comely cloþed in a cope, crouned as a kyng.   90
Hey herte hadde he of hastif hete,
He leyde his leg opon liþ at his likyng,
Ful loþ were þe lordyng his lordschipe lete,
He wende al þe world were at his weldyng
    Ful wyȝth.   95
      On knes I kyþed þat kyng:
      He seyde, 'sestou, sweting,
      How I regne wiþ ring,
      Richest in ryȝth.

79 come] comeþ.   88 rennyng] rennyg.

80 *kyngene*: 'of kings' (gen.pl.). Cf. *frendene* l. 84, *lordene* l. 125.
84–6 'Let Fortune proceed and let friends depart (lit. with the departure of friends), let the struggle to sit on the throne itself (at the top of the wheel) go ahead.'
89–92 The figure at the top of Fortune's Wheel, dressed as a king and sitting cross-legged, is splendidly depicted in fig. 5.

Versus

'Richest in ryȝth, quen and knyth   100
Kyng conne me calle;
Mest man of myȝth,
Fair folk to fote me falle.
Lordlich lif led I,
No lord lyuynde me iliche,   105
No duk ne dred I
For I regne in ryȝth as a riche.'

Of riche þenkeþ rewþe is to rede and to roune
Þat sitten on þat semeli sete and seþþe wiþ sorwe þoruout
    sout;
And I beheld on hadde an heued hor als hor-howne,   110
Al blok was his ble in bitere bales browth,
His diademe of dyamans droppede adoun,
His weyes were aweyward wroþliche iwrout,
Tynt was his tresor, tente, tour and toun,
Nedful and nawthi, naked and nawth   115
        Inome.
        Þat gome I grette wiþ griþ,
        A word he warp and wepte wiþ
        Hou he was crouned kyng in kiþ
        And caytif become.   120

        'Becomen a caytif acast,
        Kynges king couþe me calle,
        Fram frendes falle,
        Lond, luþe, litel, lo! last.
        Last litel lordene lif,   125
        Fikel is Fortune, nou fer fro,
        Here wel, here wo,
        Here knyth, her kyng, her caytif.'

110 Horehound has 'stem and leaves covered with a white cottony
pubescence' (*OED*).
112 Of the third of the figures on Fortune's Wheel in *Morte A*, the poet
relates 'His dyadem was droppede down, dubbyde with stonys' (l. 3296).
113 'His fortunes were sadly turned in the opposite direction.'
122 'Kings called me king.'
125 *Last litel*: 'lasts only a little while'.

A caytif he was become and kenned on care,
He myste many merþes and meche maistri,   130
3eth I say soriere, sikyng ful sare,
A bare body in a bed, a bere ibrouth him by,
A duk drawe to þe deþ wiþ drouping and dare.

131 sikyng] likyng.

THE THREE DEAD KINGS

INTRODUCTION

Manuscript

The poem is preserved only in Bodley MS. Douce 302, fol. 34, a collection of the poems of John Audelay, 'prest to þe lord Strange' of Knokin, Shropshire, copied at some date after 1426, perhaps at the blind poet's dictation. *Kings* is however not by Audelay, for the poet's dialect is from further to the north; see Dickins (1932).

Verse-form

This is the most complex example of the thirteen-line stanza; see Turville-Petre (1974:6–7). The rhyme-scheme complements and contrasts with the alliterative scheme as follows:

rhyme-scheme: a b a b a b a b c d c c d
alliteration: a a b b c c d d d d x f f

The first eight lines of each stanza are of four stresses rhyming alternately on the same two vowels *and on just one consonant* throughout; the last five lines (the 'wheel') are of three stresses rhyming on another two vowels and one consonant. Generally every stress is alliterated; lines alliterate in pairs and, except in the first stanza, lines 7–10 alliterate on one sound, thus binding the octave to the 'wheel'. The result is a type of rhyme, used by Wilfred Owen in *Strange Meeting*, known as pararhyme; e.g. ll. 66–78: myȝt – maȝt – syȝt – saȝt – lyȝt – laȝt – tyȝt – taȝt – trow –

trew – how – row – rew. There are similarities in *Harley Lyric* IV, above. The poet exploits to the full the devices of word-play, punning and echo to which the scheme commits him. It is an extraordinary *tour de force* of technical skill and verbal ingenuity, and yet also a work of great imaginative power.

Unfortunately, the scribe botched the job, destroying rhymes by rewriting in his own dialect, and weakening the alliteration through carelessness and misunderstanding. And yet, because of the tightness of the scheme, many of the errors can be put right, and so in this edition an attempt has been made to restore the poem to something approaching its original form, following the lead given by Dickins (1932) and McIntosh (1977).

Theme

Three kings are riding out to the hunt when they have a terrifying encounter with the figures of their dead fathers. This is the only literary account in English of the story of the Three Living and the Three Dead, a theme widespread in art, and found also in Latin, French, German and Italian versions. See W. Rotzler, *Die Begegnung der drei Lebenden und der drei Toten* (Winterthur, 1961); and Tristram (1976:162–5). In *Kings* there is a reference to church murals (l. 141), and in several English examples of these, as in the poem, the Living are hunting; see Turville-Petre (1974:8–9). Also to be compared is the most beautiful artistic representation of the story in the de Lisle Psalter, dating from the early fourteenth century (illustrated in fig. 6). Here one of the kings has a hawk, and two of the skeletons are draped in torn shrouds. Above are written lines that find an echo in *Kings*: 'Ich am afert. Lo whet ich se. Me þinkeþ hit beþ deueles þre. Ich wes wel fair. Such scheltou be. For godes loue be wer by me.'

BIBLIOGRAPHY

Edition

The poems of John Audelay, ed. E. K. Whiting, EETS 184 (1931), no. 54

Studies

B. Dickins, 'The rhyme-schemes in MS. Douce 302, 53 and 54', *Proceedings of the Leeds Philosophical and Literary Society*, 2 (1932:516–18)

A. McIntosh, 'Some notes on the text of the Middle English poem *De Tribus Regibus Mortuis*', *RES*, n.s. 28 (1977:385–92)

P. Tristram, *Figures of Life and Death in Medieval English Literature* (London, 1976:162–5)

T. Turville-Petre, 'Three poems in the thirteen-line stanza', *RES*, n.s. 25 (1974:1–14)

THE THREE DEAD KINGS

An a byrchyn bonke þer bous arne bryȝt
I saw a brymlyche bore to a bay broȝt,
Ronke rachis with rerde þai ronnon aryȝt,
Of al hore row and hore rest lytil hom roȝt;
Me þoȝt hit ful semelé to se soche a syȝt,   5
How in a syde of a salȝe a sete him he soȝt,
Fro þe noyse þat hit was new til hit was ne nyȝt,
Fro þe non bot a napwile, me þoȝt hit bot noȝt.
    Me þoȝt hit noȝt bot a þrow
    To se how he þrobyt and þrew,   10
    Hontis with hornes þai kowþ blow,
    Þai halowyd here howndys with 'how!'
    In holtis herde I neuer soche hew.

Soche a hew in a holt were hele to beholde
To se þe howndis him hent and gart him to helde;   15
Þer come barownce to þat bay with barsletys bolde,
Þai blewyn here bewgulys ful breme hore brachus to belde.
Þre kyngys þer come, trewlé itolde,
With tonyng and tryffylyng and talis þai telde;
Vche a wy þat þer was wroȝt as þai wold,   20

4 roȝt] þoȝt.   5 syȝt] seȝt.   10 þrew] þrow.   11 hontis] *altered by later hand to* honters. 17 belde] bild.   19 tonyng] donyng.

1–13 On the hunting-scene as an introduction to an encounter with death, see Turville-Petre (1974). Cf. also the boar hunt in *SGGK* 1412–67, 1561–1600, where the terms *bay*, *rachez* and *halowed* are used again.
7 'From the time that the noise (of the hunt) was new until it was nearly night.'
12 *how*: a hunting-call borrowed from French.
15 'To see that the hounds seized him and caused him to fall', i.e. 'brought him down'. For the construction after *see*, cf. *Somer Soneday* 16.
17 *bewgulys*: 'hunting-horns'; see *Parlement* 652n.
19 *tonyng*: 'making musical (i.e. hunting-horn) notes'; cf. *Wynnere* 358. In this ms. voiced and voiceless initial consonants (/d/ and /t/, /g/ and /k/) are sometimes interchanged; see Whiting (1931:xxxiii), and notes to ll. 47, 58, 132 below.

The Three Dead Kings

Þese wodis and þese wastis þai waltyn al to welde.
    Þai waltyn at here wil to ware
    Þese wodis and þe wastus þat þer were;
    Herkyns what befel of here fare –
    Ham lakyd no lorchip in lare –   25
    Þe lede þat wold lestyn and lere.

When þai weren of þese wodys went at here wyn,
Þai fondyn wyndys ful wete and wederys ful wane,
Bot soche a myst vpo molde with mowþ as I ȝoue myn,
Of al here men and here mete þai mystyn vche man.   30
'Al our awnters' quod one, 'þat we ar now inne,
I hope fore honor of erþ þat anguis be ous an.
Þaȝ we be kyngis ful clene and comen of ryche kyn,
Moche care vs is caȝt fore kraft þat I can.
    Can I mo no cownsel be Cryst,   35
    Bot couerys and cachis sum rest;
    Be morne may mend þis myst,
    Our Lord may delyuer vs with lyst,
    Or lelé our lyuys ar lest.'

21 welde] wylde.   25 lakyd] lykyd.   27 went] gone; wyn] wyl.   29 I]
om.; myn] men.   30 man] mon.   31 ar] beþ.   32 an] on.   35 be
Cryst] bot care.   39 lest] lost.

21 *waltyn*: a spelling of *waldyn*, pa.t.pl. of 'will': 'they wished to possess
entirely'.
24–6 'Listen what became of their conduct – they had no lack of lordship
on earth – anyone who wishes to listen and learn.' The parenthesis of
l. 25 is difficult; *lare* is here taken to be *MED leir* n.(2), 'earth'; it is used
again in l. 112. On the rhyme see Jordan (1974:135).
29 *with . . . myn*: 'as I relate to you.'
30 *men and mete*: 'fellowship and company'; *MED mene* n.(1), and
mette. See McIntosh (1977:387).
32 'I suppose that suffering has come upon us in consequence of our
status in the world.' The phrase *honor of erþ* is equivalent to *lorchip in
lare* (l. 25).
34 *fore . . . can*: 'despite the skill that I have'? Or 'as I understand'? (*I*,
missed by previous editors, is inserted by the scribe above the line.)
35 For the emendation, see Dickins (1932:517), though the whole line
was perhaps picked up from l. 89.

152

Where þai not forþ gone fotis bot a fewe 40
Þai fondon feldus ful fayre and fogus ful fow,
Schokyn out of a schawe þre schalkys ischeue,
Schadows vnshene were chapid to chow,
With lymes long and lene and leggys ful lew,
Hadyn lost þe lyp and þe lyuer seþyn þai were layd loue. 45
Þer was no beryn þat þer was dorst bec nor bewe,
Bot braydyn here brydilys agayne, hor blongis can blow;
    Here blonkis can blow and abyde,
    Siche barns þai can hom bede,
    Þai se no sokur hom besyde, 50
    Bot oche kyng apon Crist cryde
    With crossyng and karpyng o crede.

The furst kyng he had care, his hert ourcast,
Fore he knew þe cros of þe cloþ þat couerd þe cyst;
Forþ wold not his fole bot fnyrtyd ful fast, 55
His fayre fawkun fore ferd he fel to his fyst:
'Now al my gladchip is gone, I grue and am agast
Of þre gostis ful grym þat gare me be gryst,
Fore oft haue I walkon be wodys and be wast,

42 schalkys ischeue] schalys at eus.   43 chow] chew.   49 bede]
byde.   56 fyst] fest.   57 grue] gre.   58 gare] care; gryst] cryst.
59 oft] of.

40 *Where*: 'were'. Similarly *whe*, l. 108.
41 *fogus*: 'meadows'; see McIntosh (1977:387). *fow*: 'variegated?,
bright?'; cf. Henryson, *Fables* 1834.
42 'Having emerged from a thicket, three men come forth.'
43 '. . . were shaped to show'; i.e. 'in appearance'.
45 *layd loue*: 'dead and buried.'
47 *can blow*: 'snorted' (*can* = *gan*, as in next lines).
49 'These men (the Dead) summoned them (the Kings).'
52 'Making the Sign of the Cross and saying the Creed.'
54 'For he recognized the cross on the pall that covered the coffin.' The
Dead are shrouded in grave-clothes (l. 99), as two of them are in the de
Lisle Psalter (fig. 6).
56 In the de Lisle Psalter, as often elsewhere, one king has a falcon on
his fist (fig. 6).
58 *gare me be gryst*: 'make me terrified'; see McIntosh (1977:388). There
is strictly no need for emendation, in view of other examples of initial /k/
for /g/; see l. 19n.

Bot was me neuer so wo in þis word þat Y wyst.   60
    So wo was me neuer I wene,
    My wit is away oþer wane;
    Certis sone hit wil be sene
    Our tounyng wil turne vs to tene,
    Fore tytle I trow we bene tane.'   65

Then bespoke þe secund kyng þat mekil was of myȝt,
Was made as a man schuld of mayn and of maȝt:
'Me þenkys, seris, þat I se þe selquoþ syȝt
Þat euer segge vnder sonne sey and was saȝt
Of þre ledys ful layþ þat lorne haþ þe lyȝt;   70
Boþ þe lip and þe lyuer his fro þe lyme laȝt.
Fore ȝif we tene to þe towne as we hadyn tyȝt
Ha ful teneful way I trow þat vs is taȝt.
    Vs is taȝt, as I trow –
    I tel ȝou no talis bot trew –   75
    What helpis our hontyng with "how"?
    Now rayke we to þe ȝonder row
    Or raddelé oure rese mon we rew.'

Þen speke þe henmest kyng, in þe hillis he beholdis,
He lokis vnder his hondis and his hed heldis,   80
Bot soche a carful knyl to his hert coldis
So doþ þe knyf ore þe kye þat þe knoc kelddus.
'Hit bene warlaws þre þat walkyn on þis woldis.

64 tounyng] connyg.   66 bespoke] besopke; secund] ii.   67 maȝt]
myȝt.   71 and þe] *smudged*.   81 knyl] kynl.   82 þe knoc]
knoc.

64 *tounyng*: cf. l. 19.
65 *Fore tytle*: 'as of right, with due claim'? McIntosh (1977:388), would
read *tryfle*, 'trifling, irresponsibility'.
67 *schuld*: 'ought to be'.
69 *saȝt*: 'afflicted by' (ppl. of *seek*); cf. *Somer Soneday* 109, *sout*.
71 *his*: 'is'. Similarly *Ha*, 'A' (l. 73).
72–8 The second king suggests that running away from the Dead would
only land them in worse trouble.
81–2 'But such a sorrowful blow strikes cold at his heart, as the knife or
the key does that chills the knuckle.' MS. *kynl* may be read as either
knyl, 'knell', hence 'shock', or *kyl*, 'blow' (*MED cul* n.(2)).

Oure Lord wyss vs þe redé way þat al þe word weldus!
My hert fars fore freȝt as flagge when hit foldus,   85
Vche fyngyr of my hond fore ferdchip hit feldus.
    Fers am I ferd of oure fare.
    Fle we ful fast þerfore.
    Can Y no cownsel bot care,
    Þese dewyls wil do vs to dare   90
    Fore drede lest þai duttyn vche a dore.'

'Nay, are we no fyndus', quod furst, 'þat ȝe before ȝou fynden.
We wer ȝour faders of fold þat fayre ȝoue haue fondon.
Now ȝe beþ lytyr to leue þen leuys on þe lynden
And lordis of oche towne fro Loron into Londen.   95
Þose þat bene not at ȝour bone ȝe beton and byndon,
Bot ȝef ȝe betun þat burst in bale be ȝe bondon.
Lo here þe wormus in my wome! Þai wallon and wyndon.
Lo here þe wrase of þe wede þat I was in wondon!
    Herein was I wondon, iwys,   100
    In word wan þat me worþelokyst was;
    My caren was ful cumlé to kysse.
    Bot we haue made ȝoue mastyrs amys
    Þat now nyl not mynn vs with a mas.'

That oþer body began a ful brym bere: 105
'Lokys on my bonus þat blake bene and bare!

84 weldus] wildus.   85 foldus] feldus.   94 lytyr] lykyr; lynden] lynde.
96 byndon] bedon.   102 kysse] cusse.

91 *dore*: i.e. 'escape route'.
93 'We were your earthly fathers who have provided for you well.'
94 'Now you take more delight in living than leaves on the linden tree.'
The comparison depends upon the expression 'lyter þanne lef is on
lynde' (see *MED lind(e* n., 1(b)), and also on a pun on *leue*, 'to live, to
leaf' (*MED liven* v.(1) and *leven* v.(2)).
95 *Loron*: Lorraine? Or Lorne in Scotland.
97 'Unless you atone for that wickedness you will be bound in torment.'
Note the play on *beton*, 'beat', and *betun* 'repent of' (*MED beten* v.(2)).
For *burst* see *MED brest* n.(2).
98–9 The worms and the tattered winding-sheet are clearly illustrated in
the de Lisle Psalter (fig. 6).

Fore wyle we wondon in þis word, at worchip we were;
Whe hadon our wyfe at our wil and well fore to ware.
Þenkes ȝe no ferlé bot frayns at me fere:
Þaȝ ȝe be neuer so fayre, þus schul ȝe fare!   110
And ȝif ȝe leuyn vpon Crist and on his lore lere,
Leuys lykyng of flesche and leue not þat lare!
    Fore warto schuld ȝe leue hit? Hit lyus!
    Hit ledys ȝoue be lagmon be leus
    When þou art aldyr-hyȝtus and hyus.   115
    Away of þis word when þat þou wryus,
    Al þi wild werkys hit wreus.'

Then speke layþe vpo last with lyndys ful lene,
With eyþer leg as a leke were lapid in lyne:
'Makis ȝour merour be me! My myrþus bene mene.   120
Wyle I was mon apon mold morþis þai were myne,
Me þoȝt hit a hede þenke at husbondus to hene.

---

107 wyle we] wyle.   108 and well] *added in later hand*.   109 fere] ferys.
111 lere] lerys.   114 leus] lyus.   115 hyus] hyust.   116 wryus] wryust.

111–12 'And if you believe in Christ and study his doctrine, give up pleasure of the flesh and do not trust in that filth.' There are plays on *leuys*, 'leave' – *leue*, 'believe', and *lore*, 'teaching' – *lare*, 'earth, filth'.
113–17 'For why should you trust it? It lies! It leads you astray all over the place when are you are at your proudest and highest. When you turn away from this world it will reveal all your lascivious deeds.' The forms of the rhyme words present problems.
114 *be lagmon*: 'astray'? Cf. *SGGK* 1729. The meaning of the phrase is uncertain despite several ingenious explanations; see McIntosh (1977:390–2). *be leus*: 'over the fields', hence 'hither and thither'; *MED lei(e* n.(3)? Or possibly a form of *MED lie* n.(1), 'falsehood'.
115 *aldyr-hyȝtus*: 'proudest of all', a superlative form based on *height*, adj. Similarly, the *-us* ending needs to be restored for the rhyme in *hyus*, 'highest' and *wryus*, pr.2sg. 'turnest' (presumably originally *hyes* and *wryes*, forms found in northern texts such as *Wars*).
120 Cf. Elde's admonition, *Parlement* 290. Note the play on *myrþus*, 'joys', and *morþis*, 'homicides, heinous crimes' (previously read as *merþis*).
122–5 The ghost accuses himself of treating common people dishonourably, for which arrogance he is now suffering. *Husbondus*: 'villagers, villeins'; *hatyd . . . hyne*: 'hated by common people'.

The Three Dead Kings

Fore þat was I hatyd with heme and with hyne,
Bot þoȝt me neuer kyng of coyntons so clene.
Now nis þer knaue vnder Crist to me wil enclyne,   125
    To me wil enclyne, to me come,
    Bot ȝif he be cappid or kyme.
    Do so ȝe dred not þe dome!
    To tel ȝoue we haue no longyr tome,
    Bot turn ȝoue fro tryuyls betyme!'   130

Now þis gostis bene grayþ, to graue þai glyde;
Þen began þese gomys grayþlé to glade,
Þai redyn on þe ryȝt way and radlé þai ryde,
Þe red rowys of þe day þe rynkkys kouþyn rade.
Holde þai neuer þe pres be hew ne be hyde   135
Bot ay þe hendyr hert after þai hade,
And þai þat weryn at myschip þai mend ham þat tyde,
And þroȝ þe mercé of God a mynster þai made.
    A mynster þai made with masse
    Fore metyng þe men on þe mosse,   140
    And on þe woȝe wrytyn þis was.
    To lyte will leue þis, allas!
    Oure Lord delyuer vs from losse. Amen.

125 nis] is.   127 kyme] kymyd.   131 glyde] glydyn.   132 gomys]
comys.   133 ryde] rydyn.   136 hendyr] hengyr.   140 þe men] þen
men; mosse] masse.

124 Perhaps 'but considered there was never a king with such elegant
companions'. Or emend *neuer* to *euer*.
127 'Unless he is a madman or a fool.' The usual sense of *cappid*, 'with a
priest's cap', seems inappropriate; McIntosh (1977:390), compares Scots
cappit. See *Harley Lyric* IX.1 above.
132 *gomys*: 'men' (ms. *comys*). See note to l. 19.
134 'The men immediately (*rade*) recognised the red rays of daylight.'
135 *Holde þe pres*: perhaps 'acted oppressively', *MED presse* n., 5(a).
be hew ne be hyde: lit. 'by complexion nor by skin', hence, perhaps, 'not
at all', *MED heu* n., 2(b).
140 *mosse*: 'moor'; found in place-names of the north and NWMidl.
141 'And this (story) was written on the wall.' There are late medieval
wall-paintings of the story in a number of churches; see E. Carleton
Williams, 'Mural paintings of the Three Living and the Three Dead in
England', *Journal of the British Archaeological Association*, 3rd ser. 7
(1942:31–40).
142 'Too few will believe this, alas.'

THE SIEGE OF JERUSALEM

INTRODUCTION

Manuscripts

There are eight mss., though one, BL Cotton Vespasian E xvi, fols. 70a–75b, does not contain the extract here. The others are:

L: Bodley Laud misc. 656, fols. 1a–19a, by a late fourteenth-century Oxfordshire scribe. *Siege J* is followed by *PPl* C.

P: Princeton Univ. Lib., R. H. Taylor Collection, Petre MS, of much the same date as L, from the northern tip of the W. Riding of Yorks. according to *LALME*. The MS. begins with the *Speculum Vitae*.

A: The Thornton ms., BL Addit. 31042, fols. 50a–66a, also containing *Parlement* and *Wynnere*. See the introduction to *Wynnere* above.

D: Lambeth Palace 491 (pt. I), fols. 206a–227b, by the same Essex scribe of 1425–50 who wrote the copy of *Susan* in Huntington Lib. HM 114. D also contains the *Awntyrs*.

C: BL Cotton Caligula A ii (pt. I), fols. 111a–125a, a mid-fifteenth-century ms. that begins with a text of *Susan*; see introduction to that poem.

U: Cambridge Univ. Lib. Mm.V.14, fols. 187a–206b, copied by the London scribe Richard Frampton in the early fifteenth century. The other contents are the Latin sources of *Wars* and *Dest Troy*.

E: Huntington Lib. HM 128, fols. 205a–216a, of the first half of the fifteenth century, from Warwicks., according to *LALME*. The *Siege J* follows *PPl* B by another scribe.

On all these mss. see Doyle (1982:93–6), Guddat-Figge (1976).

The relationship between the texts in the extract here edited is far from clear. The best text, inevitably chosen as copy text here, is L, but it has the disadvantage that it has apparently been patched up by a competent versifier (see e.g. l. 607 and perhaps l. 722). P, discovered in 1952 and not previously used, is related to L, but is helpful because it is not affected by L's revisions, though it is full of omissions and clumsy misreadings. A has good readings, but is subject to typical scribal expansion and smoothing. The mss. DCUE form a rather close group, of which D is the best representative, while E has been extensively rewritten.

All departures from L are noted here, together with the authorities for the preferred readings. Other variant readings are not noted unless they have some particular interest.

Sources

The story of how Titus and Vespasian besieged Jerusalem, and how the Jews were finally starved out and the survivors sold thirty for a penny, was widely popular, and the poet seems to have drawn on several Latin accounts, on which see Kölbing and Day (1932:xv-xxiv, 83–9). However, as discovered by Moe (1970), the source for the passage edited here is Roger d'Argenteuil's *Bible en françois*. A fifteenth-century English prose translation is edited by P. Moe, Middle English Texts 6 (Heidelberg, 1977); see pp. 82–5 for the corresponding chapters. The poet follows the main outlines of the French, but expands and selects freely.

Date, place, verse-form

The only indication of date is that of the earliest mss., L and P. The author's dialect is difficult to reconstruct from the alterations of the scribes; the many parallels with *Wars* and *Dest Troy* (see, e.g., notes to ll. 532, 548, 571–2, 611–16, 654), together with some features of vocabulary and alliterative practice, would suggest a NWMidl. poet. Like *Erkenwald* and *Wars*, the poet tends to write in four-line units.

BIBLIOGRAPHY

Edition

E. Kölbing and M. Day, *The Siege of Jerusalem*, EETS 188 (1932)

Study

P. Moe, 'The French Source of the Alliterative *Siege of Jerusalem*', *MÆ*, 39 (1970:147–54)

THE SIEGE OF JERUSALEM

[Titus and his father Vespasian, miraculously cured of cancer of the lip
and a swarm of wasps on the nose respectively, vow to avenge Christ's
death, and so, accompanied by Sabinus, they attack Jerusalem. The Jews
have a great army, including dromedaries, camels and a magnificent
elephant bearing a castle containing their chief priest Caiaphas and his
twelve scribes.]

Bemes blowen anon blonkes to neȝe,
Stedis stampen in þe felde, stif steil vndere,
Stiþe men in stiropys striden alofte,
Knyȝtes croysen hemself, cacchen here helmys,
With loude clarioun cry and cormus pypys,   525
Tymbris and tabourris tonelande loude,
ȝeuen a schillande schout, schrynken þe Jewes,
As wommen welter schal in swem whan water hem neȝeþ.
Lacchen launces anon, lepyn togedris,
As fure out of flynt-ston ferde hem bytwene,   530
Doust drof vpon lofte, dymedyn alle aboute,
As þonder and þicke rayn þrowblande in skyes;
Beren burnes þrow, brosten her launces,
Knyȝtes crosschen doun to þe cold erþe,
Fouȝt faste in þe felde and ay þe fals vndere,   535
Doun swowande to swelt without swar more.
Tytus tourneþ hym to, tolles of þe beste,
Forjustes þe jolieste with joynyng of werre,

525 cormus] PAD, curyous CUE, alle kyn L.   528 women] AEUC,
womman LD; welter schal] w. solde A, wepith DCE, shullen U, schal L;
in swem] in a swem L, in swoun A, & waylith D, on hyȝe CUE; water
thaym] AU, w. her D, w. he C, hire þe w. L, þat sorwe hem E.
532 þrowblande] þrowolande L, thrymbland P, threpande A.   533 her]
DCUE, þair P, *om.* L.   537 beste] PADCUE, bestes L.
538 joynynge] APDCUE, joyned L.

521 'Then trumpets summon horses to come forward.' Cf. l. 634.
528 I.e. '. . . when childbirth approaches'.
532 Cf. *Dest Troy* 12496 (and note) below, giving support to the
emendation *þrowblande*.
537 '. . . pulls the best men off (their horses)'. Cf. *Wars* 3768, 'Tolls of
þe tirantis'.

Suþ with a briȝt bronde betiþ on harde
That þe brayn and þe blod on þe bent lefte,   540
Souȝt þroȝ an oþer side with a sore wepne,
Bet on þe broun stele while þe bladde laste,
An hey breydeþ þe brond, and as a bore lokeþ,
How hetterly doun, hente whoso wolde.
Alle briȝtned þe bent as bemys of sonne   545
Of þe gilden gere and þe goode stones;
For schymeryng of scheldes and schynyng of helmes,
Hit ferde as þe firmament vpon a fure were.
Waspasian in þe vale þe vaward byholdeþ,
How þe heþyn here heldiþ to grounde,   550
Cam with a faire ferde þe fals for to mete,
As griffouns with grame þey girden in samen.
Spakly here speres on sprotes þey ȝeden,
Scheldes as schidwod on scholdres tocleuen,
Schoken out of scheþes þat scharpe were ygrounde,   555
And mallen metel þroȝ vnmylt hertes;
Þey hewen on þe heþen and hurtlen togedre,
Forschorne gild schroud, schedered burnee,
Baches woxen ablode aboute in þe vale,
And goutes out of gold wede as goteres þey runne.   560
Sire Sabyn setteþ hym vp whan hit so ȝede,

539 betis] PDCUE, he betiþ L.   540 Þat] PADCUE, Tille L;
lefte] ACUE, ornen L, rann P.   547 schemerynge] ADCUE,
schyueryng LP; scheldis] APDCUE, schendes L.   548 þe] PADCUE,
alle þe L.   549 vauarte] PADCUE, fanward L.   551 false] ADCU,
fals men L; for] PAD, *om.* LUE.   552 gryffounes] ADCUE, greued
griffouns L, þe grimly griffons P; wiþ grame] DU, one grownde A, on
grene CE, *om.* LP; þay] ADCUE, *om.* L.   555 were] APDCUE, was
L.   556 vnmylt] L, vnmaght P, maltyn A.   557 Thay] ADCUE, *om.*
L; and ADCUE] *om.* L.   560 oute of] PADCU, fram L.

540 This use in this position of *lefte*, 'remained, was left', is
characteristic of the poet: cf. ll. 568, 595, 603 etc.
547 *schymeryng*: the obvious choice of variants is supported by
'estancellez' in the source, quoted by Moe (1970:151).
548 Very similar is *Dest Troy* 3700.
555 þat: i.e. '(swords) that'.
558 *schedered burnee*: '(they) split coats of mail.'
560 'And streams (of blood) like gutters run out of the gold clothes.'

The Siege of Jerusalem

Rideþ myd þe rereward and alle þe route folweþ,
Kenely þe castels he came to assayle
Þat þe bestes on here bake out of burwe ladden,
Atles on þe olyfauntes þat orible were, 565
And girdiþ out þe guttes with grounden speres;
Roppis rispen forþ, þat ridders an hundred
Scholde be busy to burie þat on a bent lafte.
Castels clateren doun, cameles brosten,
Dromedaries to þe deþ drowen ful swyþe, 570
Þe blode fomed hem fro in flasches aboute,
Þat kne-depe in þe dale dascheden stedes.
Þe burnes in þe bretages þat aboue were,
For þe doust and þe dyn – as alle doun ȝede
Whan hurdiȝs and hard erþe hurtled togedre – 575
Al forstoppette in stele, starke-blynde wexen,
And vnder dromedaries doun diȝede ful sone.
Was non left vpon lyue þat alofte stode,
Saue an olepy olyfaunt at þe grete ȝate
Þeras Cayphas þe clerke in castel rideþ. 580
He say þe wrake on hem wende and away tourneþ
With twelf maystres made of Moyses lawe;
An hundred helmed men hied hem after,
Er þey of castel myȝt come, cauȝten hem alle,
Bounden þe bischup on a bycchyd wyse, 585
Þat þe blode out barst eche a band vndere,

563 he] PE, thay ADCU, *om.* L.   566 And] ADCUE, *om.* L.
567 Roppis] ADCUE, Rappis L; rydders] A, redles L, redily DUC.
571 in] PADCUE, in þe L.   572 Þat] PADCUE, Þe L.
575 *follows* 576 *in* L; *line om.* P.   576 starke] PDCUE, storte L,
stane A.   577 doun] L, *om.* ADCUE; dyede] ADCUE, diȝten L;
full] A, hem L.   578 stode] PADCUE, standeþ L.   579 ane] A, *om.*
L.   583 hyed] PADCUE, hien L.   585 a] PACUE, *om.* L.   586 a]
PACE, *om.* LDU.

563 The *castels* are the protective structures filled with men on the
elephants' backs.
571–2 The picture of horses wading through pools of blood is also in
Wars 2174–5.
573–5 The *bretages* and the *hurdiȝs* are the 'castles' on the elephants.

163

And broȝten to þe berfray alle þe bew clerkes
Þer þe standard stode, and stadded hem þer.
Þe best and þe britage and alle þe briȝt gere,
Chaire and chaundelers and charbokel stones,   590
Þe rolles þat þey redden on and alle þe riche bokes
Þey broȝt myd þe bischup þoȝ hym bale þouȝte.
Anon þe feyþles folke fayleden herte,
Tourned toward þe toun and Tytus hem after,
Felde of þe fals ferde in þe felde lefte   595
An hundred in here helmes myd his honde one.
Þe fals Jewes in þe felde fallen so þicke
As hail froward heuen, hepe ouer oþer,
So was þe bent ouerbrad, blody byrunne,
With ded bodies aboute alle þe brod vale.   600
Myȝt no stede doun stap bot on stele-wede,
Or on burne, or on beste, or on briȝt scheldes –
Þe multitude was so myche þat on þe molde lafte
Þer so many were mart, mereuail were ellis.
Ȝit were þe Romayns as rest as þey fram Rome come,   605
Vnryuen eche a renk and noȝt a ryng brosten,
Myȝt no berne on hem breke, better was neuere,

587 to] PDCUE, vnto A, *om.* L; berfray] PADUE, bastyle C, bischup
& L; þe(2)] PDCUE, his L, those A.   591 on] PADCUE, *om.* L.
592 þof] PADCUE, þou L.   595 Fellide] AUCE, Felles P, Fele LD.
602 or(2)] ADCUE, oþer L.   603 Þe . . . mych] DCUE, Þe
. . . mekill A, M. was þare myche P, So myche was þe m. L.   604 mart]
(*with* red *added above line*) L, merrede ADCUE, morte P.
606 Vnrevyn] A, Ronnen ouer L.   607 Might] PDE, May U, Ther was
C; no bierne] DU, no bone C, no body E, noght þaire brayne P; on hem
breke] DUE, broken C, bresten P; better was neuer] P, b. were þey n.
C, so boldely (bigly U) þei stode DUE; *line om.* A; L *has* Was no poynt
perschid of alle here pris armure.

587–8 The *berfray* is a large and well-provisioned siege-tower that
Vespasian has set up as his *standard*, here meaning 'headquarters'.
595–6 'Of the false (i.e. Jewish) army that remained in the field he
slaughtered a hundred in their helmets with his hand alone.'
599 *blody byrunne*: 'drenched with blood' – a common b-verse; e.g.
Parlement 62.
604 *mart*: ppl. of *merren*, 'impair, kill'.
606 *ryng*: i.e. of chain-mail.
607 'No man could break in on them, the situation was never better.' L

So Crist his kny3tes gan kepe tille Complyn tyme.
An hundred þousand helmes of þe heþen syde
Were fey fallen in þe felde, and no3t a freke scaped   610
Saue seuen þousand of þe somme þat to þe cité flowen,
And wonnen with mychel wo þe walles withynne.
Ledes lepen to anon, louken þe 3ates,
Barren hem bigly with boltes of yren,
Brayden vp brigges with brouden chaynes,   615
And portecolis with pine picchen to grounde.
Þei wynnen vp why3tly þe walles to kepe,
Fresche vnfounded folke, and grete defence made,
Tyeþ into tourres tonnes ful þicke
With grete stones of gret and of gray marble,   620
Kepten kenly with caste þe kernels alofte,
Quappen out querels by quarters attonys.
Þat oþer folke at þe fote freshly assayled
Tille eche dale with dewe was donked aboute;
Withdrowen hem fro þe diche dukes and oþer,   625
For þe caste was so kene þat come fram þe walles,
Comen forþe with the kyng clene as þey 3ede,
Wanted no3t o wye, ne non þat wounde hadde.

---

610 & noght a] PUE, that no A, not o DC, or þe L; freke] PADE, fi3t
L; shapid] PADCU, ended L.   612 wonnen] wan PADCU, wymmen
L.   616 pyne] ADCUE, pynnes P, pile L.   618 Fresch] PADCUE,
Frasche L.   619 thyk] PADCUE, manye L.   622 Quappen] Whappes
P, Warppis A, Quattid DE, Quarten L; owte quarells] ADCE, doune q.
P, q. out L; be] PAC, with L, *om.* DE.   626 For] PADCUE, *om.* L.
628 Wantid] PADCU, Wounded L; wounde] PAU, woundes C, wem L.

---

has an entirely different line, perhaps authentic, but perhaps rewritten to
avoid the defective reading that evidently puzzled the other scribes.
608 The source, too, mentions Compline, the last service of the day
following Evensong.
611–16 The Jews who escape into Jerusalem lock the city gates, pull up
the drawbridge and lower the portcullises. Lines 614–15 are very similar
to *Dest Troy* 10463–4.
618 *vnfounded*: 'untried' (from *fonden*); hence perhaps 'unwearied'.
622 *by quarters*: possibly 'in all directions'. For the a-verse, cf. *Wars*
2353, 'Quirys out quarrels, quappid thur3e mayles'.
623–4 The Romans at the foot of the wall attacked until evening.
628 'Not a man was missing, and none was wounded.'

Princes to here pauelouns passen on swyþe,
Vnarmen hem as tyt and alle þe ny3t resten 630
With wacche vmbe þe walles, to many wyes sorowe:
Þey wolle no3t þe heþen here þus harmeles be lafte.

As raþe as þe rede day ros on þe schye,
Bemes blewen abrod burnes to rise;
Þe kyng comaundeþ a cry þat comsed was sone 635
Þe ded bodies on þe bent bare for to make,
To spoyle þe spilt folke spare scholde none;
Geten girdeles and gere, gold and goode stones,
Byes, broches bry3t, besauntes riche,
Helmes hewen of gold, hamberkes noble; 640
Kesten ded vpon ded, was deil to byholde,
Made weyes ful wide, and to þe walles comen,
Assembleden at þe cité, a saut to bygynne,
Folke ferlich þycke at þe foure 3ates.
Þey bro3ten toures of tre þat þey taken hadde, 645
A3en euereche 3ate 3arken hem hey,
Bygonnen at þe grettist a garrite to rere,
Grayþed vp fro þe grounde on twelue grete postes.
It was wonderlich wide and wro3t vpon hy3te,
Fyue hundred in frounte to fi3ten at þe walles; 650
Hardy men vpon hi3t hyen at þe Grecys
And bigonnen with bir þe borow to assayle;

632 þus] PADCUE, so L.   633 As rathe] D, Sone LACUE, Onone P;
rose on] PCE, rosen LD, rawede and rase one A.   634 blewen]
PADCU, blowen L; on brode] PADC, anon L; ryse] AD, arise LC,
rayse PUE.   636 bent] PA, bonke LDCU, feeld E.   640 nobill]
PADCU, riche E, manye L.   642 wayes full wyde] ADCU, wide weyes
L.   643 a sawte] PCE, assawte ADU, saut L.   648 Graythid] PDU,
Groded L, Getyn AC.   649 It] PADCUE, He L; &] PACU, *om.*
LDE.   651 highte] A, heght P, hye DUE, haste L.

632 Most of the mss. mark a major division after this line.
634 'All around trumpets summoned men to get up.'
645–8 The Romans place against the city gates the wooden towers that
had been carried by the beasts in the Jewish army, and then erect a
siege-tower against the chief gate.
651 *vpon hi3t*: 'quickly' (*MED highthe*); see L's reading.

Quarels flambande of fure flowen in harde,
And arwes vnarwely with attyr enuenymyd
Þey taysen at þe toures and tachen on þe Jewes;   655
Þroȝ kernels cacchen here deþ many kene burnes.
Brenten and beten doun bildes ful þycke,
Brosten þe britages and þe brode toures;
By þat was many bold burne þe burwe to assayle,
Þe hole batail boun aboute þe brode walles   660
Þat were byg at a bir and bycchet to wynne,
Wondere heye to byholde with holwe diches vndere,
Heye bonked aboute vpon boþe halues,
And wonder wicked to wynne bot ȝif wyles helpe.
Bowmen atte bonke benden here gere,   665
Schoten vp scharply at þe schene walles
With arwes and arblastes and alle þat harme myȝt,
To affray þe folke þat defence made.
Þe Jewes werien þe walles with wyles ynowe,
Hote playande picche amonge þe peple ȝeten,   670
Brennande leed and brynston, barels fulle,
Schoten schynande doun riȝt as schyre water.
Waspasian wendeþ fram þe walles wariande hem harde;
Oþer busked were boun, benden engynes,
Kesten at þe kernels and clustred toures,   675
And monye der daies worke dongen to grounde.
By þat wriȝtes han wroȝt a wonder stronge pale

653 in] PADC, out L.   654 vnarghely] A, arwely L, egrely P.
655 Þai] PAC, *om*. LD; &] PADC, *om*. L.   657 beldis] AD,
byggynges C, bretage P, þat bilde was L; full] A, wel L, so DC, *om*. P.
661 at a] C, at þe D, os a U, & LA, *om*. P; birre] DCU, bare A,
brode L, *om*. P.   663 abowte] ADCU, aboue LP; halues] PADC, sydes
L.   664 & wonder] PADCU, Riȝt L.   666 at] PADC, to LE.
670 playand] PA, blowande L.   671 Brynnand] PADCUE, Brennen
L.   673 harde] PAD, alle LCU.

654 Cf. *Wars* 1513 below, and in general compare the description of the
siege there.
659 'That was the signal for many bold men to attack the city.'
674 'Other men were made ready, they bent catapults.'
677–88 The Romans put up a stockade around the city, fill the moat
with corpses and dam up the city aqueduct. Moe (1970:151), compares
the French source.

Alle aboute þe burwe with bastiles manye,
Þat no freke myȝt vmfonge withouten fele harmes,
Ne no segge vndere sonne myȝt fram þe cité passe;   680
Suþ dommyn þe diches with þe ded corses,
Crammen hit myd karayn þe kirnels vnder
Þat þe stynk of þe stewe myȝt strike ouer þe walles
To coþe þe corsed folke þat hem kepe scholde;
Þe cors of þe condit þat comen to þe toun   685
Stoppen euereche a streem þer any strande ȝede
With stockes and stones and stynkande bestes,
Þat þey no water myȝt wynne þat weren enclosed.
Waspasian tourneþ to his tente with Titus and oþer,
Commaundeþ consail anon on Cayphas to sitte,   690
What deþ by dome þat he dey scholde,
With þe lettered ledes þat þey lauȝte hadde.
Domesmen vpon dese demeden swyþe
Þat ech freke were quyk fleyn þe felles of clene,
First to be on þe bent with blonkes ydrawe,   695
And suþ honget on an hep vpon heye galwes,
Þe feet to þe firmament alle folke to byholden,
With hony vpon ech halue þe hydeles anoynted,
Corres and cattes with claures ful scharpe

679 Þat . . . harmes] P, *line om.* L; myght vmfonge] P, vnfongede
A, m. found DE; fele h.] P, fresshe h. DCUE, fethyrhames A.
680 Ne] PADU, Þat L.   683 stewe] PAC, steem LU, stench
DE.   685 to þe] PADCUE, to L.   686 streem] LADCUE, strande P;
strande] A, strem LP, spryng DCE.   691 What] PDCUE, Whatekyns
A, With L.   693 dese] PADE, deþes LC.   695 Firste] PADCE,
Þen LU; þe] PAC, a L; ydrawen] ADCE, drawen PE, todrawe L.
698 halfe] PADU, side LE.

684 *coþe*: 'bring sickness to'. Illnesses such as the plague were thought
to be spread by infected atmosphere, and citizens were especially
advised to avoid the stench of mortuaries.
688 'So that they who were enclosed (in the city) might not get any
water.'
692 The clerks of ll. 587 and 705.
693–702 Moe (1970:152) quotes the source of this hideous passage.
694 'That each man should be flayed alive so that the skins were entirely
off.'
698 *þe hydeles*: probably 'those without hide', though A's reading
hiddills means 'concealed parts, crevices'.

Foure cacched and knyt to Cayphases þeyes,   700
Twey apys at his armes to angren hym more,
Þat renten þe rawe flesche vpon rede peces.
So was he pyned fram prime with persched sides
Tille þe sonne doun sett in þe sommere tyme;
Þe lered men of þe lawe a litel bynyþe   705
Weren tourmented on a tre, topsail walten,
Knyt to euerech clerke kene corres twey,
Þat alle þe cité myȝt se þe sorow þat þey dryuen.
Þe Jewes walten ouer þe walles for wo at þat tyme,
Seuen hundred slow hemself for sorow of here clerkes,   710
Somme hent here heere and fram þe hed pulled,
And somme doun for deil dasched to grounde.
Þe kyng lete drawen hem doun whan þey dede were,
Bade a bole-fure betyn to brennen þe corses,
Kesten Cayphas þeryn and his clerkes alle   715
And brenten euereche bon into browne askes,
Suþ went to þe walle on þe wynde syde
And alle abrod on þe burwe blewen þe powdere.
'Þer is doust for ȝour drynke!' a duke to hem crieþ,
And bade hem bibe of þat broþ for þe bischop soule.   720
Þus ended coursed Cayphas and his clerkes twelf,
Al tobrused myd bestes, brent at þe laste,
In tokne of tresoun and trey þat þey wroȝt
Whan Crist þrow here conseil was cacched to deþ.

---

700 cacchyd] PADU, kagges L.   704 sett] PACU, souȝt L, syed D; þe]
PADCU, *om.* L.   712 doune] PADCUE, *om.* L; daschede] ADCUE,
daschen P, daschande L.   713 doune] PADCUE, adoun L.   715 all]
PADCU, twelf L.   716 into] PAC, into þe LD, to the U.   719 for]
LP, to ADCUE; duk] PADCUE, doun L.   720 bebe] PAD, bible L;
bisshop] PAU, bischopes LDCE.   721 xij] PDCUE, alle LA.   722 *line
om.* PDCUE, *rewritten* A.   723 thay] ADCUE, he L.   724 her]
DCUE, þaire PA, his L.

706 *topsail walten*: i.e. head over heels; cf. *Dest Troy* 1219, *topsailes
ouer*.
713 *lete drawen hem*: 'had them taken'.
720 *þe bischop*: (gen.) 'Caiaphas'.

John Clerk: THE DESTRUCTION OF TROY

INTRODUCTION

Manuscript

The only text of the poem is that in Glasgow Univ. Lib. Hunterian MS. 388, copied in about 1540 by Thomas Chetham of Nuthurst, Lancs., bailiff of the Earls of Derby; see Luttrell (1958). Despite its late date, this appears to be a remarkably faithful copy, apart from a few gaps and some disordering of the last quires.

Author, place and date

The initial letters of the first 22 chapters give the author's name as John Clerk of Whalley, Lancs.; see Turville-Petre (1988). This is possibly the poet mentioned by Dunbar in 'Timor mortis conturbat me', l. 58. The list of contents in the Hunterian ms. promises also to reveal the 'nome of the knight that causet it to be made' – presumably one of the Lancashire gentry – but the promise is not fulfilled in the text as it now stands.

Clerk twice alludes to 'Troylus' (ll. 1487–8, 8053–4) in contexts that probably refer to Chaucer's *TC*, written in *c.* 1385, suggesting that *Dest Troy* was composed at a time when Chaucer's poem was well known; see Benson (1974). Parallels with *Siege J* (*ante* 1400) have commonly been taken to indicate the indebtedness of that poem to *Dest Troy*; see Day and Steele's edition, EETS 188, and Lawton (1982:5). The reverse is, however, much more probable.

John Clerk: The Destruction of Troy

Source

Clerk follows with reasonable fidelity the Latin *Historia Destructionis Troiae* by Guido de Columnis, completed in 1287; a work that became extremely popular, in part because of the belief in the Trojan ancestry of the British and other Europeans (see *SGGK* 1–15, *Wynnere* 1–2). References to Guido are to the edition by Griffin (1936). The nature and influence of Guido's work are discussed by Benson (1980:3–31), and in the introduction to the translation by Meek (1974). Clerk sometimes expands on Guido, particularly in scenes of violent action, but almost as often he abbreviates, dropping many ponderous classical allusions. Even so, at over 14,000 lines, *Dest Troy* is much the longest of all alliterative poems. For analysis of Clerk's method of translation, see Benson (1980:42–66) and Lawton (1980).

BIBLIOGRAPHY

Editions

G. A. Panton and D. Donaldson, *The 'Gest Hystoriale' of the Destruction of Troy*, EETS 39 and 56 (1869–74)
K. Sisam, *Fourteenth Century Verse and Prose* (Oxford, 1921:pp. 68–75) (ll. 1–98, 12463–547)

Source

N. E. Griffin, *Guido de Columnis, Historia Destructionis Troiae* (Cambridge, Mass., 1936)
M. E. Meek, *Guido delle Colonne, Historia Destructionis Troiae* (Bloomington, Indiana, 1974) (translation)

Studies

C. D. Benson, 'A Chaucerian allusion and the date of the alliterative "Destruction of Troy"', *NQ*, 219 (1974:206–7)
C. D. Benson, *The History of Troy in Middle English Literature*, (Woodbridge, 1980)
D. A. Lawton, '*The Destruction of Troy* as translation from Latin prose: aspects of form and style', *SN*, 52 (1980:259–70)
C. A. Luttrell, 'Three north-west midland manuscripts', *Neophilologus*, 42 (1958:38–50)
T. Turville-Petre, 'The author of *The Destruction of Troy*', *MÆ*, 57 (1988:264–9)

John Clerk: THE DESTRUCTION OF TROY

[The Greeks sack Troy, kill its king Laomedon, and abduct his daughter Hesione. Priam, son of Laomedon, is away from the city besieging a castle.]

Book V

Now as þis kyng vmbe the castell lay closing abute	
With his folke all in fere and his fyn childur,	1510
He was enfourmyt of þat fare and of his fader dethe,	
How his towne was takon and tiruyt to ground,	
His suster sesyd and soght into syde londis,	
His knightis downe kyld vnto cold vrthe.	
Soche sikyng and sorow sanke in his hert,	1515
With pyté and complaint, pyne for to here,	
He toke vp his tentis and the towne leuyt,	
Teght hym vnto Troy with tene þat he hade,	
Segh the buyldyngis brent and beton to ground.	
Soche wo for þat werke þan þe wegh thowlit	1520
Þat all his wongys were wete for weping of terus,	
Thre dayes þroly with thricchyng of hondys,	
And drowpet for dole as he degh wold.	
Þen he sesit o syther and his sorow voidit,	
Mendit his mode and his mynd stablit,	1525
Toke councell in the case and his care leuyt,	
The styfe towne to restowre and so stronng make	
For daunger and drede of enny derfe enmys;	
Gate masons full mony þat mykull fete couthe,	
Wise wrightis to wale, werkys to caste,	1530
Qwariours qweme, qwaint men of wit,	
Mynours of marbull ston and mony oþer thingis.	
Sone he raght vpon rowme, rid vp þe dykis,	

1518 hym] hom.

1509 *þis kyng*: Priam. *His suster* (l. 1513) is Hesione.
1524 *o syther*: 'later, after that' (*OED sithre*), as again in l. 13861. The earlier editors print *of sychen*.
1530 *to wale*: 'in abundance'; cf. *Erkenwald* 73n.
1533 *raght vpon rowme*: 'cleared a wide space'; *MED rechen* v.(1).

172

Serchit vp the soile þere þe citie was,
And byld vp a bygge towne of þe bare vrthe,   1535
In the nome of Neptune þat was a noble god.

The Discripcoun of Troye

This cité was sothely, to serche it aboute,
Þre jorneys full jointly to joyne hom by dayes;
Was neuer sython vnder son cité so large,
Ne neuer before, as we fynd, fourmyt in vrthe   1540
Non so luffly on to loke in any lond oute;
The walles vp wroght, wonder to se –
With grippes full grete was þe ground takon –
Bothe syker and sad þat selly were þik,
Fro the vrthe vpward vne of a mesure.   1545
Of the walle for to wete to þe wale top,
Twa hundrethe cubettis be coursse accounttid full euyn
Þat of marbill was most fro þe myddes vp,
Of diuers colours to ken craftely wroght,
Þat were shene for to shew and of shap noble;   1550
Mony toures vp tild þe toune to defende,
Wroght vp with the walle as þe werke rose,
On negh to anoþer nobly deuyset,
Large on to loke, louely of shap.
In the sercle of the cité were sex faire ȝates   1555
For entre and yssue and ease of þe pepull;
The furst and the fairest fourmet was Dardan,
Tricerda, Thetas, Troiana, þo foure,
Anchinordes, Hylias, heght þe two other,
With grete toures vmbtilde and torettis aboute,   1560
Well wroght for the werre, wacches o lofte.
Ymagry ouer all amyt þere was
Of bestis and babery breme to beholde,

1547 Twa hundrethe] CC.

1536 The dedication of Troy to Neptune is derived by Guido from
Virgil, *Aeneid* iii. 3.
1538 'Three *jorneys* altogether to reckon them up by the days.' A *jorney*
is the distance travelled in a day.
1546 'To know about (i.e. to tell you about) the wall . . .'
1547 *be coursse*: 'row by row (of masonry)'.

Bost out of þe best þe byg toures vmbe;
The wallis in werre wikked to assaile,   1565
With depe dikes and derke doubull of water.
Within the citie, forsothe, semly to ken,
Grete palis of prise, plenty of houses,
Wele bild all aboute on the best wise.
The werst walle for to wale, þere any wegh dwelt,   1570
Was faurty cubettis by coursse, to count fro the vrthe,
And all of marbill was made with meruellus bestis
Of lions and libardis and other laithe wormes.
The stretis were streght and of a stronge brede,
For ymur and aire opon in þe myddis;   1575
By the sydes, forsothe, of sotell deuyse,
Was archet full abilly for aylyng of shoures,
Pight vp with pilers all of playn marbill,
Weghis in to walke for wetyng of rayn.
There were stallis by þe strete stondyng for pupull,   1580
Werkmen in to won and þaire ware shewe,
Bothe to selle and to se as þaimselfe lyked,
Of all þe craftes to ken as þaire course askit:
Goldsmythes, glouers, girdillers noble,
Sadlers, souters, semsters fyn,   1585
Taliours, telers, turners of vessell,
Wrightis, websters, walkers of clothe,
Armurers, arowsmythis with axes of werre,
Belmakers, bokebynders, brasiers fyn,
Marchandis, monymakers, mongers of fyche,   1590
Parnters, painters, pynners also,
Bochers, bladsmythis, baxters amonge,

1575 opon] vpon.

1564 'Carved in the finest manner about the strong towers.'
1566 The town had a double moat.
1570 'The least impressive wall one could pick out (for comment) . . .'
1579 'For people to walk in to prevent (*for*) wetting from the rain.'
1584–1600 This enumeration of trades reads like a list of the medieval
guilds, such as those of York in *Records of Early English Drama: York*,
ed. A. F. Johnston and M. Rogerson (Manchester, 1979:i, 17–27).
Guido, p. 48, has a list of the same length, but in many cases Clerk has
substituted contemporary trades.

Ferrours, flecchours, fele men of crafte,
Tauerners, tapsters all the toune ouer,
Sporiors, spicers, spynners of clothe, 1595
Cokis, condlers, coriours of ledur,
Carpentours, cotelers, coucheours fyn,
With barburs bigget in bourders of the stretes,
With all maister-men þat on molde dwellis,
Onestly enabit in entris aboute. 1600
Thurgh myddis þe mekill toune meuyt a water
And disseuert the cité, þat Xanthus hight.
There were bild by the bankis of þe brode stremes
Mylnes full mony, made for to grynde,
For solas of the cité þat suet hom to. 1605
The water by wisshyng went vnder houses,
Gosshet through godardys and other grete vautes,
And clensit by course all þe clene cité
Of filth and of fen through fletyng bynethe.
In ensample of this cité, sothely to telle, 1610
Rome on a ryuer rially was set,
Enabet by Eneas after full longe,
Tild vpon Tiber, after Troy like.
Priamus pertly the pupull ylkon,
Þat longit to his lond and logit o fer, 1615
Gert sue to þe cité, sothely, to dwelle,
And fild it with folke, fuerse was þe nowmber
Of lordis of þe lond and oþer lesse pupull.
In þat cité, forsothe, as saith vs the story,
Mony gamnes were begonnen þe grete for to solas: 1620
The chekker was choisly þere chosen þe first,
The draghtes, the dyse and oþer dregh gamnes,
Soche soteltie þai sought to solas hom with;
The tables, the top, tregetre also,
And in the moneth of May mekill þai vsit 1625

1606 *by wisshyng*: 'by guidance', i.e. through a pipe.
1621–4 Guido, p. 49, mentions chess, dice, tragedy and comedy.
Probably *tregetre*, 'magic' (OFr *tresgeterie*), is an error for *tregedie*,
'tragedy' (OFr *tregedie*).
1625–7 Guido writes of 'circus games and the May festivals'. May
games, with their 'summer queens', were widely popular in England, and

With floures and fresshe bowes fecchyng of somer;
Somur-qwenes and qwaintans and oþer qwaint gamnes
There foundyn was first, and yet ben forthe haunted.

[Priam resolves to take revenge on the Greeks by abducting one of their ladies to be exchanged for Hesione. Paris, son of Priam, urges that he should be the one to do this, and recounts a propitious dream.]

Book VI

The Visyon of Paris

'Hyt is not meuyt of mynde ne mony day past   2340
Syn I was lent in a londe þat is lese Ynde,
Your biddyng to obey as my blithe fader.
In the season of somer er the sun rose,
As it come into Canser and be course entred,
Hit fell me on a Fryday to fare vppon huntyng,   2345
With myrthes in the mornyng and mony other pupull.
All went we to wod the wilde for to cacche,
And laburt full long, laytyng aboute;
Till mydday and more myght we not fynde
For to wyn as for waithe in þat wode brode,   2350
Tyll hit entrid to euyn and euynsong was past.
Þen it fell me by fortune, fer on a playne,
As I beheld þurgh a holte, a hert for to se
Þat pastured on a playn pertly hym one,

---

the *fecchyng of somer* ('inductio Maii') was condemned by Robert
Grosseteste as early as 1244. See E. K. Chambers, *The Medieval Stage*
(Oxford, 1903:i, 89–181). For illustrations of tilting at the quintain, see
Poole (1958:pl. 133).
2341 *lese Ynde*: 'India Minor', as in Guido (p. 61).
2343–78 With this description of a summertime hunt leading to a dream-
vision, cf. the opening of *Parlement*. In particular, cf. l. 2343 with
Parlement 2.
2344–5 The sun is in the sign of Cancer in midsummer; see Trevisa,
Properties, 532. Friday, the day of Venus, was considered unlucky; see
Chaucer, *CT* vii. 3341–52.
2350 'Anything to catch in the way of game . . .'
2351 *euynsong*: 'time of Vespers', hence simply 'evening'.

And I cast me be course to cum hym before.   2355
Fast fro my felowes and fuersly I rode,
Euery lede hade I lost and left me behynde,
And swaruyt out swiftly, might no swayne folo.
So I wilt in the wod and the wild holtis
Fer fro my feres, and no freike herde   2360
Till I drowgh till a derke and the dere lost.
He þrong into þicke wod, þester within,
For thornes and tres I tynt hym belyue;
Than I sesit of my sute and softly doun light,
Beheld to my horse þat hote was of rennyng,   2365
All swoty for swyme and his swift course
That stremys from hym straght and stert vpon þe erthe,
And dropis as dew or a danke rayne.
All wery I wex and wyll of my gate,
And raght to my reyne, richet o lenght,   2370
Bound vp my blonke to a bogh euyn,
And graithed me to ground as me gode liked,
In a shadow of shene tres and of shyre floures,
Ouerhild for þe hete, hengyng with leues.
My bow þat was bigge and my bright qwyuer,   2375
Arowes and other geire atled I anon,
Pight as a pyllow put vnder my hede,
And sleghly on slepe I slypped belyue.
I drow into a dreme, and dreghly me thought
That Mercury the mykill god in þe mene tyme   2380
Thre goddes hade gotten goyng hym bye
That come in his company clere to beholde:
Venus the worthy, þat wemen ay plesyn,
And Palades with pure wit þat passes all other,
And Jono, a justis of joyes in erthe.   2385
These ladis he lefte a litill besyde,
And sothely hymseluyn said me thies wordis:
"To the, Paris, I appere with þre prise goddis
That are stad in a strife here stondyng besyde,

2370 'And caught hold of my rein, pulled it out to its full length'; see
MED richen v.(1), 3(a).
2372 *graithed me*: 'threw myself'.
2384 *Palades*: Pallas Athene, goddess of wisdom.
2389 *stad in a strife*: 'involved in a dispute'.

177

And haue put hom full plainly in þi pure wit   2390
To deme as þe dere thinke and þai in dede holde,
When trouth is determynet and tried by the.
Thus it befell hom by fortune, faire as I telle,
As þai sate in hor solas samyn at a fest,
Ane appull of a new shap þat neuer man hade sen   2395
Coyntly by craft was cast hom amonge.
Hit was made of a mater meruell to shew,
With gret letturs of Grew grauyn þere vmbe;
To rede it by reson renkis might se
That the fairest of þo fele shull þat fe haue.   2400
And duly this dome haue þai done o þiselfe,
And put on þi person hor pese for to make.
The is hight for to haue highly by me
A mede of þo mighty to mend the withall,
As in rewarde for to ricche of hir þat right has,   2405
That þe faithfully shall falle and not faile of.
Yf þou juge it to Jono this joye shall þou haue,
To be mightiest on molde and most of all other;
This ho grauntis þe to gyffe of hir good wille.
And if þou put it to Palades as for þi prise lady,   2410
Thou shal be wisest of wit, this wete þou for sothe,
And know all the conyng þat kyndly is for men.
Iff þou deme it in dede duly to Venus,
Hit shall falle the to fortune þe fairest of Grice
To haue and to holde to þi hegh mede."   2415
When Mercury hade menyt this mater to ende
And graunt me þise gyftis, hit gladit my hert.
I onswaret hym esely euyn vponon:
"This dome is in dowte to demyng of me
The certayn to say, but I hom segh naked   2420
And waitid hom wele, þo worthy togedur,

2390 *in þi pure wit*: 'at your absolute discretion'.
2395 *Ane appull* alliterates *a nappull*.
2402 *þi person*: 'you'. 'And depend on you to make their peace.'
2403–6 'Through me you are firmly promised to receive from these
powerful ladies a gift that will greatly benefit you, as a reward to enrich
you from the lady who wins the judgement, (a reward) that will faithfully
be given to you and not be withheld.'
2414 'It will befall you as fortune . . .'; i.e. 'your fortune will be . . .'.

The bodies aboute with my bright ene.
Than shuld I full sone say as me thought,
And telle you the truthe, and tary no lengur."
Then Mercury with mowthe þus menit agayne:
"Be it done euyn in dede as þi dissire is." 2425
Than naknet anon full naitly were all
And broght to me bare; I blusshet hom on,
I waited hom witterly as me wele thoght,
All feturs in fere of þo fre ladys.
Hit semit me for certayn and for sothe dom 2430
Þat Venus the vertuus was verely the fairest,
Most exulent of other and onest to wale,
And I duli be dom demyt hir the appull,
And ho fayn of þat faire, and frely me het
That the mede shuld be myne þat Mercury saide. 2435
Þen wightly þai went; I wackonet with þat,
And gripet my gayre and my gate helde.
Now howpe ʒe not hertely þat þis hegh goddis
Will faithly fulfille þaire forward to ende?
I am certen and sure, be I sent forthe, 2440
The brightest lady to bryng of þo brode londys.
Now, meke fader and mylde, þis message to do,
Ye deme your dere son, and dresse me þerfore.
Hit shall glade you full godely agaynes your gret anger,
And fille you with faynhed, in faithe I you hete.' 2445
When he told hade his tale tomly to þe ende,
He enclinet the kyng and carpit no more.

2442 brightest] brightiest.

2423 *shuld*: for the alliteration Clerk uses the northern form *suld*.
2435 *ho fayn*: 'she was glad'.

John Clerk: The Destruction of Troy

[Troy is destroyed, and the priestess Cassandra is dragged from the
temple of Minerva by Ajax Telamonius. Many of the Greeks, loaded
with booty, decide to return home.]

Book XXXI

Hyt fell thus by fortune, þe fairest of þe yere
Was past to the point of the pale wintur;
Heruest with the heite and the high sun   12465
Was comyn into colde with a course low,
Trees thurgh tempestis tynd hade þaire leues,
And briddes abatid of hor brem songe;
The wynde of the west wackenet aboue,
Blowyng full bremly o the brode ythes,   12470
The clere aire ouercast with cloudys full thicke,
With mystis full merke mynget with showres,
Flodes were felle thurgh fallyng of rayne,
And wintur vpwacknet with his wete aire.
The gret nauy of the Grekis and the gay kyngis   12475
Were put in a purpos to pas fro the toune;
Sore longit þo lordis hor londys to se,
And dissiret full depely, doutyng no wedur.
Þai counted no course of the cold stormys,
No the perellis to passe of þe pale windes: 12480
Hit happit hom full hard in a hond-qwile,
And mony of þo mighty to misse of hor purpos.
Thus tho lordes in hor longyng laghton þe watur,
Shotton into ship mony shene knightis,
With the tresowre of þai token before.   12485
Relikis full rife and miche ranke godes.
Clere was the course of the cold flodis,

12476 Were] We.

12467–74 The passage is analysed by L. Benson, *Art and Tradition in Sir
Gawain and the Green Knight* (New Brunswick, N.J., 1965:176–7). For
comparison with other alliterative poems and with Guido's account, see
N. Jacobs, 'Alliterative storms: a topos in Middle English', *Speculum*, 47
(1972:695–719). The scene in *Patience* 137–64, is especially to be
compared.
12476 *Were put in a purpos*: 'were set on a plan of action', i.e. 'decided'.

180

And the firmament faire as fell for the wintur;
Thai past on the pale se, puld vp hor sailes,
Hadyn bir at þaire backe and the bonke leuyt.   12490
Foure dayes bydene and hor du nyghtis
Full soundly þai sailed with seasonable windes;
The fyft day fuersly fell at the none,
Sodonly the softe winde vnsoberly blew,
A myste and a merkenes myngit togedur,   12495
A thoner and a thicke rayne þrublet in the skewes
With an ugsom noise, noy for to here,
All flasshet in a fire the firmament ouer,
Was no light but a laite þat launchit aboue,
Hit skirmyt in the skewes with a skyre low,   12500
Thurgh the claterand clowdes clos to the heuyn,
As the welkyn shuld walt for wodenes of hete.
With blastes full bigge of the breme wyndes,
Walt vp the waghes vpon wan hilles,
Stith was the storme, stird all the shippes,   12505
Hoppit on hegh with heste of the flodes,
The sea was vnsober, sondrit the nauy,
Walt ouer waghes and no way held,
Depertid the pepull – pyne to behold –
In costis vnkowthe, cut down þaire sailes,   12510
Ropis al torochit, rent vp the hacches,
Topcastell ouerturnyt, takellis were lost.
The night come onone, noye was the more!
All the company cleane of the kyng Telamon,
With þaire shippes full shene and þe shire godis,   12515
Were brent in the bre with the breme lowe
Of the leymond laite þat launchit fro heuyn,
And euyn drownet in the depe dukis and other.

12488 *as fell for*: lit. 'as was appropriate to', i.e. 'as much as could be
expected in'.
12490 This line is identical to *Siege J* 290.
12496 Cf. *Siege J* 532. *þrublet*: 'caused commotion'? The verb is twice
used in *Cleanness*, 504, 879, apparently meaning 'jostle'.
12497 The word-division in the ms., *a nugsom*, points to the alliteration.
12508 '. . . and kept to no fixed path.'

Oelius Ajax, as aunter befell,
Was stad in the storme with the stith windes,   12520
With his shippes full shene and the shire godes;
Thrifty and þriuaund, thretty and two
There were brent on the buerne with the breme low,
And all the freikis in the flode floterand aboue.
Hymseluyn in the sea sonkyn belyue,   12525
Swalprit and swam with swyngyng of armys;
ȝet he launchet to lond and his lyf hade,
Bare of his body, bretfull of water,
In the slober and the slicche slongyn to londe,
Ther he lay if hym list, the long night ouer,   12530
Till the derke was done and the day sprang.
And than wonen of waghes, with wo as þai might,
Þan sum of his sort þat soght were to lond
Laited þaire lord on the laund syde,
If hit fell hym by fortune the flodes to passe.   12535
Þan found thai the freike in the fome lye,
And comford hym kyndly as þaire kyd lord,
With worship and wordis wan hym to fote;
Bothe failet hym the fode and the fyne clothes.
Thus þaire goddis with gremþ with þe Grekis fore,   12540
Mighty Mynerua of malis full grete,
For Telamon in tene tid for to pull
Cassandra the cleane out of hir cloise temple.
Thus hit fell hom by fortune of a foule end

12530 *follows* 12531 *at top of fol. 203b, but catchwords for* 12530 *on fol.
203a.*   12535 hym] hom.   12540 gremþ] gremy.   12541 Mynerua]
Mynera.

12519 The confusion of Ajax Oileus and Ajax Telamonius who took
Cassandra from the temple (ll. 12542–3) is inherited from Guido. See
Benson (1980:51–2).
12522–3 '. . . thirty-two ships were burnt on the sea . . .'; as in Guido
(p. 244).
12530 *if hym list*: 'whether (or not) it pleased him'. For the full
expression, see Chaucer, *LGW* 2312–3.
12531 Parallels to this stereotyped line are discussed by Turville-Petre
(1977a:86).
12540 *fore*: 'acted, dealt', pa.t. of *faren*.
12544 'Thus it happened that a terrible end befell them.'

For greuyng þaire goddes in hor gret yre.   12545
Oftsythes men sayn, and sene is of olde,
Þat all a company is cumbrit for a cursed shrewe.

THE WARS OF ALEXANDER

INTRODUCTION

Manuscripts

There are two manuscripts: Bodley MS. Ashmole 44 (A) gives the text of ll. 1–722 and 846–5803; Trinity College, Dublin, MS. 213 (D) contains only ll. 678–3424 and 3485–553. The end of the poem is lost. The edited text is based on A, except for ll. 723–40, extant only in D. Both mss. are northern copies from the second half of the fifteenth century. D, which also contains an A-text of *Piers Plowman*, is from Durham; see Doyle (1982:99–100). There are traces of a NWMidl dialect behind the northernisms, and it is probable that the author, of whom nothing is known, came from Lancs.

Verse-form

The poem is divided into passus or chapters, probably 28 in the complete text, with a half-way break at the end of passus 14. Each passus is subdivided into regular 24-line paragraphs, marked here by indentation, and each paragraph is made up of six four-line units, here indicated, where appropriate, by the punctuation. See further, Duggan (1977). The alliterative pattern is regular throughout, though this is sometimes obscured by error in the mss. The significance to the editor of this regular organization is discussed by Turville-Petre (1980 and 1987a).

Source

The Wars of Alexander is translated from the Latin prose *Historia de Preliis*, a late twelfth-century revision of a work ultimately derived from the Greek account of Pseudo-Callisthenes; see Duggan (1976). In general the poet follows his source closely, but seldom slavishly; comparison shows how the process of translation results in a wonderful metamorphosis of a sober (indeed dull) Latin history into a vividly exciting tale of marvels and adventure, using an extraordinary range of vocabulary. See Lawton (1981), and, for an appreciation of the poem's great qualities, see Turville-Petre (1977a:94–104). In these notes, quotations from the source are based on the text in St John's College, Cambridge, MS 184.

BIBLIOGRAPHY

Editions

W. W. Skeat, *The Wars of Alexander*, EETS ES 47 (1886)
H. N. Duggan and T. Turville-Petre, *The Wars of Alexander*, EETS SS 10 (1989)

Studies

H. N. Duggan, 'The source of the Middle English *The Wars of Alexander*', *Speculum*, 51 (1976:624–36)
H.N. Duggan, 'Strophic patterns in Middle English alliterative poetry', *MP*, 74 (1977:223–47)
D. A. Lawton, 'The Middle English alliterative *Alexander A* and *C*: form and style in translation from Latin prose', *SN*, 53 (1981:259–69)
T. Turville-Petre, 'Emendation on grounds of alliteration in *The Wars of Alexander*', *ES*, 61 (1980:302–17)
T. Turville-Petre, 'Editing *The Wars of Alexander*', in *Manuscripts and Texts*, ed. D. Pearsall (Cambridge, 1987:143–60)

THE WARS OF ALEXANDER

[The Egyptian magician Anectanabus sleeps with Queen Olympias while her husband Philip of Macedon is away in battle. Philip, having dreamed that Olympias will bear a child conceived by the god Ammon, returns to Macedon, where Alexander is born amid storms and earthquakes.]

Passus III

Þis barne quen he borne was, as me þe boke tellis,
Miȝt wele aprefe for his aport to any prince oute,
Bot of þe lyfe þat he liȝt off he like was to nane,
Nouþire of fetour ne of face to fadire ne to modyre.   600
Þe fax on his faire hede was ferly to schawe,
Large lyons lockis þat lange ere and scharpe,
With grete glesenand eȝen grymly he lokis,
Þat ware as blyckenand briȝt as blesand sternes.
Ȝit ware þai sett vnsamen of serelypy hewys,   605
Þe tane to breue at a blisch as blak as a cole,
As any ȝare ȝeten gold ȝalow was þe tothire,
And he wald-eȝed was as þe writt schewys.
Ȝit, it tellis me þis tale, þe tethe in his hede
Was as bitand breme as any bare tuskis;   610
His steuyn stiffe was and steryn þat stonayd many,
And as a lyon he lete quen he loude romys.
His fell fygoure and his fourme fully betakend
Þe prowis and þe grete pryse þat he apreuyd eftire,
His hardynes, his hyndelaike and his hettir myȝtis,   615
Þe wirschip þat he wan quen he wex eldire.
Þan sembled his syb men, be sent of þam all,
To consaile of þis kyng son how þai him call suld,
And so him neuyned was þe name, of his next frendis,
Alexsandire þe athill, be allirs acorde.   620

611 and] *om.* A.

597–616 This description of Alexander is considerably expanded from the *Historia de Preliis.*
599 'But he was like none of the people that he sprang from.'
619 *of his next frendis*: 'by his closest relatives'.

Þan was he lede furthe belyfe to lere at þe scole,
As sone as to þat sapient himself was of elde,
Onane vnto Arystotill þat was his awen maistir,
And one of þe coronest clerkis þat euir knew lettir.
Þan was he broȝt to a benke, a boke in his hand,   625
And faste by his enfourmer was fettild his place;
For it come noȝt a kyng son, ȝe knaw wele, to sytt
Doune in margon and molle emange othire schrewis.
Sone wex he wittir and wyse and wondir wele leres,
Sped him in a schort space to spell and to rede,   630
And seþen to gramere he gase, as þe gyse wald,
And þat has he all hale in a hand-quyle.
In foure or in fyfe ȝere he ferre was in lare
Þan othire at had bene þare elleuyn wyntir;
Þat he suld passe him in þat plite vnpussible semed,   635
Bot at God will at gaa furth qua may agaynstande?
In absens of Arystotill, if any of his feris
Raged with him vnridly or rofe him with harme,
Him wald he kenely on þe croune knok with his tablis,
Þat all tobrest wald þe bordis and þe blode folowe.   640
If any scolere in þe scole his skorne at him makis,
He skapis him full skathely bot if he skyp bettir;
Þus with his feris he faȝt, as I fynd wreten,
As wele in lettir and in lare as any laike ellis.
    Þus skilfull lange he scolaid and þe scole vsed   645
Till he was euyn of eld elleuyn wyntir,
He had na pere in na place, þat proued so his tyme,
For þe principalté of all þe pake he of aprefe wynnys.

626 enfourmer] enfourme A.   634 elleuyn] seuynte A.

621–52 The source says simply that Alexander struggled with his schoolmates both in letters and words, but the poet has a more realistic view of the struggles of schoolboys. In addition he gives Alexander an education appropriate to an aristocratic boy in the Middle Ages, beginning with basic literacy, going on to 'grammar', i.e. the use of Latin, and at the age of twelve taking up the 'craft of battle'. See N. Orme, *From Childhood to Chivalry* (London, 1984:112–19, 142–56, 181–91).
635 *him*: 'them'.
636 'But who may stand up against the one that God wishes to prosper?'

And qwen it teȝt to þe tyme of twelfe ȝere of age,
Þen was him kend of þe kynde and craft of bataile,   650
Wele and wiȝtly in were to welden a spere,
A preke on a proude stede proudly enarmed.
Þat lare was him lefe to and lerid in a qwile,
Was þare na lede to him like within a lite ȝeris,
So cheualus a chiftan he cheuys in a stonde   655
Þat in anters of armes all men he passes.
Quen Philip see him sa fers in his first elde,
His hert and his hardynes hiȝely he lofed,
Comendid mekill his knyȝthede, him callid on a day
Betwene þamselfe on a tyme and talkis þire wordis: 660
'Alexsandire,' quod þe athill, 'I augirly prayse
Þi wirschip, þi worthines, þi wit and þi strenth;
Es nane so tethe of þi tyme to tryi now olyfe.
How suld I, lede, for þi lofe bot lufe þe in hert?
Bot I am sary, forsothe, my son, at þi fourme   665
Is lickenand on na lym ne like to myselfe.
Oft storbis me þi statour and stingis me ȝerne
Þat þi personale proporcion sa party is to myne.'
Þis herd hire þe hend quene and hetirly scho dredis,
Sent eftir Anectanabus and askis him belyue,   670
Beknew him clene all þe case how þe kyng sayd,
And frayns him fast quat þe freke of hire fare thingis.
Þen con he calke and aconte and kest on his fyngirs,
Lokis him vp to þe lifte and þe lady swares:
'Be noȝt afriȝt,' quod þe freke, 'ne afrayd nouþire!   675
It sall þe noy noȝt an ege nane of his thoȝtis.'

649 twelfe] ten A.   654 lite] fewe A.   659 him] and him A.
661 athill] kynge A.

649 *twelfe*: emended to accord with the source, as well as the sense of
l. 646.
652 *A*: 'and'.
657 *first elde*: 'youth'. Discussed by Dove (1986:136–9).
660 *Betwene þamselfe*: 'the two of them privately'.
664 'What else could I do, boy, except love you deeply for your own
sake?'
672 *thingis*: 'thinks'.
673–4 Anectanabus makes astrological calculations.
676 *ege*: 'egg'; i.e. something of no account. The scribe writes *a nege*,
since the alliteration is on /n/.

With þat he heuys vp his hede and to þe heuyn lokis,
Hedis hetirly on hiȝe, behelde on a sterne
Of þe quilke he hopid in his hert sumquat to knawe
Quateuire he wald wete of his will alltogedire.   680
Quod Alexsandire to þis athill, as he his arte fandis:
'Quat is þe planet or þe poynt ȝe purpose to sene?
Quat sterne is it at ȝe stody on? Quare stekis it in heuyn?
May ȝe oȝt me in any maner to þat merke schewe?'
'Þat can I wele!' quod þe clerke, 'Ellis couthe I littill.   685
Noȝt bot sewe me, son, quen þe son is to reste,
Quen it is dreuyn to þe derke and þe day fynyst,
And þou sall sothely se þe same with þine eȝen.'
'Is oȝt þi werid to þe wissid?' quod þe wee þan,
'For þat I couet to ken if þou me kythe wald.'   690
'Sire, sothely of myne awen son slayne mon I worth,
So was me destaned to dye done many wintir.'
    As tyte as Anectanabus þis auntir had tald,
Þen treyned he doune fra þe toure to tute in þe sternes;
Þan airis sire Alexsandire eftire his fadire;   695
Þat euir he kyndild of his kynde kend he bot litill!
Þus led he furthe his leue child late on ane euen,
Sylis softely himselfe þe cité withouten,
Boȝes him vp to a brenke, as þe buke tellis,
To þe hiȝt of þe hiȝe dike and to þe heuyn waytis.   700
'Alexsandire, athil son,' quod Anectanabus his syre,
'Loo, ȝondir behald ouir þi hede and se my hattir werdis,
Þe euyll sterne of Ercules, how egirly it soroȝes,
And how þe modé Marcuré makis sa mekill ioy!

677 his] *om.* A.   678 D *begins here.*   682 sene] seme A, se D.   683 is
it] A, *om.* D.   684 merke] D, sterne A.   687 is] D, *om.* A.   688 se
þe same] A, þe same see D.   692 done] D, gane A.   694 he] D, *om.*
A.   698 himselfe] A, þaimselfe D.   699 him] A, þaim D.   700 hye]
D, depe A.

679–80 'From which he inwardly hoped to learn something, whatever he
wished to know about all his desires.'
689 'Is your fate known to you at all? . . .'
692 *done many wintir*: 'many years ago'.
698–9 *himselfe* and *him* are pl.; cf. variants.
703–4 The star of Hercules is Mars. *Marcuré*: Mercury.

Loo, ȝondir þe gentill Jubiter, how jolylé he schynes!   705
Þe domes of my destany drawis to me swythe,
Þik and þraly am I thret, and thole mon I sone
Þe slaȝtir of myne awen son as me was sett euir.'
Vnethis werped he þat worde, þe writt me recordis,
Þat Alexsandire as belyfe was at him behind,   710
And on þe bake with slike a bire he bare with his handis
Þat doune he drafe to þe depest of þe dike bothom.
Sayd 'Lo vnhappeiste vndire heuyn, þat þus on hand takis
As be þe welken to wete quat suld worth eftir!
Þou has feyned þe forwyse, and fals alltogedire.   715
Wele semys slike a sacchell to syeȝe þus of lyfe!'
    Þan Anectanabus, as him aȝt wele, augirly granys,
Dryues vp a dede voyce and dymly he spekis:
'Wele was þis cas to me knawen and kyd many wyntir
Þat I suld dee slike a dethe, be dome of my werdis.   720
Sayd I þe noȝt so myselfe here before,
I suld be slayn of my son, as now sothe worthis?'
'What! And am I', quod Alexander, 'ane of þi childer?'
'Ȝha, son! Als glad I my god, I gat þe myseluen!'
Fro he had warpyd hym þis worde, he wakens no more,   725
Bot gaue a gremly grane and þe gast ȝheldez.
That oþer wy for hys werkez wepys eueryllyke
So hard and so hertly þat neȝ hys hert brestes.
Þus plenys þis prouud knyght þe pyté of hys fader,
Cares hym downe into þe cafe þareas þe cors ligges;   730
Belife lyftes he hys liche on lofte on hys shulders
And beres hym forth vppon hys bake at þe brade ȝates.
'Sone,' sayd þe whene when sho hym see with syland teres,
'What haue ȝe done, my dere sonn?' and drowpys doun in
   swone.
'Dame, now is þare none other to do bot deme it þiseluen,   735

---

707 thraly] D, þrathly A.   710 Þat] D, Þat ne A; belyfe] D,
sone A.   714 suld worth] suld come A, worth sall D.   722 A *breaks
off here.*   725 warpyd] *om.* D; sayd *ins. after* worde D.   731 hys liche]
om. D; lofte] lofte euen D.

716 *sacchell*: probably a contemptuous and colloquial use of 'satchel';
i.e. 'old wretch'.

For as þi foly was before so foloweth aftir!'
Than makes þis man and hys moder menskfully and faire
Titely hys enterment, as þai þat tyme vsed.
Þus shamesly of hys awne childe hym chevyd such end;
And her fynes a fytt and fayr when vs likez.   740

[Alexander besieges Tyre, building a huge tower on ships. His soldiers run out of provisions, but the bishop of Jerusalem refuses his plea for supplies, and Balaan of Tyre demolishes Alexander's siege-works, killing many of the Macedonians and Greeks. Alexander builds a floating tower even bigger than before, and assaults Tyre again.]

Passus VI

   Now tenkelis vp taburns and all þe toun rengis;
Steryn steuyn vp strake, strakid þaire trumpis,
Blewe bemys of bras, bernes assemblis,   1510
Seȝes to on ilk syde and a saute ȝeldis.
Þare presis to with paues peple withouten,
Archars with arows of attir envemonde
Schotis vp scharply at shalkis on þe wallis,
Lasch at þam of loft, many lede floȝen;   1515
And þai ȝapely aȝayne ȝildis þam swythe,
Bekire out of þe burȝe bald men many,
Kenely þai kepe with kastis of stanys,
Driues dartis at oure dukis, dedly þam woundid.
Þan passe vp oure princes prestly enarmed,   1520
Into þe baistell abofe bremely ascendid,
Sum with lances on loft and with lange swerdis,
With ax and with alblastir and alkens wapen.

1508 tenkelis] tenelis A, tynkyll D.   1515 many lede floȝen] A, in mony lowd showte D.   1516 ayayn] D, aȝayne & A.   1518 kepe] D, kast of A.   1519 dedly] A, deply D.

1508–43 This vivid description of battle is one of the poet's longest additions to his source. Alexander's tower on ships is illustrated in fig. 7.
1509 'A fierce noise arose, their trumpets sounded.'
1513–14 Cf. *Siege J* 654, 666 above.
1523 The weapons and equipment used for the siege are well illustrated in the French Alexander romance, MS Bodley 264; see fig. 7; and Poole (1958:pl. 12).

Alexsandire ai elike augrily fe3tis,
Now a schaft, now a schild, nowe a scheue hentis,   1525
Now a sparth, now a spere, and sped so his mi3tis
Þat it were tere any tonge to of his turnes rekyn.
And þai within on þe wall worthili withstude,
Fersly defend of and fellid of his kny3tis,
Thristis ouir thikefald many threuyn berne,   1530
And doun bakward þam bare into þe brade watter.
   With þat oure wees without writhis þam vnfare,
Went wode of þaire witt and wrekis þam swyth,
For na wounde ne na wathe wand þai na langir,
Bot all wirkis him þe wa and wrake at þai cuthe.   1535
Sum braidis to þaire bowis, bremely þai schut,
Quirys out quarels quikly betwene,
Strykis vp of þe stoure stanes of engynes
Þat þe bretage aboue brast all in soundire,
Girdis ouir garettis with gomes to þe erthe,   1540
Tilt torettis doun, toures on hepis,
Spedely with spryngaldis spilt þaire bernes,
Many mi3tfull man marris on þe wallis;
And be þe kirnells ware kast and kutt doun before,
Be þat þe baistell and þe bur3e ware bathe elike hi3e,   1545
And all oure werke without þe wallis wetirly semed
Þe sidis of þe cité to se to o fernes.
Þan Alexsandire als belyf on þam all entris,

1525 scheue] A, swerde D.   1527 to of his turnes] A, hys tournays to D.
1528 worthili] A, wightly D.   1535 him] A, þaim D; þai] D, he A.
1537 Quirys] Whirres D, Quethirs A. 1542 springaltez] D, sprygaldis A;
bernes] D, braynes A.   1548 als] D, *om.* A.

1529 'Fiercely made defence and killed some of his knights.'
1532–5 The alliteration is on /w/ throughout.
1535 'But they all cause them as much sorrow and suffering as they
could.'
1544–7 'And when the battlements were thrown over and cut down in
front, then the tower and the town were both equally high, and all our
siege-works outside the walls seemed indeed to resemble the sides of the
city at a distance.' Once the city defences are breached, the tower is
moved forward until it touches the town-walls and, from a little way off,
is not easily distinguished from them.

Bruschis in with a brand on bernes a hundreth,
Thrange thurȝe a thousand þare thikest þai were,   1550
Wynnes worthly ouir þe wallis within to þe cité.
Þe first modire-son þat he mett or oþire man outhire
Was Balaan þe bald berne, as þe boke tellis,
And him he settis on a saute and sloȝe him belyue,
And werpid him out ouir þe wall into þe wild streme.   1555
    Sone as oure athils behind saȝe þare heued entre,
His men and all þe Messedones maynly ascendis,
And þai of Grece gredely girdis vp eftire,
Thringis vp on a thraw thousandis many.
Sum stepis vp on sties to þe stane wallis,   1560
On ilka staffe of a staire stike wald a clustir,
And qua na leddirs couth lache, as þe lyne tellis,
Wald gett þam hald with þaire hend and on hiȝe clyme.
Sa freȝt ware þire othire folke þat feȝtis within,
For Balaan þaire bald duke þat broȝt was of lyue,   1565
Þat all failis þam þe force, and so ferd worthe
Þat nothire with stafe ne with stane withstand þai
    na langir.
Sire Alexsandire with his athils and his awen sleȝtis
Þe toune of Tire þus he tuke, and othire twa burȝes
In þe quilke þe Siriens of þis sire so many soroȝes had   1570
As wald bot tary all oure tale þaire tourment to reken.
Sone as þis cité was sesid and slayne vp and ȝolden,
Þen ridis furth þe riche kynge and remowed his ost,
Gais him furth to Gasa, anothire grete cité,
And þat he settis on a saute and sesis it belyue.   1575
And quen þis Gasa was geten, he graythis him swyth
And joynes him toward Jerusalem þe Jewis to distroy.
And ȝe þat kepis of þis carpe to knaw any ferre,
Sone sall I neuen ȝow þe note þat is next eftir.

1552 þat] D, *om.* A; or] D, *om.* A.   1556 heued entre] D, he entred A.
1561 stare] D, staire staire A.   1562 na] sa AD; couth lache] D, had
nane A.   1563 hiȝe] loft AD.   1564 folke] D, *om.* A.

1552 'The first mother's son or any other man that he met'.

Passus VII

Als hastily as þai herd of in þe haly cité,   1580
And bodword to þe bischop broȝt of his come,
For Alexsandire aȝe almast he euen deis,
For he had nite him an erand noȝt bot o new time.
And now him þinke in his þoȝt him thurt noȝt haue carid
In all his mast mystir nad he þat man faylid   1585
When he for socure to þe cité sent him his lettir,
And he soyned him be his surement, þat sare him forthinkis.
'For me had leuir', quod þe lede, 'be lethirely forsworn
On as many halidoms as opens and speris,
Þan anys haue greuyd þat gome or groched him his
    erand.   1590
Þat euir I warned him his will, wa is me þat stonde!'
Þus was Jaudes of joy and jolité depryued,
And all þe Jewis of Jerusalem he joyntly asembles.
He said, 'Alexsandire is at hand and will vs all cumbre,
And we ere dredles vndone, bot Driȝten vs help.'   1595
Þan bedis þe bischop all þe burȝe, barnes and othire,
Athils of all age, eldire and ȝongire,
Comandis to ilka creatour to crie þurȝe þe stretis,
To thre dais on a thrawe be threpild togedire,
Ilka frek and ilka fante to fast and to pray,   1600
To ocupy þaire oures and orisons and offire in þaire temple,
And call vp with a clene voice to þe Kyng of Heuyn
To kepe þam at þis conquiroure encumbrid þaim neuir.
   Now seȝen þai to þaire sinagogis all þe cité ouire,
Ilka bodi þare bedis þat in þe burȝe lengis,   1605
Putt þam to prayris and penaunce enduris,
Þe vengance of þis victoure to voide if þai miȝt.

1582 euen] A, *om.* D.   1587 surement] sorement A, cas D.
1590 groched] D, warned A.   1596 barnes] A, bernes D.   1601 þaire
oures and] A, in þair D.   1602 a clene voice] A, kene cry D.

1582–7 'He nearly dies for fear of Alexander, since he had just recently
refused his request. And now he realizes that he wouldn't need to have
worried if he hadn't failed that man in his greatest hour of distress, when
he (Alexander) sent a letter to the city for help, and he (the bishop)
excused himself on the grounds of his pledge, which he bitterly regrets.'
1589 Reliquaries often have lids or doors that 'open and shut'.

Þe niȝt eftir þe note, as neuens me þe writtes,
Quen all þe cité was on slepe and sacrifis endid,
In ane abite of þe aire ane aungell aperis   1610
To Jaudas of Jerusalem, and him with joy gretis.
'I bringe þe bodword of blis, sire bischop,' he said,
'With salutis of solas I am sent fra þe trone,
Fra þe Maistir of Man, þe Miȝtfull Fadere,
Þat bedis þe noȝt be abaist, he has þi bone herd.   1615
And I amonest þe tomorne, as me was amoued,
Þat þou as radly as þou rise aray all þe cité,
Þe stretis and in all stedis stoutly and faire,
Þat it be onest all ouire, and open vp þe ȝatis.
Lett þan þe pupill, ilka poll, apareld be clene,   1620
And al manere of men in mylk-quyte clathis,
And pas, þou and þi prelatis and prestis of þe temple,
Raueste all on a raw as ȝoure rewill askis.
And quen þis conquirour comes, caire him agaynes,
For he mon ride þus and regne ouire all þe ronde werde,   1625
Be lord of ilka lede into his laste days,
And þen be diȝt to þe deth of Driȝtins ire.'
    Sone þe derke ouiredrafe and þe day springis,
Oure bischop bounes him of bed and buskis on his wedis,
And þen jogis, all þe Jewis, in generall he callis,   1630
Avaies þaim his vision how þe voice bedis.
Þan consals him þe clergy clene all togedire,
And all þe cité asentis, saraȝens and oþir,

1608 as neuen] D, & tellis A.   1613 I] A, *om*. D.   1616 me was amoved]
D, I am enjoyned A.   1626 lord of] D, lordschip in A.   1627 be] D, he A.
1630 jogis all þe] A, þat jew of all D; in] D, & A; he] D, *om*. A.
1633 saraȝens] A, sariauntez D.

1610 Aquinas argued that angels manifest themselves as condensed air.
The idea reappears in Donne's 'Aire and Angels'.
1616 'And I order you tomorrow, as it was urged upon me'.
1628–99 The rich detail of this long passage is an addition to the source.
The poet had in mind a civic pageant such as the entry of Richard II into
London in 1392. See G. Wickham, *Early English Stages 1300–1660*
(London, 1959:i, 51–111).
1630 'And then he calls together judges and all the Jews.' But the line is
corrupt in both mss.
1633 *saraȝens*: a spelling of 'sergeants', 'law-officers', as in the D ms.

To buwne furth with all þe burȝe and buske þam belyue
As him was said in his slepe, þis soverayn to mete.　　　1635
Þan rynnes he furth in a rase, arais all þe cité,
Braidis ouire with bawdkyns all þe brade stretis,
With tars and with tafeta þare he trede sulde,
For þe erth to slike ane emperoure ware ouire-feble.
He plyes ouire þe pauement with pallen webis,　　　1640
Mas on hiȝt ouire his hede, for hete of þe sone,
Sylours of sendale to sele ouire þe gatis,
And sammes þaim on aithire side with silken rapis.
And þen he caggis vp on cordis, as curteyns it were,
Euen as þe esyngis ȝede ouire be þe costes,　　　1645
All þe wawis withoute in webis of ynde,
Of briȝt blasand blewe browden with sternes.
Þus atired he þe toune, and titely þare-eftir
On ilka way wid open werped he þe ȝatis,
And quaso waitis fra without and within haldis,　　　1650
It semyd as to se to ane of þe seuyn heuyns.
　Now passis furth þis prelate with prestis of þe temple,
Reueschid him rially and þat in riche wedis,
With erst ane abite vndire all, as I am infourmede,
Full of bridis and of bestis, of bise and of purpre,　　　1655
And þat was garnest full gay with golden skirtis,
Store starand stanes strenkild all ouire,
Saudid full of safirs and oþire sere gemmes,
And poudird with perry was purer and othire.
And sithen he castis on a cape of kastand hewes,　　　1660
With riche rybans of gold railed bi þe hemmes,

1636 arayes] D, & arais A.　1650 wates] D, lukis A.　1651 to se to]
D, þe cite to se A.　1654 ane] D, & A.　1657 strenkild] strenklett D,
strekilland A.　1659 purer] D, perrour A.　1660 kastand hewes] A,
castans hewe D.　1661 rybans] D, rabies A.

1644–6 'And then he fixes up on cords, like curtains, just where the
eaves projected from the sides of the houses, blue fabrics on all the
outside walls.'
1650–1 'And to anyone who looks from outside and gazes within, it
resembled one of the seven heavens in appearance.'
1659–60 'And decorated with jewellery that was finer than any other.
And then he throws on a cope of brilliant colours.' The D reading means
'of chestnut colour'.

A vestoure to vise on of violet floures,
Wro3t full of wodwose and oþir wild bestis.
And þan him hi3tild his hede and had on a mitre,
Was forgid all of fyne gold and fret full of perrils,　　　　1665
Sti3t staffull of stanes þat stra3t out bemes,
As it ware shemerand shaftis of þe shire son.
Doctours and diuinours and othire dere maistris,
Justis of Jewry and jogis of þe lawe,
Ware tired all in tonacles of tartaryn webbis,　　　　1670
Þai were bretfull of bees all þe body ouire,
And oþir clientis and clerkis as to þe kirke fallis
Ware all samen of a soyte in surples of raynes,
Þat slike a si3t, I supose, was neuir sene eftire,
So parailed a procession a person agaynes.　　　　1675
　　Now bowis furth þe bischop at þe bur3e 3atis,
With prestis and with prelatis a pake out of nombre,
And all þe cité in sorte sylis him eftir,
Quirris furth all in quite, of qualité as aungels.
Marchands, maistir-maire, mynistris and othire,　　　　1680
Worthi wedous and wenchis and wyues of þe cité,
Be ilka barne in þe burgh, as bla3t ere þaire wedis
As any snyppand snawe þat in þe snape li3tis.
Þare passis þe procession a piple beforne,
Of childire all in chalk-quyte, chosen out a hundreth,　　　　1685
With bellis and with baners and blasand torchis,
Instrumentis and ymagis within of þe mynstire,

1670 tartaren] D, tarrayn A.　　1672 clientis and clerkis] A, clerkez and
colettes D; fallis] A, longen D.　　1678 sylez] D, felowis A.
1680 Marchaundez maister mair] D, Maistirs marchands & maire A.
1685 chalke] D, shalk A.

1663 Cf. *Wynnere* 71.
1673 'Were all together dressed alike in surplices of cloth of Rennes'; a
fine linen from Brittany (cf. Chaucer, *BD* 255). This makes the point
that the poet is visualizing a medieval civic procession.
1675 *agaynes*: 'towards'; hence 'to meet, to welcome'.
1682 Lit. 'With regard to each child . . .', i.e. 'Every child in the town
had clothes as white'.
1687–90 The procession carried 'musical instruments and statues from
inside the temple, some with censers and such like, with silver chains,

Sum with sensours and so, with siluiryn cheynes,
Quareof þe reke aromatike rase to þe welken,
Sum with of þe sayntware many sere thingis,   1690
With tablis and tapoures and tretice of þe lawe;
Sum bolstirs of burnet enbrouden with perill
Bare before þe bischop his buke on to lig,
Sum candilstickis of clere gold and of clene siluir,
With releckis full rially, þe richest on þe auutere.   1695
Þus seyis all þe semlé þe cité withoute,
Vnto a stonen stede streȝt on þe temple,
Scopulus, by sum skill, þe scripture it callis,
And þare þe come of þe kynge þis couent abidis.
    Sone Alexsandire with ane ost of many athill dukis   1700
Come prekand toward þe place with princes and erlis,
Sees slike a multitude of men in milke-quite clathis
And ilk seg in a soyte, at selly him thinkis.
Þan fyndis he in þis oþire flote fanons and stolis,
Practisirs and prematis and prestis of þe lawe,   1705
Of dialiticus and decre, doctours of aythir,
Bathe chambirlayn and chaplayne in chalke-quite wedis.
And as he waytis in a wra, þan was he ware sone
Of þe maistir of þat meneyhe in myddis þe puple,
Þat was þe bald bischop abofe all þe Jewis,   1710
Was graþid in a garment of gold and of purpree.
And þan he heues vp his eȝe, behaldis on his mytir,
Before he saȝe of fine gold forgid a plate,
Þarein grauen þe grettest of all gods names,
Þis title 'Tetragramaton', for so þe text witnes.   1715
With þat comandis þe kyng his knyȝtis ilkane,

1691 tapors] D, topoures A.   1710 þe (2)] D, þ A.   1711 purpree]
pupree A, siluer D.   1715 wittnesse] D, tellis A.   1716 ilkane] ouire
ilkane A, all D.

---

from which the aromatic incense rose to the sky, some with many
different things from the sanctuary'.
1697–8 Mount Scopus is about a mile north of Jerusalem. The Gk and
Lat word *scopolus* means 'rock'; hence the poet calls it 'a stony place'.
1706 'Doctors of both dialectics (logic) and ecclesiastical law.'
1715 The Gk *Tetragramaton* means 'the word of four letters', that is,
YHWH or Yahweh.

Bathe beron and bachelere and bald men of armes,
Na nere þat place to aproche a payn of þaire lyuys,
Bot all to hald þam behynd, heraud and othire.
Þan airis he furth all him ane to þis athill meneȝe,   1720
Bowis him doun of his blonke þe bischop beforne,
And kneland on þe cald erth he knockis on his brest,
And hersouns þat haly name at he byheld wreten.
    Þan þe Jewis of Jerusalem, justis and othire,
Lordis and ladis and þe litill childere,   1725
Enclynes þam to þe conquirour and him on kneis gretis,
Kest vp a kene crie and carpis þire wordis:
'Ay moȝt he lefe! Ay moȝt he lefe!' quod ilka lede twyse,
'Alexsandire þe athilest aire vndire þe heuyn!
Ay moȝt he lefe! Ay moȝt he lefe, þe lege emperoure!   1730
Þe wildire of all þe werde and worthist on erthe!
Ay moȝt he lef! Ay moȝt he leue!' quod loude all at anys,
'Ouircomere clene of ilka coste, and ouircomyn neuir,
Þe gretest and þe gloriosest þat euir God formed,
Erle or emperoure or any erdly prince!'   1735

[Having defeated first Darius of Persia and then Porus of India,
Alexander arrives at the Ganges where the Brahmans explain to him
their way of life. Erecting a pillar to mark the extent of his march, he
turns back from the Ganges.]

Passus XXII

    Now gase he fra Gangan and all his ginge eftir,
Fondis forth with his folke and a fild entris,
Vmfaldin with a faire wod, florischst out ouire,
Of appils and almands and all manere of frutis.   4845
All þe chiere of þe champe was chargid with floures,
Acrea, sais oure autour, þat angill is hatten.

1723 hersouns þat] D, reuerencez þis A; byheld] D, seis A.   1725 and
(2)] & þe A, þe D.   1728 lede] D, man A.   1729 athilest] athelfullest
D, athill A.   1730 þe] quod þe A, þis D.   4842–5200 A *readings
only*.

1718 *a*: 'on'.
1720 *him ane*: 'alone'.

3it wont men in þa woddis, as þe writt tellis,
Of joynttours as jeants in jopons of hidis,
And þai ware fedd all of frute and of na fode ellis,   4850
Of grapis and of gernets and othire gude spices
Of sike as growis in þe grewis I galed of before;
Þai ware as rughe as a resche, þe rige and þe sidis.
Quen þai persayued of oure prince and slik a pake armed,
Þan stode þai glorand on his gomes with grisely mawis,   4855
And he mas heraud and heres to hant for þe nanes,
And sett vp a scharp schoute at all þe schaw ryngis;
And þai for skere of þe skrike into þe schow fledd,
For þai hadd herd neuire of 'how!' ne of heremans noyse;
And sex hundreth was slane and sesid with oure kni3tis,   4860
And foure and threti as I fynd was in þe fild drepid,
And sex score on þis side and seuen at was armed
Was with þe churles in þe chace choppid to deth.
Þus thre daies in þat thede thurghout þai lengid,
And dietis þam with damysens and oþir dere frute.   4865
    Þan ferd he furth to a flumme and ficchid þare his tentis,
And newly eftir þe none, or nere þareaboute,
Þare coms a bonde of a brenke and breed þaim vnfaire,
A burly best and a bigge, was as a berne shapen.
Vmquile he groned as a galt with grysely latis,   4870
Vmquile he noys as a nowte as an ox quen he lawes,
3armand and 3erand, a 3oten him semed,
And was as bristilé as a bare all þe body ouire.
Dom as a dore-nayle and defe was he bathe,

4848 writt] buke.   4852 galed] tald.   4853 rige] bake.   4855 gomes]
gome.   4859 heremans] mans.   4861 fynd] flode *substituted in margin.*
4862 sex] iiij *in margin.*   4866 ficchid] sett.   4869 berne]
man.   4873 bristilé] bristils.

4858 *schow*: 'wood' (ON *skógr*); alliterating on /sk/ despite its spelling.
4859 For *how*! as a hunting call, see *Kings* 12.
4862–3 The Latin similarly says '127 of Alexander's men were killed by
them'.
4868–77 The poet is influenced by descriptions of the 'wild man', such as
that in *Ywain and Gawain*, EETS 254, ll. 244–70. See L. D. Benson, *Art
and Tradition in Sir Gawain and the Green Knight* (New Brunswick,
1965:77); and Bernheimer (1952).
4871 The scribe writes *a nox*, to indicate the alliteration.

With laith leggis and lange and twa laue eres,   4875
A heuy hede and a hoge, as it a hors ware,
And large was his odd lome þe lenthe of a ȝerde.
With þat comands oure kyng his kniȝtis him to take,
And þai asaillid him sone, bot he na segge dredis,
For nouthire fondis he to flee ne na fens made,   4880
Bot stude and stared as a stott and stirred he na forthire.
Þan callis to him þe conquirour a comly mayden,
Bad hire be broȝt before þe best and bare to be nakid,
And he beheld on þat hend and hissis as a neddire,
He wald haue strangild hire streȝt ne had stiffe men bene.   4885
He wald haue schowid on þat schene had noȝt schalkis halden,
And to þe prince pauelion prestly him lede;
Quen he had ferlied his fill on his foule schapp,
He gers þaim bynde him at a braid and brent him to poudire.

  Þen rade he fra þat reuir and remowid his ost   4890
Intill a brade bent-fild and bildid vp his tentis;
Þare fande he lindis on þat lande, þe lenthe of a spere,
And þai ware frett full of frute þe fairest of þe werde.
It ware to tere any tong to tell of þa trees kinde,
For þai wald sett with þe son and with þe son rise;   4895
Fra morewane to þe mydday merely þai springe,
And þan discende þai doun as þe day passis.
Lo, þis was a wondirfull werk, bot Gods will ane,
Þat þai suld wax soo and wane within a wale time,
For fra it droȝe to þe derke ay till it dawid eftir,   4900
It was bot vacant and voide as vanité it were.
Þe kyng in his caban with his kniȝtis ligis,
Tutand out of his tents and þe trees waitis,
A bad a berne of a bobb bring him an appill.
Þan bowis furth a bachelere his bedinge to fill,   4905
And he was sodanly sesid and slane with a sprete;
With þat enverrouns all þe vale a voice fra þe heuen,
Said, 'Quaso fangis o þis frute bees fey in a stounde!'
Ȝit bred þare briddis in þa braunches at blith was and tame,

4886 schalkis] men.   4898 werk] werek; will ane] awen will.
4902 ligis] he ligis.

4904 *A*: 'he'.

201

And if a hathill had þaim hent or with his hand touchid   4910
Þan floȝe þare flawmes out of fire before and behind,
And quare it liȝt on his like it lichid him for euire.
   Now bowis furth þis baratour and bidis na langire,
Vp at a maȝtene mountane he myns with his ost,
And aȝt daies bedene þe driȝe was and mare   4915
Or he miȝt couire to þe copp fra þe caue vndire.
Quen he was comen to þe crest his kniȝtis wald haue esid,
And namely a new note neghis on hand
Of dragons and of dromondaris and of diuerse neddirs,
Of liones and of leopards and othire laith bestis.   4920
Þare was hurling on hiȝe, as it in hell ware,
Quat of wrestling of wormes and wonding of kniȝtis;
As gotis out of guttars in golanand wedres
So voidis doun þe vemon be vermyns schaftis!
At oþir time of oure tulkis was tangid to dede   4925
And slayn with þa serpents a sowme out of nounbre;
So hard þai hampird oure heere and herid oure erles,
Vnneth it chansid þaim þe cheke þe cheffire to worthe.
Quen he sckonfet and skerrid all þa skathill fendis,
Þen metis he doun of þe mounte into a mirk vale,   4930
A dreȝe dale and a depe, a dym and a thestir,
Miȝt þare na saule vndire son see to anothire.
Þai ware vmbethourid in þat thede with slike a thike
   cloude
Þat þai miȝt fele it with þaire fiste as flabband webbis;
With all þe bothom full of bournes briȝt as þe siluire,   4935

4910 hathill] man.   4922 of(1)] oft.   4925 of] of of.   4932 Miȝt] Miȝ.

4912 '. . . it healed him forever.' The Latin says 'it burnt him cruelly';
either the poet's source had a different reading, or *lichid* is an error.
4913–36 In this extraordinary passage, the poet uses simile and
descriptive detail to convert the dry Latin account into a tale of wonder
and imagination.
4919 To the poet a dromedary is, like a dragon, an exotic and fearsome
beast. Cf. Spenser, *Fairie Queene* IV, viii. 38–9: 'a Dromedare . . . Of
stature huge, and horrible of hew'.
4923–4 'The venom pours down from the jaws of foul creatures like
streams out of gutters in howling storms.'
4928 i.e. 'with difficulty they managed to get the upper hand'.
4932 'Nobody anywhere could see anyone.'

And bery bobis on þe braes brethand as mirre.
   Þus drafe þai furth in derknes a neȝen daies euen,
So lange þaim lackis at þe last þe liȝt of þe son;
Þan come þai blesnand till a barme of a brent lawe,
Neȝe throtild with þe thik aire and thrange in þare andes.   4940
Þai labourde vp agayn þe lift an elleuen dais,
And quen þai couert to þe crest, þen clerid þe welkyn,
Þe schaftis of þe schire son schirkind þe cloudis,
And Gods glorious gleme glent þam emaunge.
Þan past þai doun fra þat pike into a playn launde   4945
Quare all þe gronde was of gols and growen full of impis,
A cubete lenth, sais þe clause, cald was þe maste,
Quareof þe feloure and þe frute as fygis it sawourd.
Þare fand þai revers, as I rede, ricchest of þe werd,
Þof it ware joly Jurdan or Jacobs well,   4950
Was neuir no mede ne no milke so mild vndire heuen,
Ne cliffe of cristall so clere at cried was euire.
A hundreth daies and a halfe he held be þa playnes,
Till he was comen till a cliffe at to þe cloudis semed,
Þat was so staire and so stepe, þe storé me tellis,   4955
Miȝt þare no wee bot with wyngis win to þe topp.
Ȝit fand he clouen þurȝe þe clynt twa crasid gatis,
Ane to þe noke of þe north, anothire to þe est;
Sire Alexsandire him avises, and all him awondres,
And trowid it was wroȝt of na lede werkis.   4960
   With þat stairis he forth þe stye þat streȝt to þe est,
And seuen dais with his seggis he soȝt be þa costis,
And on þe aȝtent day, eftire þe prime,
A basilisk in a browe breis þaim vnfaire;

4941 labourde] babourde.   4952 cried was euire] euire god fourmed.
4957 crasid] trasid.   4962 seggis] men.

4950 The river Jordan where Christ was baptized, and Jacob's Well
where the Samaritan woman gave him water; see Matthew iii. 13, John
iv. 6.
4952 The emended half-line is used elsewhere by the poet (l. 1831).
4957 'Yet he found two rough paths cut through the cliff.'
4960 'And he concluded it was constructed by no human workmanship.'
But the line fails to alliterate.
4964–8 It was well known that the stinking breath and the sight of the
basilisk were fatal to every creature except the weasel.

A straȝtill and a stithe worme, stinkand of elde,   4965
And es so bittir and so breme and bicchid in himselfe
Þat with þe stinke and þe strenth he stroyes noȝt allane,
Bot quat he settis on his siȝt he slaes in a stonde.
He vemons in þe vaward valiant kniȝtis,
Maistirs out of Messedone, of Mede and of Persee;   4970
Þai seȝe doun sodanly slane of þaire blonkis,
To step and to stand dede, and in þe strete liggis,
With þat areris all þe route, and radly þai said,
'Þe writh of þe wale god vs of þe wai lettis!'
Þe kyng, to knaw of þat case, vp to þe cliffe wendis,   4975
Saȝe quare þe same serpent slepit in a roke;
Þan mas he bonds in a braide at sall na berne pas,
In bole and in balan buskes he his fotes,
A blason as a berne-dure þat all þe body schildis,
And fiches in a fyne glas on þe fere side.   4980
Þe screwe in þe schewere his schadow behaldis,
And so þe slaȝtir of his siȝt into himselfe entris.
Þan cals oure kyng him his kniȝtis and comandis him to
    bryn,
And þai, as sone as þai him saȝe, him for his sleȝt thankis.
    Sone as þis balefull best was broȝt out of lyfe,   4985
Þan ridis furth oure riche kyng and remowis his ost,
And of þis way at he went sone worthis him an ende,
So at he flitt may na ferre, ne his fokke nouthire.
Þare was so hedous and so hoge hillis þam beforn,

4977 berne] pepill.   4985 Sone] Cone.

4967–8 'That he destroys not only with the stink and the strength, but he
slays instantly whatever he fixes in his sight.'
4972 The meaning of the first half-line is unclear. The source says only
that 'they fell lifeless'.
4977–80 'Then he hurriedly sets limits that no-one must pass, he fits out
his feet in wood and in whalebone, (gets) a shield the size of a barn door
that protects all his body, and fixes a clear glass (as a mirror) on the
outside.'
4982 *slaȝtir*: 'slaying power'.

204

Cloȝes at was cloude-he, clyntirand torres,   4990
Rochis and rogh stanes, rokkis vnfaire,
Scutis to þe scharpe schew sckerres a hundreth.
Þan ȝaris he him ȝapely and aȝayne turnes,
And past into þe proud playn I proued to ȝow first,
Þat all was brettfull of bowis and blossoms so swete,   4995
Þat bawme ne braunche o aloes bettir was neuire.
Fra þens oure note men be northe nymes þaim þe way,
And þat þan fonde all þe flote fiftene dayis,
And þai croke ouire crosse to cache þaim anothire,
Þat led þam to þe left hand, and þat a lange quile.   5000
And þus þai dryfe furth þe driȝt of daies foure score,
Till at þai come till a cliffe, as þe clause tellis,
Ane egge þat was all ouire of adamand stanes,
With, hingand in þe rughe roches, rede gold cheynes.
Þan was þare graythed of degreces, for gomes vp to wynde,   5005
Twa thousand be tale and fyue trew hundrethe,
And þai ware sett so in soute of safers fyne,
Þat of þe noblay to neuen it neyd any Cristen.
    Þare logis þe leue kyng late on an euen,
Vndire þis maȝté mountayne, and on þe morne eftir   5010
Þare setts he furth of sere gods a sellé nounbre
Þat he honours, and his ost, and offirs ilkane.
Syne tas he with him titly his twelue tried princes,
Gas him vp be degreces to þe grete lawe,
Trenes to þe top-ward þat touched to þe cloudis,   5015
Þat he miȝt lend þare o loft and laite eftir wondirs.
Vpon þe cop of þe cliffe a closure he fyndis,

5013 princes] prince.   5016 laite] waite.

4990–2 'Cliffs high as the clouds, rocky peaks, boulders and rough
stones, dreadful crags, a hundred rocks jut out to the cold sky.' A
dramatic description, using many topographical terms that are found in
place-names of the NWMidl. See R. W. V. Elliott, 'Hills and valleys in
the *Gawain* country', *LSE*, n.s. 10 (1978:18–41).
4996 *aloes*: not the bitter sort, but the fragrant spice in which Christ's
body was wrapped; John xix. 39–40.
4998–9 'And all the army went along that (path) for fifteen days, and
then they turn off in another direction to pick up another (path).'
5007–8 'They (the steps) were uniformly set with fine sapphires so that it
would be difficult for any person to describe the splendour.'

A palais, ane of þe precioussest and proudest in erth,
A bild, as þe buke sais, with twelfe brade ȝatis,
And seuenty wyndows beside of serelepé werkes.   5020
Þe ȝatis ware of ȝeten gold ȝarkid of platis,
Þe windows on þe selfe wyse, as þe writ schews,
And þai ware coruen full clene and clustrid with gemmes,
Stiȝt staffull of stanes, stagis and othire.
Ȝit was a mynstir on þe mounte of metall as þe nobill,   5025
Vmbegildid with a garden of golden vynes,
Was chatrid full of chefe frute of charbocle stanes,
Withouten mesure emaunge of margrite grete.
þis hame at houes on þis hill was in þe hiȝe est,
Forthi ȝit hedirto it hat þe Hous of þe Son,   5030
It was so precious a place and proudly atired,
þare was na place it a pere bot Paradyse selfe.

Passus XXIII

þen aires furth sire Alexsandire into þis athill temple,
With Caulus and with Cleopas and othire kidd princes,
And fand a berne in a bedd bawnand alane,   5035
Ane of þe graciousest gomes þat euire God fourmed.
All lemed of his letere þe loge as of heuen,
For it was gayly begane with golden webbis;
A blewe bleant obofe brad him al ouire,
Was browden all with brent gold full of briȝt aungels;   5040
Þe testre trased full of trones with trimballand wingis,
Þe silloure full of seraphens and othire sere halows,
With curtyns all of clene silke and coddis of þe same,
With cumly knottis and with koyntis and knopis of perle.

5019   twelfe] twa.   5020 serelepe] sereleps.

5035–52 This is vividly expanded from the source, which says: 'they
found a man lying in a golden bed under a golden coverlet wonderfully
adorned. And this man was exceedingly large of body and very good-
looking, and his head and beard seemed like the purest snow'. The
description of the guardian of the trees shows interesting parallels with
SGGK, particularly with the description of the Green Knight; with
ll. 5048–9, 5055, 5057–8, cf. *SGGK* 2148, 847, 818 and 303–8. Also cf.
l. 5050 with *Parlement* 112.

It ware to tere me to tell þe tirement togedire,　　　　　5045
Or any kid clerke þe cost to devise;
And he þat ristis in þat rowme, þe romance it tellis,
Was ane of þe borliest bernes þat euire body hade,
With fell face as þe fire and ferly faire schapen,
Balgh, brade in þe brest, and on þe bely sklendire,　　　　5050
His cheuelere as chanuele for changing of eld,
And as blaȝt was his berd as any briȝt snaw.
Sone as oure prince with his peris his person avyses,
He gesse him wele to be god and of na gome kind;
He knelis doun with his kniȝtis on þe cald erthe,　　　　5055
With 'Haile!' him hailsis on heȝe, and oþir hend wordis.
　　þe renke within þe redell þan raxsils his armes,
Rymed him full renyschly and rekind þire wordis:
'Haile, Alexsandire,' quod þis athill, 'at all þe erth weldis!
Þou ert welcum, iwis, and all þi wale princes.　　　　　5060
Sire, þou sall see with þi siȝt slike signes, or þou passe,
As neuire segge vndire son saȝe bot þine ane;
And þou sall here apon happis, or þou hethen founde,
Þat neuire hathill vndire heuen herd bot þiselfe.'
'A! A! Happy haly hereman!' quod þis hathill þan.　　　　5065
'How þat þou neuynes my name and þou me neuire kend?'
'Ȝis, sothly, sire,' saied þe segge, 'þiselfe and þi werkis,
Or any drope of þe deluuie drechet had þe erd.
List þe noȝt loke on þe lindis þat leuys euiremare,
Þat has þe surname of þe son and Cynthia alls –　　　　5070
Þat is to mene bot of þe mone – and miȝt has to speke,
And tell þe trewly all þe text quat tide sall here-eftir?'
'Ȝis, by my croune!' quod þe kyng, and kyndly was joyed.
'Þis word I wald, be ȝour will, noȝt all þe werd leuir.'
'Sire, waite at þou be wemles for woman touchinge,　　　5075
Þan may ȝe leuely on þam loke and lesten ȝour wirdis.
For be ȝe pure of þat pliȝt, ȝe may þis place entre,

5046 any kid] a nany.　5051 chanuele] chaaele.　5068 þe (1)] þi.
5070 Cynthia] of þe mone.

5066 'How is it that you mention my name if you never knew me?'
5070 For Cynthia as the name of the moon, see Chaucer, *TC* iv. 1608.
5074 'With your permission, I'd like to have this information more than
all the world.'

Þat is þe sette of þat sire þat sett all þe werd.'
'Sire, I am clene of þat craft, I knaw wele myselfe.
Be þou oure gide to þe greuys, apon Gods name!'   5080
   With þat bownes him þat berne and fra his bed ryses,
Cled all in clene gold, kirtill and mantill,
A grym grisely gome with grete gray lokis,
Al glitired þe ground for glori of his wedis.
'Sirs, 3e þat will has to wend, 3our wapens deuoidis,   5085
Nymes of 3our nethirgloues and nakens 3oure leggis,
Pesan, pancere and platis, all to 3oure preué clathis,
Jopon and jesserand, and joyntly me folows!'
Þe kyng at his comaundment him with his kni3tis spoilis,
Puttis of to þe selfe serke, senture and othire,   5090
Takis with him Sire Telomew, an of his twelfe princes,
And Antioc an athill duke, and eftir him wendis.
Þai ferd furth all in fere, þire foure all togedire,
Þe lede at was þaire ladisman, þe lord and his kni3tis,
Went þur3e a wale wode, was wondire of to tell,   5095
As it ware hi3tild in þat hill with handis of aungels.
For þare ware tacchid vp trees, þe triest of þe werd,
A hundreth fote to þe hede þe hi3t was and mare,
Lyke oleues out of Lebany and lores so grene,
With sichomures and sipresses and sedrisse eblande.   5100
Þare trekild doun of þa treis teres of gummes,
Boyland out of þe barke, bawme and mirre,
Of scence and of othire salue as sechis out of wellis,

5086 nethirgloues] nethirgloue. 5088 joyntly] radly. 5089 him with
his kni3tis] with his kni3tis him. 5091 twelfe] *om* A. 5092 Antioc]
Antiet. 5100 sichomures] sicho*u*rmes. 5101 treis] *om.* A; gummes]
iemmes.

5095–104 The description of the site of the Trees of the Sun and Moon
has been influenced by legends of Alexander's journey to the Earthly
Paradise; see Lascelles (1936). The source says the trees in the wood
'were like laurel and olive, and from these trees frankincense and balm
flowed copiously'. The poet's additions are influenced by the paradisaical
description in the *Song of Songs*, whence the reference to Lebanon, the
sichomures (fig-trees, not the modern sycamores), the cypresses and
cedars, the aromatic spices and so on.
5103–4 'Of incense and other unguent such as comes from springs, so
that nowhere did such aroma ever rise from fragrant spice.' Magical and

Þat rase neuire of aromitike sike rekils in erth.
Þai fande a ferly faire tre quareon na frute groued,   5105
Was void of all hire verdure and vacant of leues,
A hundreth fote and a halfe it had of heȝt large,
Withouten bark ouþir bast, full of bare pirnes.
Þare bade a brid on a boghe abofe in þe topp,
Was of a port of a paa with sike a proude crest,   5110
With bathe þe chekis and þe chauyls as a chykin brid,
And all gilden was hire gorge with golden fethirs.
All hire hames behind was hewid as a purpure,
And all þe body and þe brest and on þe bely vndire
Was finely florischt and faire with frekild pennys,   5115
Of gold graynes and of goules full of gray mascles.
Þan waitis on hire þe wale kyng and wondire him thinke,
Was in þe figure of hire fourme noȝt ferlid a littill.
'Quat loke ȝe?' quod þe ladisman. 'Do lendis on forthire!
Ȝone is a fereles foule, a fenix we call.'   5120
Þan bowe þa forthe all ebland and to þire bolis comes,
Þe plants of þe proud son and of þe pale mone,
'Behalds now', quod þis hare man, 'to þire haly bowis!
And quat þou will of þaim to wete, wis in þi saghe.
Appose þaim all in preuaté, bot make na playn wordis,   5125
And þou may swythe haue a sware at swike sall þe neuire.
Þan may þou gesse in þi gast it is a gude sprete
Þat sends þe sike asouerance and sees to þi thoȝtis.'
  Þire boles was, as þe boke sayes, borly and hiȝe,

5107 heȝt] leȝt.   5121 Þan] Þam; bolis] treis.
5128 asouerance] asouerante.

healing liquids rose from the ground, often where saints had been
buried. For examples, see *MED oil(e* 4(b).
5105–8 This is the Dry Tree, found by Seth in the Earthy Paradise, as
described in *Cursor Mundi*, ed. Bennett and Smithers (1968:XIV.
183–92).
5111 Some illustrations of the Phoenix depict it with wattles like a
chicken.
5120 *fereles*: 'without companion'; cf. 'Ase feynes wiþoute fere',
Bennett and Smithers (1968:VIII. E. 75). The Phoenix was often cited as
an emblem of uniqueness and peerlessness.

Þe lind of þe liȝt son louely clethid   5130
With feylour as of fine gold þat ferly faire lemes,
Þat oþir loken ouire with leues as it ware liȝt siluir.
Þan Alexsandire at þis athill askis a demande:
'In quatkyn maner of lede sall me þire treis sware?'
'Sothly, sire, þe Son-Tree', said þe segge þan,   5135
'Entris in with Yndoyes and endis in Greke;
And mast-quat ay þe Mone-Tree, þurȝe miȝt of hire kynde,
Quen it kithis vs any carpe, þe contrarie spekis,
For scho begynes all in Grew and endis in Ynde,
And þus be twinlepi tongis tell þai oure wirdis.'   5140
Þan knelis doun þe conquirour vnto þe cald erthe,
And aithire bole eftir bole blithly he kissis,
And þoȝt if he suld with þe thra of all þe thedes wete
If he suld move agayn to Messedon quare his modire duellid.
Þan schogs hire þe Son-Tree and schoke hire schire leues,   5145
And with a sweȝand swoȝe þis sware scho him ȝeldis:
'Sire, þou ert lelé of ilk lede þe lorde and þe fadire,
Bot þi sire soile in na side see sall þou neuire.'
Þan list him lithe of his lyfe and of his last ende;
'So maideux,' quod þe Mone-Tree, 'þi meere bees na langir   5150
Bot out þis anlepi ȝere and aftir aȝt monethis.
Þan sall he duale þe with a drinke at þou full dere traistis.'
    Þan makis he mournyng and mane and in his mynd thinkis
Qua suld þat trecherous trayne of treson him wirke.

5148 *Following this is* For þi modire nor ȝit Messedon þou seȝis þaim na mare.

5130–2 The Latin says: 'The Tree of the Sun had leaves like the purest gold, shining red; the Tree of the Moon had leaves white and bright as pure silver'.
5134 Here, and in l. 5139, the alliteration is defective.
5143–4 'And wondered if, with (i.e. having achieved) the victory of all the countries, he might learn whether he would go back to Macedonia where his mother lived.'
5151 *out*: 'to the end of'.
5152 'Then he whom you trust very dearly will poison you with a drink.' Jobas, a young favourite of Alexander, who was angry at a blow the king had given him, dropped poison into his wine. Alexander asked for a feather to make himself vomit, and Cassander, brother of Jobas, gave him one smeared with more poison.

He said, 'Hende, haly tree!' and halsid hire in armes,   5155
'Quat person sall do me depresse? I pray þe me tell!'
'Sire, sothely,' said þe Son-Tree, 'if I þe sothe neuened
Qua suld þe wite out of þe werd and þe þi werdis dele,
Þan suld þou slaa þe same segge, and so my sawis faile;
And þat may worthe be na wai, for ay my wordis standis.'   5160
Þan lokid on him his ladisman, said, 'Lefe of þi wordis,
For writhing of þire wale treeis, and willne þaim na mare;
Bot graythe þe, gome, on Gods behalue, and agayn turne,
For ouire þe lemetis of þire lindis may no lede founde!'
Þen bownes agayn þe bald kyng, bittirly he wepis,   5165
Þat he so skitly suld skifte and for his skars terme,
So did his princes, sais þe prose, for peté of himselfe,
With ȝedire ȝoskingis and ȝerre ȝett out to grete.
Þan bedis þaim þe barotour, on bathe twa þaire eȝen,
Þat þai suld neuire neuyn þis note to nane of his ost,   5170
Quat þai beheld in þe hill and herd with þaire eres;
And he þan styntis of his stoure and steris his hert.
'If ȝe will gange', quod þis gide, 'agayn to ȝoure kniȝtis,
Nymes ȝow to þe northward, next I it hald.'
Þan passis he to þis proud place and oure prince leues;   5175
And he gose doun be grece agayn to his tentis.
   Þare logis he fra þe late niȝt till efte þe liȝt schewis,
With sare sighingis and sadd for sake of his wirdis;
Constreynes him with his contenance to with his kniȝtis play,
Bot þat bot sprang of þe splene; þe sprite was vnesid.   5180
Sone as þe day-rawe rase, he risis vp belyue,
Riches him radly to ride and remows his ost,
Driues on with his dukis day eftir othire,
Till he was meten to þe meere quare he þe monte entird,

5165 bittirly] baldly.   5166 for] fra.   5170 neuyn] *in margin*.
5174 Nymes] Moves; northward] nethireward.   5175 prince] kynge.
5179 Constreynes] Costreynes.   5182 ost] l ost.

5164 'No-one may go beyond the limits of these trees.'
5174 'Keep to the northward route, I regard it as nearest.'
5175 *place*: 'palace'.
5176 *he*: Alexander.
5180 The spleen was regarded as the seat of laughter; see Trevisa,
Properties, 250.

Þat was þe proud playn fild I proued ȝow before,   5185
Quare all þe face of þe fild was of fyne goules.
Þare piȝt he doun his pauylions and with his princes bidis,
And þe driȝt of a day he duellis in þa costis,
Betwene þa styes, in a stound, þat strekis þurȝe þe mountis
He mas twa pylars doun to pycche all of playn marble,   5190
And tacchis vp of treid gold a table in þe myddis,
With a prolouge in þat plate on aithire post writen:
'I, Alexsandire þe athill, eftire þe date
Of þe prince of Persye and Porrus, þire pilars enhaunsid.
Qua list þis lymit ouirlende, lene to þe left hand,   5195
For þe rake on þe riȝt hand þat may na renke passe!'
Þis titill was of þa tongis tane out and grauen:
Of Ebru and of Yndoys, and of þire ald lettres
Of Latine and of othire lare, and leues out of Grece,
Proudly prikid all in prose; and here a pas endis.   5200

5190 pycche] pynche.   5191 table] pelare.   5193 date] dat*ere*.
5194 of(2)] &.   5192 renke] man.   5197 þa] twa.

5194 Darius and Porus, both of whom had been vanquished by
Alexander.

SELECT BIBLIOGRAPHY

See p. xi for a list of primary sources

Bennett, H. S. (1937) *Life on the English Manor* (Cambridge)

Bennett, J. A. W. and Smithers, G. V. (1968) *Early Middle English Verse and Prose* (2nd edn, Oxford)

Benson, L. D. (1965) 'The authorship of *St. Erkenwald*', *JEGP* 64, 393–405

Benson, C. D. (1974) 'A Chaucerian allusion and the date of the alliterative "Destruction of Troy"', *NQ* 219, 206–7

—— (1980) *The History of Troy in Middle English Literature* (Woodbridge)

Bernheimer, R. (1952) *Wild Men in the Middle Ages* (Cambridge, Mass.)

Bestul, T. H. (1974) *Satire and Allegory in Wynnere and Wastoure* (Lincoln, Neb.)

Booth, P. H. W. (1981) *The Financial Administration of the Lordship and County of Chester 1272–1377*, Chetham Soc., 3rd ser. 28 (Manchester)

Brook, G. L. (1933) 'The original dialects of the Harley Lyrics', *LSE* 2, 38–61

Brown, C. (1932) *English Lyrics of the XIIIth Century* (Oxford)

—— (1939) *Religious Lyrics of the XVth Century* (Oxford)

—— (1952) *Religious Lyrics of the XIVth Century* (2nd edn, Oxford)

Burrow, J. A. (1965) *A Reading of Sir Gawain and the Green Knight* (London)

—— (1986) *The Ages of Man* (Oxford)

Dickins, B. (1932) 'The rhyme-schemes in MS. Douce 302, 53 and 54', *Proceedings of the Leeds Philosophical and Literary Society* 2, 516–18

Dobson, E. J. (1971) Review of *Susannah*, *NQ* 216, 110–16

Dove, M. (1986) *The Perfect Age of Man's Life* (Cambridge)

Doyle, A. I. (1974) 'The shaping of the Vernon and Simeon Manuscripts', in *Chaucer and Middle English Studies*, ed. B. Rowland (London), 328–41

213

—— (1982) 'The Manuscripts', in *Middle English Alliterative Poetry and its Literary Background*, ed. D. Lawton (Cambridge), 88–100

Duggan, H. N. (1976) 'The source of the Middle English *The Wars of Alexander*', *Speculum* 51, 624–36

—— (1977) 'Strophic patterns in Middle English alliterative poetry', *MP* 74, 223–47

—— (1986a) 'The shape of the b-verse in Middle English alliterative poetry', *Speculum* 61, 564–92

—— (1986b) 'Alliterative patterning as a basis for emendation in Middle English alliterative poetry', *Studies in the Age of Chaucer* 8, 73–105

—— (1988) 'Final -*e* and the rhythmic structure of the b-verse in Middle English alliterative poetry', *MP* 86, 119–45

Guddat-Figge, G. (1976) *Catalogue of Manuscripts Containing Middle English Romances* (Munich)

Jacobs, N. (1985) 'The typology of debate and the interpretation of *Wynnere and Wastoure*', *RES*, n.s. 36, 481–500

Jordan, R. (1974) *Handbook of Middle English Grammar: Phonology*, trans. E. J. Crook (The Hague)

Kane, G. (1986) 'Some fourteenth-century "political" poems', in *Medieval English Religious and Ethical Literature*, ed. G. Kratzmann and J. Simpson (Cambridge), 82–91

Kernan, A. (1974) 'Theme and structure in *The Parlement of the Thre Ages*', *NM* 75, 253–78

Lascelles, M. M. (1936) 'Alexander and the Earthly Paradise in mediaeval English writings', *MÆ* 5, 31–47, 79–104, 173–88

Lawton, D. A. (1980) '*The Destruction of Troy* as translation from Latin prose: aspects of form and style', *SN* 52, 259–70

—— (1981) 'The Middle English alliterative *Alexander A* and *C*: form and style in translation from Latin prose', *SN* 53, 259–68

—— (1982) *Middle English Alliterative Poetry and its Literary Background* (Cambridge)

Lewis, R. E. (1968) 'The date of the *Parlement of the Thre Ages*', *NM* 69, 380–90

Luttrell, C. A. (1958) 'Three north-west midland manuscripts', *Neophilologus* 42, 38–50

McAlindon, T. (1970) 'Hagiography into art: a study of *St. Erkenwald*', *SP* 67, 472–94

MacCracken, H. N. (1910) 'Concerning Huchown', *PMLA* 25, 507–34

McIntosh, A. (1977) 'Some notes on the text of the Middle English poem *De Tribus Regibus Mortuis*', *RES*, n.s. 28, 385–92

Maddicott, J. R. (1975) 'The English peasantry and the demands of the Crown 1294–1341', *Past and Present*, Supplement 1

Mann, J. (1973) *Chaucer and Medieval Estates Satire* (Cambridge)

Meek, M. E. (1974) *Guido delle Colonne, Historia Destructionis Troiae* (Bloomington, Ind.)

Menner, R. J. (1949) 'The Man in the Moon and Hedging', *JEGP* 48, 1–14

Select bibliography

Moe, P. (1970) 'The French source of the alliterative *Siege of Jerusalem*', *MÆ* 39, 147–54

Mustanoja, T. F. (1960) *A Middle English Syntax* (Helsinki)

Newton, S. M. (1980) *Fashion in the Age of the Black Prince* (Woodbridge)

Oakden, J. P. (1930) *Alliterative Poetry in Middle English: The Dialectal and Metrical Survey* (Manchester)

Osberg, R. H. (1984) 'Alliterative technique in the lyrics of MS. Harley 2253', *MP* 82, 125–55

Patch, H. R. (1927) *The Goddess Fortuna in Mediaeval Literature* (Cambridge, Mass.)

Pearsall, D. (1977) *Old English and Middle English Poetry* (London)

Peck, R. A. (1972) 'The careful hunter in *The Parlement of the Thre Ages*', *ELH* 39, 333–41

—— (1973) 'Number structure in *St. Erkenwald*', *Annuale Medievale* 14, 9–21

Petronella, V. F. (1967) '*St. Erkenwald*: style as the vehicle for meaning', *JEGP* 66, 532–40

Poole, A. L. (1958) *Medieval England* (2nd edn, Oxford)

Reliquiæ Antiquæ, ed. T. Wright and J. O. Halliwell (London, 1841)

Revard, C. (1979) 'Richard Hurd and MS. Harley 2253', *NQ* 224, 199–202

—— (1981) 'Three more holographs in the hand of the scribe of MS. Harley 2253 in Shrewsbury', *NQ* 226, 199–200

—— (1982) '*Gilote et Johane*: an interlude in B.L. MS Harley 2253', *SP* 79, 122–46

Rowland, B. (1975) 'The three ages of *The Parlement of the Three Ages*', *Chaucer Review* 9, 342–52

Salter, E. (1978) 'The timeliness of *Wynnere and Wastoure*', *MÆ* 47, 40–65

Scattergood, V. J. (1983) '*The Parlement of the Thre Ages*', *LSE*, n.s. 14, 167–77

Seymour, M. C. (1974) 'The scribe of Huntington Library MS. HM 114', *MÆ* 43, 139–43

Smallwood, T. M. (1973) 'The interpretation of *Somer Soneday*', *MÆ* 42, 238–43

Speirs, J. (1957) *Medieval English Poetry: The Non-Chaucerian Tradition* (London)

Stemmler, T. (1962) *Die englischen Liebesgedichte des MS. Harley 2253* (Bonn)

Stern, K. (1976) 'The London "Thornton" miscellany', *Scriptorium* 30, 26–37, 201–18

Trigg, S. (1986) 'Israel Gollancz's "Wynnere and Wastoure": political satire or editorial politics?', in *Medieval English Religious and Ethical Literature*, ed. G. Kratzmann and J. Simpson (Cambridge), 115–27

Tristram, P. (1976) *Figures of Life and Death in Medieval English Literature* (London)

Turville-Petre, T. (1974) ' "Summer Sunday", "De Tribus Regibus Mortuis", and "The Awntyrs off Arthure": three poems in the thirteen-line stanza', *RES*, n.s. 25, 1–14
—— (1977a) *The Alliterative Revival* (Cambridge)
—— (1977b) 'The ages of man in *The Parlement of the Thre Ages*', *MÆ* 46, 66–76
—— (1979) 'The Nine Worthies in *The Parlement of the Thre Ages*', *Poetica* 11, 28–45
—— (1980) 'Emendation on grounds of alliteration in *The Wars of Alexander*', *ES* 61, 302–17
—— (1987a) 'Editing *The Wars of Alexander*', in *Manuscripts and Texts*, ed. D. Pearsall (Cambridge), 143–60
—— (1987b) 'The prologue of *Wynnere and Wastoure*', *LSE*, n.s. 18, 19–29
—— (1988) 'The author of *The Destruction of Troy*', *MÆ* 57, 264–9
Vale, J. (1982) *Edward III and Chivalry* (Woodbridge)
Waldron, R. A. (1972) 'The prologue to *The Parlement of the Thre Ages*', *NM* 73, 786–94
Whatley, G. (1986) 'Heathens and saints: *St. Erkenwald* in its legendary context', *Speculum* 61, 330–63
Whiting B. J. (1968) *Proverbs, Sentences, and Proverbial Phrases from English Writings Mainly Before 1500* (Cambridge, Mass.)
Woolf, R. (1968) *The English Religious Lyric in the Middle Ages* (Oxford)
—— (1969) 'The construction of *In a fryht as y con fare fremede*', *MÆ* 38, 55–9

GLOSSARY

The glossary includes forms and senses of words that might present difficulties. Regular inflected forms and common variant spellings, such as pl. *-is/-es*, adv. *-ly/ -liche*, or ppl. *-ede/-yt*, are not generally listed. Sigils for the texts are as follows: A – *The Wars of Alexander*; E – *St Erkenwald*; H – *The Harley Lyrics*; J – *The Siege of Jerusalem*; K – *The Three Dead Kings*; P – *The Parlement of the Thre Ages*; S – *A Pistel of Susan*; SS – *Somer Soneday*; T – *The Destruction of Troy*; W – *Wynnere and Wastoure*.

In the order *y* and *i* are treated as forms of the same letter, as are þ and *th*; ȝ follows *g*, and *u/v* are distinguished as vowel and consonant. The swung dash, ~, represents the head-word in any of its forms.

abaist *pp.* dismayed A 1615
abatyd *pp.* demolished E 37
abyde *v.* stop K 48
abilly *adv.* effectively T 1577
abyme *n.* abyss E 334
abite *n.* garment
ablode *adj.* full of blood J 559
aboht *pp.* paid for H I. 18
abrod *adv.* far and wide
acast *pp.* cast down H III. 10, cast out SS 121
ache *n.* wild celery H II. 14
aconte *v.* compute A 673; **accounttid** *pp.* reckoned up T 1547
acorde *n.* agreement A 620
acorde *v.* agree S 345
acounte *n.* reckoning E 209
adred *pp.* frightened H VII. 20
affinité *n.* kindred S 180
affray *v.* frighten J 668; *pp.* P 356
afretye *pr.3sg.subj.* devour H VIII. 8, 38
afriȝt *ppl.adj.* afraid A 675
after *prep.* for E 126, according to E 195, in accordance with W 429
agayne(s), agein, aȝayne, aȝen *adv.*

back, in return; *prep.* towards, against; in the face of T 2445
agaynstande *v.* withstand A 636
aghe, aȝe *n.* fear E 234, dread A 1582
aght, aȝt *num.* eight E 210, A 4915
aghtene *num.* eighteen E 208
aght(es), aȝt *see* **ow(e)the; aȝayne, aȝen** *see* **agayne(s)**
aȝtent *adj.* eighth A 4963
ah *conj.* but
ay *adv.* always, ever
aylyng *n.* discomfort T 1577
ayre *n.* smell S 94
aire *n.* ruler A 1729, **eyre** heiress S 15; **ayers** *pl.* heirs P 577
airis *pr.3sg.* goes
aithire *see* **oþer**
al *quasi conj.* although E 226
alast *adv.* in the end H III. 12
alblastir *n.* crossbow A 1523
albus *pl.* finches? W 494
ald *adj.* old A 5198
alder *n.* ancestor E 295
alder-grattyst *adj.* greatest of all
alees *pl.* garden paths S 11

217

Glossary

alisaundre *n.* horse-parsley H II. 14
alkens *adj.* every sort of A 1523
all *adv.* entirely
allane *adv.* only A 4967
allirs *gen.pl.* of all A 620
allþofe *conj.* although W 420
alowes *pr.3sg.* gives credit for E 267
als *adv. & conj.* as, also
amad *adj.* mad H VI. 14
amblande *ppl.adj.* ambling W 417
ames *pr.3sg.* goes P 493; *(refl.)* resolves; **amyt** *pp.* shaped T 1562
amylliers *pl.* almond trees S 80
amys *adv.* wrongly K 103
amonest *pr.1sg.* order A 1616
amorelle *n.* emir P 515
amorewen *adv.* in the morning H II. 8
amounte *v.* be sufficient E 284
amoued *pp.* urged A 1616
an *prep.* on K 1, 32, J 543
and *conj.* if P 106, than A 1659; **ant** and H *passim*
andes *pl.* breathing A 4940
angill *n.* place A 4847
anguis *n.* suffering K 32
anys *see* ones
anlepi *adj.* single A 5151
anoye *n.* suffering E 211
anoynted *pp.* smeared J 698
ant *see* and; **anters** *see* auntoure
apeched *pa.t.* accused S 303
apele *n.* accusation S 294
apert *adj.* open S 294
aport *n.* bearing A 598
appaire *v.* reduce W 372
ap(p)on, opon, vppon *prep.* upon
appose *imp.* question A 5125
aprefe *n.* in *of* ~ by excellence A 648
aprefe *v.* show himself equal A 598; **apreuyd** *pa.t.* demonstrated A 614
araide *pp.* dressed E 77, **arayed** provided S 4
araye *n.* appearance; sequence SS 51
arblastes *pl.* crossbows J 667
ar(e) *see* er, hy; **aren** *see* be(n)
areris *pr.3sg.* retreats A 4973
areste *see* erst
arewen *v.* regret H VIII. 32
ariht, aryȝt *adv.* properly S 112, well K 3
arne *see* be(n)
aromitike *n.* fragrant spice A 5104

aroste *ppl.adj.* roasted H VIII. 8
arrerage *n.* shortfall H VIII. 32
arste *see* erst
art *n.* province E 33
arwes *pl.* arrows
as *see* habben
ascenteþ *pr.pl.* agree H IX. 14
ashunche *v.* escape from H V. 45
askes *pl.* ashes J 716
askes *pr.3sg.* demands
asluppe *v.* escape H V. 40
asouerance *n.* certain knowledge A 5128
aspieþ *imper.pl.* check S 122
assay *v.* put to test S 64
as(s)eg(g)ede *pa.t.* besieged P 303, 574; *pp.* P 356
at *adv.* to (with infin.)
at *conj. & rel.pron.* that, who, the one whom, which A *passim*
ataynt *v.* convict S 207
aþel *n.* excellence H IV. 67
athell, athill *adj.* noble; *as n.* nobleman; **athilest** *sup.* noblest
athes *pr.3sg.* binds by oath P 499
atles *pr.3sg.* advances J 565; **atled** *pa.t.* arranged T 2376, **aughtilde** intended P 483
atluppe *v.* escape H V. 44
atraht *pp.* taken away from H V. 30
atte *prep.* at the J 665
attyr *n.* poison
attonys *adv.* at once J 622
augarte *adj.* arrogant W 267
aughte *see* ow(e)the; **aughtilde** *see* atles
augirly *adv.* greatly A 661, 717; **augrily** violently A 1524
auntirs *pr.3sg.(refl.)* ventures P 375; **aunterde** *pa.t.* P 543
auntoure, -er, -ir, aventure *n.* fate P 317, fortune T 12519, story A 693, danger P 451; **anters, awnters** *pl.* dangers K 31, deeds A 656
auay *v.* inform E 174, A 1631
auenaunt *adj.* gracious S 30; **auenauntliche** *adv.* excellently S 8
aueroyne *n.* southernwood (medicinal plant) S 115
avyses *pr.3sg.* looks at A 5053, *(refl.)* considers A 4959; **auisyd** *pa.t.* studied E 53
avoutri *n.* adultery

awe *v.* frighten H VI. 11
aweyward *adv.* in a contrary direction SS 113
awen *adj.* own A 691
awnters *see* **auntoure**
awondres *pr.sg.impers.* it amazes A 4959
axles *pl.* shoulders P 113

babery *n.* grotesques T 1563
bac-bite *pp.* defamed H VI. 34
bachelere *n.* young knight
baches *pl.* streams J 559
bade *see* **bede**
bagge *n.* money-bag P 139
bay *n.* defensive position K 2, 16
bayly *n.* bailiff H VII. 32
baistell *n.* tower A 1521, 1545; **bastiles** *pl.* J 678
bayþeþ *pr.3sg.* grants H II. 35; **baythes** asks E 257
bake *n.* in *one ~ back* P 369
baken mete *n.* pies W 335
balan *n.* whalebone A 4978
bald(ore) *see* **bolde**
bale *n.* suffering, pain, misery, sorrow, wickedness; damage S 307; *pl.* misdeeds H VI. 23, destruction S 189
bale *adj.* wicked W 292
balefull *adj.* murderous A 4985; **balefully** *adv.* with distress E 311
balghe *adj.* rounded P 112, A 5050
balkede *pa.t.* bellowed P 56
ballede *adj.* bald P 158
baratour, barotour *n.* warrior A 4913, 5169
barbet *n.* cloth band H I. 31
bare *n.* boar A 610, 4873
bare *adj.* destitute H III. 52
bare *see* **beren**
baret *n.* wretchedness S 147
barme *n.* lap W 418, brow of hill A 4939
barnakes *pl.* barnacle geese W 349
barne *n.* child
barotour *see* **baratour**
barownce *pl.* lords K 16
barre *n.* court S 189
barsletys *see* **ber(e)selet(t)**; **barst** *see* **brestes**
bashis *pr.3sg.* disconcerts E 261;

baschede *pa.t.* dismayed P 369
bastiles *see* **baistell**
bastons *pl.* verses SS 47
batail, batell *n.* army
bathe *pron.& adj.* both; *adv.* also A 4874
bawdkyns *pl.* silks A 1637
bawme *n.* balm
bawnand *pr.p.* dwelling A 5035
baxters *pl.* bakers T 1592
be *see* **by**
bec *v.* nod K 46
beckneþ *pr.3sg.* indicates H III. 16; **bikken** *imper.* beckon with W 480
bedagged *pp.* bespattered P 245
bede *v.* (**bydde** *pr.1sg.*; **bedis, biddes, byt** *3sg.*; **beden** *pl.*; **bed(e), bade** *pa.t.*; **bede, boden, boded** *pp.*) offer E 243, ask S 328, ask for W 239, P 390, demand H III. 59, challenge H II. 44, give H I. 4, exchange E 214, bid, command H IV. 4, A 1615 etc., order H V. 7, 36, J 714 etc., summon K 49, give instructions W 437, pray A 1605
bedels *pl.* town-officials
bedene *see* **bydene**
bedinge *n.* order A 4905, **biddyng** demands H III. 28
beeren *pr.pl.* cry out S 79; **beryd** *pa.t.* rang out E 352
bees *pl.* jewels A 1671; **byes** precious things J 639
bees *see* **be(n)**
before, byfore *adv.* in front; **beforne** *prep.* in front of
begane *pp.* adorned A 5038
behaldis *pr.3sg.* sees A 4981
behalue *n.* in *on Gods ~* in the name of God A 5163
beyen *pr.pl.* restore H IV. 40
bekire *pr.pl.* attack A 1517
beknew *see* **biknowe**
belde *v.* encourage K 17
belde *see* **byld**
bele *adj.* lovely P 390
belyfe *adv.* quickly; *as ~* quickly
beme *n.* cross E 182
bemes *pl.* trumpets
be(n) *v.* be; **be** *pr.1sg.*, (as fut.) will be H IV. 3, S 147; **arte, ert** *2sg.*; **er, is** *3sg.*, **bees** (as fut.) will be A 4908, 5150; **beon, bene, beþ,**

bueþ, aren, arne, ere *pl.*; **bue**
  3sg.subj.; **was, wos** *pa.t.sg.*; **weore,**
  ware *pl.*; **ware, were** *subj.* would be;
  bene *pp.*, **ibe** S 304
benche, bynche, benke *n.* judicial seat
  S 307, throne W 87, bench A 625;
  bynche *pl.* benches W 314
bende *n.* heraldic stripe W 149
bende *pp.* stretched E 182; **ibente**
  ppl.adj. arched SS 68
benefetis *pl.* financial rewards P 143
benes *pl.* services P 143
bent *n.* battlefield; **bent-fild** meadow
  A 4891
beralles *pl.* beryls P 123
bere *n.*[1] bier SS 132
bere *n.*[2] speech K 105
beren *v.* (**beren** *pr.pl.*; **bere, bare**
  pa.t.; **ybore** *pp.*) bear, carry; force
  P 369, stab J 533, push A 711, 1531;
  (refl.) behave P 439; ~ *in* support
  H I. 22, ~ *doun* lower E 311
ber(e)selet(t) *n.* hunting dog P 39, 69;
  barsletys *pl.* K 16
berfray *n.* siege tower J 587
beryd *see* **beeren**
beryn, berne, burne *n.* man, knight;
  barns *pl.* K 49
besantes *pl.* gold coins (or depictions)
beside *adv.* in addition W 170,
  nearby SS 33
besiet *pa.t.* busied E 56
best *n.* beast J 589, A 4883
best *adj.* in *of þe* ~ in the finest way
  T 1564
betakend *pa.t.* presaged A 613
bete *pa.t.* drove E 9
beþ *see* **be(n)**; **betyme** *see* **bytyme**
betyn *v.* kindle J 714; **beteþ** *pr.3sg.*
  heals H II. 21; **betun** *pr.pl.* repent
  K 97 **bet** *pp.* made amends for
  H IV. 3
betwene *adv.* at intervals A 1537
bew *adj.* fine J 587
bewe(de) *see* **bogh**
bewells *pl.* bowels P 69
bewile *v.* trick S 54; **biwiled** *pp.*
  deluded S 333
by *adv.* to one side E 72; **by, be** *prep.*
  by; with regard to A 1682; *conj.*
  when A 1544; ~ *þat* (by) then, when
bibe *v.* drink J 720
bycchyd, bycchet *ppl.adj.* dreadful

J 585, difficult J 661, foul A 4966
bycomen *pp.* gone P 507
biddyng *see* **bedinge**
byde *v.* (**bid(is)** *pr.3sg.*; **bade** *pa.t.*)
  wait, remain; suffer H VII. 5
bydene, bedene *adv.* together;
  bideene immediately S 310
byes *see* **bees**; **byfore** *see* **before**
big(ge) *adj.* strong; **bigly** *adv.* J 614
biggede, -et, bugged *pp.* built,
  founded, established
bigripid *pa.t.* encircled E 80
byhete *pr.1sg.* promise P 178; **byhyht**
  pp. H V. 24
bikken *see* **beckneþ**
biknowe *imper.* make known E 221;
  beknew *pa.t.* informed A 671
bil *n.* pickaxe H III. 44
bild *n.* building
byld *pa.t.* built T 1535, **bildid** erected
  A 4891, **belde** settled P 658; *pp.*
  built T 1603
biledes *pr.pl.* persecute H VI. 3
bileue *n.* belief E 299
billed *ppl.adj.* long-billed W 349
bymodered *ppl.adj.* covered with
  mud H VI. 58
bynche *see* **benche**
byrchyn *adj.* with birch-trees K 1
birde, burde *n.* lady
byronnen, byrunne *pp.* drenched
  P 62, J 599
bir(re) *n.* instant W 292, violent
  attack J 661, blow A 711, force of
  wind T 12490
bis *n.* linen H II. 17
bise *n.* grey A 1655
byswykeþ *pr.pl.* deceive, persuade
  H VI. 68
byt *see* **bede**
bitand *ppl.adv.* bitingly A 610
bytyme, betyme *adv.* quickly
bitok *pa.t.* handed over S 21; **bitan**
  pp. given E 28
bitt *n.* sharp point P 228
bittir *adj.* cruel A 4966; **bitterly** *adv.*
  fiercely P 228
byweuede *pp.* covered P 122
biwiled *see* **bewile**
blaȝt *ppl.adj.* white A 1682, 5052
blanchede, blawnchede *pp.* whitened
  P 156, 285
blasand, blesand *ppl.adj.* shining

Glossary

W 342, A 1647, blazing A 604, 1686
blason *n.* shield A 4979
blaunderers *pl.* kind of apple S 97
bleant *n.* robe A 5039
bleo, ble(e) *n.* colour
blerren *v.* blear W 278
blesand *see* **blasand**
blesenande *ppl.adj.* illustrious W 168;
  blesnand *pr.p.* staring A 4939
blessyd *pp.* ordained E 3
blethely *see* **blith; blewen** *see* **blow**
blyckenand *pr.pl.* shining A 60
blynne *v.* stop E 111; **blynes** *imper.*
  W 457
blyot *n.* mantle P 482
blisch *n.* in *at a* ~ in appearance
  A 606
blisfull *adj.* lovely
blysnande *ppl.adj.* shining E 87
blith *adj.* joyful S 77, gracious
  T 2342, gentle A 4909; *(as n.)*
  beautiful one H II. 35; **blithly** *adv.*
  joyfully A 5142, **blethely** merrily
  P 214
blo *adj.* dark E 290
blode *n.* noble blood W 194
blok *adj.* pale SS 111
blonke *n.* horse; **blongis** *pl.* K 47
blostme *n.* blossom SS 68
blow *v.* snort K 47; *pr.pl.* command
  (of trumpets) J 521; **blewen** *pa.t.*
  J 634
blussche *n.* shining W 187
blusshet *pa.t.* looked T 2428
bo *pron. & adv.* both
bobb *n.* branch A 4904; *pl.* A 4936
bochers *pl.* butchers T 1592
bode, boode *n.* command
boded, boden *see* **bede**
bod(e)word *n.* message, report
bodi *n.* person A 1605
bogh *n.* branch; **bowes, bous, bewes**
  pl.
bogh, bewe *v.* (**bowes, bewes** *pr.3sg.*;
  bewe, boȝes *pl.*; **bouwed, boghit,**
  bewede *pa.t.*; **bown** *pp.*); bend S 97,
  turn aside K 46, submit E 194, go
  P 370, E 59, S 232 etc, *(refl.)* A 699;
  ~ *hym to fote* submit to him P 490,
  (refl.) ~ *doun* dismount A 1721
boyes *pl.* low fellows, servants
boyland *pr.p.* overflowing A 5102
bolde, bald *adj.* bold; shameless

H III. 67, great E 106; **baldore**
  comp. H II. 44
bole *n.* tree, tree-trunk; wood A 4978
bole-fure *n.* pyre J 714
bolle *n.* goblet W 278; *pl.* W 214
bolstirs *pl.* cushions A 1692
bonde *n.* bondsman H III. 30, churl
  A 4868
bonds *see* **boundes**
bone *n.*[1] bidding, command, request
bone *n.*[2] murderer E 243
bone *adj.* obedient E 181
bones *pl.* in *lawe* ~ lower limbs W 111
bonke *n.* bank, slope; shore T 12490;
  bonkes *pl.* hills E 32
boode *see* **bode**
borde, burde *n.* table W 335, 342;
  bordis *pl.* writing-tablets A 640
bordon *n.* staff H III. 34
bor(e)ly, borlich *adj.* large, massive;
  borliest *sup.* A 5048; **bureliche** *adv.*
  excellently S 195
borewe *v.* redeem H VII. 32
bor(o)w *see* **burgh**
borstax *n.* axe H III. 44
boskeþ *pr.pl.* adorn H VIII. 26
bost *pp.* embossed T 1564
boste *n.* arrogance, threatening
bote *n.* help, remedy
bot(en) *adv. & conj.* but, unless; *noȝt*
  ~ only, ~ *if* unless, if not; *prep.*
  apart from, all except
botet *ppl.adj.* wearing boots W 476
bot-forke *n.* hay-fork H VII. 2
bothen *pron.* both P 276
bothum *n.* bottom E 76
botours *pl.* bitterns W 379
boun *see* **bown(n)**
boundes, bonds *pl.* limits; *Ercules* ~
  Pillars of Hercules P 334
bounes *see* **buwne**
bounty *n.* in *to* ~ as an honour E 248
boure *n.* lady's chamber
bourne *n.* stream; **buerne** sea T 12523
bous *n.* booze H VII. 29
bous *see* **bogh**
bout *n.* loop of material (?) H I. 31
boute *prep.* without H V. 15
bouwed, bowes, bown *see* **bogh**
bowndes *pl.* bands W 252
bowne *adv.* quickly SS 48
bown(n), boun *adj.* ready, prepared,
  equipped, dressed

221

Glossary

bown(n)es, bownede *see* **buwne**
brachus *pl.* hunting-dogs K 17
brad *see* **braidis; brade** *see* **brode**
braes *pl.* banks A 4936
braid *n.* instant A 4889, 4977
brayde(n) *see* **breydeþ**
braidis *pr.3sg.* spreads A 1637;
 brayden *pa.t.* in ~ *owte* unfurled
 W 52; **brayde** *pp.* unfurled W 163,
 brad covered A 5039
brayed *pa.t.* roared P 56, cried out
 E 190
brak *pa.t.* broke S 322; **broken** *pp.*
 committed H IV. 4
brakans *pl.* bracken P 62
brande *see* **bronde**
brase *n.* strap W 158
brasiers *pl.* brass-workers T 1589
braste *see* **brestes; brauden** *see*
 breydeþ
braundesche *v.* in ~ *hym* swagger
 W 241; **brawndeschet** *pa.t.*
 brandished P 504
brawnche *n.* share E 276
bre *n.* sea T 12516
brede *n.*[1] breadth
brede *n.*[2] roast meat H II. 47
bredeþ *pr.pl.* multiply H III. 67
breydeþ *pr.3sg.* (**brayden, braidis** *pl.*;
 brayde *pa.t.*; **brayden, brauden,**
 brouden, browden *pp. & ppl.adj.*)
 pull P 69, 371, J 615, draw tight
 K 47, brandish J 543, rush A 1536;
 pp. & ppl.adj. embroidered;
 fashioned W 113, linked J 615
breis *pr.3sg.* frightens A 4964; **breed**
 pa.t. A 4868
breme *adj.* fierce; loud T 12468,
 sharp A 610, lovely H IV. 40; *adv.*
 loudly SS 11, K 17; **bremly** fiercely
 T 12470, A 1536, quickly A 1521,
 loudly W 41
brenke *see* **brynke**
brenn(en), brene, bryn *v.* (**brynneth**
 pr.3sg.; **brennynde, -ynge** *pr.p.*;
 brent *pp.*) burn; be burnt A 4983;
 ppl.adj. burnished; refined A 5040
brent *adj.* steep A 4939
brerdes *pl.* borders W 164
brere *n.* briars H VII. 23; **breris** *pl.*
 brambles P 62
brestes *pr.3sg.* (**brosten** *pr.pl.*; **barst,**
 braste, brosten *pa.t.*; **brosten** *pp.*)

break; crush P 231, crash down
 J 569, burst P 55, J 586
bretage *see* **britage; bretenet** *see*
 bryten
brethand *pr.p.* smelling A 4936
brethe *n.* anger W 457
bret(t)full *adj.* quite full T 12528,
 A 1671, 4995
breue(n) *v.* put on record H VI. 23;
 tell P 424, report E 103, describe
 A 606
brewe *v.* contrive S 189, 307
brid *n.* bird
brigges *pl.* drawbridges J 615
briȝtned *pa.t.* shone J 545
bryht *adj.* lovely
brym *adj.* stern K 105; **brymlyche**
 fierce K 2
bryme *n.* river P 7
brynke, brenke *n.* river-bank
 H III. 70, edge of ditch A 699,
 river's edge A 4868
bryn(neth) *see* **brenn(en)**
brynston *n.* sulphur J 671
britage, bretage *n.* battlements,
 defensive structure
bryten *v.* destroy S 351; **bretenet** *pp.*
 torn apart S 147
britouns *pl.* Breton apples S 97
broche *n.* spit W 348
broched *pa.t.* spurred W 121
brode, brade *adj.* broad, wide; large
 W 333, outspoken W 457; *adv.* all
 around P 51
broȝt, browth, ybroht, ibrouth *pp.*
 brought; summoned H VI. 26,
 introduced H I. 15; ~ *of lyue* killed
 A 1565
broken *see* **brak**
bronde, brande *n.* sword
brosten *see* **brestes; brouden** *see*
 breydeþ
brouderde, -irde *pp.* embroidered
 W 91, 96
broun *adj.* bright W 113, J 542
browden *see* **breydeþ**
browe *n.* steep bank A 4964; *pl.*
 eyebrows SS 68
browth *see* **broȝt**
bruches *pl.* sins H IV. 4
brude *n.* lady, bride
bruschis *pr.3sg.* rushes A 1549; *pa.t.*
 P 56

brust *adj.* bristling with anger H III. 51

buerne *see* **bourne; bue(þ)** *see* **be(n); buggid** *see* **biggede**

bugging *n.* farm H III. 52

buk-tayles *pl.* hind-quarters of deer W 333

burde *pa.t.impers.* ought to E 260

burde *see* **birde, borde; bureliche** *see* **bor(e)ly**

burgeys *pl.* freemen of city E 59

burgh, burwe, bor(o)w *n.* city, town, borough; **borowes** *pl.*

burgons *pl.* buds P 11

burynes *n.* tomb E 142, 190

burne *see* **beryn**

burnee *n.coll.* coats of mail J 558

burnet *n.* dark cloth A 1692

burst *n.* wickedness K 97

burþen *n.* load H VII. 2, 23

burwe *see* **burgh**

buske *v.* get ready A 1634, equip W 110, A 4978, hurry E 112, put A 1629, cover P 22; ~ *boun* get ready J 674

busmare *n.* insult E 214

buturs *pl.* bitterns W 349

buwne *v.* go A 1634; **bounes, bown(n)es** *pr.3sg.* prepares P 265, *(refl.)* goes A 1629, gets ready A 5081; **bownede** *pa.t.* P 43

caban *n.* tent

cac(c)he *v.* (**caught(en), kaghten** *pa.t.*; **caȝt, cacched** *pp.*) obtain W 274, receive E 148, S 59, J 656, get H III. 61, take P 362, 443, K 36, take hold E 71, pick up J 524, A 4999, fasten J 700, drive J 724, come upon K 34

cafe *n.* cave A 730

caggis *pr.3sg.* fastens A 1644

caynard *n.* old rascal H VII. 20

cayre, kayre *v.* go, travel; **cares** *pr.3sg.(refl.)* A 730; **ycayred** *pp.* separated H V. 35

cayser, kaysser *n.* emperor

caytif, caytef(fe) *n.* villain, wretch

cald *pp.* reckoned A 4947

calke *v.* calculate A 673

calle *n.* head-dress H VI. 60, S 158; **kelle** S 128; **chelle** hairnet H I. 21

calsydoynnes *pl.* chalcedonies P 124

camelyn *n.* fine material E 82

can, kan, con(ne) *pr.* (**couþe, cuthe, kouþyn** *pa.t.*) can, know; recognise K 134, are skilful SS 5, know how S 249

canel *n.* cinnamon H II. 39, cinnamon tree S 83

cape *n.* cope A 1660

capill, kaple *n.* horse; **capel-claweres** *pl.* those who curry horses H VIII. 25

capped *ppl.adj.* mad H IX. 1, K 127

caprons *pl.* hoods P 237, 212

care *n.* sorrow, trouble

careles *adj.* generous E 172

caren *n.* body K 102; **karayn** corpses J 682

cares *see* **cayre**

carf *pa.t.* carved H II. 47; **coruen** *pp.* A 5023

carful *adj.* sorrowful

carieþ *pr.pl.* lament H III. 9

carpe *n.* story A 1578, speech A 5138

carpe *v.* (**carped, -it, kerpede** *pa.t.*) speak; cry out H III. 9

carpynge, karpyng *n.* speech P 168, speaking K 52, complaint SS 46

case *n.* event W 448, situation S 331

caste *n.* throwing of stones; **kastis** *pl.* throwing A 1518

caste(n), kest *v.* (**cast, kast, kest** *pa.t.& pp.*) throw P 80, J 641, throw over A 1544, cast (stones) J 675, place E 83, utter S 153, arrange W 77, construct T 1530, add up A 673, attempt T 2355, send A 1727, remove H IV. 52, H V. 11; ~ *on* put on H V. 13, ~ *vp* turn over P 68

caudels *pl.* broths W 353

caughte(n) *see* **cac(c)he**

causes *pl.* legal actions E 202

cauteles *pl.* lies S 205

cely *adj.* wretched W 414

celydoyne *n.* celandine H II. 18

cenacle *n.* dining-room E 336

certys *adv.* indeed

cessyd *see* **sese**

chaffare *n.* goods H VI. 73

chamber *n.* dwelling W 474

champe *n.* field A 4846

chansid *pa.t.* happened to A 4928

chanuele *adj.* grey (?) A 5051

chapitre *n.* ecclesiastical court H VI. 73

chaplet *n.* circlet P 118

charbiande *adj.* grilled? W 336

charbocle *n.* carbuncle

charge *pr.1sg.* value S 247; **chargit** *pa.t.* pledged, dedicated E 18; *pp.* filled A 4846

chatrid *pp.* crammed (?) A 5027

chaule *v.* gossip H VIII. 36

chaundelers *pl.* candlesticks J 590

chaunged *pp.* exchanged H IX. 11

chawylls, chauyls *pl.* jaws P 72, A 5111

chechun *n.* escutcheon, shield W 116

chefe *v.* prosper W 496, succeed P 243; **cheuys** *pr.3sg.* becomes A 655; **cheuede** *pa.t.* turned out P 98, *impers.* it happened to A 739

chefe, cheue *adj.* best P 255, S 105, prominent P 121, excellent A 5027; **cheffire** *comp.* more powerful A 4928; *adv.* first P 72; **chefely, cheuely** quickly P 89, especially P 235, first of all E 18

chefelere *n.* hair P 118; **cheuelere** A 5051

cheke *n.* success A 4928

chekker *n.* chess T 1621

chele *n.* cold H VII. 5

chelle *see* **calle**

chepe *pr.1sg.* buy H VI. 73

cheping, chepyn *n.* market H III. 43, market-place H VI. 82

chere *n.* face; behaviour W 429, spirits W 383; **chiere** surface A 4846; *appon* ~ in appearance W 24

cheres *pr.3sg.* encourages P 235

cherl(d) *n.* fellow H VII. 34, 40

chese *v.* (**chosen** *pr.pl.*; **ches** *pa.t.*) choose H II. 10, go P 243, 538, (*refl.*) go W 474, P 255, decide P 531; **chosen** *ppl.adj.* excellent P 118, conspicuous P 121, lovely S 93

chete *n.* hall H IV. 28

cheualus *adj.* chivalrous A 655

cheue- *see* **chefe-**

cheuerol *n.* chervil S 106

chewettes *pl.* meat pies W 336

chibolle *n.* spring onion S 105

chiere *see* **chere**

childur *pl.* children

chynede *pa.t.* removed meat from backbone P 89

chyn-wedys *pl.* beard W 24

choisly *adv.* suitably T 1621

chollet *n.* cabbage S 105

chosen *see* **chese**

chost *n.* quarrelling H III. 43

chouwet *n.* cabbage? S 106

cyst *n.* coffin K 54

cladden *see* **cleþe**

claht *pp.* grasped H V. 36

clansyd *pa.t.* cleansed E 16

clastreþ *pr.pl.* enslave? H VI. 42

claterand *ppl.adj.* resounding T 12501

claures *pl.* claws J 699

clause *n.* (Latin) account

cled *see* **cleþe**

clene *adj.* pure, elegant; complete J 627; *adv.* elegantly, entirely; **clenly** neatly W 77

cleopeþ *pr.3sg.* calls H VI. 57; **clepen** *pl.* call W 355

clerc, clerke *n.* cleric, learned man

clere, cleer *adj.* beautiful P 621, 623, pure S 24

clergye *n.* learning S 24

cleþe *v.* clothe H V. 12; **cladden** *pa.t.* dressed E 249; **cled** *pp.* A 5082, **clethid** adorned A 5130

cleuyen *v.* be attached H I. 21, stick H V. 36; **cleue** *pr.pl.* cling S 111

clientis *pl.* attendants A 1672

clynt *n.* cliff A 4957

clyntirand *ppl.adj.* rocky A 4990

clyp *v.* embrace P 248; **cluppe** H V. 38

clogges *pl.* lumps H I. 21

cloȝes *pl.* ravines A 4990

cloise *adj.* enclosed T 12543

cloyster *n.* enclosed area E 140

clos *n.* cathedral precinct E 55

closing *pr.p.* besieging T 1509; **closede** *pa.t.* fortified P 411

closure *n.* castle A 5017

cloþe *n.* clothes H V. 37

clottes *pl.* clumps S 111

cloude-he *adj.* high as the clouds A 4990

cloutes *pl.* shreds E 259

clouen *pp.* split W 340, cut A 4957

cluppe *see* **clyp**

cocke *v.* fight H I. 2

Glossary

coddis *pl.* pillows A 5043
cofre *n.* chest H II. 39
coyfe *n.* cap (of lawyer) E 83
coynte, coyntly *see* **quaynt**
coyntons *n.* fellowship K 124
colde *adj.* chilling (of care); *adv.*
bitterly H III. 9
coldis *pr.3sg.* sends cold K 81
colle *n.* trickery H VI. 42
coloppe *n.* tasty dish P 33
come *n.* arrival A 1581, 1699
come *v.* (**com(e)** *pa.t.*) come; suit
A 627
comeliche, cumly *adj.* lovely K 102,
A 5044, attractive E 82; *adj.as n.*
attractive man H V. 37, lovely lady
S 199; *adv.* beautifully H V. 12,
S 96, elegantly W 90
comford *pa.t.* helped T 12537
comforth *n.* relief E 168, 172
comyn *n.* cumin (spice) H II. 38, 39
committid *pp.* appointed E 201
communnates *pl.* communities E 14
companage *n.* meal, board
H VIII. 31
compaste *pa.t.* designed P 409
complaint *n.* weeping T 1516
comsed *pp.* carried out J 635
con *v.* did (forming pa.t.)
condit(he) *n.* aqueduct P 409, J 685
condlers *pl.* candlemakers T 1596
confourmyd *pa.t.* formed E 242
conyng *n.* knowledge T 2412
conynges *pl.* rabbits W 353
con(ne) *see* **can**
consail, conseil, counsell, cownsel *n.*
legal officers J 690, judgement J 724,
understanding E 167, 172, wisdom
E 266, advice K 35, A 618
constory *n.* consistory court
H VI. 76, 85
constreynes *pr.3sg.* forces A 5179
contenance *n.* demeanour A 5179
copp *n.* top A 4916, 5017
corbyns *gen.* raven's P 80
coriours *pl.* curriers T 1596
cormus pypys *pl.* hornpipes J 525
cornells *pl.* battlements P 411
coron *n.* crown; **crone** head H II. 38;
crownes *pl.* tonsures E 55
coronest *adj.* most distinguished
A 624
corres *pl.* dogs J 699

cors *n.* corpse, body
cors *see* **course; coruen** *see* **carf**
cosyns *pl.* relatives S 170
costardes *pl.* apples S 96
coste *n.* region; *pl.* sides A 1645
cot *n.* cottage H III. 62
cotelers *pl.* knife-makers T 1597
coþe *v.* infect J 684
couche *n.* bed P 165
coucheours *pl.* makers of
bed-hangings T 1597
counsell *see* **consail**
counte *n.* account H III. 62
counted *see* **cownten**
countene *gen.pl.* shire H VI. 46
countours *pl.* accountants P 148
courbede *see* **cowrbed**
coure(n) *v.* squat H VI. 46, cower
H VI. 76
course *n.* flowing T 1608, 12487, path
of sun T 2344, 12466, pursuit
T 2355, running T 2366, force
T 12479, trade T 1583; **coursse** line
of stone T 1547, 1571; **cors** water-
course J 685
coustage *n.* expenditure H VIII. 29
couþe *see* **can**
couthely *adv.* knowledgeably P 462,
plainly E 98
couent *n.* congregation A 1699
couerys *imper.* take cover K 36
couet *pr.1sg.* desire A 690
couetys *n.* lust; avarice E 237
couire, keuere *v.* recover H III. 10,
reach A 4916; **couert** *pa.t.* reached
A 4942, **keuered** rose S 252
cowchide *pa.t.* made (dog) lie P 39
cownsel *see* **consail**
cownten *pr.pl.* regard as P 307;
counted *pa.t.* were bothered about
T 12479
cowpe *n.* cup P 401
cowpe *v.* fight P 203
cowples *pr.3sg.* fastens P 237
cowrbed *pa.t.* bent P 287; **courbede**
ppl.adj. P 154
cowschote *n.* wood-pigeon P 13
craft, kraft *n.* skill; cleverness E 167,
structure E 346, business A 5079; *pl.*
poetic skills H IV. 66
crafty *adj.* clever E 44; **craftely** *adv.*
skilfully; **creftly** SS 46
crakede, -it *pa.t.* knocked hard

P 373, resounded E 110

crasid *ppl.adj.* rough A 4957

creatour *n.* person A 1598

creftly *see* **crafty**

crepite *pa.t.* crept P 42; *pp.* P 64

cried *pp.* created A 4952

cristen *n.* honest person A 5008

croysen *pr.pl.* make sign of cross J 524

croke *pr.pl.* turn aside A 4999; **crokede** *ppl.adj.* stooped H VII. 20, curled W 151

crommeþ *pr.3sg.* crams full H VIII. 17

crone *see* **coron**

crop *n.* belly H VIII. 17; **croppes** *pl.* buds S 83

crosschen *pr.pl.* smash J 534

crosse *n.* in *ouire* ~ in another direction A 4999

crowes *pl.* crowbars E 71

crownes *see* **coron**

cubete *n.* measure (length of forearm)

cud, cuyþe *see* **kythe**

cumbre *v.* destroy A 1594; **cumbrit** *pp.* afflicted T 12547

cumly *see* **comeliche**

cumpere *n.* companion S 345

cunde *see* **kynde**; **cundelet** *see* **kendles**

cure *n.* heed E 168

curtest *adj.as n.* most excellent one E 249

cusse *v.* kiss

custadis *pl.* tarts W 353

cuthe *see* **can**; **cuþþes** *see* **kythe**

cuttede *ppl.adj.* gelded W 240

daderande *pr.p.* trembling W 97

dadillyng *n.* chattering W 44

daies, dawes, dawen *pl.* days; *on* ~ during the day S 40

dayntethes *pl.* delicacies W 330

day-rawe *n.* ray of dawn A 5181

dale, dole *n.* distribution W 303, 305, portion W 337, part E 6

dalfe *pa.t.* dug E 45; **doluen** *pp.* buried P 258, E 99

dalte *see* **dele**

damesene *n.* damson S 89

dampned *pp.* condemned S 267

dare *n.* grief SS 133

dare *v.* cower K 90

dariols *pl.* pastries W 354

dartis *pl.* arrows A 1519

date *n.* period of time E 205, lifetime A 5193

daunceden *pa.t.* ran about SS 12

daungerde *pa.t.* made liable E 320

dawe *v.* dawn; **dewe** *pa.t.* S 174

dawen, -es *see* **daies**

debonerté *n.* mercy E 123

declare *v.* pass judgement on S 175

declynet *pa.t.* deviated E 237

decre *n.* ecclesiastical law A 1706

dede *n.*[1] action E 169

dede *n.*[2] death; dead body E 116; **dede-day** death day W 441

dede(n) *see* **do(o)**

dedifie *v.* consecrate, dedicate E 6, 23

defaute *n.* damage E 148

degh, dee *v.* (**deis** *pr.3sg.*; **deghed, diʒede** *pa.t.*) die

degreces *pl.* steps

deil *see* **dole**

deis, dese *n.* judicial bench

del *n.* devil H VII. 34

dele, -yn *v.* (**dalte** *pa.t.*) distribute W 441, P 403, hand out S 292, bestow on P 660

deluuie *n.* Flood A 5068

deme *v.* judge, pass judgement, arbitrate between, assign to T 2444, award T 2413, 2434, order S 175, declare P 331, vow P 367; ~ *to* inflict upon P 472

demyng *n.* verdict T 2419

dene *n.* dean E 144

denede, denyed *pa.t.* resounded E 246, SS 13, 14

deny *v.* refuse S 140

deol *see* **dole**; **deolfolich** *see* **dulfully**; **deorly** *see* **dere**

departede, depertid *pa.t.* separated P 77, dispersed T 12509

depresse *v.* vanquish A 5156

deputate *n.* deputy E 227

dere *n.* evil intent S 243

dere *v.* injure P 36

dere *adj.* valuable, precious, noble, excellent; proper T 2391; **derrest** *superl.* most honoured E 29; **dere, duere** *adv.* dearly H I. 18, fondly A 5152; **deorly** heartily H VII. 29

derfe *adj.* great E 99, terrible T 1528,

Glossary

shameless S 40, 131, wicked S 278;
derfliche *adv.* cruelly S 242

derke *n.* dark place T 2361

derne *n.* dark W 413, secrecy S 131

derne *adj.* secret; *adv.* secretly
H II. 36

dese *see* **deis**

deue *pr.pl.* deafen S 235

deuyne *pr.pl.(subj.)* conjecture E 169

deuyse *n.* construction T 1576

deuyse *v.* explain to E 225; *pa.t.*
described E 144, 309; *pp.*
constructed T 1553

deuoydes *pr.3sg.* eliminates E 348;
pl. remove A 5085; *pa.t.* went away
E 116

dewe *see* **dawe**

dialiticus *n.* dialectics A 1706

dietis *pr.pl.* feed A 4865

digges *pl.* ducks P 245

dighte *v.* (**dyght, dyȝt** *pa.t.& pp.*;
(i)diht *pp.*) prepare, set; adorn
H II. 6, place P 125, establish P 597,
provide S 8, assign E 23, build E 45,
condemn, put (to death) S 246, 267,
A 1627; ~ *vs* condemn us to E 294

digne *pr.3sg.subj.* grant E 123

diȝede *see* **degh**

dike *n.* ditch, moat

dymedyn *pa.t.pl.* made dark J 531

dynges *pr.3sg.* knocks P 650; **dongen**
pa.t. J 676

dynt *n.* blow P 447, W 103

dische-metis *pl.* pies W 354

diseuered *pa.t.* parted S 300

dismale *pl.* evil days S 305

disparage *v.* sully S 253

disseuert *pa.t.* divided T 1602

ditoyne *n.* dittany (herb) S 114

ditte *pa.t.* shut E 116

diuinours *pl.* wise men A 1668

doctours *pl.* learned men A 1668

doghety *adj.* valiant P 181

dole, deil, deol, dul *n.* sorrow

dole *see* **dale; doluen** *see* **dalfe**

dom *n.* judgement, decree

domesmon *n.* judge

dommyn *pr.pl.* dam up J 681

donged *pp.* manured H IX. 9

dongen *see* **dynges**

donkede *pa.t.* was moist P 10; *pp.*
moistened J 624

do(o) *v.* cause W 220, S 236, K 90;

imper. make W 478, behave K 128;
dede(n), dide *pa.t.* placed P 557, put
S 174; **done** *pp.* placed T 2401

doren *pl.* gaps H VII. 14

dotest *pr.2sg.* become feeble-minded
S 305

doughty *adj.as n.* brave man P 344

doussypers *see* **dussypere**

doust *n.* dust

doute *n.* fear H VII. 4, anxiety P 102

douth *n.* army P 348

doutyng *pr.p.* fearing T 12478

dowkynge *n.* diving P 245

drafe *see* **driue**

drawe *v.* (**drewe, droghe(n), drow(gh)**
pa.t.; **drawe(n), ydrawe** *pp.*) draw
SS 133, J 695, drag H VIII. 20, pull
E 6, get near J 570, A 4900, move
T 2379, come T 2361, go S 40, *(refl.)*
P 410, withdraw P 381

drechet *pp.* afflicted A 5068

drede *n.* in *withouten eny* ~ certainly
S 274, 326

dredis *pr.3sg.* is afraid A 669;
dred(d)e *pp.* P 488, S 32

dredles *adv.* without doubt A 1595

dreghe *v.* experience P 3

dreghe, dreȝe *adj.* mighty A 4931,
excellent T 1622, troubled P 102;
dreghly *adv.* in reality T 2379

dreynt *pp.* drowned H VII. 31

dreme *n.* voice E 191

dremed *pa.t.(impers.)* dreamed P 102

drepide, drepit(t) *pa.t.* killed

drery *adj.* mournful E 191

dresse *v.* deliver E 236, send S 274,
T 2444

dreuyn *see* **driue; drewe** *see* **drawe**

drye *n.* drought W 276

dryft *n.* driving of deer SS 14

driȝe *n.* period A 4915

driȝt *n.* period A 5001, 5188

driȝten *n.* God

drynke *v.* provide drink H VII. 29

dryt *n.* shit H VIII. 31

driue *v.* (**drafe** *pa.t.*; **dreuyn** *pp.*)
hasten A 5183, run P 19, come
A 687, travel A 4937, 5001, fall
A 712, send A 718, 1519, endure
J 708

droghe(n) *see* **drawe**

dropeles *adj.* without rain W 276

drouping *n.* suffering SS 133

227

Glossary

drow(gh) *see* **drawe**

drowpys *pr.3sg.* sinks A 734; **drowpet** *pa.t.* mourned T 1523

du *adj.* accompanying T 12491; **duly** *adv.* properly T 2401, justly T 2413

duale *v.* poison A 5152

duere *see* **dere**; **dul** *see* **dole**

dulfully *adv.* sorrowfully; **deolfolich** shamefully S 267

dures *pr.3sg.* lasts W 108

durre *n.* door E 116

dussypere *n.* famous knight; **d(o)ussypers** *pl.* princes P 403, twelve peers P 521

dutten *v.* close H VII. 14, K 91

dwynande *pr.p.* languishing E 294

ebland *adv.* together

Ebru *n.* Hebrew A 5198

ecchekkes *pl.* false game P 235

eche *see* **iche**

efte *adv.* again

egge *n.* ridge A 5003

eggit *ppl.adj.* sharp-edged E 40

eghe *n.* eye; **eghne, eyene, ene** *pl.*; *tofore/byfore with myn* ~ in my presence W 434, P 549; *on/for bothe myn* ~ on pain of my life W 126, E 194, A 5169

egheliche *adv.* extraordinarily P 28

egre *adj.* fierce W 79; **egirly** *adv.* bitterly A 703

egretes *pl.* white herons W 494

eyre *see* **aire**

eke *adv.* also

elde *n.* age, old age; *first* ~ youth A 657

eldes *pr.3sg.* grows old W 9

elike *adv.* **equally** A 1545; *ai* ~ continually A 1524

ell(i)s *adv.* besides, otherwise; other A 644, in another way E 121

emaunge *adv.* here and there A 5028

enabet *pp.* established T 1600, 1612

enbawmyd *pp.* enbalmed

enbelicit *pp.* decorated E 51

enbroddirde *pp.* embroidered P 123

enbrouden *pp.* embroidered A 1692

enchaunte *v.* delude S 46

enclyne *v.* bow K 125, *(refl.)* A 1726, bow to T 2448

encrampeschet *pa.t.* twisted P 287; *ppl.adj.* P 154

encumbrid *pp.* overcame A 1603

ende *n.* district W 47

endes *pl.* ducks P 220

ene *see* **eghe**

enewede *pp.* driven into water P 245

enfourmer *n.* instructor A 626

engynes *pl.* siege-engines J 674, A 1538

enhaunsid *pa.t.* erected A 5194

enjoynyd *pp.* appointed E 216

enprise *n.* achievement E 253

ensample *n.* example W 421, imitation T 1610

entent *n.* objective S 355

enterment *n.* burial A 738

entouchid *pp.* poisoned E 297

entris *pl.* passages T 1600

entris *pr.3sg.* in ~ *in* begins A 5136

enuenymyd *pp.* envenomed J 654, **envemonde** A 1513

enverrouns *pr.sg.* surrounds A 4907

envyous *adj.* full of ill-will P 163

eode *see* **ȝede(n)**

er, are, or *adv. & conj.* before, previously

er *see* **be(n), euer**

erand, ernde *n.* request; decree W 125, business H VII. 22

erber *n.* garden S 104

erberi *n.* flowers S 8, 11

erbes *pl.* plants S 8

erdly *adj.* earthly A 1735

ere *see* **be(n)**

eren *pl.* ears H I. 23

ernde *see* **erand**

ers *n.* arse H I. 14

erst, ar(e)ste *n., adj.& adv.* first

eschewe *v.* avoid S 46

esely *adv.* politely T 2418

esid *pp.* rested A 4917

esyngis *pl.* eaves A 1645

estres *pl.* estates W 403

euel *adv.* hardly E 276

euen *n.* eve, evening

euen, euyn *adv.* just, exactly; nearby T 2371, also T 12518; ~ *vponon* at once T 2418

euene *n.* character H VI. 38

euer, er *adv.* always

euerech, -uch *adj.* each, every; ~ *a* every

eueryllyke *adv.* continually A 727

euer(r)ous *adj.* eager

228

euynsong *n.* evening T 2351

face *n.* surface A 5186
faʒt *see* **feʒtis**
fay *n.* truth S 87
faile *v.* be lacking (to); **faylid,
  fayleden** *pa.t.* was without E 287,
  disappeared E 342, lost J 593
fayly *adj. & n.* delinquent H VI. 43,
  77
fayne *adj.* happy; ready E 176
faynhed *n.* joy T 2446
faire *see* **fare, feire**
fayth *n.* allegiance W 329; *in* ~ truly
  T 2446
faithly *adv.* faithfully T 2440
falle *v.* (**valle** *pr.3sg.subj.*; **fell** *pa.t.*;
  fallen *pp.*) fall H VII. 4, befall
  P 317, happen (to) W 448,
  T 2352, 12463 come to pass T 12493,
  belong A 1672, be allotted to
  T 2406; *pr.sg.impers.* it is necessary
  W 378; ~ *to fote* submit (to)
  H VI. 66, SS 103
falshede *n.* lying
falsleke *n.* falsehood H IV. 34
falsly *adj.* deceitful H IV. 31
falsshipe *n.* dishonesty H III. 32
fande *see* **fynde; fandis** *see* **fonde;
  fangis** *see* **fonge(n)**
fanons *pl.* vestments A 1704
fante *see* **fa(u)nt**
fantome *n.* illusion P 184
fare *n.* behaviour P 59, K 24,
  entertainment W 295, circumstances
  K 87, A 672, situation T 1511; **faire**
  action T 2435
fare *v.* (**fars** *pr.3sg.*; **ferd(en), fore**
  pa.t.; **faren** *pp.*) go; seem (to be)
  J 530, 548, act K 85, T 12540, get on
  K 110; **fayr** *pr.pl.subj.* let us
  continue A 740
fason *n.* appearance S 17
faste *adj.* firm H V. 19; *adv.* eagerly
  A 672; ~ *by* close to A 626
fastynge *n.* confirmation E 173
fatills *pr.3sg. (refl.)* gets ready P 20;
  fittilled *pa.t.* P 542; **fettild** *pp.* fixed
  A 626
fatte *see* **fet**
fatteþ *pr.3sg.* grows fat H III. 32
faucoun *n.* falcon H II. 25
fa(u)nt *n.* child S 329, A 1600

faute *n.* lack H IX. 16
fawked *pp.* caught (by falcons) W 98
fax *n.* hair A 601
fe *n.* prize T 2400; **fees** *pl.* rewards
  S 86
fecchyng *n.* bringing-in T 1626
fede *v.* please H II. 46; **yfed** *pp.*
  brought up H VII. 18
fee *v.* reward W 434
feere *see* **fere**
feetur *n.* projection of antler P 27
feʒe *v.* match H I. 31
feʒtis *pr.3sg.* fights A 1524; **faʒt** *pa.t.*
  fought A 643
feh *n.* cattle H III. 65
fey *adj.* dead
feylour *see* **feloure**
feyned *pp.* made (yourself) appear
  A 715
feire, faire *adj.* lovely, fine; **feyrore**
  comp. more beautiful H II. 46; *adv.*
  splendidly H III. 42, excellently
  P 71, 77, well K 93
felde *n.* (battle)field
felde *see* **fellid; feldus** *see* **folde**
fele, feole *adj.* many
fele *adj.as n.* worthy ones T 2400
fell *see* **falle**
felle *n.* skin
felle *adj.* treacherous W 228, terrible
  T 12473, formidable A 613, fierce
  A 5049
fellid *pa.t.* killed A 1529; **felde** J 595
fellys *pl.* hills P 59
felonse *adj.* treacherous E 231
feloure, feylour *n.* foliage
  A 4948, 5131
fen *n.* mud T 1609
fend *n.* devil, wicked creature; **fyndus**
  pl. fiends K 92
fenge *n.* prize H V. 2
fens *n.* defence A 4880
fer *see* **ferre(re)**
ferd *ppl.adj.* afraid; *as n.* fear
ferdchip *n.* fear K 86
ferde *n.* army, company
ferdede *pp.* assembled W 138
ferd(en) *see* **fare**
ferdere *adj.* keener W 287
ferdnes *n.* fear W 98
fere, feere *n.*[1] husband, wife, mistress
fere *n.*[2] (noble) company W 21,
  companions K 109; *in* ~ together; *to*

229

~ as a companion S 48

fereles *adj.* unique A 5120

ferforthe *adv.* far E 242

ferkes *pr.3sg.* goes P 20; **ferkede** *pa.t.* went P 655

ferly, ferlé *n.* marvel, strange thing; *pl.* strange events

ferly *adj.* surprising, wonderful, *adv.* very, marvellously, wonderfully

ferli(e)d *pp.* marvelled A 4888, amazed A 5118

fernes *n.* in *o* ~ at a distance A 1547

ferre(re) *adj.* further W 311, more advanced A 633; **fer(re)** *adv.* far (off); *o* ~ at a distance T 1615; **ferrere, fyrre** *comp.* further

ferrours *pl.* blacksmiths T 1593

ferse, fuerse *adj.* fierce; huge T 1617; *adv.* violently K 87; **fuersly** fiercely T 2356, violently T 12493

fersely *see* **freschely**

feste *pa.t.* fastened P 91

festes *pl.* feasts P 385

fet *pa.t.* fetched P 378; **fatte** H III. 65

fete *n.* skill T 1529

fettild *see* **fatills; fewl(l)es** *see* **foule**

fiches *pr.3sg.* fixes A 4980; **ficchid** *pa.t.* pitched A 4866

fygers *pl.* fig trees S 86

fykel *adj.* sinful H IV. 31

filbert *n.* hazel S 92

filet *n.* headband H I. 32

fill *v.* fulfill A 4905

filmarte *n.* polecat P 18

fynde *v.* (**fande, fond** *pa.t.*; **fondon, foundyn, ifounde** *pp.*) find; invent T 1628, provide for W 428, nourish K 93

fyndus *see* **fend**

fine *n.* end S 344

fyne *adj.* pure E 173, clear A 4980

fyned *pp.* refined S 193

fynes *pr.3sg.* ends A 740

fynyst *pp.* finished A 687

fynour *n.* refiner P 587

firmament *n.* sky

fyrre *see* **ferre(re); fittilled** *see* **fatills**

flabband *ppl.adj.* flapping A 4934

flagge *n.* rush K 85

flayede *pp.* put to flight P 428

flayre *n.* smell S 98

flakerande *pr.p.* flapping W 92

flambande *pr.p.* flaming J 653

flasches *pl.* pools J 571

flecchours *pl.* arrow-sellers T 1593

fleh *n.* flea H VIII. 12; **fles** *pl.* H VIII. 10

fleyn *see* **flewe**

fleis *n.* flesh H VIII. 38

fleschliche *adj.* bodily S 271

flete *v.* swim W 386

fletyng *n.* flowing T 1609

flewe *pa.t.* flayed P 78; **fleyn** *pp.* J 694

fly3th *n.* departure SS 84

fly3tte *n.* struggle SS 85

flyte *imper.* dispute P 264

flitt *v.* move A 4988, proceed SS 85

flyttynge *n.* debate W 154

flode *n.* water, river, sea

flo3en *see* **flowen**

florence *pl.* florins W 281

floreschede, florisch(s)t *pp.* grown fat P 71, adorned with flowers A 4844, adorned A 5115

flote *n.* army, company A 1704, 4998

floterand *pr.p.* tossing T 12524

flowen, flo3en *pa.t.* fled J 611, A 1515, flew J 653; *pp.* fled P 498

flumme *n.* river A 4866

fnyrtyd *pa.t.* snorted K 55

fodemed *pp.* grown S 92

fogus *pl.* meadows K 41

fokke *n.* people A 4988

fol *adj.* immoral H VI. 43

fol *see* **ful**

folde *n.* earth; *on* ~ there

folde *v.* bend over W 35, bend K 85; **feldus** *pr.3sg.* grows weak K 86

fole *n.* horse K 55

foles *pl.* fools S 290

folowe *v.* flow A 640; **foloen** *pr.pl.* follow W 502

folwe *pr.1sg.* baptise E 318; **fologhed** *pa.t.* P 545; *pp.* P 552

fomen *pl.* enemies P 356

fond *see* **fynde**

fonde *v.* deal with SS 41; **fandis** *pr.3sg.* carries out A 681

fondis *see* **founde; fondon** *see* **fynde**

fonge(n) *v.* (**fangis** *pr.3sg.*; **fonge** *pa.t.*; **fongen** *pp.*) receive, take, capture

fonnes *pr.2sg.* are foolish P 183

foode *n.* young person S 17, 283

for *prep.* before H VI. 67, to avoid

Glossary

S 57, to prevent T 1579; *conj.*
because
forced *pp.* strengthened W 170
forewardes *see* **forward**
forfrayed *pp.* rubbed (of horns) P 27
forfrayede *pp.* terrified P 59
forgid *pp.* fashioned A 1665, 1713
forgo *v.* avoid E 276
forhaht *pp.* rejected H V. 34
forjustes *pr.3sg.* unhorses J 538
forlaped *pp.* filled with drink
H VIII. 19
forlore *pp.* abandoned H III. 23
forme *see* **fo(u)rme**
forschorne *pa.t.pl.* cut to pieces J 558
forsoht *pp.* sought out H II. 20
forsothe *adv.* indeed
forst *n.* frost H VII. 5
forstoppette *pp.* smothered J 576
forswat *ppl.adj.* sweaty H VI. 70
forswore, forsworn *pp.* perjured
H VI. 49, A 1588
forte *prep.* to, in order to
forthe *adv.* since then T 1628
forthi *adv.* therefore; *conj.* since
W 286
forthinkis *pr.sg.(impers.)* is
displeasing A 1587
forthir *v.* benefit, show favour to
W 429, 464
forward *n.* promise T 2440;
forewardes *pl.* contracts H V. 19
forwyse *adj.* prescient A 715
forwrast *pp.* seized E 220
foster *v.* care for
fostere *n.* in ~ *of the fee* forester by
heritable right P 94
fote *n.* footing E 42; **fotes** *pl.* feet
A 4978
fothire *n.* cart-load P 189
foul *adj.* wretched H III. 47
foule *n.* bird P 15; **fewl(l)es** *pl.*
(water) birds
founde *v.* (**fondis** *pr.3sg.*; **fonde** *pa.t.*)
go, hasten; turn A 4880, travel
A 5063
foundyn *see* **fynde**
founte *n.* font P 549
fourche *n.* haunch P 91, 88
fourme *n.*¹ in *in* ~ *of* in accordance
with E 230
fo(u)rme *n.*² lair H IX. 13, W 13,
P 20

fourmyt *pp.* constructed T 1540, 1557
fourte *see* **furþe**
frayne *v.* ask, ask about
fra(m) *see* **fro**
frape *n.* company S 289
fre *adj.* noble, honourable; gracious
E 318, excellent T 2430; *adv.* nobly
W 434
freȝt *n.* terror K 85
freȝt *ppl.adj.* frightened A 1564
freke, freike *n.* man
frekild *pp.* spotted A 5115
freli(ch), freoly *adj.* noble, excellent,
lovely; **fre(e)ly** *adv.* eagerly P 222,
generously T 2435
fremede *adv.* as a stranger, alone
H V. 1
frendis *pl.* relatives P 354, A 619
freschely *adv.* again W 217, 367,
vigorously P 372; **fersely** eagerly
P 216, 226
fresse *n.* harm S 43
frete *v.* devour W 386
fret(t) *pp.* covered A 1665, 4893
frythe *n.* wood; **friht** H II. 25,
H V. 1
fro, fra, fram *prep.* from; *conj.* when
W 200, as soon as W 26; *adv.* away
frountel *n.* band across forehead
H I. 31
froward *prep.* from J 598
frowarde *adj.* disobedient E 231
frumentee *n.* wheat porridge W 334
fuers(ly) *see* **ferse**
ful, fol *adv.* very, entirely
full *imper.* fill up W 217, 367
fulloght *n.* baptism E 299
fulsen *pr.3sg.subj.* help E 124
fulþe *n.* filth, wickedness S 344
fundement *n.* foundation E 42
fure *n.* fire J 548, 653
furme *adj.* earliest H VI. 7; **furmest**
adv. first H I. 15
furrit *pp.* trimmed with fur E 81
furþe *adj.* fourth H III. 8; **fourte**
W 163

gaa *v.* go A 636; **gase** *pr.3sg.* A 631;
(refl.) A 5014; **go** *pp.* ago H VII. 21
gabbyng *n.* deception H VI. 62
gadir *see* **gedir**
gaye *adj.* fair P 351; **gayliche** *adv.*
splendidly S 42, beautifully S 95

231

Glossary

gaynly *adv.* quickly P 281
gayre *n.* equipment T 2438
gale *n.* singing H II. 26
galed *pa.t.* spoke A 4852
galegs *pl.* sandals W 157
galt *n.* boar A 4870
gameliche *adj.* joyful SS 45; *adv.* SS 67
gan, gon(ne) *pa.t.* did (forming pa.t.)
gange *v.* go A 5173
gare *v.* cause (to be done); **gers** *pr.3sg.*; **gart, gert** *pa.t.*
garettis *pl.* turrets A 1540
gargeles *pl.* gargoyles E 48
garnettes *pl.* pomegranates S 95
garnysht, -est *pp.* decorated E 48, adorned A 1656
garrite *n.* siege-tower J 647
gast *n.* spirit A 726, soul A 5127
gate *n.* street, road, path, way
gat(te) *see* **gete**
gedelyng *n.* low fellow H VIII. 36; *pl.* H VIII. 2, 5
gedir *pr.1sg.* gather W 231; **gadir** *pl.* accumulate W 227; **gadird, gedrid** *pp.* assembled W 432, E 134; ~ *of* assembled from H VIII. 5
geyneþ *pr.3sg.* helps H III. 43
generall *n.* in *in* ~ together A 1630
gentil, jentil(le), jentel *adj.*[1] noble, gracious; **gentilly** *adv.* nobly P 439
gentil *adj.*[2] pagan E 216, 229
gentrise *n.* graciousness S 41
gere, geire *n.*[1] armour, equipment
gere *n.*[2] mood H V. 4
gerede *pp.* dressed P 122; ~ *of* adorned with W 63
gerner *n.* storehouse H VIII. 16
gernet *n.* garnet H II. 4
gernets *pl.* pomegranates A 4851
gers, gert *see* **gare**
gesse *v.* imagine A 5127; *pr.3sg.* supposes A 5054
gesserante *n.* coat of armour P 180
gete *v.* guard P 608
gete, gat(te) *pa.t.* got P 281, T 1529, conquered P 416, 491, brought E 241, begot A 724
gett *n.* fashion W 410
gigelot *n.* tart H I. 17, 25
gyle *n.* deceit H V. 48
gylofre *n.* clove H II. 40
gynful *adj.* treacherous E 238

gynge *n.* company E 137, A 4842
girde *see* **gurden**
girden *v.* (**girde, gurte** *pa.t.*) strike P 343, knock SS 45, push A 1540, press A 1558, rush P 318, J 552, cut J 566
girdillers *pl.* belt-makers T 1584
gyse *n.* custom A 631
glad *adj.* beautiful H II. 16; **gladly** *adj.* happy H V. 4
gladchip *n.* joy K 57
glade *v.* rejoice K 132, become happy W 227, gladden T 2445, please W 391, A 724; **gladit** *pa.t.* T 2417
glayfe *n.* sword P 202
glede *n.* ember SS 57
glees *pr.pl.* rejoice
glent *v.* deviate E 241
glent *pa.t.* shone A 4944
gleterand *ppl.adj.* glittering W 275
glystnede *pa.t.* shone H V. 3; **glisnande, glesenand** *ppl.adj.* shining E 78, A 603
glode *n.* space E 75
gloes *pr.sg.* glows P 188; **gloud** *pa.t.* shone SS 57
glorand *pr.p.* staring A 4855
glotte *n.* filth E 297
glow *pr.pl.(subj.)* call E 171
gnewen *pa.t.* gnawed P 50
gnoste *n.* spark(?) H VIII. 5
go *see* **gaa**; **godardys** *see* **guttars**
goddes *pl.* goddesses T 2381, 2388, 2439
godely *adv.* very much T 2445
golanand *ppl.adj.* howling A 4923
golyone *n.* simple tunic P 138
gols *see* **goules**
gome *n.* man
gon(ne) *see* **gan**
gore *n.* dress, clothing
gorge *n.* throat A 5112
gosshet *pa.t.* gushed T 1607
goules, gols *n.& adj.* red colour A 4946, 5116, 5186
goullyng *n.* howling W 359
go(u)tes *pl.* streams J 560, A 4923
graythe, greyþe *v.* (**gra(y)thed, greiþed** *pa.t.*; **grayþ(ed), graþid** *pp.*) make P 588, 608, A 5005, build J 648, dress A 1711, finish K 131, set P 85, pay H III. 38, *(refl.)* prepare, (prepare to) go

graythely *adv.* firmly P 202, fittingly P 642, swiftly P 494; **grayþlé** at once K 132

graythist *adj.* most eminent E 251

grame *n.* rage J 552

grane *n.* groan A 726

granys *pr.3sg.* groans A 717

graunte *n.* in *hade* ~ was granted E 126

graunte *v.* (**graunt** *pa.t.*) grant T 2417, agree T 2409, admit S 298

grauen *pp.* engraved; buried P 629

grece *pl.* steps A 5176

grede *v.* shout SS 20, revile H VI. 9

gredely *adv.* eagerly A 1558

gree *n.* dignity P 473

gregeis *pl.* Greeks P 318

grey frere *n.* Franciscan H VII. 19

greyþe, greiþed *see* **graythe**

gremede *pa.t.impers.* in *hire* ~ she grew angry H V. 7

gremly *adj.* terrible A 726

gremþ *n.* anger T 12540

grene *n.* field SS 38

grete *n.* earth E 41, sandstone J 620

grete *v.* weep A 5168; **grette** *pa.t.* E 126

grete *adv.* much W 224

greue *n.* thicket; **greuys, grewis** *pl.* woods A 4852, 5080

greue *v.* cause trouble S 138; *pr.3sg.* torments H III. 55; *pa.t.* became angry P 182, 194, annoyed P 50

greuyng *n.* offending T 12545

Grew *n.* Greek T 2398, A 5139

grym *adj.* formidable A 5083; *adv.* cruelly P 202

grippede *pa.t.* pulled P 85

grippes *pl.* trenches T 1543

grys *n.* in *gro ant* ~ grey furs H II. 16

gryse *n.* grass P 8

grisely *adj.* forbidding A 5083

gryst *pp.* terrified K 58

griþ *n.* friendship SS 117

griþele *adj.* splendid SS 19

gro *see* **grys**

groched *pp.* begrudged A 1590

grom *n.* servant; *pl.* attendants SS 20; **gromene** *gen.pl.* H VIII. 16

gromyl *n.* gromwell H II. 37

grone *n.* seed H II. 37

grounde *n.* earth; *appon* ~ anywhere W 173

grounden *pp.* disposed of W 269

grownden, grounden *pp.* sharpened P 202, J 566

grubber *n.* digger E 41

grucchyng *n.* grumbling H VIII. 36

grue *n.* bit E 319

grue *pr.1sg.* shudder K 57

gude *n.* money; **gudes** *pl.* goods

gurden *pa.t.* clothed E 251; **girde** *pp.* wrapped round W 94, P 138

gurte *see* **girden**

guttars *pl.* gutters A 4923; **godardys** T 1607

ȝaf *see* **ȝeuen**

ȝape *adj.* lively; clever W 75; **ȝapeste** *superl.* liveliest W 119; **ȝapely** *adv.* quickly, nimbly, **ȝepply** S 118, **ȝepely** freshly E 88

ȝare *adv.* greatly S 191, soon S 228, well A 607

ȝaris *pr.3sg.(refl.)* gets ready A 4993

ȝarken *pr.pl.* place J 646; *pp.* fashioned W 75, made A 5021

ȝarmand *pr.p.* howling A 4872

ȝate *n.* gate

ȝe *pron.* you; **ou** *acc.* H VIII. 38; **or** *gen.* your H V. 17

ȝede(n), eode, ȝeoden, ȝode *pa.t.* went, walked

ȝedire *adj.* frequent A 5168

ȝee *adv.* yes W 368

ȝef, ȝif *conj.* if; *bot* ~ unless

ȝeȝe *v.* cry out H VI. 55, VII 35

ȝeldis, ȝheldez, ȝildis *pr.* gives A 5146, gives up A 726, make A 1511, repay A 1516; **ȝolden** *pp.* surrendered A 1572, handed over P 398, 575

ȝeme *v.* guide W 419, care for W 376, protect W 114, 152; *pa.t.* governed E 202

ȝeolumon *n.* crier? H VI. 55

ȝepely, ȝepply *see* **ȝape**

ȝerand *pr.p.* yelling A 4872

ȝerde *n.*[1] garden S 118, **ȝorde** precinct (of cathedral) E 88; **ȝerdes** *pl.* enclosed lands W 289

ȝerde *n.*[2] rod H VI. 55, yardstick A 4877

ȝerne *v.* long for, be eager for

ȝerne *adv.* eagerly, thoroughly,

Glossary

vigorously; greatly P 183, painfully
A 667

ȝernynge *n.* desire P 535

ȝerre *n.* loud cry A 5168

ȝeten *pr.pl.* pour J 670; **ȝett** *pa.t.*
gushed out A 5168; **ȝeten** *ppl.adj.*
cast A 607, 5021

ȝet(t)e *pp.* granted P 398, 535, 575

ȝeuen *pr.pl.* give J 527; **ȝaf** *pa.t.*
S 280

ȝheldez *see* ȝeldis; **ȝif** *see* ȝef

ȝiftes *pl.* gifts S 280

ȝildis *see* ȝeldis

ȝis *adv.* yes A 5067

ȝit(t) *adv.* yet, also, still

ȝode *see* ȝede(n); **ȝolden** *see* ȝeldis

ȝolow *adj.* yellow S 192

ȝone *pron.* that one A 5120

ȝorde *see* ȝerde

ȝore *adv.* for a long time, long ago

ȝoskyd *pa.t.* sobbed E 312

ȝoskingis *pl.* sobbings A 5168

ȝoten *n.* giant A 4872

ȝouþehede *n.* youth S 280

habben, ha *v.* (**ha** *pr.1sg.* H IV.5; **as**
3sg. H IX.1; **han** *pl.*; **habbe** *subj.*
H I.17; **hade, hedde** *pa.t.*) have; ~
in bring in E 17

habyde *v.* (**habade** *pa.t.*) remain, wait

hayfre *n.* heifer H VIII. 27

hailsis *pr.3sg.* greets A 5056

hald *see* holde

haldis *pr.3sg.* beholds A 1650

hale *n.*[1] hiding-place H III. 35

hale *n.*[2] tent W 70

hale *see* hole

halfe, halue *n.* side

haly *adj.* holy A 5065

halidoms *pl.* holy relics A 1589

halymotes *pl.* court meetings H I. 28

hallede *pa.t.* in ~ *to* drew back P 53

halowes *pl.* saints E 23, holy ones
A 5042

halowyd *pa.t.* shouted at K 12

halse *n.* neck P 373; **haulse** P 90

halsid *pa.t.* embraced A 5155

halt *see* holde; **ham** *see* hy;
hamberkes *see* hawberkes

hame *n.* building A 5029

hames *pl.* plumage A 5113

hampird *pa.t.* encumbered A 4927

hande-while, hond-qwile *n.* short time

hant *v.* assemble Ā 4856;
haunteþ *pr.pl.* indulge in
H VIII. 13; **haunted** *pa.t.* resorted
S 31; *pp.* practised T 1628

hap *n.* happiness H IV. 68; *pl.* events
A 5063

happede *pp.* enclosed W 298

happit *pa.t.* turned out for T 12481

harde *adv.* close W 11, P 19, firmly
P 201

hardy *adj.* bold J 651

hardynes *n.* boldness

hare *see* hore

harlotes *pl.* low servants
H VIII. 3, 13

harme *n.* evil W 68; *pl.* injuries
E 232, J 679, indignities H V. 10

harmeles *adj.* unharmed J 632

haspede *pp.* fastened P 201

hasteletez *pl.* roast meats W 492

hastif *adj.* impetuous SS 91

hat *n.* order H VI. 71

hat *see* hete

hates *pl.* hatreds W 219

hathel(l) *n.* man

hatt(en) *see* hete

hattfull *adj.* wrathful W 73

hattir *see* hettir

hattren *pl.* clothes H VII. 6

haulse *see* halse; **haunted** *see* hant

hauande *pr.p.(as n.)* wealth W 323

hauer *adj.* skilful H VI. 2

hawberkes *pl.* coats of mail W 50;
hamberkes J 640

hawes *pl.* hedges P 19

hawtayne *adj.* noble P 209

hawteste *adj.* noblest P 213

he *see* heh, heo, hy; **he(o)re, huere** *see*
hy; **hedde** *see* habben

hede *n.* in **haue (to)** ~ pay attention
to H II. 48, notice SS 59

hede *adj.* splendid K 122

hedes *pr.3sg.* rules S 188, looks
P 508, A 678

hedire *adv.* hither; **hedirto** up to
now A 5030

hedous *adj.* hideous A 4989

heere *see* here, herie

hefe *v.* (**heuys** *pr.3sg.*; **heef** *pa.t.*) lift
P 288, A 677, 1712, push P 92, raise
S 262

hegge *n.* hedge H VII. 8

heghely, highly *adv.* solemnly

P 178, 204, T 2403

heght(e) *see* **hete, highte**

heghwalles *pl.* woodpeckers W 38

heh, hegh, heȝe, he(y), heþ *adj.* high; noble T 2415, 2439, distinguished E 137; *an, (vp)on, of* ~ on high H VI. 56, VII 35, W 64, out loud A 5056; **heghe** *adv.* loud W 358

heilse *v.* greet S 133

heyse *n.* ease H VII. 28

helde *n.* grace H V. 9

helde *v.* fall down K 15, J 550, bow K 80, E 196; **heldyt** *pa.t.* went E 137

helde *see* **holde**

hele *n.* well-being P 177, happiness K 14

heltre *n.* halter W 418

hem *see* **hy**

heme *n.* yokel H VI. 22; **heme** *pl.* villagers K 123

heme *adj.* fitting H IV. 42

hend *adj.* gracious, noble, worthy; submissive H IV. 28; *as n.* gracious one(s) W 419, S 31, A 4884, noble lady S 133; **hendy** lovely one H II. 49; **hendore** *comp.* H II. 48, **hendyr** kinder K 136; **hendest** *superl.* H V. 9; **hendely** *adv.* graciously P 267

hend *see* **honde**

hendelec *n.* nobility H IV. 70

hene *v.* scoff K 122

hene *adj.* contemptible H III. 29

hengeth *see* **hongen**

henyng *n.* insult H V. 8

henmest *adj.* hindmost K 79

hent *v.* (**hent** *pa.t. & pp.*) take, seize, receive; come in contact J 544, grasp J 711, catch A 4910, treat H IV. 42

heo, ho *pron.* she; **he** H I. 14; **hire** *gen.* her

heo, heore *see* **hy**

heowe *n.* family H V. 33

hep *n.* group J 696

heraud *n.coll.* heralds

herbarewen *v.* live H VIII. 40

herbergages *pl.* houses S 6

herdmans *gen.* retainer's W 364; **hyrdmen** *pl.* H VI. 40

here, heere *n.* army

here *v.* hear; **yhere** *imper.* listen to H V. 9; ~ *apon* hear about A 5063

here *see* **hy**

hereman *n.* lord A 5065; **heremans** *gen.* man's A 4859

heres *pl.* sirs W 212, warriors A 4856

here-wedys *pl.* armour P 201

herghdes *pa.t.* harrowed E 291; **heryett** dragged P 66, **herid** tormented A 4927

herie *pr.1sg.* praise H IV. 53, **heere** E 339; **herid** *pp.* E 325, **heryet** exalted P 427

herygoud *n.* cloak H VI. 22

herken *v.* listen; ~ *after* listen for E 307

hersouns *pr.3sg.* honours A 1723

herston *n.* hearth-stone H IX. 4

hertelich *adv.* sympathetically S 268, fully T 2439

heruest *n.* autumn T 12465

heste *n.*[1] fury T 12506

heste *n.*[2] promise P 178

hete *n.* eagerness SS 91

hete *v.* (**hete, hatt(en)** *pr.*; **het, hat, heght, hight** *pa.t.*; **hatt(en), highte, hiht, hiȝt** *pp.*) promise, call, be called; command W 211, threaten H III. 15, shout out H VI. 56, offer H III. 28, acknowledge H IV. 67

heþ *see* **heh**

hethe *n.* heather P 93

heþe *v.* mock H V. 10

hethen *adv.* from here A 5063

heþyn *adj.* heathen J 550

hethyng *n.* shame W 68

hettir, hattir *adj.* fierce A 615, cruel A 702; **hetterly, hetirly** *adv.* fiercely J 544, keenly A 669, earnestly A 678

heued *n.* head; chief A 1556

heuenriche *n.* the kingdom of heaven P 427

heuyn *n.* sky

heuys *see* **hefe**

hew *n.* din K 13

hewe *n.* colour, complexion

hewede *pp.* coloured P 157, A 5113

hewen *v.* cut W 196, strike J 557; **how** *pa.t.* J 544; **hewen** *pp.* fashioned J 640

hi *n.* haste S 159

hy, hue, he, heo *pron.* they; **hem, huem, hom, ham** *acc. & dat.* them, themselves, **him** P 416, A 635; **he(o)re, hore, hire, huere, ar** *gen.*

Glossary

their; **hemselue** *acc. & dat.*
themselves

hyde *n.* concealment H IV. 18

hydeles *adj. as n.* skinless J 698

hideward *adv.* to this H VIII. 39

hidis *see* **hude**

hye *v.* (**hyeghte, hyes** *pr.3sg.*;
hyen(n), hyghes *pl.*; **highid, hi3ed,**
hyede *pa.t.*) hasten, hurry; rush
J 651, approach rapidly W 453

highly *see* **heghely**

highte, heghte, hi3t, hiht *n.* top
A 700; *one, appon, uppon* ~ on
high, out loud

highte, hi3t, hiht *see* **hete, hiþte**

hi3tild *pa.t.* adorned A 1664; *pp.*
A 5096, **hightilde** repaired W 438

hil(le)de *pa.t.* covered W 76, P 93

him *see* **hy**

hyndelaike *n.* courtesy A 615

hyne *n.* servant, farm-worker;
hyne(n) *pl.*

hing- *see* **hongen; hipped** *see* **hup(p)e;**
hire *see* **hy**

hyrd, hyrt *n.* company H V. 34,
assembly H IV. 67, court H VI. 2,
56, public H IV. 54

hyrdmen *see* **herdmans**

hyrne *n.* corner W 238; **hurne** place
of refuge H III. 35

hit, yt *pron.* it; **hit** *gen.* its E 309

hiþte *n.* haste H VII. 11; **vpon hi3t**
quickly J 651

ho *see* **heo**

hodes *pr.3sg.* puts hoods on P 236

hodirde *pp.* heaped up W 298

hoge *adj.* huge

hokes *pl.* catches (of crossbow) P 53

holde *n.* castle P 413

holde *v.* (**hald** *pr.1sg.*; **halt** *3sg.*; **helde**
pa.t.; **holden** *pp.*) hold, keep, regard
(as); keep to T 2438, retain
H III. 11, contain E 249, consider
H IV. 64, agree T 2391, *(refl.)*
behave H III. 33; ~ *byhynde* be
worse off W 9, ~ *be* keep to A 4953

hole *adj.* whole J 660; **hale** complete
A 632; **holliche** *adv.* wholly S 188

holte *n.* wood, wooded hill

holwe *adj.* excavated J 662

hom *see* **hy**

homelyde *pa.t.* cut P 90

homliche *adv.* impudently S 200

hond *n.* dog SS 30

honde *n.* hand; *on, appone* ~ near
(by) W 11, A 4918; **hend** *pl.* hands
A 1563

hond-qwile *see* **hande-while; honest**
see **onest**

hongen *v.* (**hynges, hengeth** *pr.3sg.*;
hingand, honginde, hengyng *pr.p.*;
hynged *pp.*) hang; cover T 2374

hongren *v.* starve H V. 33

hontis *see* **hunte**

hope *v.* (**howpe** *pr.pl.* T 2439)
believe; expect H III. 11; ~ *aftir*
hope for W 374, expect W 290

hopynge *n.* estimation P 164

hoppit *see* **hup(p)e**

hor, hare *adj.* with grey hair

hore *v.* grow grey H V. 23, W 470

hore *see* **hy**

hore-mosse *n.* hair-moss P 93

hor-howne *n.* horehound SS 110

horlynges *pl.* whoremongers
H VIII. 13

hors-knaues *pl.* stable-boys H VIII. 3

hose *see* **whoso**

hosede *pp.* wearing hose H VII. 37

houres *pl.* prayers E 119; **oures**
A 1601

houes, houen *pr.* wait; hover P 215, is
situated A 5029

how *see* **hewen**

howes *pl.* lawyers' caps W 150, 314

howpe *see* **hope**

hude *n.* skin H VIII. 27; **hidis** *pl.*
A 4849

hude *v.* hide H IX. 13, cover
H III. 22

hue, huem, huere *see* **hy**

hulle *n.* hill H III. 57

hummyd *pa.t.* muttered E 281

hunte *n.* huntsman P 96; **hontis** *pl.*
K 11

hup(p)e *v.* leap H V. 42, hop
H VII. 37; **hipped** *pa.t.* W 38,
hoppit T 12506

hurcle *v.* crouch W 13; **hurkles** P 19

hurdes *pl.* buttocks W 436

hurdi3s *pl.* wooden structures J 575

hure *n.* cap H VI. 19

hurlede *pp.* fallen P 57

hurling *n.* uproar A 4921

hurne *see* **hyrne**

husbondus *pl.* husbandmen K 122

Glossary

y *prep.* in H III. 39, V 37
ibe *see* be(n); ibente *see* bende; ybore
 see beren; ybroht, ibrouth *see* bro3t;
 ycayred *see* cayre
Ich *pron.* I; me *acc. & dat.*; my *gen.*,
 me K 109
iche, eche, oche, vche, ilk(a), *adj.*
 each; ~ a every; icheon, ichone,
 vschon, ylkon, ilkane *pron.* each
 person, each one
Ichot *see* wete; ycud *see* kythe; idiht
 see dighte; ydrawe *see* drawe; yfed
 see fede; ifounde *see* fynde
yhaht *pp.* hatched H VIII. 7
yhere *see* here
ylike, iliche *adv.* equally W 48,
 likewise P 113; *prep.* like SS 105
ilk(a), ilkane *see* iche
ilke *adj.* same
yloren *see* leosen
ymagry *n.* sculpture T 1562
ymbryne dayes *pl.* ember days W 310
imene *adv.* together SS 37
impis *pl.* saplings A 4946
ymur *n.* moisture of atmosphere
 T 1575
inde *n.* blue W 62, A 1646
Ynde, Yndoyes *n.* the Indian
 language A 5136, 5139, 5198
innes *pl.* buildings S 5
innocens *gen.pl.* of innocents S 284
inome *see* nymes
ynowe, ynewe *adj.* many; sufficient
 W 282
inwith *prep.* within E 307
ipiht *see* pycche
yre *n.* anger T 12545, A 1627
irkede *pa.t.(impers.)* grew tired P 277
ys *pron.* his
ischeue *pr.pl.* come forth K 42
ysope *n.* hyssop S 115
ysped *see* spede
yssue *n.* exit T 1556
ytake *see* take; itened *see* tene
ythes *pl.* waves T 12470
iþeuwed *pp.* cultivated S 73
ytold *see* told
ywedded *ppl.adj.* married H V. 39
ywis *adv.* indeed
iwrout *see* worche

jangle *v.* chatter W 26; *pa.t.*
 screeched W 40

japes *pl.* comic stories W 26,
 wrongful decisions E 238
jarmede *pa.t.* twittered W 40
jaspe *n.* jasper H II. 3
jeants *pl.* giants A 4849
jentil(le) *see* gentil
jesserand *n.* coat of armour A 5088
jeu3 *n.* Jew S 2
jewry *n.* the Jewish people A 1669
jogis *pl.* judges A 1630, 1669
joyeþ *pr.3sg.* has pleasure H II. 50;
 pp. pleased A 5073
joyne *v.* add up T 1538; *pr.3sg.(refl.)*
 proceeds A 1577; jonyng *pr.p.*
 linking S 71
joyned *pp.* assigned E 188
joynyng *n.* encounter J 538
joyntly *adv.* in company P 180,
 together A 1593, 5088, added
 together T 1538
joynttours *pl.* limbs A 4849
joly *adj.* vigorous P 459, amorous
 P 620, lovely A 4950; jolieste
 superl.as n. strongest men J 538
jopon, jupown *n.* tunic W 115,
 A 5088; *pl.* A 4849
jugge *pr.pl.* judge, consider P 422;
 juggid *pp.* decided E 180,
 condemned E 188
juste *adj.* well-fitting W 115
justede *pp.* jousted P 180
justers *pl.* warriors P 459
justifiet *pa.t.* acted as judge to E 229
justis *n.* ruler T 2385; justis *pl.*
 justices, judges A 1669, 1724

kayre, kaysser, kan, kaple, karayn,
 karpyng, kast *see* c-
kastand *ppl.adj.* brilliant A 1660
katour *n.* buyer W 491
kelddus *pr.3sg.* chills K 82
kelde *n.* suffering H V. 11
kembid *pp.* combed W 151
kempes *pl.* warriors P 251
kendles *pr.pl.* give birth H IX. 4;
 kyndild *pa.t.* was born A 696,
 cundelet gave rise to S 224
kene *adj.* brave, lively, fierce, sharp,
 loud; kenely *adv.* eagerly P 362,
 S 83, fiercely J 621, sharply A 639,
 firmly S 214, very E 63
kenede *pa.t.* gave birth to H V. 5;
 kynned was born E 209

kenettes   *pl.* hunting dogs SS 5, 10
ken(ne)   *v.* (**kend** *pa.t.& pp.*) know;
  teach H VI. 85, W 491, A 650,
  explain E 124, show W 479, guide
  P 553, perceive T 1549, 1567; ~ *on*
  instruct in SS 129
kepe, keppyn   *v.* (**kepten, kepide**
  pa.t.) keep, preserve, look after,
  protect; defend J 617, 684, A 1518,
  occupy E 66, pull P 212, wish
  H III. 4, A 1578, greet P 353
kernels, kirnel(l)s   *pl.* battlements
kerpede   *see* **carpe; kest** *see* **caste(n)**
kete   *adj.* bold SS 89
keuercheue   *n.* head-cloth S 158
kyd(de)   *see* **kythe**
kye   *n.* key K 82
kiluarde   *adj.* treacherous P 516
kyme   *n.* fool K 127
kyn   *n.* family K 33; *pl.* kinds E 63
kynde, cunde   *n.* nature; physical
  appearance E 157, family S 184,
  birthright SS 78, parentage A 696
kynde   *adj.* abundant W 274
kyndeli   *adv.* lovingly S 249, heartily
  A 5073, by (human) nature T 2412
kynned   *see* **kenede**
kippe   *pr.1sg.* receive H III. 61
kirke   *n.* church
kirnel(l)s *see* **kernels**
kirtill   *n.* gown A 5082
kystes   *pl.* chests W 255
kythe, kiþ   *n.* country; **cuþþes** *pl.*
  families S 249
kythe, cuyþe   *v.* make known;
  proclaim W 104, tell A 690, express
  A 5138, acknowledge SS 96;
  kyd(de), (y)cud *pp.& ppl.adj.* made
  known, named, famous, remarkable,
  acknowledged, recognised; ~ *for*
  recognised as E 222; **kiddeste** *superl.*
  P 299
kny3thede   *n.* knightliness A 659
knyl   *n.* shock K 81
knyt   *pp.* tied J 700, 707
knoc   *n.* knuckle K 82
knoppe   *n.* stud W 81; *pl.* buttons
  A 5044
koyntis   *see* **quontyse; kouþyn** *see* **can;
  kraft** *see* **craft**

laburt   *pa.t.* were busy T 2348
lac(c)he   *v.* (**laughte, laghton, lacched**

pa.t.; **la(u)3t** *pp.*) take; catch W 406,
  fetch E 316, seize J 529, capture
  J 692, remove K 71, obtain A 1562;
  ~ *till/to* pick up P 52, 239
lad   *see* **lede**
ladde   *n.* servant, low-born fellow
ladisman   *n.* guide
laft(es)   *see* **leue(n); lagh** *see* **lawe;
  laghton, la3t** *see* **lac(c)he**
lay   *n.* law H VI. 5, faith P 197,
  practice S 135
layke   *n.* game A 644, quarry P 49,
  SS 32
layke   *v.* amuse P 259; *pa.t.* played
  SS 71
layne   *v.* hide the truth S 282; *imper.*
  remain silent E 179
laite   *n.* flash of lightning
  T 12499, 12517
laite   *v.* search (for)
laithe   *see* **loþ**
lake   *n.* moat S 229, pit E 302
lakyd   *pa.t.* was lacking K 25
lande, launde   *n.* clearing
lanerettis   *pl.* male hawks P 220
laners   *pl.* female hawks P 220
lant   *see* **lene**
lappyn   *v.* fold P 247; **lap(p)ed** *pa.t.*
  enclosed W 111; *pp.* covered W 350,
  swathed K 119
lare   *n.* earth K 25, filth K 112
lare   *see* **lore**
lasch   *pr.pl.* let fly A 1515; **lasshit**
  pa.t. flashed E 334
last   *n.* in *vpo* ~ lastly K 118
laste   *n.* sin H IV. 27, H V. 15
laste   *adv.* least P 283
late   *see* **lete**
later   *adj.* in ~ *ende* last part E 136
lathe   *v.* invite (to a meal) E 308
latis   *see* **lot**
laughte, lau3te   *see* **lac(c)he**
launchit   *pa.t.* darted T 12499, 12517,
  hastened T 12527
launde   *see* **lande, lond**
launsyng   *pr.p.* sprouting S 109
lauande   *ppl.adj.* flowing E 314
laue   *adj.* drooping A 4875
laueroc   *n.* lark H II. 24
lawe   *n.*[1] hill W 49, A 4939, 5014;
  lowe SS 29
lawe, lagh   *n.*[2] law; law (of hunting)
  P 240, (Christian) faith S 3, 164,

E 34, system of religion E 187, 203, 287, Mosaic law S 23, 32, Jewish rite J 705, A 1705, what is right H VII. 36, fashion H I. 10

lawe, lawly *see* **loghe**

lawes *pr.3sg.* bellows A 4871

lebarde *n.* leopard W 74; **libardis** *pl.* T 1573

leces *see* **less(ch)es**

leche *v.* cure H II. 33

lede, lued *n.*[1] person, man; country, nation A 1626, A 5147; **leodes** *pl.* properties H III. 27

lede *n.*[2] language A 5134

lede *n.*[3] lead seal W 146

lede *v.* (**lad, lede** *pp.*) conduct H VI. 10, bring H VIII. 19, take A 621, control W 15

ledyng *n.* guidance W 223

ledur *n.* leather T 1596

leefe *see* **leue; leende** *see* **lende**

lees *v.* be damned S 358; **les** *pa.t.* lost SS 32

le(e)se *n.* lie

leeue, lefte *see* **leue(n)**; **lefe** *see* **leue, libben**

lege *adj.* sovereign A 1730

legyance *n.* allegiance W 501

leye *adj.* uncultivated H III. 64, W 234

leymond *ppl.adj.* blazing T 12517

leiþ *see* **loþ**

lele *adj.* loyal S 3, lovely P 115; **lel(el)y, lelé** *adv.* faithfully W 430, P 274, sincerely E 268, certainly K 39, truly A 5147

leman, lem(m)one, *n.* mistress W 428, S 136, lover S 163, dear one P 174

leme *n.* beam of light E 334

leme *v.* shine, gleam

lemetis *pl.* limits A 5164

lende, leende *v.* stay S 125, dally SS 8, come T 2341, go A 5016, A 5119; **lent** *pp.* situated S 68

lene *v.*[1] incline A 5195; **lenyde** *pa.t.* bent over P 152, sat down SS 9, 32

lene *v.*[2] grant, give H I. 1, E 315; **lente** *pa.t.* S 353, SS 72; **lant** *pp.* E 192, 272

lene *adj.* infertile H III. 27

lengare *adv.comp.* longer W 259; **lengeste** *sup.* W 449

lenge(n) *v.* remain, linger; exist E 68, live A 1605

lenght *n.* in *o* ~ to its full length T 2370

leodes *see* **lede**

leosen *v.* (**lest, lorne, yloren** *pp.*) lose

lepe(n), leop *pa.t.* hurried P 76, leapt E 61, S 229

lere *n.* face; complexion E 95; *pl.* cheeks H II. 12

lere *v.* learn; instruct W 223, teach S 23, study K 111; **lered** *ppl.adj.* learned J 705, *(as n.)* learned men H VI. 3

les(e) *see* **lees, le(e)se**

lesinge *n.* loss H III. 6

less(ch)es, leces *pl.* leashes P 211, 238, SS 18

lesse *conj.* lest W 98, P 82; ~ *and* lest W 395

lest *see* **leosen; leste** *see* **list**

lesten *v.* listen to A 5076

lete, late *v.* (**lete** *pa.t.*; **let(t)** *pp.*) let; have (something done), cause (to do) S 185, 296, J 713, give up SS 93, forfeit H IV. 5, emit sound A 612; ~ *be* leave off W 263; *pp.* in ~ *of* appreciated W 27

letere *n.* bed A 5037

lethe *v.* cease E 347

lethirely *adv.* shamefully A 1588

lettes *pr.3sg.* hinders E 165, A 4974

lettir *n.* learning A 624, writing A 644

lettrure *n.* learning S 18

leue *n.*[1] leaf S 109; *pl.* written matter A 5199

leue, lefe *n.*[2] leave W 469, permission E 316

leue, le(e)fe, luef *adj.* dear; willing W 465, pleasing H V. 48, pleasant A 653; **leuere** *comp.* preferable; *me were* ~ I should rather; **leuest** *superl.* dearest (thing) H III. 12; **leuir** *adv.* rather, more dearly

leuedy *n.* lady

leuely *adv.* lawfully A 5076

leue(n), leeue *v.*[1] believe; trust K 113; ~ *vpon* believe in K 111

leue(n) *v.*[2] (**leuyt, lefte, laftes, lafte(n)** *pa.t.*; **leuyd** *pp.*) leave; remain E 328, J 540, 568, 603, give up T 1526

leuys *pr.3sg.* produces leaves A 5069

lew *adj.* frail K 44
lewed *ppl.adj.* unlearned, lay H VI. 1
lyame *n.* leash P 38, 61
libardis *see* **lebarde**
libben, lefe *v.* live H VI. 1, A 1728
lyche *n.* corpse E 146, body A 731;
  like A 4912
liche *prep.* like S 3
lichid *pa.t.* healed A 4912
lickenand *ppl.adj.* resembling A 666
lyfe, lyue *n.* living people A 599;
  vpon ~ alive
lifte *n.* sky A 674, 4941
lygge, lye *v.* (**ligis, lyes, liþ** *pr.3sg.*)
  lie; be fitting W 428, remain intact
  E 264, lay A 1693
lighte, lightten *v.* (**light(en), li3t** *pa.t.*)
  fall P 323, E 322, A 1683, swoop
  down P 220, 222, dismount T 2364,
  land A 4912, gladden W 406; ~ *off*
  be descended from A 599
lighte *adj.*[1] bright W 306; **li3tly** *adv.*
  E 334
lighte *adj.*[2] agile W 74, eager P 352
ly3thhed *n.* fickleness SS 59
likame, lykhame *n.* body P 275,
  E 179
like *see* **lyche**
liked *pa.t.impers.* in *me gode* ~ it
  pleased me T 2372
lykyng *n.* pleasure K 112
lympe *v.* be obliged W 449 ~ *of*
  happen to W 369; **lympis**
  pr.sg.impers. it happens W 284
lynage *n.* noble family S 16
lynde *n.* (linden) tree
lyndys *pl.* loins K 118
lyne *n.*[1] cloth, clothing; *adj.* linen
  H I. 22
lyne *n.*[2] story A 1562
lyngwhittes *pl.* linnets W 350
lyre *n.* appearance? W 415, flesh
  E 149
lyst *n.* in *with* ~ by some means K 38
list *pr.3sg.* wishes A 5195; **liste, luste**
  pr.sg.impers. it pleases; **leste** *pa.t.*
  SS 8
lite *adj.* few
liþ *n.* leg SS 92
liþ *see* **lygge**
lythe *n.* property P 185, 207; **luþe**
  SS 124
lithe *v.* hear A 5149

littill-whattes *pl.* small amounts
  W 225
lyue *see* **lyfe**
lyuynde *ppl.adj.* living SS 105
lodely *adj.* horrible E 328
lofed *pa.t.* praised A 658
lofte *n.* in *o(f)*, *on*, *vpon* ~ above
  E 81, A 1515, up J 531, A 731, on
  top T 1561, to the top A 5016
loge *n.* palace A 5037
loge *v.* camp, stay P 542,
  A 5009, 5177; **lugede** *pa.t.* sheltered
  P 659, **logit** lived T 1615
loghe, lowe, lawe *adj.* low; *on* ~
  below; deep down E 147; **loughe**
  adv. low P 460; **lawly** *adv.* quietly
  SS 29
loke *v.* watch over H I. 1; ~ *on* see
  T 1554; **lokande** *pr.p.* staring W 74
loken *see* **lowked**
loket *n.* curl of hair H I. 29
lokyngges *pl.* glances SS 72
lome *n.* tool; container E 68, 149;
  odd ~ penis A 4877
lond *n.* land; field SS 25; **laund syde**
  n. shore T 12534
longen *pr.pl.* belong E 268; **longit**
  pa.t. T 1615, **longede** lived P 57
longyng *n.* eagerness T 12483
lorchip *n.* lordship K 25
lore, lare *n.* learning; wisdom E 264,
  doctrine K 111, statement H V. 25,
  language A 5199
lorere *n.* laurel tree; **lores** *pl.* A 5099
lorne *see* **leosen**
loselles *pl.* villains S 161
losynger *n.* rascal H VIII. 24
lossum *see* **louesum**
lostlase *adj.* listless H VII. 36
lot *n.* behaviour H IV. 27; **latis** *pl.*
  sounds A 4870
loþ, laithe, leiþ *adj.* foul P 275, K 70,
  T 1573, displeasing H V. 25,
  horrible, terrible A 4875, 4920,
  hateful S 291, ugly P 152, unwilling
  SS 93; *as n.* loathsome figure K 118
loughe *see* **loghe**
loure *v.* scowl H I. 17
louse, lowsen *v.* set free E 165, P 211;
  louset *pa.t.* loosened P 61, uttered
  E 178
lout(t)ed *pa.t.* bent P 52, bowed
  (head) S 237

louache   *n.* lovage (herb) S 109
loue   *adj.* beloved E 34
loueli(che)   *adj.* lovely S 154; *as n.* handsome man SS 72; **loueloker**   *comp.* more lovely SS 54; *adv.* graciously S 237, lovingly W 456
loves   *pl.* hands E 349
louesum   *adj.* lovely S 275; **lossum** H II. 12
louyng   *n.* praising E 349
low   *n.* light, fire T 12500, 12516, 12523
low   *pa.t.* laughed SS 71
lowe   *see* **lawe, loghe**
lowed   *pa.t.* praised, glorified; **louyd** *pp.*
lowked   *pa.t.* closed W 45; **loken** *pp.* enclosed W 49, E 147, covered A 5132
lowppes   *pr.3sg.* attaches with a loop P 238
lowsen   *see* **louse; lued** *see* **lede; luef** *see* **leue; lugede** *see* **loge**
lure   *n.* defeat P 323; *pl.* deprivations E 328
luste   *see* **list; luþe** *see* **lythe**
luþer   *adj.* harmful H III. 13
luþernesse   *n.* wickedness H VIII. 30

macers   *pl.* mace-bearers E 143
madde   *adj.* grief-stricken SS 37
maghty, maʒtene   *see* **mighty; maʒt** *see* **miht**
mai   *n.* girl, maiden
maideux   *phrase* may God help me A 5150
maiʒt   *pr.2sg.* (**mou, mowe** *pl.*; **moʒt** *pa.t.subj.*) may, be able
mayne   *n.* strength, force
maynly   *adv.* with force A 1557
mayster   *n.* master; ~ *maire* chief civic leader A 1680, ~ *mon* chief official E 201, ~ *men* master-craftsmen T 1599, ~ *toun* chief town E 26
maisterful   *adj.* tyrannous S 288
maistri   *n.* power SS 130, compulsion E 234; *for þe* ~ as much as possible H VII. 28; **maystries** *pl.* arts P 469
maistris   *n.* superiority S 227
makande   *n.* comfort P 278
make   *n.* lady W 446

make   *v.* make; **mas** *pr.3sg.* makes; puts A 1641; **makkyd** *pa.t.* built E 43; **made, makyd** *pp.* appointed J 582; ~ *opon* opened E 128
malis   *n.* ill-will T 12541
mallen   *pr.pl.* thrust J 556
malte   *v.* melt E 158
manas   *n.* threat E 240
mane   *see* **mon**
manerly   *adv.* with ritual E 131
maners   *pl.* kinds E 60
marbre   *n.* marble E 48
marche   *n.* district P 151
marciall   *n.* officer in charge of feast E 337
mare   *n.* more
marg(a)rite   *n.* pearl H II. 9, A 5028
margon   *n.* mud A 628
marke   *v.* cut S 320; **marked** *pp.* declared S 19, **merkid** inscribed E 154
marke   *see* **merke**
marlede   *pa.t.* spread fertilizer P 279
marlelyng   *n.* using fertilizer P 142
marreþ   *pr.3sg.* destroys H III. 32, VIII 18; **marris** *pl.* injure A 1543; **marred** *pp.* confined S 176, **mart** killed J 604
martilage   *n.* burial register E 154
mas   *see* **make**
mascles   *pl.* spots A 5116
mase   *n.* blow S 320
mast   *see* **most**
mast-quat   *adv.* mostly A 5137
mater   *n.* substance T 2397; *pl.* subjects W 20
matyd   *pp.* overcome E 163
maulerdes   *pl.* mallards P 221
maumene   *n.* dish of chopped meat W 355
maundement   *n.* commandment S 19
mawe   *n.* stomach, guts; *pl.* jaws A 4855
mawngery   *n.* feast W 304
me   *see* **Ich, mon; meche** *see* **muche; mecul** *see* **mekill**
mede   *n.*[1] mead A 4951
mede   *n.*[2] reward; bribe H III. 53, VI 29, gift T 2415; *pl.* good deeds E 270
meere   *n.* place E 114, A 5184, allotted time A 5150
meynye   *see* **meneyhe**

Glossary

meke *adj.* sweet H IV. 63, kind
T 2443; **mekest** *as n.* most
benevolent one E 250

mekill, mecul, mychel *adj.* much,
great; *adv.* greatly A 659

n.ele *v.* speak S 288, W 264

mellyd *pp.* mingled E 350

men *n.* fellowship K 30

mend *v.* benefit T 2404, P 146,
improve W 383, K 37; *pa.t.* T 1525,
helped K 137; *pp.* cured E 298

mendys *n.* reparation P 359

mene *v.*[1] lament H V. 20, E 247;
ment *pa.t.* P 160

mene *v.*[2] remember P 630, E 151;
menit *pa.t.* spoke T 2425; *pp.* T 2416

mene *adj.* contemptible H IV. 44,
small K 120

meneyhe, meneȝe, meynye *n.*
company, retinue E 65,
A 1709, 1720

menge *v.* blend P 592; **myngit** *pa.t.*
mingled T 12495; *pp.* mixed T 12472

menyuer *n.* miniver (white fur) E 81

menske *n.* honour; favourable
treatment H VI. 29

menskes *pr.3sg.* honours E 269;
menskid *pa.t.* E 258

menskfully *adv.* gracefully P 114,
E 50, honourably A 737

mercie *n.* favour H II. 41

mere *n.* lake P 500

mere *adj.* excellent H II. 9; **merely**
adv. excellently A 4896

mereuail *n.* wonder J 604

mery *adj.* pleasant P 12, lively E 39;
murgest *superl.* happiest H IV. 64

merion *n.* noontime S 51

meritorie *adj.* meritorious E 270

merke, marke *n.*[1] mark, two-thirds of
a pound H IX. 11, W 356

merke *n.*[2] point A 684

merke *adj.* dark T 12472, **mirk**
A 4930

merkenes *n.* darkness T 12495

merkid *see* **marke; meschefe** *see*
mischeue

mese *n.* course W 344, 356

message *n.* errand S 20, mission
T 2443

mest *see* **most**

mesters mon *n.* craftsman E 60

mesure *n.* restraint A 5028; *of a ~* of

the same size T 1545

mete *n.*[1] company K 30

mete *n.*[2] food P 52

meteles *adj.* without food S 177

metely *adv.* suitably E 50

methful *adj.* gentle H IV. 51

metis *pr.3sg.* travels A 4930; **meten**
pp. in ~ *to* arrived at A 5184

meuyt *see* **move; miche** *see* **muche;**
mychel *see* **mekill**

mychewhate *n.* many things P 105

mid *prep.* with

middelert *n.* earth S 263

myddis *n.* middle; waist W 94

mye *pr.pl.* grind H VII. 39

mighty, maghty, maȝte(ne) *adj.*
mighty E 27, A 4914, 5010; *as n.*
powerful ones T 2404

miȝtfull *adj.* powerful A 1543

miht, myȝth *n.* power, force; **maȝt**
vigour K 67; **miȝtis** *pl.* A 1526

mylnes *pl.* water-mills T 1604

myndale *n.* commemorative
celebration W 304

mynde *n.* record E 154, mental
power E 163

myngit *see* **menge**

mynistris *pl.* officers A 1680

myn(n)e, *v.* remember H V. 20,
P 530, K 104, relate K 29, mention
E 104

mynnyng *n.* observing E 269,
munnyng remembering H V. 21

myns *pr.3sg.* goes A 4914

mynstir *n.* temple A 5025

mynte *see* **munte; mirk** *see* **merke**

mirre *n.* myrrh A 4936, 5102

myrthes, murþes *pl.* entertaining
stories W 20, joys P 1, K 120,
delightful events S 52

mischeue, meschefe *n.* affliction
E 240, distress S 239; **at myschip** in
trouble K 137

mysdone *pp.* done wrong P 359

mysmotinde *ppl.adj.* falsely accusing
H VI. 38

mysse *n.* sin P 640

myste, -yn *pa.t.* lacked SS 130, lost
K 30; *pp.* done without E 300

mystir *n.* time of need A 1585

mo, moo *pron.& adv.* more

moccheþ *pr.3sg.* munches H VIII. 18

mode *n.*[1] mood T 1525

Glossary

mode *n.*² mud P 433
mody, modé *adj.* proud, brave, noble
modire-son *n.* person A 1552
moeth *n.* blast on horn SS 15
moght-freten *adj.* moth-eaten E 86
moȝt *see* **maiȝt**
molde *n.* earth, land; *on* ~ anywhere; *pl.* clods of earth E 343
momeleþ *pr.3sg.* mumbles H VIII. 18; **momelide** *pa.t.* babbled P 160
molle *n.* dirt A 628
mon *n.*¹ man
mon *n.*² lamentation H III. 1; **mane** A 5153
mon, man, me *pron.* one
mon *pr.* must
mondrake *n.* mandrake H II. 31
monen *v.* remember SS 73
moneþ *n.* month H VI. 14
mony *adj.& pron.* many T 12482; ~ *one* many E 214
monkune *n.* mankind H I. 6
monlokest *adj.as n.* noblest one E 250
monte *n.* mountain A 5184; **mountis** *pl.* A 5189
moo *see* **mo**
morowen, morewane *n.* morning E 306, A 4896
morþis *pl.* wicked crimes K 121
mosse *n.* moor K 140
most, mast, mest *adj.* greatest
mot *pr.* (**moste** *pa.t.*) may, must, have to
mot *adj.* sad H IV. 29
mote *pr.1sg.* have dealings with H VI. 4; **moten** *pl.* speak P 105
motes *pl.* spots E 86
mou *see* **maiȝt**
moulyng *n.* mould E 86
mountes *pr.3sg.* amounts E 160
mountis *see* **monte**
mousede *pa.t.* pondered P 140, **muset** wondered about E 54
mouth *n.* in *to* ~ out loud E 54
move *v.* go A 5144; **meuyt** *pa.t.* ran T 1601; *pp.* in ~ *of* passed from T 2340
mowe *see* **maiȝt**
muche, meche, miche *adj.* much; large E 81, great S 315, J 603
muge *n.* nutmeg H II. 31

mukkede *pa.t.* manured P 279
mukkyng *n.* manuring P 142
munnyng *see* **mynnyng**
munte *imper.* think H V. 21; **mynte** *pa.t.* pointed to E 145; **myntid** *pp.* taken aim P 48
munte(n) *v.* pay H III. 53, VI 29
murgest *see* **mery; murþes** *see* **myrthes; muset** *see* **mousede**

nad *see* **nauy**
na(y)mely *adv.* particularly; then A 4918
nayttede *pa.t.* practised P 607; **naityd** *pp.* recited E 119
nayt(t)ly *adv.* properly, promptly
nakens *imp.* make bare A 5086
naknet *pp.* made naked T 2427
name *see* **nymes**
nane *pron.* none A 599
nanes *see* **nones**
nappe *v.* sleep W 43, 435
napwile *n.* short while K 8
nas *see* **nes**
naþeles *adv.* nonetheless SS 49
nauy *pr.1sg.* (**nast** *2sg.*; **naþ** *3sg.*; **nabbe** *pr.subj.*; **nad** *pa.t.*) (I) have not
nawth *adj.* powerless SS 115
nawthi *adj.* in want SS 115
ne *see* **neih**
neddire *n.* adder
nede, neode *n.* time of need H IV. 55; *a, for* ~ necessarily H IV. 58, S 295; *pl.* desires S 140
nedeles *adv.* pointlessly W 401
nedful *adj.* poor SS 115
negardes *pl.* misers W 435
neghe, neȝe *v.* (**neghande** *pr.p.*; **neghede, neiȝed** *pa.t.*) approach, be near
neȝen *see* **nyȝe; neyd** *see* **noy**
neih, neghe, ne *adj.* near, close; ~ *honde* close at hand S 348; **next** *adj.* nearest A 619, 5174; **ne(ghe), neȝe** *adv.* nearly W 16, K 7; **ner(r)e** *comp.* more closely W 106, nearer A 1718
nempneþ *imper.* mention H II. 29; **nemnede** *pa.t.* H IV. 56
neode *see* **nede**
ner *adv.* never
nes, nis *pr.3sg.* (there) is not; **nes,**

nas *pa.t.*

nes(s)e *n.* nose P 45, 99

nethirgloues *pl.* shoes A 5086

neuen *v.* name, tell, call, call out;
describe A 1579, 5008, mention
A 5170, 5066

neuer-þe-lattere *adv.* nevertheless
W 29

new *adv.* anew; **newely** immediately
W 18

next *see* **neih**

nyckenay *pr.1sg.* deny H IV. 55

nygromancye *n.* sorcery P 607

ny3e *num.* nine H V. 32; **ne3en**
A 4937

nikke *pr.1sg.* refuse S 148

nyl *see* **nul(l)**

nymes *pr.pl.* take A 4997;
imper.(refl.) go A 5174; ~ *of* take
off A 5086; **name** *pa.t.* took; **inome**
pp. brought down SS 116

nynedele *n.* ninth part W 4

nis *see* **nes**

nysely *adv.* foolishly W 410

nysottes *pl.* fools W 410

nite *pp.* refused A 1583

nobill *n.* gold coin A 5025

noblay *n.* splendour A 5008

no3t *n.& adv.* nothing, not; **noþt**
H IX. 8; ~ *bot* only

noy *n.* harm; suffering E 289

noy *v.* harm A 676; **noyede** *pa.t.*
angered P 573; **neyd** *pa.t.subj.* would
have caused difficulty to A 5008

noys *pr.3sg.* cries A 4871

noke *n.* direction A 4958

nolde *see* **nul(l)**

nolle *n.* head H VI. 45

nombles *pl.* innards P 86

nome *n.* name

non *n.* noon K 8

none *adv.* not at all W 127, E 157

nones, nanes *n.* in *for the* ~ indeed;
for the occasion A 4856

note *n.*[1] matter, business; fuss, effort
W 338, E 101, construction E 38,
occasion A 1608

note *n.*[2] reputation E 152

note *ppl.adj.* famous A 4997

noþir *adv.* neither

noþt *see* **no3t**

nounbre *n.* number; *out of* ~
innumerable A 4926

nourne *v.* state, tell; **nournet** *pp.*
addressed E 195

nowmbron *pr.pl.* number P 308

nowte *n.* bull A 4871

nul(l), nyl *pr.* (**nolde** *pa.t.*) will not,
do not want

o *num.* one

o *prep.*[1] of, from

o *prep.*[2] on

o *see* **one**

obofe *adv.* on top A 5039

oche *see* **iche**

ocupy *v.* perform A 1601

of(f) *prep.* from W 202, away from
S 138, 151

offirs *pr.3sg.* makes sacrifice to
A 5012

ofþunche *pr.sg.impers.* it displeases
H V. 47

oftsythes *adv.* often T 12546

ogh *see* **ow(e)the**; **o3t** *see* **oughte**

oynement *n.* ointment S 121

olepy *adj.* single J 579

olyfaunt *n.* elephant

olyfe *adj.* alive A 663

olofte *adv.* on top E 49

olonke *adv.* stretched out H VI. 21

onane *adv.* at once A 623

one, ane, o *pron.& adj.* one J 628,
alone W 132, P 149, A 4898, itself
W 430; *apon* ~ together S 58, *al,
myn/þine/hire* (etc.) ~ me (etc.)
alone W 32, S 49, A 5062

onere *n.* honour P 180

ones, anys *adv.* once

onest, honest *adj.* proper T 2433,
splendid A 1619, dignified S 30,
lovely S 94; **onestly** *adv.* respectably
T 1600

one-vnder *adv.* underneath E 70

opon *see* **ap(p)on**; **or** *see* **er, 3e**; **ou** *see*
3e

orisons *pl.* prayers A 1601

ost *n.* army

oþe *n.* oath H V. 43

oþer, owthir, outhire, aithire, eyþer
pron.& adj. both, each W 196,
K 119, either W 245, else A 1552;
pron.pl. other people J 674, 689, all
others T 2433, other things
A 5024, 5090; **oþer, ouþir, owthir**
conj. or; ~ . . . *oþir* either . . . or

oughte *n.* anything W 186; **oȝt** *adv.* at all A 684, 689

oures *see* **houres**

ourlede *pp.* trimmed W 412

ous *pron.* us; **vr(e)** *gen.* our

oute *adv.* anywhere T 1541, A 598

ouerbrade *pp.* covered W 342, J 599

ou(er)cast *pa.t.* became overcast T 12471, grew troubled K 53

ouerdrofe, ouiredrafe *pa.t.* moved away E 117, passed away A 1628

ouerhild *pp.* shaded T 2374

ouire-feble *adj.* too poor A 1639

ouirlende *v.* pass beyond A 5195

ow(e)the, ogh *pr.3sg.* **(a(u)ghte** *pa.t.*, **aghtes** 2sg. E 224) owns, possesses, obtains; owes W 329, ought W 287; **aȝt** *pa.t.impers.* it was necessary for A 717

owthir *see* **oþer**

owttrage *n.* excess W 267

paa *see* **po(o)**

paye *v.* please W 408; **payes** *pr.sg.impers.* it pleases W 297 433; **paied** *pp.* punished S 202

paynym *n.* pagan

pake *n.* company, group

pale *n.* stockade J 677

palefreiours *pl.* grooms H VIII. 6

pales *n.* palace W 498; **palis** *pl.* T 1568

pallen *adj.* cloth A 1640

pancere *n.* stomach armour A 5087

papejai *n.* parrot H II. 21; **popejayes** *pl.* S 75, 81

pappis *pl.* breasts P 176

parage *n.* high rank E 203

parailed *pp.* dressed A 1675

paramoures *adv.* passionately; *as n.* courtly love P 172, love-sickness P 176; *pl.* lovers P 633

parnters *pl.* furriers T 1591

parossh *n.* parish H VI. 41; **parischen** members of the parish W 376

parte *n.* share W 382

party *adj.* different A 668

partyd *pp.* departed E 107

pas *n.* road P 296, crossing SS 26, 27, chapter A 5200

passenep *n.* parsnip S 107

passeþ *pr.3sg.* surpasses H II. 13; **paste** *pa.t.* died P 325; **passyd** *pp.* surpassed E 163

pastured *pa.t.* fed T 2354

pauelion *n.* tent A 4887; *pl.* J 629, A 5187

pauement *n.* paved street A 1640

paues *pl.* shields A 1512

pedders *pl.* peddlers W 377

pelers *pl.* pillars W 301

peletre *n.* pellitory (herb) S 116

peloure *n.* fur W 393

pendant *n.* hanging end of belt W 183

penn *n.* quill P 232; *pl.* feathers A 5115

perche *v.* pierce P 82; **perset** *pa.t.* pierced P 380; **persched** *pp.* lacerated J 703

pere *n.* equal A 647, 5032; **peris** *pl.* nobles A 5053; **peere** *adj.* equal S 33

peren *pl.* pears S 82

pergett *v.* plaster W 301

perill *n.* pearl A 1692; *pl.* A 1665

perken *pr.pl.* perch S 81

perlous *adj.* dangerous S 53

perry *n.* jewellery

persayued *pa.t.* saw A 4854

persel *n.* parsley S 107

perset, persched *see* **perche**

pertly *adv.* openly, publicly; clearly S 355

pertrikes *pl.* partridges W 493

peruenke *n.* periwinkle H II. 13, P 9

pesan *n.* chest armour A 5087

pycche *v.* **(pycchynde** *pr.p.*; **piȝt**, **pight** *pa.t.*; **picchit, pight, ipiht** *pp.*) place; set E 79, set in place J 616, be placed A 5190, pitch A 5187, erect H VII. 13; ~ **vp** erect T 1578

pye *n.* magpie H VII. 37

pike *n.* hill A 4945

piked *pp.* stolen H III. 24

pileþ *pr.3sg.* oppresses H III. 19

piliole *n.* pennyroyal (flower) P 9

pinchid *pa.t.* pressed E 70

pine *n.*[1] bolt for gate J 616

pyne *n.*[2] sorrow, trouble, suffering, torment

pyned *pp.* tortured J 703

pynkes *pr.pl.* stab H VI. 25

pynnede *pp.* nailed P 555

pynners *pl.* nail-makers T 1591

pyon *n.* peony S 108

pirie *n.* pear tree S 70

pirnes *pl.* branches A 5108

pistel *n.* epistle S 363
pyté *n.* sad fate A 729
playande *ppl.adj.* boiling J 670
playe, pleye *v.* amuse oneself, enjoy oneself, be glad
playn *n.* paved area E 138
playn *adj.* open A 4945, 5185
playnt *see* **pleint**
playstere *n.* cure P 176
planed *pp.* smoothed E 50
plat *adj.* flat P 319
plates *pl.* armour plating W 114
plauntoyne *n.* plantain S 116
plawe *n.* social occasion H I. 8, sexual sport H VIII. 13
plee *n.* court H VI. 79
pleide *pr.1sg.* plead H VI. 79
pleye *see* **playe**
pleint, playnt *n.* charge
plenys *pr.3sg.* laments A 729; **pleynede** *pa.t.* P 172
plied *pa.t.* gathered E 138
plyes *pr.3sg.* covers A 1640
pliȝt *n.* sin A 5077
plyȝtles *adj.* guiltless E 296
plite *n.*[1] covenant E 285
plite *n.*[2] manner A 635
plontes *pl.* herbs W 332
plunket *n.* light blue W 65
poynte *n.* deed P 380; *pl.* dots W 65, accusations S 160
polayle *n.* poultry P 144
poles *pl.* fish-ponds W 235
polkeþ *pr.pl.* make exactions H VI. 41
polle *n.* head H VIII. 3, person A 1620
pomeri *n.* orchard S 63, 209
pontificals *pl.* bishop's vestments E 130
po(o), paa *n.* peacock H VI. 87, P 365, A 5110
poretes *pl.* leeks S 107
port *n.* figure A 5110
portours *pl.* bearers P 241
posterne *n.* gate S 159
poudird *pp.* decorated A 1659
poure *adj.* sheer W 370; **purer** *comp.* finer A 1659
practisirs *pl.* lawyers A 1705
praye *n.* stolen property P 341
prechours *pl.* Dominican friars W 169

preye *v.* invite H VII. 27
prelacie *n.* body of prelates E 107
prematis *pl.* bishops
prese, prece *n.* thick of battle P 368, crowd E 141
presidens *pl.* leaders S 33
prest(ly) *see* **priste**
preuaté *n.* secrecy A 5125
preue *see* **prouen**; **preué** *see* **priué**
pryke, preke *v.* (**prekand** *pr.p.*; **prikkede** *pa.t.*; **prikid** *pp.*) ride W 318, A 652, 1701, incite H IX. 12, sew W 232, inscribe A 5200
prikyares *gen.pl.* horsemen's H III. 24
prime *n.* sunrise
primerole *n.* cowslip H II. 13
principalté *n.* top position A 648
prine *n.* holm-oak S 342
pryne *pr.1sg.* stitch together W 232
pris *n.* value; account H III. 19, praise H I. 8, glory A 614, dignity W 377, excellence P 449, T 1568
prise, price *adj.* noble, excellent, worthy
prises *pl.* levers E 70
priste, prest *adj.* ready W 169, S 160, bold P 421, 618, lively S 75; **pristly, prestly** *adv.* promptly; quickly P 241
priué, preué *adj.* secret S 159; ~ *clathis* underclothes A 5087; **priueliche** *adv.* in private S 28, alone SS 27
proces *n.* legal procedure S 294
prode, proud *adj.* lordly W 433, splendid A 4994, 5185; **proudly** *adv.* splendidly A 5200
profers *pl.* vows P 205
prouen, preue *v.* taste, eat S 107, prove P 205, 532; **proued** *pa.t.* described A 4994, 5185; **preued** *pp.* tested P 328, 478
prouidens *n.* divine power E 161
prowis *n.* prowess A 614
prude *n.* pride; finery H I. 12
pruynen *pr.pl.* preen S 81
pufilis *pl.* parcels of land P 144
pulled *ppl.adj.* plucked W 493
purer *see* **poure**
purpre(e), purpure *n.* red (or purple) A 1655, 1711, 5113
putten *pr.pl.* in ~ *vpe* drive up P 241

Glossary

qu- *spelling of* wh- in **qua, quare, quaso, quat, quen, quere, quy, quil, quite, quo**

quaynt, coynte *adj.* elegant H II. 15, E 133, T 1627, clever T 1531; **waynt** cunning S 205; **coyntly** *adv.* ingeniously T 2396

quappen *pr.pl.* shoot J 622

quelle *v.* kill SS 10; *pa.t.* P 233

queme *adj.* pleasant E 133, skilful T 1531

quere *n.* choir E 133

querels, quarels *pl.* crossbow-bolts J 622, 653, A 1537

querrye *n.* reward for hawks P 233

questede *pa.t.* barked at prey SS 10

questis *pl.* sounds E 133

queþer *conj.* whether; yet E 153

quibibe *n.* cubeb (spice) H II. 38

quyk *adj.* alive J 694

quilke *pron.* which

quirris *pr.3sg.* moves noisily A 1679; **quirys** *pl.* let whizz A 1537

quod *pa.t.* said

quontyse *n.* marvel E 74; **koyntis** finery A 5044

quopes *pr.3sg.* cries 'whoop' P 233

qwaintans *pl.* tilting at a post T 1627

qwariours *pl.* stoneworkers T 1531

raches *pl.* hounds

radde *adj.* frightened; *for* ~ for fear P 429

radde *see* rede

radly, rad(de)lé *adv.* quickly, soon; **rade** at once K 134

rade *see* rode

rafte, refte *pa.t.* deprived H IV. 15, P 563

raged *pa.t.* fought A 638

ragged *adj.* thorny S 72

raght, raȝt *see* rechen

rayke *pr.pl.* go K 77; *pa.t.* proceeded E 139

raylede *pp.* adorned, decorated, arrayed, arranged

raymeþ *pr.3sg.* plunders H III. 26

raynes *n.* linen from Rennes A 1673

raysed *pp.* assembled W 438

rake *n.* path A 5196

rakill *adj.* rash P 481

rane *n.* thicket S 72

ranke *see* ronke

rapis *pl.* ropes A 1643

rase *n.* hurry A 1636; *at a* ~ with one movement P 73

rase *see* ryse

raþe *adv.* quickly S 347, soon J 633; **rathere** *comp.* sooner W 322

ratons *pl.* rats W 254

rattes *pl.* tatters E 260

rau *adj.* raw H VIII. 8

raughten *see* rechen

raunged *pp.* set out S 112

raueste *see* reueschid; **raw** *see* row

rawnson *n.* huge sum W 363

rawnsone *v.* (**rawnsede** *pa.t.*, **rawnnsunte** *pp.*) ransom

raxillyng *n.* stretching W 436

raxsils *pr.3sg.* stretches A 5057

real *see* ryall

reame, rewme *n.* realm

reche *pr.3sg.subj.* may care P 447; **rohte** *pa.t.* cared H VI. 17, **roȝt** *impers.* in *hom* ~ they cared K 4

rechen *v.* (**raght, raȝt, raughten** *pa.t.*) give (to); hand over W 363, grasp P 75, catch hold T 2370, extend P 29, sound W 42; ~ *forþ* hand over H VI. 39

reches *see* rycheis

recordet *pa.t.* remembered S 60

red, reed *n.* advice, guidance; *pl.* decrees H VI. 6

rede *v.* (**radde** *pa.t.*) advise, guide H V. 28, relate SS 108, say H IV. 60, utter H II. 42, SS 53, read, interpret H II. 30, VIII 11, decree H VI. 28, offer advice W 57, decide K 133, control E 192

redeles *adj.* baffled E 164

redell *n.* curtain A 5057

redy, redé *adj.* wise E 245, sensible SS 51, direct K 84; **redely** *adv.* promptly

reed *see* red

refetyd *pp.* fed E 304

refreyte *n.* poem W (title)

refte *see* rafte; **reghte** *see* ryht

reke *n.* incense A 1689

rekene *adj.* capable H II. 42, upright E 245; **rekenest** *superl.(as n.)* noblest ones E 135

rekils *n.* incense A 5104

rek(k)en, rekyn *v.* (**rykeneþ** *pr.3sg.*; **rekened, rekind** *pa.t.*) settle accounts

H VIII. 29, count W 192, P 141,
relate W 344, describe P 107, P 166,
tell P 250, give account (of) A 1527,
1571, utter A 5058
releues *pr.3sg.* assists P 377
reme *v.* weep W 258
remows *pr.3sg.* removes A 5182;
remewit *pa.t.* departed E 235
renaide, reneyed *ppl.adj.* apostate
E 11, perfidious S 198
rengis *pr.3sg.* resounds A 1508;
ronge *pa.t.* rang E 117
renyschly *adv.* violently A 5058
renke *n.* man, knight; **rynkkys** *pl.*
K 134
rent *n.* revenue
rent *pa.t.* slit P 87, tore T 12511
reowe *see* **rew**
repairen *pr.pl.* go E 135
repaste *n.* meal W 363
rerde *n.* noise K 3
rere *v.* build W 474, J 647, drive
P 217; **rerede** *pa.t.* brought about
P 453; *pp.* pitched (of tent) W 59
rereward *n.* rearguard J 562
resche *n.* rush A 4853
rese *n.* wantonness K 78
resorte *pa.t.* returned P 58
reso(u)n *n.* wisdom; intellect T 2399,
sensible conversation H II. 42; *pl.*
words
rest *ppl.adj.* fresh J 605
restorment *n.* restitution E 280
restowre *v.* repair T 1527
reþly *adj.* fierce S 341
reuerence *n.* respect E 338, deference
E 239
revers *pl.* rivers A 4949
reueschid *pa.t.* arrayed in vestments
A 1653; **reuestid, raueste** *pp.* E 139,
A 1623
rew, reowe *v.* lament K 78, regret
H VI. 6, cause sorrow H V. 29;
pa.t. made sorry P 562
rewe *n.* company H I. 35
rewe *pr.3sg.subj.* dawns H VIII. 21
rewill *n.* religious code A 1623
rewlyn *v.* control W 57
rewme *see* **reame**
rewthe, routhe *n.* sorrow W 258,
sadness SS 108, pity E 240; **rouþes**
pl. misfortunes H VI. 28
ryall, real *adj.* royal E 77, high-born

S 29, noble P 468, arrogant W 128,
exquisite W 339; **ryally** *adv.*
splendidly, nobly
rybans *pl.* bands A 1661
rybaudz *n.* serving man H VIII. 21;
pl. H VIII. 1; *gen.pl.* dissolutes
H I. 35
ricche *v.* enrich T 2405
riche *adj.* fine, noble; powerful
E 212, A 1573; *as n.* noble person
SS 107; *adv.* richly E 139; **richely**
profusely P 29
rycheis, riches, reches *n.* wealth
riches *pr.3sg.* prepares A 5182; **richet**
pa.t. pulled T 2370
ridde *v.* separate combatants W 57;
pa.t. cleared T 1533
ridders *pl.* scavengers J 567
ryfe *n.* profusion W 258
rife *adj.* abundant T 12486, P 282;
ryfly *adv.* SS 7
rygalté *n.* rule P 598
rig(g)e *n.* back; **rugge** hill SS 7
right, ry3t(h) *n.* justice; judgement
T 2405, authority SS 99, 100, 107;
pl. things that are just E 269
ry3twis *adj.* righteous E 245
ryht, ri3t, reghte *adv.* correctly
H VIII. 11, fully S 4, exactly W 165,
right P 73, just J 672
rykeneþ *see* **rek(k)en**
rym *n.* poem H IV. 62
ryme *v.* clear W 289; *pa.t.* drew
(himself) up A 5058
ryne *v.* touch E 262
rynge *n.* rim SS 43, 88
rynkkys *see* **renke**
ryotte *n.* noisy revelry P 253
rys *n.* branch
ryse *v.* happen H III. 18; **risinde**
pr.p. rising SS 2; **rase** *pa.t.* A 5104
rispen *pr.pl.* burst J 567
riste *n.* rest P 572
ristyth, ristis *pr.3sg.* rests, lies
W 200, reclines A 5047
ritte *pa.t.* cut P 73, 75
roches *pl.* boulders A 4991, 5004
rode *n.*[1] complexion H II. 11, red
colour E 91
rode *n.*[2] crucifix W 343
rode, rade *pa.t.* rode A 4890, rode
across P 514
roe *n.* wheel SS 43

Glossary

rofe *pa.t.* attacked A 638
ro3t, rohte *see* **reche**
roynyshe *adj.* mysterious E 52
rolle *n.* scroll (of names)
romys *pr.3sg.* roars A 612
ron *n.* song H IV. 62; **rounes** *pl.*
  words SS 53
ronge *see* **rengis**
ronynge *ppl.adj.* moving SS 43
ronke, ranke *adj.* abundant W 322,
  healthy E 91, fierce K 3, rebellious
  E 11, foul E 262
ro(o), row *n.* peace; rest K 4
roon *pl.* roe deer SS 7, 16
roppis *pl.* intestines J 567
rosett *n.* coarse cloth P 137, 261
rothelede *pa.t.* spoke wildly (?) P 261
rottok *n.* decayed object E 344
rounde *n.* circumference SS 88
roune, rowne *v.* whisper, talk
  privately; speak SS 52, 53
rounes *see* **ron; route** *see* **rowte;**
  routhe, rouþes *see* **rewthe**
routten *pr.pl.* snore W 436
row, raw *n.* group of people K 77,
  procession A 1623
row *see* **ro(o)**
rowys *pl.* rays K 134
rowme *n.* place E 338
rowmly *adv.* amply P 137
rowte, route *n.* army W 202, 270,
  armed men W 128, J 562, crowd
  E 62, company A 4973
rugge *see* **rig(g)e**
rughe *adj.* hairy A 4853
ru3e *n.* rye H III. 68, 69
ruyde *adj.* violent W 42; **ruydely** *adv.*
  S 341
ruls *n.* rubbish (?) H III. 68, 69

sable *n.* black W 157
sacryd *pp.* consecrated E 3, 159
sad(de) *adj.* heavy W 146, solid
  P 333, T 1544, dignified E 324,
  determined W 193; **sadly** *adv.*
  heavily W 215, seriously W 17,
  firmly P 322, fully S 203
safe *see* **saue**
safers *pl.* sapphires A 5007
sage *adj.* wise S 14
saghe *see* **sawe; sa3e, say** *see* **sene;**
  sa3t *see* **seche**
saylen *pr.pl.* attack

sayne *see* **suggen**
sayntuaré *n.* sanctuary E 66, A 1690
sake *n.* accusation S 204
sakeles *adj.* guiltless S 240
sale *n.* hall H II. 23, S 301
sal3e *n.* willow K 6
sall *pr.sg.* (**suld** *pa.t.*) shall, should
salutis *pl.* greetings A 1613
salue *n.* unguent A 5103
samen *adv.* together
sammes *pr.3sg.* fastens A 1643
samples, sampills *pl.* proverbs
  P 263, 602
sandisman *n.* herald W 204
sapient *n.* wisdom A 622
sara3ens *pl.* sergeants A 1633
sare *see* **sore**
satillede *pa.t.* settled P 437
saudid *pp.* set A 1658
sauge *n.* sage (herb) H II. 18, S 110
saule *n.* soul P 103, person A 4932
sauns *prep.* without S 181
saut *n.* attack
sauue *v.* heal H II. 20, 34
saue, safe *prep.* except
sauyne *n.* savin, red cedar S 69
sawe, *n.* saying, remark, story; **saghe**
  words A 5124; **sawen** *pl.* speech
  S 240
sawourd *pa.t.* tasted A 4948
sawtries *pl.* psalms P 162
scapen *v.* escape H VI. 8; **skapis**
  pr.3sg. A 642; *pa.t.* J 610
scaþe *n.* injury, harm H VI. 15
scence *n.* incense A 5103
schadow *n.* image A 4981; *pl.* ghosts
  K 43
schaft *n.* spear A 1525
schaftis *pl.* jaws A 4924
schaggen *pr.pl.* waggle S 106
s(c)hake *v.* move H VII. 11, go
  W 403; **schoke(n)** *pa.t.* brandished
  J 555, shook A 5145; **schokyn** *pp.*
  gone K 42
s(c)halke *n.* man
scharpe *adj.* rough A 602, cold
  A 4992
schatereden *pa.t.* ran in all directions
  (?) SS 17
schathed *pp.* impoverished W 362
schawe *n.* thicket
schawe *see* **s(c)hewe**
schedered *pa.t.* split J 558

schelfe *n.* bank P 657

schenchipe *n.* dishonour W 432

s(c)hene *adj.* bright, fair, lovely; splendid J 666; *as n.* lovely one A 4886

schent *pp.* destroyed W 317, S 359

schert *n.* chemise S 197

scheue *n.* sheaf of arrows A 1525

s(c)hewe, schawe *v.* show; display S 85, look at P 275, T 2397, see T 1550, A 601

schewere *n.* mirror P 291, A 4981

schidwod *n.* split wood J 554

schye, schew *n.* sky J 633, A 4992; **skewes** *pl.*

s(c)hilde *v.* protect H I. 7, A 4979

schillande *pr.p.* resounding J 527

schiltrons *pl.* groups of armed men W 53

s(c)hyre *adj.* beautiful S 194, T 2373, bright J 672, A 1667, noble T 12515

schirkind *pa.t.* brightened A 4943

schirlé *adv.* cleanly P 643

scho *pron.* she

schogs *pr.3sg.(refl.)* shakes A 5145

schoke(n) *see* **s(c)hake**

schonn *v.* shun W 432

schoten, schut *pr.pl.* throw J 672, shoot A 1536; **shotton** *pa.t.* rushed T 12484

schow *n.* wood A 4858

schowen *pa.t.* rushed W 53; **schowid** *pp.* made attack A 4886

s(c)hrewe, screwe *n.* wicked person, wretch

schrynken *pr.pl.* terrify J 527; **scrynkeþ** recoil H VI. 59

schryue *v.* confess P 643

schroud *n.* clothing J 558, plumage S 85

schunte *imper.* avoid P 291; **shont** *pr.pl.* shrink back S 166; **schunte** *pa.t.* drew back S 231

schurtted *pa.t.* amused P 657

schut *see* **schoten**

schutt *v.(refl.)* finish P 585

sckerres *pl.* rocks A 4992

sckonfet *pp.* defeated A 4929

scolaid *pa.t.* studied A 645

score *n.* register H VI. 8

scrynkeþ *see* **schrynken**

scripture *n.* (Latin) text A 1698

scutis *pr.pl.* jut out A 4992

se *see* **sene**

seche *v.* (so(u)ȝt, soughten *pa.t.*; sou(ȝ)t, soght, saȝt *pp.*) seek P 63, S 7, try to obtain H III. 63, S 146, go P 434, proceed A 4962, come A 5103, examine E 41, pierce J 541, practise T 1623; *pp.* sent T 1513, afflicted (by) SS 109, K 69; *were ~ to* had reached T 12533

sectours, sektours *pl.* executors W 302, 443

sedewale *n.* valerian (a plant) H II. 40

sedrisse *pl.* cedars A 5100

seere *see* **sere**

sege *n.* chair W 483, episcopal seat E 35

segge *n.* man, knight

seghe, seȝe, seiȝ, sey *see* **sene; seȝe(n), seyis** *see* **syeȝe; sei(dest), seyn** *see* **suggen; sekire** *see* **syker**

selcouþ *adj.* wonderful S 69; **selquoþ** strangest K 68

selcouthes *pl.* marvels W 3, P 501

sele *n.* happiness, bliss

sele *v.* cover with roof A 1642

selfe, selue *adj.* very SS 86, itself A 5090, same A 5022

selken *adj.* silk S 197

selli *n.* wonder S 155

selly, sellé *adj.* strange W 99, amazing A 1703, extraordinary A 5011; *adv.* very much T 1544

selþe *n.* joy H IV. 71

semblaunt *n.* deceitful behaviour S 216, 222

semblen *pr.pl.(refl.)* assemble P 322; *pa.t.* gathered P 83, A 617

semeli(che), semly *adj.* lovely, elegant; *as n.* lovely one; **semelyeste** *superl.* most handsome P 135

semen *v.* befit, be proper; **semys** *pr.sg.impers.* it suits, it seems

semys *pl.* seams P 126

semlé *n.* assembly A 1696

semsters *pl.* those who sew T 1585

sende *pa.t.* sent a message E 111, has sent W 125

sendell, sendale *n.* silk W 180, 394, A 1642

sene, se(gh) *v.* see, look at; (illustration of forms: **seghe** *pr.1sg.* W 188; **sestou** *2sg.* you see SS 76;

syht, syþt *3sg.* H II. 19, H VII. 11;
sawe P 512, **sey, say** SS 16, 33, **sei3**
S 222, **se(3e)** S 313, 316, **say** J 581,
segh T 1519, **sa3e** A 1556, **see** A 733
pa.t.); **sene** *ppl.adj.* evident K 63
seneke *n.* old man S 301
sengeliche *adv.* singly S 196
sensours *pl.* censers A 1688
sent *n.* agreement A 617
senture *n.* girdle A 5090
seraphens *pl.* seraphim A 5042
serche *v.* examine T 1537; *pa.t.* dug
T 1534
sercles *pl.* circlets W 394
sere, seere *adj.* various, many,
several; *as n.* in *on* ~ separately
S 300; **serely** *adv.* individually
P 218, 225
serelypy, serelepé *adj.* different
A 605, various A 5020
seris *see* **syre**
serke *n.* undergarment A 5090
sert *n.* sake S 223
seruauns *pl.* servants S 155
seruede *pp.* deserved P 570
serwe *n.* sorrow S 145
serwful, serwfol *adj.* sorrowful
S 144, 261; **serwfuller** *comp.* S 254
sese *v.* stop S 45; **sesit** *pa.t.* ceased
T 1524, 2364; **cessyd** *pp.* ended
E 136
sesyn *pr.pl.* (**seside, sessede** *pa.t. &
pp.*) seize; establish E 345
sestou *see* **sene**
sete *n.* position K 6
seþe(n), -yn, sythen, -on, suþ *adv.*
then, afterwards, subsequently; *conj.*
after, since; ~ *that* since
sette *n.* seat P 100
settis *pr.3sg.* in ~ *on a saute* attacks
A 1554, 1575, *(refl.)* in ~ *vp* gets
moving J 561; **sett** *pa.t.* seated P 98;
pp. furnished P 31, placed P 602,
appointed A 708, leased W 407; ~
of established for E 24
seuer *v.* disperse W 443
sewes *pl.* sauces W 339 381
sewet *n.* suet P 83
sewe(t), sewid *see* **sue**
sewte *n.* pursuit P 63
sextene *n.* sexton E 66
sh- *see also* **sch-**
shabbes *pl.* scabs H VIII. 22

shadde *pa.t.* spawned H VIII. 9
shamesly *adv.* shamefully A 739
shaped *pa.t.* ordained H V. 44;
shupte created H VIII. 9; **shope**
(refl.) got ready E 129
shemerand *ppl.adj.* shimmering
A 1667
shereþ *pr.3sg.* changes direction
H VII. 4
shoddreþ *pr.3sg.* trembles H VII. 4
shome *n.* disgrace
shomeþ *pr.pl.* are ashamed H VI. 59
shon *pl.* shoes H VIII. 27
shont *see* **schunte**; **shope** *see* **shaped**;
shotton *see* **schoten**
shoures *pl.* showers T 1577
shrapeþ *pr.3sg.* scratches H VIII. 22
shrude *v.* clothe H I. 13
shuppare *n.* creator H VIII. 9
shupping *n.* shape-shifting H V. 45
shupte *see* **shaped**
syb men *pl.* relatives A 617
siche *pron. & adj.* such, such things,
these K 49
sichomures *pl.* fig trees A 5100
side *n.* part A 5148
syde *adj.* long H V. 16, distant
T 1513
sye3e *v.* (**seyis** *pr.3sg.*, **se3e, -n, -s** *pl.*)
depart A 716, go A 1604, 1696, sink
A 4971; ~ *to* advance A 1511
syht *see* **sene**
sike *v.* sigh
sike *adj.* such A 5104, 5110
syker *adj.* firm T 1544; **sekire** certain
P 635; *adv.* certainly W 193
sikyng *n.* grief T 1515
sylis *pr.3sg.* goes A 1678; **sylis** *pl.*
pass A 698; **syland** *ppl.adj.* flowing
A 733; **syled** *pp.* sunk P 654
silloure *n.* canopy A 5042; **sylours** *pl.*
A 1642
symple *adj.* unadorned W 414
syne *adv.* then A 5013
sypres *n.* cypress tree S 69; *pl.*
A 5100
syre *n.* master; leader A 1570, lord
A 5078; **sire** *gen.* father's A 5148;
seris *pl.* sirs K 68
siþen *pl.* times over H III. 40
sythen, -on *see* **seþe(n)**; **syþt** *see* **sene**
sitte *v.* sit in judgement J 690
skayled *pp.* dispersed P 383

Glossary

skapis   *see* scapen
skars   *adj.* restricted A 5166
skathill   *adj.* evil W 443, harmful
   A 4929; skathely *adv.* with injury
   A 642
skelton   *pr.pl.* hasten E 278
skere   *n.* fear A 4858
skere   *v.* clear of a charge H VI. 15
skere   *adv.* entirely H VI. 8
skerrid   *pp.* frightened A 4929
skewes   *see* schye
skifte   *v.* be removed A 5166; skyftede
   pp. divided P 383
skilfulle   *adj.as n.* righteous E 278;
   adv. moderately A 645
skill   *n.* in *by (sum)* ~ with good
   reason W 362, A 1698
skyp   *pr.3sg.subj.* should run A 642
skyre   *adj.* bright T 12500
skirmyt   *pa.t.* flashed T 12500
skitly   *adv.* swiftly A 5166
skorne   *n.* insult A 641
skrike   *n.* shouting A 4858
slaa, slayne   *see* sle
slabbande   *ppl.adj.* trailing in mud
   W 411
slat   *ppl.adj.* hunted H I. 23
slaughte   *n.* murder P 314
sle, slaa   *v.* (slo3e, slo(u)ghe, slowe
   pa.t.; slayne *pp.*) slay, kill; ~ *vp*
   destroy A 1572
slee, sle3e   *adj.* cunning W 6, skilfully
   made W 411; sleghe *adv.* craftily
   P 36; sleghely skilfully P 81, with
   trickery P 314, gently T 2378
sleght   *pp.* brought level W 411
sleghte, sle3t   *n.* trickery P 36, 445,
   magic P 511, clever device A 4984;
   pl. stratagems A 1568
slekkyd   *pa.t.* alleviated E 331
slent   *n.* splash E 331
sleuen   *pl.* sleeves H VI. 22
slicche   *n.* mire T 12529
slike   *adj.* such
slipped   *pp.* fallen E 92
slyt   *pr.3sg.* slides H VII. 3; slode *pp.*
   fell E 331
slober   *n.* mud T 12529
slome   *adj.* sleepy P 101
slomerde   *pa.t.* slumbered P 101
slongyn   *pp.* flung up T 12529
slo(u)ghe, slo3e, slowe   *see* sle
smale   *adj.* slender P 658

smok   *n.* undergarment H I. 14
snape   *n.* pasture A 1683
snyppand   *ppl.adj.* dazzling A 1683
snyppes   *pl.* snipes W 349
socure   *see* sokur
sodeynly   *adv.* without delay S 301
soght, so3t   *see* seche; sogoure *see*
   sucre
soyned   *pa.t.* excused A 1587
soyte, soute   *n.* in *of/in (a)* ~ dressed
   alike A 1673, 1703, uniformly
   A 5007
sokur, socure   *n.* help K 50, A 1586
solas   *n.* comfort T 1605, pleasure
   T 2394
solas   *v.* amuse T 1620
solempnest   *adj.* most sacred E 30
solsecle, sor-   *n.* marigold H II. 20,
   S 110
somme   *see* sowme
sonde   *n.*[1] errand H IV. 45
sonde   *n.*[2] land P 333
sondire, sondree   *adj.* in *in* ~ apart
sondrit   *pa.t.* scattered T 12507
sone   *adv.* soon, at once
songe   *pa.t.* sank H VI. 24; sonkyn
   pp. T 12525
son(ne)   *n.* in *vndere* ~ anywhere
sor   *n.* grief H VI. 81
sore, sare   *adj.* cruel J 541; *adv.*
   greatly, keenly; bitterly S 171, 222,
   A 1587, eagerly T 12477; sorely
   cruelly P 322
soriore   *comp.adj.* sadder S 255;
   soriere *adv.* more sorrowfully SS 131
sorsecle   *see* solsecle
sort   *n.* company T 12533, A 1678
sotell, -il, sutile   *adj.* clever S 14,
   expert E 132, skilful T 1576
soteltie   *n.* skill T 1623
sothe   *n.* truth
sothe   *adj.* true; sothely *adv.* truly
sotted   *pa.t.* blurred P 286
sottes   *pl.* fools P 266
sought, sou3t   *see* seche
soun, sowne   *n.* voice
sounde   *n.* good health E 92
soupen   *pr.pl.* eat E 336
soure   *adv.* bitterly H I. 18
sout   *see* seche; soute *see* soyte
souters   *pl.* cobblers T 1585
souereyn   *n.* husband S 223
sowdane   *n.* sultan P 568

252

sowede *pa.t.* (it) pained W 215, P 286
sowme, somme *n.* sum W 192, army J 611
sowne *see* **soun**
sownnde *adj.* safe P 434; **soundly** *adv.* T 12492
sowpped *pa.t.* drank W 215
sowre *n.* young stag P 34, 45, 58
sowssches *pr.pl.* beat up P 218
space *n.* time
spaclyche, spakly *adv.* quickly H V. 29, E 335, swiftly J 553, frequently E 312
spare *v.* save W 224, desist J 637
sparrede *see* **spradde**
sparthe *n.* battle-axe W 238, A 1526
speche *n.* statement E 152
spede *n.* success E 132
spede *v.* (**sped** *pa.t.*; **ysped** *pp.*) succeed H VII. 22, P 366, help P 260, make haste S 103, perform A 1526, *(refl.)* manage A 630
spedfully *adv.* profitably W 224
spedles *adj.* worthless W 325, profitless E 93
spelle *v.* relate H VIII. 37
spelunke *n.* tomb
spene *v.* spend H III. 48
spere *n.* church-spire A 4892
speris *pr.pl.* close A 1589; **sperde** *pp.* fastened S 122
sperl *n.* bolt E 49
spilles *pr.2sg.* go to ruin P 193; **spilt** *pa.t.* killed A 1542; *ppl.adj.* J 637
spyr *v.* ask E 93
spyres *pl.* shoots W 398
spoyle *v.* despoil J 637, undress A 5089
sporiors *pl.* makers of spurs T 1595
spournede *pa.t.* kicked P 550
spradde *pa.t.* fastened E 49; **sparrede** *pp.* shut away W 238
sprent *pa.t.* leapt E 335
sprete, sprite *n.* (evil) spirit A 4906, 5127, 5180
spryng *v.* (**sprange** *pa.t.*) grow S 103, arise E 217, A 1628
spryngaldis *pl.* catapults A 1542
sprynge *n.* sapling W 398
sprotes *pl.* splinters J 553
stablyd *pa.t.* established E 2, settled T 1525; *pp.* E 274
stadded *pa.t.* confined J 588; **stad(de)**

pp. placed E 274, T 2389, caught T 12520
staf(f)e *n.* rung A 1561, spear A 1567
staffull *adj.* quite full A 1666, 5024
stagis *pl.* window-bars A 5024
staire *n.* ladder A 1561
staire *adj.* sheer A 4955
stairis *pr.3sg.* advances A 4961
stake *n.* framework for hedge H VII. 13
stale *see* **stond(en)**
stalken *pr.pl.* (**stalked, stelkett** *pa.t.*) move cautiously P 51, SS 17, walk SS 23
standard, -erte *n.* standard P 376, headquarters J 588
standes *see* **stond(en)**
stanys *pl.* stones
stap *v.* step J 601
starand *ppl.adj.* shining A 1657
stede *n.*¹ horse
stede, stude *n.*² place H III. 33, P 21, A 1697; *pl.* A 1618
steere *v.* guide S 304; **steris** *pr.3sg.* controls A 5172
stekis *pr.3sg.* is fixed A 683
steles *pr.3sg.* captures by stealth H IX. 6
stele-wede *n.* armour P 200, J 601
stelkett *see* **stalken; steryn** *see* **sturne**
sterlynges *pl.* silver coins W 252
sterne *n.* star
stert *pa.t.* fell T 2367
steuene, -yn *n.* voice S 268, A 611, noise A 1509
stewe *n.* moat J 683
sty *n.* path H VII. 26, A 4961; *pl.* A 5189
styes *pl.* ladders H IX. 6, A 1560
stiffe *adj.* strong, proud
stiȝt *pp.* set A 1666, 5024
stike *v.* cling A 1561
stilly *adv.* quietly P 41
stingis *pr.3sg.* afflicts A 667; **stonge** *pa.t.* penetrated P 446
stynte *v.* stop; **stunte** *pa.t.* H IV. 17
stird *pa.t.* drove along T 12505
stirkes *pl.* young cattle P 147, 190
stith *adj.* violent T 12505, 12520, A 4965, valiant J 523
styþye *n.* excellent person H IV. 17
stockes *pl.* tree-trunks J 687
stoken *pp.* enclosed P 200

stonayd *pa.t.* amazed A 611
stond(en) *v.* (**stont, standes** *pr.3sg.*; **stode** *pa.t.*) stand; exist W 382, remain E 97; *stale* ~ stand up P 289
stonge *see* **stingis**
stont, sto(u)nde *n.* while A 655, time E 288, A 1591, moment S 167, A 4908, instant A 4968; *in a* ~ for a short time A 5189
storbis *pr.3sg.* disturbs A 667
store *adj.* large A 1657
stotayde, -eyd *pa.t.* stood still P 51, halted S 285
stott *n.* ox A 4881
stounde *see* **stont**
stour(r)e *n.* battle P 272, army A 1538, fuss A 5172
stoutly *adv.* magnificently A 1618
straght, straȝt *see* **strekis**
straȝtill *adj.* stretched out A 4965
strake *see* **strike**
strakid *pa.t.* sounded A 1509
strande *n.* water-flow J 686
strangild *pp.* killed A 4885
streghte *pa.t.* straightened P 116
streȝt *adv.* properly E 274, at once A 4885; ~ *on* right by A 1697
strekis *pr.pl.* lead A 5189; **straȝt, straght** *pa.t.* sent A 1666, led A 4961, flowed T 2367
stremys *pl.* currents W 460
strende *n.* stream S 123
strenkild *pp.* spangled A 1657
strete *n.* path A 4972
strif *n.* force H I. 4, attack H IV. 17
strike *v.* go J 683, drive A 1538; **strake** *pa.t.* rose A 1509
strit *pr.3sg.* strides H VII. 1
stroye *v.* destroy W 243, 229, A 4967; ~ *vp* destroy W 265
stronge *adj.* massive T 1574
stude *see* **stede**
stuffede *pp.* armed W 142; supported W 168
stunte *see* **stynte**
sturne, steryn *adj.* severe H I. 4, stern A 611, fierce A 1509
sturte *n.* quarrelling W 265
sucre *n.* sugar, sweetness H II. 34; **sogoure** W 350
sue *v.* (**sewe** *imper.*; **suet, -ede, sewet, -id** *pa.t.*) follow; come T 1616, go T 1605

suggen, sey(n) *v.* (**sei** *pr.1sg.*; **sayne** *pl.*; **seidest** *pa.t.*) say
suld *see* **sall**
sulle *v.* sell H III. 46
sunne *n.* sin H I. 7
surement *n.* pledge A 1587
surname *n.* name A 5070
sute *n.* pursuit T 2364
suþ *see* **seþe(n)**; **sutile** *see* **sotell**
swayne *n.* attendant T 2358
swalprit *pa.t.* tossed about T 12526
swapped *pa.t.* cut P 551
sware *n.* answer, word
sware *v.* answer A 647, 5134
swarues *pr.3sg.* swerves E 167; **swaruyt** *pa.t.* turned aside T 2358
sweȝand *ppl.adj.* rushing A 5146
swelt *v.* die J 536
swem *n.* swoon J 528; **swyme** giddiness T 2366
sweped *pp.* carried off W 46
sweuen, -ynn *n.* dream W 46, P 102
swike *v.* prove false to A 5126
swynde(n) *v.* waste away H III. 20, 72; *pa.t.* vanished E 342
swyngen *v.* strike W 320
swynk *n.* toil H III. 20
swynke *v.* work H III. 72
swythe *adv.* quickly, greatly, fully
swo *adv.* thus H III. 20
swoȝe *n.* murmur A 5146
swot *n.* labour H III. 20
swoty *adj.* sweaty T 2366
swowande *pr.p.* swooning J 536

table *n.* tablet A 5191; *pl.* writing-tablets A 639, 1691, backgammon T 1624
tabourris *pl.* drums J 526; **taburns** A 1508
tacchis *pr.3sg.* sets A 5191; **tachede** *pa.t.* fixed P 67; **tacchid** *pp.* set A 5097
tachen *pr.pl.* make attack J 655
tadde *n.* toad H VIII. 10
taȝt, taht *see* **teche**
taysen *pr.pl.* shoot (arrows) J 655; *pa.t.* aimed P 44
tayte *adj.* drunk W 477
tayttely *adv.* quickly P 219
take *v.* (**tast** *pr.2sg.*; **takeþ, tas** *3sg.*; **token** *pa.t.*; **ytake, tane, takon** *pp.*) take; capture K 65, afflict S 149,

excavate T 1543; ~ *an hond*
undertake H V. 23, A 713, ~ *out*
copy A 5197, ~ *to* reach E 57
tale   *n.* tally P 308; *be* ~ in number
A 5006
tale   *adj.* argumentative P 105
talent   *n.* wish E 176
tane   *pron.* in *þe* ~ one A 606
tane   *see* **take**
tangid   *pp.* stung A 4925
tapoures   *pl.* tapers A 1691
tapsters   *pl.* ale-sellers T 1594
taryen   *pr.pl.* wait P 242
tars   *n.* Tharsian silk A 1638
tartaryne   *n.* silk from Tartary P 132;
adj. A 1670
tas(t)   *see* **take**
tec(c)he   *n.* stain E 85, guilt E 297
teche   *imper.* show W 477; **taȝt, taht**
pp. appointed H III. 58, decreed
K 73
teeld   *see* **tild; teght, teȝt** *see* **tighte**
teh   *pl.* teeth H VII. 39
telde   *see* **told**
tele   *n.* wicked speech H IV. 35
telers   *pl.* tile-makers T 1586
telys   *pl.* teal (small ducks) P 219
temyd   *pa.t.* adhered E 15
tene, teone   *n.* sorrow, suffering,
trouble, vexation, rage
tene   *v.* annoy W 247; **teone, tenys,**
-yth *impers.* it pains, vexes
H VII. 39, W 341, 358; **tenyn** *pr.pl.*
injure P 242; **teneden** *pa.t.* were
angry P 321; **itened** *pp.* afflicted
H III. 2
tene   *pr.pl.* go K 72; **tyeþ** drag J 619
tenefull   *adj.* sorrowful
tenkelis   *pr.pl.* sound A 1508
tent   *n.* notice W 445
tentid   *pa.t.* attended P 313
tercelettes   *pl.* male peregrine falcons
P 219, 242
tere   *adj.* difficult
terme   *n.* lifespan A 5166
testre   *n.* head-board A 5041
tethe   *adj.* excellent A 663
text   *n.* account A 5072
þa   *see* **þo**
þah, þagh, þof   *conj.* although
thare, þarf   *pr.sg.impers.* (it) is
necessary (for), need W 201,
S 120, 137, 358; *3sg.* may E 262;

thurt *pa.t.* A 1584
þare   *see* **þer**
that   *pron.* that which, what H V. 44,
W 286, he that W 455
þe   *v.* prosper S 335
thede   *n.* country, place A 4864, 4933;
pl. A 5143
thedir, þider   *adv.* to there;
þiderwardes in that direction
thefe   *n.* rascal W 228, 242
þeyes   *pl.* thighs J 700
þen   *conj.* than H V. 20
þenke   *n.* thing K 122
thenke   *see* **thynke; þeos** *see* **þis**
þer, þare   *adv.& conj.* where;
(introducing wish) P 660; ~ *as*
where, ~ *fro* from there P 97, ~ *till*
to that place E 69; ~ *to* to it E 70, in
addition P 32; ~ *vntill adv.* to that
place W 473
þester   *adj.* dark T 2362, A 4931
þeþorn   *n.* hawthorn S 73
þider(wardes)   *see* **thedir**
þik   *adv.* severely A 707
thikefald   *adv.* in crowds A 1530
thynke   *v.* (**thenke** *pr.1sg.*; **thingis,**
þenkeþ *3sg.& impers.*; **þouȝte** *pa.t.*)
think, intend; *(impers.)* it seems
þynne   *adj.* thin, slight H V. 18;
þunne meagre H VI. 75
þire   *adj.* these
þis, þeos   *pron.& adj.* this, these
þo, thoo, þa   *pron.& adj.* those, they
þo   *adv.* then; *conj.* than
þof   *see* **þah**
thole   *v.* suffer A 707; **tholede, thowlit**
pa.t. P 403, T 1520
thoner   *n.* thunder T 12496
þonke   *n.* gratitude
þoruout, þorw-, thurgh- *prep.*
throughout; *adv.* through and
through SS 109, in all A 4864
þoste   *n.* turd H VIII. 7
þou   *pron.nom.sg.* you; **the** *acc.&*
dat.; **þi(ne)** *gen.*
þouȝte   *see* **thynke**
þourh, þroȝ, þrow   *prep.& adv.*
through
thowlit   *see* **thole**
thra   *n.* victory A 5143
þraly   *see* **þro; thrange** *see* **thrynges**
þrat   *pp.* threatened H VI. 69; **thret**
A 707

Glossary

thraw   *see* **þrow**
threnen   *adv.* thrice E 210
threpe   *n.* quarrel P 268
threpen   *pr.pl.* contend (in song)
  W 37, quarrel P 14; **threpden** *pa.t.*
  disputed P 104; **threpid** *pp.*
  quarrelled P 262
threpild   *pp.* added up A 1599
thret   *see* **þrat; thretty** *see* **þritty;**
  threuyn *see* **þryue(n)**
þrew   *pa.t.* twisted K 10
thricchyng   *n.* wringing T 1522
thrid   *adj.* third E 31
thrifty   *adj.* successful T 12522
thrynges   *pr.* (**þrong, thrange** *pa.t.*;
  thrange *pp.*) rush P 368,
  A 1550, 1559, push T 2362, oppress
  A 4940
thristis   *pr.pl.* thrust A 1530
þritty, thretty   *num.* thirty P 133,
  E 210, T 12522
thriuand   *ppl.adj.* excellent S 73,
  prosperous T 12522; **thryuandly** *adv.*
  gracefully E 47
þryue(n), threuyn   *ppl.adj.* fair
  H II. 23, vigorous H VI. 74, well-
  grown P 133, mighty A 1530
þro   *adj.* noble H II. 23, quarrelsome
  P 104; **throly, þraly** *adv.* fiercely
  W 37, P 14, A 707, vigorously
  P 133, violently T 1522
þrobyt   *pa.t.* beat around K 10
throgh   *n.* coffin E 47
þrong   *see* **thrynges; throstills** *see*
  þrustle
throtild   *pp.* suffocated A 4940
þrow, thraw   *n.* brief time K 9,
  moment A 1559; **on a ~** together
  A 1599
þrow   *see* **þourh**
þrowblande   *pr.p.* causing commotion
  J 532; **þrublet** *pa.t.* T 12496
þrustle   *n.* song-thrush H II. 23;
  throstills *pl.* P 14
þunne   *see* **þynne; thurghout** *see*
  þoruout; thurt *see* **thare**
tyde   *n.* time
tyde   *v.* (**tyd(de)** *pa.t.*) befall, happen
tidyng   *n.* message H VIII. 39
tyeþ   *see* **tene**
tighte, teght, teʒt   *pa.t.*[1] pulled P 79,
  (refl.) went T 1518; **~ to** approached
  A 649

tighte, tyʒt   *pa.t.*[2] set P 44, 361,
  intended K 72
tiht   *adj.* thick S 74
tyke   *n.* mongrel H VIII. 10
tild   *pp.* built T 1551, 1613; **teeld**
  situated S 56
tylere   *n.* stock of crossbow P 44
tilyynge   *n.* cultivation H III. 2
tyl(l)   *prep.* to
tilt   *pa.t.* overturned A 1541
tymbris   *pl.* small drums J 526
tyme   *n.* life A 647
tyne   *pr.2sg.subj.* lose S 340; **tynt** *pa.t.*
  T 2363; *pp.* SS 114, T 12467
tynen   *v.* harrow W 288
tired   *pp.* attired A 1670
tirement   *n.* ornamentation A 5045
tiruyt   *pp.* overturned T 1512
tyte   *adv.* soon A 693; **as ~** at once
  J 630; **tit(e)ly** quickly
title, titill   *n.* document E 102,
  inscription A 5197
titmoyses   *pl.* tits W 352
to   *conj.* until
to   *prep.* by way of H V. 2
tobrest   *v.* break in pieces A 640
tobrused   *pp.* severely injured J 722
tocleuen   *pr.pl.* split apart J 554
todrawe   *pr.3sg.subj.* pull apart
  H VII. 34
tofore   *adv.* in front SS 56; **tofore(n)**
  prep. in front of H VII. 10, before
  S 329
toʒede   *pa.t.* fled from SS 16
token, tokne   *n.* evidence E 102; **in ~**
  as a sign J 723
token   *see* **take**
told   *pa.t.* payed H III. 40; **telde**
  spoke K 19; **(y)tolde** *pp.* recognised
  H II. 32, counted K 18; **~ of**
  reckoned as E 31
tolyuer   *pr.1sg.* hand over H VIII. 4
tolle   *n.* in **to ~** as tribute H VIII. 4
tolles   *pr.3sg.* in **~ of** pulls off J 537
tome   *n.* opportunity E 313, K 129;
  tomly *adv.* without haste T 2447
tomorne   *adv.* tomorrow A 1616
tonacles   *pl.* vestments A 1670
tonelande   *pr.p.* thundering J 526
tonyng   *see* **to(u)nyng; tonnes** *see*
  to(u)nnes
torent   *pp.* torn to shreds E 164
torettis   *pl.* turrets T 1560, A 1541

256

Glossary

torfer *n.* difficulty S 149
torochit *pa.t.* tore in pieces T 12511
torres *pl.* peaks A 4990
tortle *n.* turtle-dove H II. 22; **turtils** *pl.* S 90
tos *pl.* toes S 305
toshrude *pp.* covered H VIII. 25
toswolle *ppl.adj.* puffed up H VI. 48, 49
totereþ *pr.pl.* tear H VII. 6
toþer *pron.* in *the* ~ that other (one)
toune *n.* company H IV. 37
toune-hede *n.* upper part of town W 277
tounen *pr.pl.* sound W 358
to(u)nyng *n.* trumpeting K 19, 64
to(u)nnes *pl.* tuns W 189, casks J 619
tourneþ *pr.3sg.(refl.)* in ~ *to* goes forward J 537; **turnyd** *pa.t.* consecrated E 15
trayfoyles *pl.* trefoil (clover) P 120
traylen *pr.pl.* drag S 356
trayne *n.* deceit A 5154
traistis *pr.2sg.* trust A 5152
trased *pp.* ornamented A 5041
tregetre *n.* magic T 1624
trey *n.* treachery J 723
treid *see* **tryi**; **treyned** *see* **trynes**
trenchore *n.* knife P 79
trenes *see* **trynes**
tres *pl.* wooden structures S 356, **trene** trees S 90
tretice *pl.* treatises A 1691
treuþe *n.* faith H V. 43
trewe *adj.* faithful, excellent; exact A 5006; *as n.* faithful ones E 336
trewloues *pl.* true-love knots P 120
triacle *n.* remedy H II. 32
tryffylyng *n.* frivolity K 19
tryi *v.* choose A 663; **tried** *pp.* selected P 301, decided T 2392; *ppl.adj.* fine, excellent P 120, 525, trusty A 5013; **treid** excellent A 5191; **triest** *superl.* A 5097
trillyd *pa.t.* rolled E 322
trimballand *pr.p.* quivering A 5041
trynes, trenes *pr.3sg.* hurries W 122, goes A 5015; **trinet, treyned** *pa.t.* went S 225, A 694
tristé, -i *adj.* trusty; **tristyly** *adv.* faithfully P 326
tryuyls *pl.* trifles K 130
troches *pl.* horns P 67

trompe *pr.pl.* blow trumpets S 356
trompers *pl.* trumpeters W 358
trone *n.* throne; *pl.* angels A 5041
tronyd *pp.* enthroned, seated E 255, S 90
troubull *n.* perplexity E 109
trous *n.* bundle H VII. 15, 25
trouthe *n.* honour W 452
trowe *v.* believe
trumpis *pl.* trumpets A 1509
tuly *adj.* red (originally of silk from Toulouse) W 82
tulke *n.* man
turners *pl.* potters T 1586
turnes *pl.* feats A 1527
turnyd *see* **tourneþ**
tute *v.* look A 694; **tutand** *pr.p.* peeping A 4903; **tuttynge** projecting W 82
twey, twayne *num.* two
twybyl *n.* two-edged axe H VII. 15
twinlepi *adj.* two A 5140
twinne *v.* part S 296

vche *see* **iche**
vghten *n.* dawn E 118
ugsom *adj.* terrible T 12497
vmbe *prep.* about, around
vmbegildid *pp.* gilded all over A 5026
vmbestonde *adv.* sometimes W 100
vmbethourid *pp.* surrounded A 4933
vmbycaste *v.* sniff around P 61
vmbygone *pp.* encircled W 62
vmbiloke *imper.* look about S 291
vmbtilde *pp.* built around T 1560
vmbtourne *adv.* around W 412
vmfaldin *pp.* surrounded A 4844
vmfonge *v.* attack? J 679
vmquile *adv.* sometimes
vnarwely *adv.* swiftly J 654
vnbliþe *adj.* unhappy H IV. 3
vnbredes *pr.pl.* close? H VI. 12; **vnbrad** *pp.* H VI. 13
vnburneschede *pp.* not polished P 26
vnclosede *pp.* released P 336
vndertake *v.* promise S 208
vndide *pa.t.* destroyed P 311
vndireȝode *pa.t.* got the better of P 283
vnduwe *adj.* unjust S 236, unfitting S 292; **-liche** *adv.* wrongfully S 325
vne *adv.* exactly T 1545
vnesid *pp.* disturbed A 5180

vnfaire *adj.* terrible A 4991; *adv.* terribly
vngnede *adj.* unsparing S 276
vngreiþ *adj.* wicked S 293
vnhapnest *adj.* most unfortunate E 198
vnhappeiste *adj.* most wretched A 713
vnkowthe *ppl.adj.* unknown T 12510
vnlouke *v.* release E 162
vnmylt *adj.* fierce J 556
vnneth, vnethis *adv.* scarcely
vnpereschede *ppl.adj.* alive P 431
vnpreste *adj.* unprepared E 285
vnridly *adv.* violently A 638
vnryuen *pp.* uninjured J 606
vnsaʒt *adv.* hostilely E 8
vnsamen *adv.* not matching A 605
vnsele *n.* bad luck P 438
vnsete *adj.* improper H IV. 30; *adv.* wrongly S 360
vnshene *adj.* horrible K 43
vnskathely *adj.as n.* innocent E 278
vnsober *adj.* wild T 12507; **-ly** *adv.* T 12494
vnsparid *ppl.adj.* unrestrained E 335
vnþeufol *adj.* feeble H VI. 74
vnthrifte *n.* extravagance W 267
vntill *prep.* towards W 58
vntoun *adj.* improper H IV. 37
vnwemmyd *ppl.adj.* unspotted, unsullied
vnwerde *adj.* unguarded S 124
vnwis *adj.* foolish H I. 9
vnwraste *adj.* unreliable H V. 17
vpbrayde *pp.* raised W 149; taken up W 208
vphalden *pp.* raised E 349
vppon *see* ap(p)on
vpwacknet *pa.t.* was stirred up T 12474
vr(e) *see* ous; **vschon** *see* iche
vsen *pr.pl.* practise; **vsit** *pa.t.* inhabited E 200, performed T 1625, attended A 645
vttire *adv.* out; further out W 468

vacant *adj.* empty A 4901, 5106
vayles *pr.3sg.* avails E 348
valle *see* falle
vanité *n.* nothing A 4901
vautes *pl.* large sewers T 1607
vaward *n.* vanguard J 549, A 4969

vemon *n.* venom A 4924
vemons *pr.3sg.* envenoms A 4969
verdure *n.* greenness A 5106
vermyns *gen.pl.* of foul creatures A 4924
verray *adj.* clear E 53; **verraylé** *adv.* truly P 594; **verely** indeed T 2432
vertus *pl.* powers P 594, E 174
vertwells *pl.* varvels P 238
vestoure *n.* garment A 1662
vigures *pl.* characters E 53
vise *v.* look A 1662
void *adj.* empty A 5106
voide *v.* ward off A 1607; *pr.3sg.* pours A 4924; **voidit** *pa.t.* banished T 1524
vouche safe *pr.pl.* permit W 427

wa *see* wo
wacches *pl.* guard-posts T 1561
wade *pp.* passed SS 21
waghes *see* wawes; **waynt** *see* quaynt
waite, waytten *v.* look (at), look for; guard P 99, make sure A 5075
waiteþ *pr.3sg.* inflicts on H III. 17
waithe *n.* game T 2350
waiwordes *adv.* pervertedly S 55
wake *v.* (**woke** *pa.t.*) lie awake; stay vigilant P 35
wakeneþ *pr.3sg.* arises H III. 71, begins S 297; **wackonet** *pa.t.* awoke T 2437, was aroused T 12469
wakynge *n.* revelling at night W 266
wald *see* wol(le)
wald-eʒed *ppl.adj.* with eyes of different colours A 608
wale *n.* choice; *to* ~ in abundance E 73, T 1530
wale *v.* choose; **walon** *pp.* gathered E 64
wale *adj.* lovely, noble; swift W 460, short (of time) W 396, A 4899
walkers *pl.* fullers T 1587
wallon *pr.pl.* swarm K 98
walshenotes *pl.* walnuts S 99
walt *v.* be overturned T 12502; **walt(en)** *pa.t.* tumbled J 709, rolled T 12504, 12508; *pp.* overturned J 706
walt *see* welde
waltered *pp.* tossed W 248
wand *see* wonde

wane *v.* decline A 4899
wane *adj.*[1] dark K 28, T 12504
wane *adj.*[2] lacking K 62
wanhope *n.* despair W 309, 373
wan(n)e *see* **wynn; wanted** *see*
  wontyd
wardons *pl.* pears S 99
ware *n.* goods H VI. 90
ware *v.* use K 22, possess K 108
ware *see* **be(n), war(r)e; wariande,**
  waryed *see* **wery**
warlaws *pl.* devils K 83
warned *see* **werne**
warnestorede *pa.t.* stored P 412
warp(yd) *see* **werpe**
war(r)e *adj.* aware W 85, A 1708;
  warliche *adv.* cautiously S 121
warto *see* **where**
wast . *n.* wild country K 59
wate *see* **wete**
water *n.* river T 1601
wathe *n.* danger A 1534
wawes, waghes *pl.* waves W 12,
  T 12504
wawis *see* **woȝe**
waxen *v.* (**wax, wex(en), woxen** *pa.t.*)
  grow, become
webbe *n.* fabric; *pl.* cobwebs A 4934
websters *pl.* weavers T 1587
wed *n.* pledge H VII. 24, 25; *pl.*
  W 284
wed(e)res *pl.* storms H III. 70, K 28,
  A 4923
wederlyng *n.* codling (apple) S 102
wedous *pl.* widows A 1681
wee *see* **wy, wo**
weede *n.* dress S 26; **wedes** *pl.* clothes
weende *see* **wende; wegh, wehes** *see*
  wy
wey *n.* course of movement SS 69;
  weyes *pl.* fortunes SS 113
wel *adv.* very
welde, wielde *v.* (**walt** *pa.t.*) have,
  possess; wield A 651, rule E 161,
  A 5059
weldyng *n.* command SS 94
wele, weole *n.* happiness, wealth;
  goods H III. 66
wele-dede *n.* good behaviour E 301
welken *n.* sky
wellande *pr.p.* boiling W 262, 351
welnegh *adv.* nearly
welter *v.* toss about J 528

wemles *adj.* spotless E 85, S 151,
  A 5075
wenches *pl.* maids S 213, girls A 1681
wende, weende, wiende *v.* (**went** *pp.*)
  turn, go; turn over H VI. 13, come
  J 581; ~ *of* go from K 27
wene *n.* what is expected H III. 31
wene *pr.1sg.* think, believe, know;
  weneþ *3sg.* intends H III. 16; *pl.*
  hope H III. 10; **wende** *pa.t.*
  purposed SS 21, thought SS 94
weole *see* **wele; weore** *see* **be(n), were**
wepmon *n.* man H I. 3
werd *n.* world; **word** K 60, 84, 101
werdes *see* **werid**
were *n.* man P 581
were, weore *v.* wear H V. 14,
  H V. 15
were *see* **be(n), wer(r)e**
wery *v.* (**wariande** *pr.p.*) curse
  W 285, 437, J 673; **weryed, waryed**
  ppl.adj. accursed W 242, P 536
werid *n.* fate A 689; **werdis, wirdis**
  pl.
werien *pr.pl.* defend J 669
werk *n.* affliction H IV. 26
werke *n.* deed; fortification T 1552,
  structure A 1546; **werkys** *pl.* deeds
  K 117, artifacts T 1530,
  workmanship A 4960, designs
  A 5020
werne *v.* refuse S 137; **warned** *pa.t.*
  A 1591
werpe *v.* (**werpe(d), warp(yd)** *pa.t.*;
  werpede, warpyd *pp.*) cast W 423,
  heap W 250, put (clothes on) SS 4,
  throw A 1555, 1649, take S 124,
  rescue H IV. 48, speak E 321, 329,
  SS 118, A 725, utter A 709, weave
  W 64
wer(r)e *n.* war; *one* ~ in battle P 544
werres *pr.pl.* fight H IX. 5
wet *pp.* made wet H IV. 1
wete *n.* moisture E 321
wete, wiete, wyte *v.* (**wote** *pr.1sg.*;
  wost *2sg.*, **wot** *3sg.& pl.*; **wate**
  imper.; **wiste** *pa.t.*) know, learn;
  Ichot *pr.1sg.* I know
wetirly *see* **wittir**
weue *v.* move to and fro SS 34, 69
wex *see* **waxen**
what, whet, quat *adj.pron.& adv.*
  what; ~ *of* as a result of A 4922;

quatkyn *adj.* what kind of A 5134

whene *n.* queen A 733

where, quare *adv. & conj.* where, wherever; **quareof** of which A 4948; **warto** to what purpose K 113

whider *adv.* whither H VII. 9; **whedirwardes** P 294

why3tly *see* **wightly**

while *n.* time; *no* ~ never P 291

while, whil(e)s *conj.* until; as long as J 542

whylome *adv.* once W 19

whyt *see* **wi3t**

who, qua *pron.* who, whoever

whon *adv.* when

whoso, (w)hose, quaso *pron.* whoever

wy, wee, weghe *n.* man, person; **wyghes, wehes** *pl.* P 584, E 73

wickede, wikked *adj.* dreadful H III. 70, difficult J 664, T 1565

wyde *adv.* far and wide; *one* ~ around W 213

wydwhare *adv.* far and wide W 257, 326

wielde *see* **welde; wiende** *see* **wende**

wies(e)ly *adv.* carefully P 40, prudently P 412

wiete *see* **wete**

wyf *n.* woman; **wifman** SS 34

wyghes *see* **wy**

wightly, w(h)y3tly *adv.* quickly W 104, swiftly T 2437, J 617, bravely A 651

wi3t, whyt, wy3t, wy(3)th *n.* person

wy3t(h) *adj.* strong E 69, powerful SS 95

wikked *see* **wickede**

wild *adj.* lecherous K 117

wildire *n.* ruler A 1731

wyle *n.* sorceress H V. 46

wyled *pa.t.* tricked S 213, 219

wyles *pl.* tricks; skilful devices J 664, 669

wylyliche *adv.* craftily S 213

wil(l) *n.* desire; wilfulness H III. 23

wyll *adj.* gone astray T 2369

wilnes *pr.3sg.* wishes; **willne** *imper.* request A 5162

wilt *pa.t.* wandered T 2359

wymmene *gen.pl.* of women H VI. 36, 90

wyn *see* **wyn(ne)**

wince *n.* quince S 102

wynde *v.* (**wond** *pa.t.*; **wondon** *pp.*) turn, go; wrap K 99

wyndide *pa.t.* sniffed the air P 46

wynliche *adj.* lovely S 127, excellent S 99

wynn *v.* (**wan(ne), wonnen** *pa.t.*; **wonen** *pp.*) win, get, obtain; produce W 274, make money W 390, gain E 301, go J 617, reach J 612, persuade to come W 162, bring T 12538; ~ *to* seize P 230, ~ *of* escape from T 12532

wyn(ne) *n.* joy; *at here* ~ in their enjoyment K 27

wynnynge *n.* money-making W 161

wyntere *pl.* years

wirche *see* **worche**

wirchip, worchip, -ship *n.* honour; *at* ~ in honour K 107

wirdis *see* **werid**

wyre *n.* gold thread S 192

wise *n.* manner, way

wis(se) *v.* arrange W 308, make known A 5124, show K 84; **wysses** *pr.3sg.* guides W 226; **wysede** *pa.t.* led P 451; **wissid** *pp.* known A 689

wisshyng *n.* guidance T 1606

wiste *see* **wete; wyt** *see* **wit(t)**

witand *n.* knowledge S 250

wyte *n.* in *make* ~ blame H VI. 35

wite *v.* cause to depart A 5158

wyte *see* **wete**

witere *imper.* inform E 185

with *prep.* with; ~ *that* then; *adv.* in addition SS 118

wyth, wyþt *see* **wi3t**

withdrawen *pp.* removed

within *adv.* inside E 75

without(en) *adv. & prep.* outside

withstand *pr.pl.* resist A 1567

witnes *pr.3sg.* attests A 1715

wit(t) *n.* good sense H IV. 2, W 223, skill W 171, thought P 149, discretion T 2390

wittyly *adv.* smartly P 46

wittir *adj.* knowledgeable A 629; **wit(t)erly, wetirly** *adv.* certainly; indeed A 1546, closely T 2429

wittnesse *n.* testimony W 189

wlonke *adj.* proud H VI. 27; **wlonkest, wlankest** *sup.* noblest S 26, finest S 186

wo, wa, wee *n.* woe, distress, sorrow,

injury; *me was* ~ I was miserable
K 60

wod *adj.* mad

wodenes *n.* fierceness T 12502

wodewale *n.* woodpecker H II. 24;
pl. W 351

wodwyse *n.* wild man W 71; **wodwose**
pl. A 1663

woȝe *n.* wall K 141; **wawis** *pl.* A 1646

woke *see* **wake**

wol(le) *pr.1sg.* (**wulleþ** *pr.*; **wolde,**
wald *pa.t.*) will, wish to, want;
demand A 631

wome *n.* belly K 98

won *n.* course of action H III. 5

wond *see* **wynde**

wonde *v.* (**wand** *pr.pl.*) hesitate

wonder *adj.* wonderful SS 34, 63;
adv. extremely J 677, surprisingly A
629

wonding *n.* wounding A 4922

wondire *n.* strange thing A 5117

wondirs *pr.sg.impers.* it amazes W
392; **wounder** *3sg.subj.* marvel W
236;

wondred *pp.* amazed S 173

wondred *n.* poverty H III. 31, 71

wondrede *pa.t.* travelled H VIII. 33

wone *n.*¹ dwelling S 54, 134

wone *n.*² lack H IV. 2

won(e), wonne *v.* (**wonnes** *pr.3sg.*;
wonie *2sg.subj.*; **wont, wonnede,**
wondon *pa.t.*; **wont** *pp.*) live; dwell
E 279, remain P 193, stay T 1581;
pp. accustomed S 168

wonges *pl.* cheeks

won(n)en *see* **wynn**

wontyd, wanted *pa.t.* were lacking
E 208, lacked J 628

worche, wirche *v.* (**wirkis** *pr.pl.*;
wroghte *pa.t.*; **wroȝt, wroht, iwrout**
pp.) work, make, cause, write;
compose H IV. 11, W 25, 30, act
W 201, E 274, behave H IV. 13, do
E 301, bring about E 226, utter W
22, fashion W 71, decorate A 1663,
turn SS 113

worchip *see* **wirchip**; **word** *see* **werd**

worme *n.* serpent A 4965; *pl.* T 1573

worth *v.* be, become, come, happen;
worthis *impers.* in *him* ~ he reaches
A 4987; ~ *vp* climb up W 282, ~ *fey*
die W 300

worth(i)liche, worþi, wurþé *adj.*
worthy H V. 22, fine W 34, excellent
SS 55, 60, 83; **worly, worthy,**
wor(th)liche *as n.* worthy person,
excellent one S 54, 134, 150;
worþelokyst *sup.* most excellent
K 101; **worthist** noblest A 1731

worttes *pl.* vegetables W 346

wost, wot *see* **wete**

wothe *n.* danger P 37, E 233

wounder *see* **wondirs; woxen** *see*
waxen

wra *n.* corner A 1708

wrake *n.* harm W 198, destruction
J 581, suffering A 1535

wrakeful *adj.* vengeful E 215

wranges *pl.* injuries E 243

wrase *n.* bundle K 99

wreit *pp.* written H VI. 33

wrekis *pr.pl.* avenge A 1533

wrethe *v.* (**writhis** *pr.pl.*; **wraþþed**
pa.t.) make angry; (*refl.*) grow angry
A 1532

wriche *n.* wretch W 309

wryeth *pr.3sg.* betrays W 6; **wreus**
reveals K 117; **wryghede** *pp.*
discovered P 97

wriȝtes *pl.* workmen J 677,
carpenters T 1530, joiners T 1587

writh *n.* anger A 4974

wrythen *pr.pl.* twist P 230; **wrethen**
pa.t. turned S 55; *pp.* twisted W 71

writhing *n.* angering A 5162

writhis *see* **wrethe**

writ(t) *n.* writing, source

wryus *pr.2sg.* turn K 116

wroghte, wroȝt *see* **worche**

wrong *pa.t.* wrung S 171

wrongwys *adj.* false S 37

wroþe *adj.* angry, violent H V. 39;
wrothely *adv.* angrily; **wroþliche**
sorrowfully SS 113

wulleþ *see* **wol(le); wurþé** *see*
worth(i)liche